LAW COURTS AND LAWYERS IN THE CITY OF LONDON, 1300–1550

Between 1300 and 1550, London's courts were the most important English lay law courts outside Westminster. They served the most active and innovative of the local jurisdictions in which custom combined with the common law to produce different legal remedies from those contemporaneously available in the central courts. More importantly for the long term, not only did London's practices affect other local courts, but they influenced the development of the national common law, and quite possibly the development of the legal profession itself.

This book provides a detailed account, accessible to non-legal historians, of the administration of the law by the medieval and early modern city of London. In analysing the workings of London's laws and law courts and the careers of those who worked in them, it shows how that administration, and those involved in it, helped to shape the modern English law.

PENNY TUCKER now works in Devon as a designer, but continues to research history and to write part-time.

CAMBRIDGE STUDIES IN ENGLISH LEGAL HISTORY

Edited by
J. H. BAKER
Fellow of St Catharine's College, Cambridge

Recent series titles include

The Rise and Fall of the English Ecclesiastical Courts, 1500–1860
R. B. OUTHWAITE

Law Courts and Lawyers in the City of London, 1300–1550
PENNY TUCKER

Legal Foundations of Tribunals in Nineteenth-Century England
CHANTAL STEBBINGS

Pettyfoggers and Vipers of the Commonwealth
The 'Lower Branch' of the Legal Profession in Early Modern England
C. W. BROOKS

Roman Canon Law in Reformation England
R. H. HELMHOLZ

Sir Henry Maine – : A Study in Victorian Jurisprudence
R. C. J. COCKS

Sir William Scott, Lord Stowell
Judge of the High Court of Admiralty, 1798–1828
HENRY J. BOURGUIGNON

The Early History of the Law of Bills and Notes
A Study of the Origins of Anglo-American Commercial Law
JAMES STEVEN ROGERS

The Law of Treason in England in the Later Middle Ages
J. G. BELLAMY

William Sheppard, Cromwell's Law Reformer
NANCY L. MATTHEWS

LAW COURTS AND LAWYERS IN THE CITY OF LONDON, 1300–1550

PENNY TUCKER

CAMBRIDGE
UNIVERSITY PRESS

CAMBRIDGE UNIVERSITY PRESS
Cambridge, New York, Melbourne, Madrid, Cape Town,
Singapore, São Paulo, Delhi, Mexico City

Cambridge University Press
The Edinburgh Building, Cambridge CB2 8RU, UK

Published in the United States of America by Cambridge University Press, New York

www.cambridge.org
Information on this title: www.cambridge.org/9780521866682

First published 2007

A catalogue record for this publication is available from the British Library

ISBN 978-0-521-86668-2 Hardback

CONTENTS

ACKNOWLEDGEMENTS

As the footnotes make plain, this book owes a great deal to information supplied by Professor Sir John Baker; but what the footnotes reveal is only part of the story. Without Professor Baker's encouragement, the book would almost certainly never have been written at all. Without his help, and that of Dr Paul Brand, the most meticulous, challenging and well-informed of commentators, whose lot it has been to offer his views on almost everything I have written to date, it would almost certainly not have been worth publishing. I owe a very great deal to both of them.

I am also most grateful to the anonymous readers who have commented both on this book and on related papers. Those attending the British Legal History Conferences over the past decade or so have provided a welcoming and kindly forum in which to try out ideas, and, more importantly, to acquire them. For even longer than that, the staff of the Corporation of London Record Office have offered friendly help and support. Through the good offices of the former Archivist, Mr Jim Sewell, I was granted financial assistance by the Corporation towards my work on the Husting Rolls, without which it could not have been carried out in anything like the same detail.

Finally, among the many others who have helped me down the years and are too numerous to name individually here, Professor Caroline Barron, my former tutor, stands out. I, like all her students, have benefited very greatly indeed from her advice, guidance and generous support.

ABBREVIATIONS

Adm	Admissions
AG	Attorney–General
Ald	Alderman
AMJLH	*American Journal of Legal History*
Att	Attorney
Aug	Augmentations
B(Ex)	Baron (of the Exchequer)
BH	Bridge House
[BI]HR	*[Bulletin of the Institute of]Historical Research*
BL	British Library
C	Chief
Cal	Calendar
CalCorR	*Calendar of Coroners' Rolls*
CalCR	*Calendar of Close Rolls*
CalEMCR	*Calendar of Early Mayor's Court Rolls*
CalFR	*Calendar of Fine Rolls*
CalHW&D	*Calendar of Husting Wills & Deeds*
CalLB	*Calendar of Letterbooks*
CalPR	*Calendar of Patent Rolls*
CalPMR	*Calendar of Plea and Memoranda Rolls*
CCL	[Fitch] *Commissary Court of London*
Chanc	Chancellor
Chirog	Chirographer

CI	Clement's Inn (of Chancery)
ClI	Clifford's Inn (of Chancery)
Clk	Clerk
CLRO	Corporation of London Record Office
Cmn	Common
comm	communication
CP	Common Pleas
CS	Common Serjeant
Ct	Court
dep	deputy
edn	edition
ed(s).	editor(s)
EH	[Williams] *Early Holborn*
EHR	*English Historical Review*
Ex	Exchequer
Exec(s).	Executor(s)
fo(s).	folio(s)
GHLibrary	Guildhall Library
GI	Gray's Inn
GM	*The Guildhall Miscellany*
Gt Chron	*Great Chronicle*
GSLH	*Guildhall Studies in London History*
HB	Husting Book
HR	Husting Roll
HRO	Hampshire Record Office
HRW&D	Husting Rolls of Wills and Deeds
IT	Inner Temple
J	Justice
JLH	*Journal of Legal History*
Jor(s).	Journal(s) of the Common Council
Jun	Junior

KA	King's Attorney
KB	King's Bench
LAssNuis	[Chew, Kellaway] *London Assize of Nuisance*
LB	Letterbook
LCC	[Darlington] *London Consistory Court Wills*
LI	Lincoln's Inn
LQR	*Law Quarterly Review*
LPossAss	[Chew] *London Possessory Assizes*
LyI	Lyon's Inn (of Chancery)
m(m).	membrane(s)
Mich.	Michaelmas (term)
Misc.	Miscellaneous
MS	Manuscript
MT	Middle Temple
OSaL	[Baker] *Order of Serjeants at Law*
pb	paperback
PCC	Prerogative Court of Canterbury
photo.	photograph
PL	Pleas of Land
Plr	Pleader
PRO	Public Record Office
Protho	[Sheriff's] Prothonotary
R&M	[Thorne, Baker] *Readings & Moots*
Rec	Recorder
Recog	Recognizance
Reg.	Register
Rep	Repertories
Ser.	Series
Serg	sergeant
Serj	serjeant
Soc.	Society

SRO	Southampton Record Office
TNA	The National Archives
TRHS	*Transactions of the Royal Historical Society*
US	Undersheriff
v.	versus
vol(s).	volume(s)
WP	Weekly Payments (Bridge House)

FIGURES

INTRODUCTION

AIMS AND JUSTIFICATIONS

This book originated over a decade ago, during a study of the government of medieval London, in the need to understand the place of the administration of the law in that government.

What had seemed likely to be a short and straightforward investigation led to years of study and to an abiding interest in this aspect of the early history of the English common law. It soon became clear that anyone interested in either what the law of London was or how it was administered would have to look at a large number of books and articles in order to build up a detailed picture.[1] That picture would, moreover, in a few important respects be incomplete or misleading. These problems matter because London's law courts were the most important medieval English lay law courts outside Westminster in terms of the quantity of civil litigation brought in them: in the fifteenth century, the London Sheriffs' Court may well have been second only to the central Court of the Common Bench in this respect. They served the most active and probably the most innovative of the local jurisdictions in which custom combined with the common and merchant laws to produce different legal remedies from those contemporaneously available in the central courts. The practices and procedures of the city's courts also differed in some respects from those which were most commonly employed at Westminster.

[1] The Introductions to the *CalEMCR* (for city law courts, types of actions and procedures) and *CalPMR 1381–1412* (for merchant law and law courts, customs relating to methods of proof, liability, and negotiable instruments), *CalPMR 1413–37* (for the language of the courts, gifts of deeds and chattels) and *CalPMR 1437–57* (for gifts of deeds and chattels); also Cam, *Law-finders and Lawmakers*, pp. 85–94; Jones, 'City Courts of Law'; Harding, *Law Courts of Medieval England*, pp. 41–2.

Moreover, London's privileges, customs and procedures influenced those of other local courts. By 1216, over a dozen boroughs had adopted London's customs either directly or indirectly.[2] Finally, although there is little doubt that developments in the principles and procedures of the central court(s) had considerable influence on the administration of the law by London until the early fourteenth century, for the next two centuries, at certain times and in certain situations, influence worked in the opposite direction.

Even this might not be enough to justify devoting an entire book to the topic of the administration of the law by London, were it not for the fact that almost everything which has just been said is to a lesser or greater extent controversial and therefore requires to be demonstrated. Take the assertion that London's Sheriffs' Court in the fifteenth century may well have been second only to the Court of the Common Bench in terms of the amount of civil litigation brought there. This is controversial for two reasons. First, there is no direct evidence to support it; the records of the medieval Sheriffs' Court have almost entirely disappeared. Secondly, local courts generally are thought to have been largely eclipsed by the central courts in the course of the Middle Ages. There is no period between 1200 and 1550 when historians have not detected a strong flow of litigation from local courts into the central ones at Westminster, in particular, to the Court of the Common Bench (or Common Pleas). The work of that court undoubtedly burgeoned for most of the period. In the first century after 1200, the number of membranes in the Common Bench plea rolls multiplied twenty-fold.[3] Although growth was less rapid thereafter, the number of membranes had nevertheless almost doubled again by 1450.[4] The traditional explanation for this growth, particularly in the thirteenth century, is that litigants were abandoning local courts for the central ones. This was the result of what has been called the 'birth of the common law': the development of a system of initiating and moving legal actions in

[2] Ballard, *British Borough Charters*, pp. 10, 12, 13, 13–14, 14, 15, 23, 27, 29, 32, 34; Hudson, Tingey, *Records of Norwich*, I, pp. 12–13.

[3] Brand, *Origins of the Legal Profession*, p. 24.

[4] There were *c.* 360 membranes (excluding those recording the appointments of attorneys) in the roll for Mich. 1299 and *c.* 670 membranes in that for Mich. 1449: TNA (PRO), CP Plea Rolls, CP40/130, /755.

and between courts by means of a writ obtained from the royal Chancery. The writs, while preserving the fiction 'that access to the royal courts [meaning, the central courts at Westminster] was limited and exceptional and that the local courts were and remained the ordinary courts of law for the country at large', in fact enabled litigants to abandon local courts for the central ones. Consequently, 'the old local courts . . . sank into the comparative insignificance in which they have remained for many centuries'.[5]

Although these conclusions clearly relate primarily to the loss of business which private, seigneurial courts are thought to have sustained, both rural county and borough courts are also believed to have been affected.[6] If, in the minds of these commentators, London was the exception that proved the rule, they do not say so. And in some respects the evidence from the central court records supports those who would include London among the local jurisdictions which lost business to the central courts. There are few cases marginated 'London' in the early Common Bench records, by the fifteenth century, such entries appear by the hundred.[7] At this date, moreover, not only were London cases appearing in their hundreds in the records of the Court of the Common Bench, they could also be found, if in lesser quantities, in those of King's Bench and the Court of Chancery.[8] In the Common Bench, cases marginated 'London' often involved plaintiffs who were free of the city. The city had jurisdiction over such cases and had the right to forbid city freemen from bringing them elsewhere if they

[5] Van Caenegem, *Birth of the Common Law*, Chapter 1 and pp. 24, 29; and see also, for example, Harding, *Law Courts of Medieval England*, p. 84 (*c*. 1160 to *c*. 1290), Pollock, Maitland, *History of the English Law*, I, p. 202 (Edward I's reign, 1277–1307), and Musson, Ormrod, *Evolution of English Justice*, pp. 9–10 (fourteenth century); for the sixteenth century, see Baker, 'High Court of Battle Abbey', p. 263.

[6] Palmer, *County Courts of Medieval England*, pp. 220–1, 262, 254–5, 304–6; van Caenegem, *Birth of the Common Law*, p. 24.

[7] Palgrave, *Rotuli Curiae Regis*, I, pp. 220–304 (Easter 1199); *idem*, *Rotuli Curiae Regis*, II, pp. 1–153 (Mich. 1199), and Nicol, *Curia Regis Rolls, XVII*, pp. 83–236 (Mich. 1242); compare with TNA (PRO) CP Plea Rolls, CP40/802, /806, /825 (1460s and 1470s). The change was well under way by the later fourteenth century. Of 8 attorney appointments marginated 'London' in the rolls for Mich. 1336, only 3 definitely involved Londoners: TNA (PRO), CP Plea Rolls, CP40/308, Att. rolls, mm. 10, 10v (Robert le Ropere of London 'cyteyn' and Henry Wymond of London 'laver', *bis*), 11v. By contrast, there were 60 such appointments in Mich. 1375: CP Plea Rolls, CP40/460, Att. rolls.

[8] Tucker, 'London's Courts and the Westminster Courts', pp. 119–20.

could be brought in the city's courts. This suggests that the city courts were no longer functioning effectively or that the city's governors were powerless to stem the outflow of litigation.

Then there is the fact that local courts, London's included, do not appear to have been doing much that the central courts were not doing better. Their rolls are full of brief entries relating mainly to common-law actions like debt. As a legal profession emerged, probably before the end of the thirteenth century, the increasing penetration of professional lawyers into local courts brought central court ways of doing and thinking to the inferior jurisdictions. Apparently every little manor court was, by about 1300, tending to deal with the same sort of actions in the same sort of ways.[9] And contrariwise, insofar as they had their own customs, or usages, they were so varied and so localised in their effect as to be little more than a curiosity.

Finally, for the legal historian, there is nothing in the local courts to match the wealth of legal learning revealed in the yearbooks (though not normally in the rolls of the central courts themselves). This is as true of London as of the smallest manor court. Its half-a-dozen custumals may record custom, but they do not usually attempt to explain it. Even where the originating ordinances are preserved in its administrative records, they tend merely to state the problem and provide a solution, which, to later observers, may not even seem to have much of a bearing on the problem concerned. Only rarely do its judges explain their reasoning; they hardly ever discuss on the record the arguments which presumably informed their judgments.[10] One is left to draw what conclusions one may from the judgment itself and any surviving depositions. To scratch around in this unyielding soil for the few crumbs there are seems a painful waste of effort, when so much more can be so much more easily gleaned elsewhere.

All this would be very discouraging, were it true. One of the purposes of this book is to demonstrate that it is not. The argument advanced here is that the Common Bench rolls did not swell after 1200, nor probably indeed at any period before 1550, because cases which would formerly have been brought in the

[9] Baker, *Oxford History of the Laws of England*, vi, p. 291, Hyams, 'What did Edwardian Villagers Understand by "Law"?', esp. pp. 80–1.

[10] For exceptions, see *CalEMCR*, pp. 168–9, 183–4.

London courts were being brought in the central courts instead. Rather, it was, firstly, because litigation in both Westminster and London increased at this period; secondly, because, by the later fourteenth century, Londoners were using the central courts for actions which could not at any time have been brought successfully, or solely, in the city; and, thirdly, because litigants may have been bringing cases in the central courts which they abandoned at an early stage, as a way of 'flushing out' and securing evasive defendants who could then be made to appear in the local courts. The only city court which lost business permanently before 1500 was the Husting. And this was not because lawsuits were being attracted away from it by the central courts, but because the old common-law writs used to initiate most types of legal action there went out of fashion in the local courts. Its loss, moreover, was the other city courts' gain.

In addition, the superficial similarity of the local and central courts' administration of the law is deceptive. Not only procedures but also remedies and judicial attitudes in courts in which private (civil) actions were initiated mainly by written bill or (oral com)plaint differed from those in which they were begun by royal writ. This was the fundamental difference between the two busiest city courts and the Common Bench. Moreover, if it is the case that local jurisdictions were still handling the bulk of civil and criminal cases even in the 1500s (and it is), we need to examine them, not only in order to make sure that they really were doing no more than mimicking the central courts, but also to see what the trends in litigation were.[11] Finally, as has been pointed out in relation to modern contract law, there are laws which are quite well-developed in theory but which are of little or no practical use, or simply are not used.[12] It is possible, if admittedly not at all likely, that the yearbook discussions had hardly more relevance to medieval law in action outside Westminster than had academic debates about angels on heads of pins to the religious practices of the laity and their priests.

Furthermore, the ways in which London's law offices (and, to a lesser extent, the city's judgeships) changed over time throw a sidelight on developments in the law generally. One of the themes

[11] Harrison, 'Manor Courts and the Governance of Tudor England'.
[12] Hedley, 'Needs of Commercial Litigants'.

of this book is the suggestion that three things which happened from the late fourteenth century onwards influenced the development of both city custom and the common law considerably. First, the city's law offices ceased to exist in semi-isolation from the law offices at Westminster, and came to be merely four of the many posts open to late-medieval common lawyers. This must have had some effect on the conduct of the city courts. Secondly, a sizeable proportion of the justices on the Westminster benches (excluding Chancery) were, from about 1400 until about 1500, former city law officers. Presumably this had an effect both on relations between the central and city courts and on the attitudes of the justices of the central courts. Thirdly, from about 1500 onwards, it became much less common than it had been for much of the fifteenth century for city law officers to be created serjeant at law or to achieve a central court judgeship. This was part of a well-established problem of recruitment to the central courts, but it was nevertheless a belated response. The reasons behind this reversal have a tale to tell about the administration of the law by London and in other jurisdictions.

These changes reflected, and may have contributed to, fundamental developments in the law which took place over the same period. By the end of the sixteenth century, local courts at all levels appear to have become much more closely aligned, in terms of their principles and procedures, to the central courts. For the first time, the national 'system' of law courts might properly be so called. It could be argued that this was merely a culmination of the process of assimilation of custom and local courts by the common law and central law courts which had been going on at least since the twelfth century. The evidence discussed in Chapter 10, however, suggests that it was in the central courts that the most important changes of the later fourteenth and fifteenth centuries occurred, and that these changes brought the central courts and the common law and custom as practised at Westminster closer to the local courts and the common law and custom practised in them, rather than the other way around. This did not of course herald the triumph of local law courts and 'flexible' custom over central law courts and the 'rigid' writ system. On the contrary, it destroyed some of the distinctiveness and advantages of the local courts in relation to the central ones. They thus became less useful at the very moment when political factors were encouraging attacks on any institution or procedure which was not fully in conformity with and under the control of the common law.

Either way, it is interesting, and often informative, to compare developments in the city courts with those at Westminster at an important time for the common law. For that reason, the administration of the law by London is worth studying both in its own right and as part of research into medieval and early modern law as a whole. Understanding what was administered, how, why and when, is also a prerequisite for those who want to use the court and legal records of London, and indeed of other courts of law and custom, to undertake research in other historical disciplines. Without that understanding, as we shall see shortly, those records can be seriously misleading.

THE MAIN SOURCES OF EVIDENCE

One of the reasons why the significance of London's law courts has not been fully appreciated is that virtually all the records of its busiest court have disappeared. As with so many other medieval and early modern archives, the London collections contain either splendid runs of records relating to one, or one aspect, of its law courts, or almost nothing at all. Having a splendid run of any records might be considered an advantage, but, where records are almost entirely absent or are patchy and of unascertainable representativeness, the temptation to extrapolate from the richer sources to the poorer can mislead badly. This is especially true when one of the reasons for the different survival rates is that the types of records and the business of the courts differed. The aim here is to highlight some of the implications of the types and limitations of the source material for our understanding of the administration of law by medieval London.

EARLIEST SURVIVALS AND SUBSEQUENT LOSSES

Like most if not all English towns, London has lost many of its records to fire: not just the Great Fire of 1666, but also to conflagrations which affected individual administrative departments. Neglect had no doubt destroyed some of its legal records long before the 1660s; and even once the rise of antiquarianism led to more care being taken, the antiquarians themselves were (notoriously) not above removing records and retaining them in their own collections.[13] The result is that London has proportionately fewer surviving legal records from our period than have other, smaller and probably less well-administered, towns. There are, for example, far fewer surviving full court rolls (that is, complete except for piecemeal damage and loss) for the London Mayor's Court than for the Winchester City Court.

Possibly more surprising at first sight than this is the fact that London does not appear to have been significantly ahead of towns like Winchester – or indeed of some manor courts – in establishing formal series of legal records. The late thirteenth and early fourteenth centuries were periods which saw great changes in London's record-keeping. This affected practices in its three main courts, the Husting, the Mayor's Court and the Sheriffs' Court. A series of rolls registering property transactions and testamentary provisions (the Husting rolls of deeds and wills) probably started before 1250. While it could be that the earliest known Husting rolls, apparently of the 1230s, were a combined record, containing entries relating to legal disputes as well as deeds and wills, the earliest of the surviving rolls which record the Husting's activities as a court of law is from 1272.[14] Mayor's Court records which include, among other administrative business, the details of lawsuits, survive from 1298. It is certain that the Sheriffs' Court, or the sheriffs themselves, also kept records of cases heard in that court by this date. Although the earliest surviving full record is of a single case from 1318, which is embedded in a larger portion of a roll of 1320, there are some extracts recorded in the Mayor's Court rolls relating to individual Sheriffs' Court cases. The first of these concerns a case heard in 1300. There is also an order in a Husting roll of 1293 to produce the record of a Sheriffs' Court case in which error was alleged.[15]

SURVIVING CITY LEGAL SOURCES

The Court of Husting

The survival rate and organisation of the city's court records considerably affect our ability to understand the administration of

[13] Sharpe, *CalLBA*, pp. 11–12.
[14] Martin, *Husting Roll of Deeds and Wills*, pp. 7–9.
[15] *CalEMCR*, pp. 89–91; CLRO, HR CP22, m. 5v.

the law by medieval London. The Husting rolls, which are almost complete from 1272 on, are until 1448 arranged in a similar way to most contemporary court records. Session headings are followed by a note of business undertaken at that session, from the bringing of writs, through the process (the formal stages by which a case progressed), to the pleadings and to judgments.[16] From 1448 onwards, a 'session book' was employed, in which the briefest of entries recorded the type of lawsuits, process and judgments under session headings. From this date, separate plea rolls recording every stage, including the pleadings, in a few individual cases also survive (rolls relating to individual cases may once have existed for all actions which resulted in pleadings: Husting of Common Pleas Roll 21 concerns a single case, although, because it involved properties forfeited for treason, one cannot be sure that this reflected normal practice). As a result, it is possible both to examine the detailed workings of those cases which resulted in pleadings, which are often given at some length, and to analyse the court's business in terms of its nature and activity levels.

The Mayor's Court

Unfortunately, the Husting is the only city court for which records survive in a virtually unbroken series. The original series of Mayor's Court rolls, which contain details of, usually, several cases under a session heading, ends in 1307, and a new series, the plea and memoranda rolls, does not start until 1323 and ends in 1482. The plea and memoranda rolls, as their title suggests, are only in part a record of legal proceedings in the Mayor's Court, a reflection of the fact that this was originally a general court which did not distinguish clearly between legal and administrative activities ('administrative', in the sense, for example, of enforcing price or quality controls on basic necessities offered for sale).[17] It is possible that there continued to be a separate roll, concerned

[16] In 1329/30, there was another general Husting file which included all the paperwork relating to actions which were pending: CLRO, HR CP53, m. 13.

[17] E.g. on 17 July 1364, the court's business included swearing in the Tanners Company surveyors, taking of mainprises to keep the peace, and the presentation of a royal writ of protection: *CalPMR 1323–64*, p. 272. By the 1480s, these rolls recorded little except writs of protection and acknowledgements of deeds, receipts and bonds: e.g. *CalPMR 1458–82*, pp. 142–8.

purely with litigation and related business. A. H. Thomas, editor of the early Mayor's Court rolls, believed that these rolls were written up by the mayor's (personal) clerk and retained by each mayor when he left office, which might explain the complete disappearance of Mayor's Court rolls after 1307.[18] There is no doubt that this was the case with the Sheriffs' Court rolls in the early fourteenth century, for it was stated in the 1321 eyre that each sheriff 'took his rolls away with him as he pleased' at the end of his term.[19] Whether or not this was the case for the city's mayors, the number of legal disputes entered in the plea and memoranda rolls was probably never an accurate guide to the numbers of bills and plaints presented to the Mayor's Court (for instance, virtually all the entries in the plea and memoranda rolls relating to actions at law record a determination, whereas only a minority of cases recorded in the few surviving court rolls did so). Unfortunately, the mismatch between the numbers of cases brought in this court and recorded in the plea and memoranda rolls clearly grew greater over time. The Mayor's Court roll for 1305/6 (Roll H) contains thirty-four personal actions, whereas the plea and memoranda roll for 1354/5 (Roll A7) contains ten entries relating to this type of case.[20] Even allowing for the aftermath of the first onslaught of the Plague and the probability that the Mayor's Court was more constrained in the types of personal pleas it could hear then than it had been in the early 1300s, it seems unlikely that it was really entertaining as few as this in the 1350s. Moreover, at a time when we know from two files of bills of the 1450s that the Mayor's Court was handling several hundred personal pleas a year, the equivalent plea and memoranda roll contains just five entries relating to actions of this type.[21]

The evidence to be discussed in Chapter 3 suggests the Mayor's Court underwent a major development and expansion of its common-law side sometime between the late-fourteenth and mid-fifteenth century. These changes may have affected the way in which the plea and memoranda rolls were used. Certainly in 1460 individuals were paying to have certain matters (especially the

[18] *CalEMCR*, p. viii. [19] Cam, *Eyre 1321*, II, pp. 113–14.

[20] *CalEMCR*, pp. 228–52, *CalPMR 1323–64*, pp. 241–57.

[21] CLRO, Mayor's Court Files of Original Bills, MC1/3A; *CalPMR 1437–57*, pp. 151–7, *CalPMR 1458–82*, pp. 1–3; see Chapter 4 for further discussion of this evidence.

acknowledgement of deeds) enrolled in this series.[22] This is the only date at which payments were noted, so the payments themselves could possibly have been a short-lived experiment. On balance, however, it seems more likely that all entries in the plea and memoranda rolls relating to private affairs, including personal actions, had to be paid for by this stage.

Whether or not the Mayor's Court of the later fourteenth century onwards did keep a full set of 'session-and-plea rolls', therefore, nothing now survives in the city's own archives for the period 1307 to 1550 apart from the minority of cases enrolled in the plea and memoranda rolls and a large number of individual bills. There are well over a thousand bills relating to common-law and non-common-law cases (known as original bills and petitions respectively) still in existence for the period up to 1550.[23] A file of bills from the 1450s contains both the means of assigning the bills to particular years and occasional contemporary numerations.[24] This makes it possible to establish with fair confidence the minimum size of the original files (the present file probably includes parts of at least two original files) and the extent to which the survivals represent a reasonable sample of what once existed. In addition to the entries in the plea and memoranda rolls, the records of the Court of Aldermen (records known, confusingly, as the journals of the Common Council for most of the fifteenth century and, from the 1490s onwards, as the repertories), contain entries relating to a number of Mayor's Court cases.[25] (This is because the informal or non-common-law side of the Mayor's Court was the Court of Aldermen 'sitting judicially': that is, the mayor and aldermen dealt with disputes informally in the margins of their administrative work.) A seventeenth-century 'Book of Precedents' also includes details of actions brought in the Mayor's Court in the two preceding centuries: mainly, however, from after 1550.[26]

[22] *CalPMR 1458–82*, p. 16.

[23] CLRO, Mayor's Court Files of Original Bills, MC1/1 to MC1/3A, with a few items in MC1/158B.

[24] CLRO, Mayor's Court File of Original Bills, MC1/3A.

[25] CLRO, Jors. 1–8, CLRO, Reps. 1–12/2.

[26] CLRO, Book of Precedents, 205C/3.

The Sheriffs' Court

If outgoing medieval sheriffs continued to retain their rolls on leaving office, it is perhaps not surprising that no rolls at all, apart from the part-roll for 1320, appear to survive for the medieval period. Once the last of the London eyres had taken place, which happened in 1341, there was little incentive to maintain a central archive of Sheriffs' Court records. (Eyres were the periodic judicial visitations to the localities of the central court justices, whose duties included hearing 'pleas of the crown' such as criminal prosecutions and checking that the local judges were not defrauding the king or abusing their powers.) Because it was often difficult to recover the record of individual Sheriffs' Court actions, particularly ancient ones, the city did on occasion to try to force the sheriffs to hand over certain types of records on leaving office. The attempt was only partially successful.[27] Moreover, efforts at preservation related to records of legal disputes over rights to and arising out of real property: to the possessory assizes of freshforce and *in natura mortis antecessoris* (the city's equivalents to the national assizes of novel disseisin and mort d'ancestor), sessions of which were held separately before the sheriffs and coroner.[28] Indeed, however they were initiated, whether begun by writ, by bill or by plaint, the legal actions for which records were most carefully preserved were those which involved disputes over real property and rights arising from it. The differences in practice therefore probably partly reflect, not some arbitrary distinction in the way that bits of parchment were treated, but the particular respect accorded to the protection of rights in land, and the need to preserve evidence about possession and ownership for far longer than it was necessary to preserve evidence about debts, trespasses and the like. (Records of the property-related assizes of nuisance, which were held before the mayor and aldermen, have also survived in relatively large numbers.) The consequence is that, although many thousands of Sheriffs' Court cases are mentioned in the city and central records during our period, most of that evidence amounts to no more than the briefest of notes,

27 Riley, *Munimenta Gildhallae*, II, i, p. 89 or *CalLBC*, p. 14 (1304); *ibid.*, p. 108 (1356) and *CalLBG*, p. 199 (1365); Chew, *London Possessory Assizes*, pp. xiii, 46–72 (Roll BB, 1370–84).

28 Chew, *London Possessory Assizes*, pp. xiv–xv, xxiv–xxv.

telling us what type of action was involved, who the litigants were, and when it was initiated. Of, probably, several hundreds of thousands of pleas which were brought in that court between 1300 and 1550, we have detailed evidence relating to a few hundreds.

Two other factors probably militated against the establishment of a central archive for the Sheriffs' Court rolls. The first is that, in the early part of our period at least, the sheriffs had a personal relationship with 'their' courts and may have regarded both the staff and the paperwork produced by the court as 'theirs' (rather as owners of private courts usually kept court rolls among their own muniments instead of creating a separate repository).[29] Secondly, the fact that many actions were begun by bill seems of itself to have encouraged informality. No original Sheriffs' Court bill is known to survive from this period. Judging by practice in the Mayor's Court, however, by the second half of the fourteenth century the practice was to enter any process on the bill. Bills were then filed, or strung together, according to the term in which the action had been determined.[30] (Practices in the Mayor's Court, and possibly therefore also the Sheriffs' Court, were different again by the sixteenth century. At this period, the attorneys themselves (who were the Mayor's Court clerks) held their clients' bills. That the clerk-attorneys were controlling the files will probably have led to even greater informality.)[31]

It is by no means inconceivable that sometime after 1350 the Sheriffs' Court abandoned the practice of keeping a formal session-and-plea roll altogether. Only in the case of determined pleas, or perhaps only if the record was ordered to be produced, would the clerks write up a consolidated record of the case in question. Two pieces of evidence suggest that, in the Sheriffs' Court as in the Mayor's, the formal rolls might indeed have been replaced around 1380 by an informal session or case book, with documents relating to pending litigation being kept on file *pro tempore*, and those relating to determined cases being filed separately and on a semi-permanent basis (or even written up and then filed). We are told that in 1382 Mayor's Court bills relating to terminated cases were

[29] *CalEMCR*, p. viii, fn. 2. [30] *CalPMR 1381–1412*, pp. 16–17.

[31] CLRO, MS Book of Precedents, p. 518, for 'Coys' File [Roger Coys, a Mayor's Court clerk-attorney from the 1540s on] for the month of January, [Mayor] Champion's time.

being filed separately, 'term' by 'term'.[32] Less than three years previously, however, there had been a file of bills 'terminated in the time of Philipot mayor' (1379/80); that is, apparently these bills were then contained in an annual file.[33] If indeed the annual file of bills had been divided into four in the early 1380s, it could be that this was the point at which the court's workload had first begun to expand dramatically. Even a significant increase, however, would not necessarily lead to a sub-division of the file. What probably would have encouraged division into smaller and more chronologically restricted files was a change of use, from, perhaps, a depository of documents which were destroyed as soon as the case was determined to a semi-permanent archive that was consulted (and so had to be of manageable size and orderly) and, more importantly, had to be relied upon because the only other record then being kept was a session book.[34] If so, and if a similar reorganisation occurred at the same time in the Sheriffs' Court, it was almost certainly the sheriffs' clerks, not the sheriffs themselves, who made the change. It is from the 1380s or 1390s that we have the first evidence to suggest that, although the sheriffs and former sheriffs remained in theory responsible for producing the record of cases heard before them if it was challenged or appealed to, it was in practice the undersheriffs who kept the records, sometimes going back many years.[35] Undersheriffs are first mentioned in similar administrative capacities in the Husting rolls of the 1390s, and such references become common by the early 1400s.[36] It seems quite possible, therefore, that the 1380s saw a reorganisation of the way in which records were made and kept in both the Mayor's and Sheriffs' Court, with the undersheriff acquiring a responsibility for maintaining and producing on demand 'the record', not only of his own time, but also of his predecessors'. Whether or not this is so, it no more preserved the Sheriffs' Court records for the longer term than did the sheriffs who removed their rolls with them on leaving office. Perhaps

[32] *CalPMR 1381–1412*, pp. 16–17.
[33] CLRO, Mayor's Court File of Original Bills, MC1/1, item 163.
[34] For a reference in 1394 to 'the paper', probably meaning a book of some kind: CLRO, Mayor's Court File of Original Bills, MC1/2, item 159.
[35] Chew, *London Possessory Assizes*, p. 46.
[36] CLRO, HR CP117, m. 8v, HR CP120, m. 4, HR CP126, m. 3v, HR CP127, m. 2, HR CP128, mm. 9, 13, HR CP129, m. 10, HR CP130, m. 6, HR CP131, mm. 3, 4, *et seq.*

because the Sheriffs' Court was, as will be argued later, a far busier court than the medieval and early modern Mayor's Court, or perhaps because few of their rolls and files ever reached the relative safety of Guildhall, almost nothing original has survived.

Fortunately, the Husting rolls have, as has already been mentioned, a number of copies of Sheriffs' Court records embedded in them, and details of a few dozen pre-1550 records of individual Sheriffs' Court cases, known by the 1540s at the latest as *querelae levatae* after their preamble ('Plaint brought [*querela levata*] in Sheriff X's counter . . .'), survive among the Mayor's Court bills.[37] Even the latter records, brief and few though they are, are useful, in that they provide evidence of process. The full record of pleadings and list of errors which survive in cases summoned into the Husting on error can be very revealing. At worst, since they note when a case was initiated, when further process occurred, and when it ended, they provide evidence of the time it took to determine a case and similar procedural matters. At best, they throw light on questions of jurisdiction, the court's powers, its reception of legal representatives, and the like.

Other sources

What neither these chance survivals from the Sheriffs' Court nor the Mayor's Court plea and memoranda rolls and files of original bills allow one to do, however, is to find out exactly how much business the two courts were entertaining at different periods or what sort of actions were brought most frequently. Nor, even when large numbers of individual bills and petitions survive, is it possible to be sure whether observed changes over time reflect actual changes, and, if they do, whether they reflect them accurately.

In the absence of complete sets of session records, apart from the Husting rolls, one of the best sources of evidence for the type and level of Mayor's Court and Sheriffs' Court business from the early fifteenth century onwards are the Chancery *corpus cum causa* writ files held in The National Archives.[38] The returns made to

[37] CLRO, Sheriffs' Court Rolls [*sic*], 1407–1578 (Box 1A), 238C; Dummelow, *Wax Chandlers of London*, p. 160 (16*d* paid 'for a querelaint removinge out of the Sherifes Court').

[38] TNA (PRO), Chancery *Corpus Cum Causa* Writ Files, C244.

these writs give brief details of any action, and sometimes of several actions, brought against the petitioner. Of course they are neither comprehensive nor necessarily representative. They also suffer from changes over time which make long-term comparisons impossible.[39] However, they do provide evidence of the minimum level of activity in both city courts, year by year, and, in the short term, the basis for an attempt to work out what the probable true levels were. In addition, by comparing the number of writs contained in the *corpus cum causa* files in the years for which numbered Mayor's Court bills survive, one can get an idea of the proportion of original bills which then resulted in petitions to the chancellor.

Other major sources of evidence about the administration of the law by the city, and indeed about who was involved, are the city's custumals and letterbooks. Insofar as we know or can guess at the circumstances of their compilation, the former were usually produced under the aegis of city officers: the chamberlain, Andrew Horn ('Liber Horn'), in the early fourteenth century and common clerks John Carpenter ('Liber Albus') and William Dunthorne ('Liber Dunthorne') in the early and later fifteenth. The earliest surviving custumal is the 'Liber de Antiquis Legibus', compiled in the mid-1270s, by and for Alderman Arnald fitzThedmar; the latest is 'Liber Fletewode', presented to the city in 1576 by the then recorder, William Fletewode. The custumals are more or less (generally less) well-organised compilations of city regulations with accompanying exemplars, together with, particularly in the case of the earlier custumals, much else: the 'Liber de Antiquis Legibus', for example, contains city annals partly written by fitzThedmar himself.[40] Many entries are consequently of relevance to the administration of the law by the city: royal charters, ordinances which modified or generated city custom, declarations about custom, and examples of custom in action, as well as other matters of continuing interest to the city. London's custumals do not seem to contain many examples of outright forgeries (its 'Henry I' charter being a rare example of a recorded document of doubtful authenticity).[41] Although they cannot be assumed to

[39] See pp. 153–4, 158.

[40] Ker, *Medieval Manuscripts in British Libraries, vol. I*, pp. 18–42 and *idem*, '*Liber Custumarum*, and other Manuscripts formerly at the Guildhall', pp. 37–45.

[41] Reynolds, 'Henry I's Charter for London'.

provide wholly reliable evidence of contemporary custom and practice, the compilers undoubtedly intended that their custumals be used and useful, and city magistrates did indeed turn to them when in doubt.[42] The fact that any city custom was liable to be challenged by a litigant or indeed by the central court justices, and that antiquity alone would not suffice to protect it, explains the long-lasting fondness of the city for custumals which not only recorded its customs, but also included royal writs allowing its customs or granting privileges and which provided details of cases which had been resolved in its favour on this basis.[43]

The letterbooks were a general record of business relating to the city, the Court of Aldermen and, in due course, the Common Council. The first three volumes in their present arrangement overlap considerably in terms of chronology, with substantial portions of Letterbooks A and B consisting largely of records of private recognizances, or acknowledgements of debts, and other private deeds, which were not recorded in the later volumes.[44] They may well owe their origin to an attempt, possibly during the period when the city was governed directly on the king's behalf by a warden (1285–98), to centralise and secure existing city records, particularly those of a type later held by the chamberlain, and to discover and record all hitherto unrecorded city ordinances. By the 1310s they had developed into formal records in which entries derived from other sources (notably, in the fifteenth century, the city's journals and, later, its repertories, which contain marginalia presumably written by the common clerk or another senior clerk, ordering that an entry be copied into the relevant letterbook), which were considered to be worthy of lasting remembrance, were engrossed. They include some ordinances relating to the administration of the law among a great deal of other matter, and also, erratically, the appointment of officers, including law officers. National legislation, too, sometimes found a place either in the custumals or in the letterbooks, where it affected the city. Some of

[42] For the compilers' motives, see Bateson, *Borough Customs*, I, pp. xv–xviii; Catto, 'Andrew Horn', esp. pp. 371–82, esp. 370, 372; Riley, *Munimenta Gildhallae*, I, pp. 3–4.

[43] For the use made by the city's magistrates of its custumals, see e.g. CLRO, Jor. 3, fo. 173, CLRO, Rep. 7, fo. 148, *CalLBK*, pp. 90–1 (a response to a writ of certiorari which refers to several city custumals) and pp. 151–60.

[44] Tucker, 'First Steps towards an English Legal Profession'.

this throws light on relationships between the city courts and the central courts at Westminster. Letterbook A, for example, contains a copy of the Statute of Westminster I and (extracts from) that of Gloucester.[45] (Chapter 12 of the Statute of Gloucester was apparently introduced and subsequently amended at the city's behest. This allowed London citizens who 'vouched a foreign [non-freeman] to warranty' (which required whoever had sold or given the property to them to defend the case instead of them, on the grounds that the former owner's right to give or sell it had been challenged, and to recompense them with property of equivalent value should the case be lost) to stay proceedings in the Husting until the vouchee, the former owner, had been summoned before the justices of the Common Bench and the question of the warranty had been determined there.[46] The procedure is frequently referred to in the late fourteenth-century Husting rolls.) While there is no reason to suspect that the letterbooks were subject to even the relatively modest amount of manipulation of their contents which might have affected the custumals, given the use made of the latter, they were clearly written up later than the events they record, sometimes considerably later, and only ever offer a selective view of the city's government and administration.[47]

In summary, it should be borne in mind that the sources of the evidence for much of what follows are very unbalanced. They are unbalanced chronologically: far fewer city court records survive from the late fifteenth and the first half of the sixteenth centuries than from any earlier period; the further back in time one goes, until 1300 at least, the more material there is. As a result, the seventy years or so before 1550, during which period the practices and activity levels of two of the city's courts may have changed considerably, are exceptionally obscure. There is an even more marked imbalance in terms of the material produced by and referring to different courts. We have a great deal relating to the Husting, some evidence about the Mayor's Court in terms of the details of particular actions but not much about the overall picture, and very little indeed, relative to what there must once

[45] CLRO, LBA, fos. 118–25v, 125v–6; *CalLBA*, pp. ix–xi.

[46] Sayles, 'Two Revisions of the Statute of Gloucester, 1278', especially pp. 470–1.

[47] See, for example, *CalLBL*, p. 280, where the sheriffs said to have been present at a meeting of the Common Council were in fact in office the year before.

have been, about the Sheriffs' Court either in terms of detail or of the overall picture. Conjecture therefore plays a much larger part in the reconstruction of the latter court than of the other two. Although that is not a fatal difficulty, it is disappointing. There is no doubt that the Sheriffs' Court was by far the most important of the city courts in the sense that it was the most active, rivalling the common-law side of the Mayor's Court in the importance of those who litigated there and the matters over which they fought. It was almost certainly also the most sophisticated, legally speaking.

1

THE ADMINISTRATION OF THE LAW BY THE CITY IN CONTEXT

INTRODUCTION

A large, wealthy and well-organised entity, corporate if not in fact formally incorporated, medieval London was far more important than any single other English borough or county (throughout our period it was itself a county). For present purposes, the significance of this is that the city was in a better position than almost anyone or anything else in England to shape and influence its context and to protect its own interests.[1] Conversely, it could not afford to ignore its context, and its very size and wealth meant that it tended to attract more attention than lesser cities and towns, some of it hostile or greedy, from other powerful individuals and organisations. The aim of this chapter, therefore, is to set London in its historical and legal context.

HISTORICAL CONTEXT

Economic and demographic context

Just how large London was is the subject of considerable doubt. A modest estimate would give it a population of about 25–35,000 in 1300, roughly equivalent to Bruges at the same period.[2] This may

[1] Campbell, 'Power and Authority', pp. 75–8; Rigby, Ewan, 'Government, Power and Authority, pp. 292–300; Barron, 'London 1300–1540', pp. 409–12. But see also Bolton, 'The City and the Crown', pp. 11–24; Postan, 'Economic and Political Relations of England and the Hanse', pp. 91–154; Tucker, 'Government and Politics', pp. 340–6, 353–7, 368, 373–6; and see *ibid.*, p. 222, for the kind of concessions the city could and did obtain.

[2] Nicholas, *The Later Medieval City*, p. 70; but see p. 51, for the suggestion that 'London may have declined from 100,000 to 60,000 in the late fourteenth century'.

be a considerable underestimate, however. Evidence of the intensification of land use in London during the thirteenth century suggests that, like England as a whole, its population grew rapidly after 1200. It might well have had as many residents in 1300 as it may have had by 1550, 80,000 or more.[3] If so, it was among the 'top ten' European cities of the period.[4] Its resident population may have constituted about one in a hundred of the population of England as a whole.[5]

In 1300, the economy as a whole was a lively one, because demand for the basics of life was strong. As labour was cheap, those in a position to exploit this demand grew wealthy.[6] The result was a sharply divided society, with a wide gap between the very rich and the very poor. Consequently, there was also a market for the most luxurious of luxury goods. The requirement that goods such as silks and spices be transported great distances from their places of origin, combined with the relative lack of commercial sophistication among English traders and merchants at this period, meant that foreign merchants dominated the lucrative import and export trade. Most notable among these were the Flemings, who bought up English wool to supply the flourishing Flemish cloth towns, German and Scandinavian merchants from northern Europe, who had access to Russia, and the Italians, who controlled much of the trade with the East. As importantly, the Italians took over some of the financial activities as well as the trade of the Jews after the latters' expulsion in the 1290s, their role as financiers to the crown giving them considerable influence over royal policies, if at a price.[7]

The dramatic population loss which followed the first onslaught of the Black Death in 1348–9 punctured this buoyant economy. Towns and markets which had mushroomed to support a high level of trading decayed and in some cases reverted to villages. After a period of adjustment, wages rose and rents and land prices fell.[8] Consequently, differences in wealth became less

[3] Keene, 'A New Study of London before the Great Fire', pp. 11–21, esp. 18–19, and *idem*, 'Cheapside before the Great Fire', pp. 19–20.

[4] Nicholas, *The Later Medieval City*, p. 70.

[5] Bolton, *The Medieval English Economy*, Chapter 2, esp. p. 51, for national population estimates ranging from 3.7 to 7 millions, *c.* 1300.

[6] *Ibid.*, Chapters 3 and 4 and pp. 67, 68, 70.

[7] Brooke, Keir, *London 800–1216*, pp. 266–76.

[8] Bolton, *Medieval English Economy*, Chapters 7 and 9.

marked. Trade not only reduced in volume but changed in nature. There was more demand for goods of middling quality and cheap frivolities than there had been, and, perhaps, less for the most extravagant luxuries. More importantly in terms of later developments, although England remained an exporter of semi-processed materials such as lead and tin and, above all, wool, increasingly it was manufacturing and exporting good quality, finished cloth as well. The importance of this lay not merely in the 'added value' of manufacturing but also in the fact that it was no longer necessary for wool or unfinished cloth to be exported via continental cloth-manufacturing and -finishing towns.[9] English merchants were able to control the cloth-making networks and started to challenge alien merchants for the control of internal trade generally. They grew wealthier as a result, better able, in a few cases as individuals but more often as syndicates, to influence royal policy in their favour. They even aspired to challenge alien merchants in the highly lucrative business of international trade and transport. And although these aspirations were initially frustrated, English merchants both contributed to and benefited from the political changes of the seventeenth century. Even by 1550, a kingdom where foreign merchants had, two hundred and fifty years previously, financed and organised overseas trade and native seafarers had tended not to venture far from the English coast, was being transformed into a high-seafaring, mercantile nation.

One consequence of these developments was that London acquired an ever more commanding position as a focus of national and international trade, with its merchants controlling, not merely the trade in materials and commodities, but also the production and marketing of manufactured goods.[10] Even in the fourteenth century, before it started to overshadow a number of provincial cities and towns to such an extent that they withered in its shade, it was a giant by English standards: York and Bristol, the largest provincial cities in 1377, had perhaps 11–14,000 inhabitants at a time when London had perhaps 40–45,000. By the 1520s, when the two largest provincial cities at that time, Bristol and Norwich,

[9] Munro, *Wool, Cloth and Gold*, pp. 214–15. Cloth was worth, at the very least, 37% more than the wool used to make it: Bolton, *Medieval English Economy*, p. 301.

[10] Dyer, *Decline and Growth*, pp. 18, 25–6; Bolton, *Medieval English Economy*, pp. 254–5; Britnell, *Growth and Decline in Colchester*, pp. 176–7.

had perhaps 7–8,000 inhabitants apiece, London's population was perhaps as much as ten times this. In terms of wealth, the ratios appear to have been even more in the capital's favour by the first half of the sixteenth century.[11]

Political and social context

Of this population, only a minority were freemen or freewomen of the city. In the mid-thirteenth century, men were evidently accounted freemen if they owned city properties and paid city rates (were 'in scot and lot'), even if they were not residents, and regardless of whether or not their fathers had been freemen.[12] A man whose father had been a freeman at the time of his birth could exercise his own rights as a freeman without more ado unless his status was challenged in the course of a legal action, when the question would be tried by a jury of the neighbourhood in which he claimed to have been born.[13] By 1300, however, owning city property probably did not of itself confer the freedom. There were then three main methods of gaining it: if not a man's by birth ('by patrimony'), then it had to be obtained 'by apprenticeship' (as a time-served or released apprentice; later, as a former apprentice who was a member of one of the city's trade companies) or 'by redemption' (purchase).[14] Sometimes it was granted *ex officio* or, relatively rarely, as an honour. And the rules governing the freedom continued to be tightened after 1300. From 1387 onwards, even those who had a right to claim the freedom because their father had been a freeman at the time of their birth were required to claim it formally, by registering with the city chamberlain and being sworn in as freemen.[15] In 1433, residence became obligatory for all freemen who were merchants or other

[11] Britnell, 'The Economy of British Towns', pp. 313–33, esp. 329–30; Dyer, *Decline and Growth*, Chapter 4 and pp. 25–6, 32–3, or *idem*, 'Appendix: Ranking Lists of English Medieval Towns', pp. 747–70. For a subsidy collected in 1541 and 1542, London's 89 wealthiest residents had an assessed liability of £7,100 *p.a.*, equal to 15% of the total actually raised: Lang, *Tudor Subsidy Rolls*, pp. lxxvii–lixviii; Jurkowski, Smith, Crook, *Lay Taxes in England and Wales*, p. 142. In contrast, in 1524/5, all the subsidy payers in the most highly taxed provincial city, Norwich, contributed at most £749 *p.a.*: Dyer, *Decline and Growth*, p. 62.

[12] *CalPMR 1364–81*, pp. xix; Riley, *Munimenta Gildhallae*, I, pp. 142–3, 391.

[13] *CalPMR 1364–81*, p. xxi, Riley, *Munimenta Gildhallae*, I, p. 206.

[14] *CalPMR 1364–81*, p. xxvii. [15] *Ibid.*, p. xxix, *CalLBH*, p. 310.

traders (that is, who were not honorary freemen), and the freedom could be lost if the holder lived outside the city for more than a year.[16]

It is unlikely that at any time before 1550 more than twelve per cent of all residents were themselves freemen of the city (as with population estimates, estimates of freemen vary widely). None of the registers of freemen, which probably began in 1275, survive for our period.[17] Lists of those who purchased the freedom or entered by apprenticeship over a period of thirty-eight months from 1309 to 1312 are however incorporated in Letterbook D, and part of a register listing all those who entered the freedom in twenty-one months from 1551 to 1553 also exists. In the early fourteenth century, on average some twenty-four individuals a month were admitted to the freedom by redemption or apprenticeship.[18] How many others exercised the freedom by patrimony at this date is unfortunately unknowable, although it is likely that proportionately more did so in 1309–12 than in 1551–3. In the early 1550s, on average fifty-two individuals a month became free of the city, of whom forty-eight did so by apprenticeship (the predominant method) or redemption. A few of these were the children of freemen; overall, at this period about one in seven of those admitted could have claimed the freedom by patrimony.[19] The probability is that about one in sixteen residents at the beginning of our period and about one in eight or nine at the end was a city freeman (or, rarely, a freewoman).[20] It should be remembered, however, that a good many of the others will have belonged to the families of freemen and so will have been entitled, directly or indirectly, to some of the benefits of the freedom of the city.

Freemen enjoyed a number of privileges denied to other city residents: they could sell wholesale, they could play some part in determining how the city would be governed, and in return they supported city government financially and practically. They also benefited from the legal privileges won by the city on their behalf. Other residents were in theory not much better off than non-Londoners – and were lumped together with non-Londoners as

[16] *CalLBK*, pp. 161–6. [17] *CalPMR 1364–81*, p. xxvii.
[18] *Ibid.*, pp. xxxii–xxxiii. [19] *Ibid.*, pp. xxix–xxx and xxxiv.
[20] Williams, *Medieval London*, p. 48; Thrupp, *Merchant Class of Medieval London*, p. 51; *CalPMR 1364–81*, p. lxii.

'foreigns', that is, Englishmen who were not city freemen – when they were involved in legal disputes in the London courts, although no doubt being local could confer benefits. Having said that city freemen were an elite group among London residents, however, it is not the case that they were all wealthy merchants. Such men dominated city government, but there were something like fifty trade companies in London by the fifteenth century, some of them with tiny memberships and modest resources.[21]

A feature of government and politics in London after 1300 is the gradual elimination of the relatively long-lasting London dynasties which had played a prominent part in city government before that date.[22] No doubt the city had always acted as a magnet for aspiring men, but the tendency for those who governed it to have made their fortunes elsewhere before moving to London becomes a noticeable feature of city life by the fifteenth century.[23] It has been suggested that this change reflected a shift from rule by a patriciate with knightly aspirations to government by merchants with professional administrators to assist them. The occasionally extreme factionalism of the later thirteenth century can, according to this theory, be seen as part of a struggle for power between the conservative dynasts and a modernising, populist group which included a significant number of 'new men'.[24] Although this exaggerates the extent of the change (even at the end of our period, some aldermen came from gentry backgrounds and a number certainly had knightly aspirations), it is true that aldermen had largely ceased to be 'hands-on' administrators by 1300, leaving that sort of work to clerks.

The period between the 1190s and the later fourteenth century saw the emergence of structures of government which were to last for centuries.[25] By 1400, the city was governed by the mayor and aldermen sitting several times a week as the Court of Aldermen, and the more important of their decisions had to be approved (and

[21] Thrupp, *Merchant Class of London*, pp. 43, 46 (for 1501); Tucker, 'Government and Politics', pp. 103–5, 151–2 (for the 1460s/1470s).

[22] Thrupp, *Merchant Class of London*, pp. 39–40.

[23] Tucker, 'Government and Politics', pp. 77–85 and Appendix 2A.

[24] Williams, *Medieval London*, p. 322 (the proportion of aldermen belonging to city dynasties fell from 82% before 1230 to 4% by 1327–40, while the proportion of those described as 'English immigrants' rose from 5% to 58%).

[25] For what follows, unless otherwise stated, see Barron, *London in the Middle Ages*.

were occasionally the result of petitioning) by the much larger Common Council, which was convened less often – as infrequently as eight times a year by the 1470s, although this represented a considerable reduction on practice earlier in the century. This structure echoed that of national government: king, a great council of earls (or noblemen) who were his near-equals and advisers, advised by officials, and the Commons in Parliament, a body representative of 'the better sort' elected by their peers on a regional basis. Similarly, government in the city rested on an administrative substructure of wards, the areas into which the city was divided, much as national government rested on an administrative substructure of counties and hundreds or their equivalent. On the other hand, throughout our period the mayor and aldermen maintained an active interest in the daily running of the city, and even when they were meeting relatively infrequently, common councils were far more regularly engaged with the major decisions of government than were contemporary parliaments. Moreover, the small size of most London wards (twenty-four of them lying wholly or partly within the 'square mile' enclosed by the city walls), the existence of ward as well as shrieval administrations and the aldermen's position at the head of the former, meant that city government and ward administration were much closer than was national government to local administration.

This was, however, probably less true by the end of our period than it had been in 1300. An attempt to create a formal place for all the city trade companies in the city's government in the 1380s failed, and elections to the Common Council and aldermanry continued thereafter to be made by the city wards. By 1550, however, there were twelve 'great' or 'livery' companies to which every aspiring governor, if he wanted to get to the top, had to belong or transfer.[26] From the later fifteenth century on, the leading companies played an increasingly prominent role in city government and politics, offering an alternative and often more effective and efficient means of raising money, mobilising manpower, and even controlling and defending the city.[27] The effect of this, as with a number of other developments of the later

[26] Barron, 'London 1300–1540', pp. 405–9; Nightingale, 'Capitalists, Crafts and Constitutional Change, pp. 3–35; Tucker, 'Government and Politics', p. 103.
[27] Tucker, 'Government and Politics', pp. 161, 163–6.

medieval period, was probably to detach London's higher-level government from Londoners born and bred. By 1500, Londoners by birth seem to have had hardly more in common with their governors than have today's Cockneys with the mayor and aldermen of the city of London.

On the other hand, London's governors and, to a lesser extent, its officers were a comparatively open elite (compared to other English towns of the period, that is). The city's increasing dominance meant that it had influence on other towns. Equally, however, men who moved to London in order to enhance their fortunes brought with them different ideas and ways of doing things. As a result, the capital was a force for change as well as interchange.[28] Exposure to new ideas may also have encouraged some of the men who governed and administered the city to take a broader view of their world than they would have done even in the leading provincial cities. It is noteworthy that the two lawyers of the fifteenth and early sixteenth centuries who are best known for what they had to say about politics as well as the law, Sir John Fortescue and Sir Thomas More, had held a city undershrievalty before going on to greater things at Westminster and beyond.

THE LEGAL CONTEXT

City law and custom in the national context

From the second half of the twelfth century, developments in England had resulted in the establishment of a number of legal remedies and of routine methods of initiating legal actions which were available nationally. These are generally regarded as critically important landmarks in the formation of the system of English national law known as the common law.[29] The 'possessory assizes', which were designed to provide a way of recovering lands or tenements rapidly in the event that the occupier or his heir had recently been 'disseised' (ousted), were developed as a nationally available remedy in the second half of the twelfth century.

[28] E.g. Hughes, 'Guildhall and Chancery English', especially p. 59, arguing that 'Chancery Standard' English of the mid-fifteenth century, the forerunner of modern written English, may have owed a debt to earlier developments at Guildhall.

[29] Brand, 'Local Custom in the Early Common Law', p. 150.

A feature of the assizes was that the method of trial was an inquiry by a jury, rather than a duel.[30] At much the same time there emerged what was to become the main mechanism both for transferring cases between courts and for initiating lawsuits in courts which would not normally entertain the case in question: the 'writ system'. Would-be plaintiffs were in due course able to buy from the royal Chancery a writ to the holder of a court, usually in standard form and for a predictable cost, which ordered him to hear and determine the case in his court (alternatively, the local sheriff might be told to get the appropriate court to deal with the case, or to do so himself if the court failed to act). These related developments have been called 'the birth of the common law'.[31]

Associated with these developments was the emergence of two specialised law courts. One of these was by 1300 settled at the Palace of Westminster, just to the west of the city of London, and the other came increasingly, over the course of the fourteenth century, to be based there.[32] By far the most active of the two specialised law courts was the first, the Court of the Common Bench or Common Pleas; its sister, and superior, court was the Court of King's Bench. Broadly speaking, the former dealt with lawsuits between private individuals or organisations: what would later be known as civil actions. Initially, King's Bench dealt mainly with civil suits of concern to the king himself and with criminal prosecutions. There were other courts: the 'departments' of the Exchequer and, later, Chancery both developed courts which could deal with disputes involving their own activities or staffs; and the king's Council, through parliaments when they sat, accepted petitions relating to private disputes and complaints about crimes and offences, which it might deal with itself rather than pass to one of the central common-law courts. The principal and only routinely available national sources of justice at this date were, nevertheless, the Courts of the Common Bench and King's Bench.

By 1250, the usual way of initiating a private suit in the central courts was by buying a writ from Chancery, which ordered and authorised the court to hear the case. Although the central courts

[30] Sutherland, *Novel Disseisin*, pp. 1–5.
[31] Van Caenegem, *Birth of the Common Law*, pp. 26–8.
[32] For what follows, unless otherwise stated, see Baker, *Introduction to English Legal History*, or Harding, *Law Courts of Medieval England*.

could and did entertain cases which concerned goods and chattels ('personalty'), the focus of legal learning was on the different actions available for the assertion, protection and recovery of rights in and to land and tenements ('realty'). This reflected both the importance of land at the time as a source of wealth and the interest of kings, in whose court King's Bench and the Common Bench had their origins, in resolving disputes concerning their greatest subjects and the land from which, indirectly, they themselves drew money, men and provisions.

The emergence of specialised law courts was accompanied by the emergence of specialist lawyers. These lawyers, as judges, advisers to the court, and advocates, had already done much work in establishing or approving the procedures which would be employed in their courts; or, as the legal treatise known as *Glanvill* put it as early as the 1180s, in deciding what 'general rules [would be] frequently observed in [the king's chief] court'.[33] During the 1200s, they had turned their attention increasingly to the legal principles which guided the remedies offered by their courts and the ways in which disputes could and should be determined there, a development reflected in the difference in focus between *Glanvill* and *Bracton*, a legal treatise of the 1250s. In tandem, they were developing a specialist legal language.[34] By 1300, they had largely displaced the unspecialised or less specialised men who had formerly served as justices and had represented litigants in the central courts. An elite, the serjeants at law, which enjoyed a monopoly of pleading (advocacy) in the Common Bench, was also emerging.[35]

None of this happened in a vacuum.[36] A number of the features which were characteristic of the medieval common law existed before 1150: for example, the arrangement of England into counties, most of which had a county court presided over by a sheriff or his deputy, where private suits as well as what would later be described as crown pleas could be brought, and sometimes were brought by royal writs directed to the sheriffs. There were also royal justices, whose judgments would be enforced by sheriffs locally; equally, there were also local, normally private,

33 Hall, *Glanvill*, p. 3. 34 Baker, 'Three Languages of the Common Law'.

35 See generally Baker, *Order of Serjeants at Law*; Brand, *Origins of the English Legal Profession*.

36 Van Caenegem, *Birth of the English Common Law*, pp. vii–xv.

lay courts which were not county courts.[37] While all this was both substantially extended upwards and outwards after 1150 and fragmented, even perhaps undermined, with many new courts and ways of resolving disputes emerging, it is at least arguable that what happened constituted a reorganisation and expansion of something that was not entirely unsystematic before. It is of course possible that some of the remedies and procedures adopted by the central courts were entirely new inventions, or such complex marriages of existing ones as to be innovations. It is, however, equally possible that the Chancery and central courts normally adapted to their own purposes the most suitable, or perhaps just the most widespread (or 'common'), of the remedies and procedures that were already available in other courts. If so, arguably the most significant aspect of what was created in the years around 1200 was a mechanism which opened the doors of English lay courts (not just the central courts) to all free men and women whose disputes could sensibly be handled by them, and then attempted to regulate that access by various means, the most enduring of which proved to be the creation of specialised high courts.

What the developments of the late twelfth century onwards do undoubtedly seem to have generated, or for other reasons to have been followed by, was a surge in private litigation. It may well be that the king's counsellors and justices had not anticipated either the increase in litigation or the number of plaintiffs who would try to make use of the central courts for purposes for which they had not been intended. Consequently, in the first century or so after the emergence of the central courts, attempts were made to restrict the types of remedies they would offer and the sorts of case they would entertain. This necessarily involved some decisions about the remedies which would be offered in other courts and the sorts of cases that other courts would entertain. This was as true of London's courts as of other local courts. The city's jurisdiction, however it first came into existence, was by 1300 far from unconstrained.

That the city law and custom to which its records make frequent reference was a part of a national law is nevertheless not a truth universally acknowledged. This is hardly surprising, given

[37] Morris, *Medieval English Sheriff*, pp. 87–91.

comments such as those made by Serjeants Shardlow and Deanham in the 1321 London eyre, when they claimed that Londoners, like those living on ancient royal demesne lands, were 'persones especials', not bound by the common law, and that they were 'gens de usage, et lour usage est lour ley'.[38] It is of course understandable that lawyers acting on behalf of the city should seek to claim that the central court justices had no right to interfere with its jurisdiction; and the claim was of course rejected. But the city was still making assertions which sound very similar in very different circumstances many years later. In 1388 it was argued on the city's behalf that a litigant who claimed that the mayor and commonalty had disseised him ought to proceed at common law (that is, at Westminster) and not before the mayor and sheriffs in the city's Court of the Husting.[39] Such references can be multiplied: the city's early fifteenth-century common or town clerk, John Carpenter, who compiled 'Liber Albus', the best-known of the city's custumals, wrote, in a section on the legal practices of the city which he seems to have composed himself instead of simply copying it from elsewhere, of the circumstances in which a plaintiff could be required to abandon an action in the city courts and sue 'at common law'.[40] In cases brought in the central courts, city custom was repeatedly contrasted with the common law.[41]

There is however abundant evidence that the city courts dealt with legal actions according both to the common law and to city law and custom, with certain exceptions which were, by the fifteenth century, always clearly highlighted. The regulations made in about 1285, for the period when the city was directly ruled on Edward I's behalf, tell us as much: actions brought by writs of customs and services, which were nevertheless governed by city custom, were to be 'pleaded and determined in the manner that they have been hitherto; but let other judgments [in the Husting] be awarded, according to the Common Law ... devised lands excepted, in respect to which the King wills that the custom shall be maintained'.[42] Common Clerk Carpenter's description of city customs includes an account of procedures in the Husting, where

[38] Cam, *Eyre 1321*, I, pp. lxii, 15. [39] CLRO, HR PL110, m. 15.
[40] Riley, *Munimenta Gildhallae*, I, p. 210.
[41] E.g., *Les Reports de les Cases ..., The Seconde part of Henry the Sixt ...*, pl. 29.
[42] Riley, *Munimenta Gildhallae*, I, pp. 186, 291.

actions originated by writs of right are said to be partly dealt with according to the custom of the city (which he proceeded to describe), 'and other process, as at Common Law'; the same was true of those actions 'brought without the king's writ according to the custom of the city'.[43]

The sheriff who, in 1384, made a return into Chancery saying that there was 'no custom in the city with regard to a writ of *justicies* other than the common law' came closest to expressing the nature of the relationship between the common law and local custom generally.[44] Viewed broadly, the common law of England was the entire gamut of the laws and customs of all lay courts in which free men and women litigated. In the narrow sense of 'the law approved by and practised in the central courts, especially the Court of the Common Bench', the common law applied whenever a court did not have a different custom of its own that was applicable to the particular circumstances at issue. The main difference between the Common Bench and other courts, including other common-law courts at Westminster, was that the former's custom was – in that narrower or more precise sense – the common law; but it was not 'the whole common law'.[45] All English lay courts, therefore, with the exception of ones that regulated only the affairs and disputes of unfree men and women, were courts both of (common and local or particular) law and custom. And as by 1300 relatively few courts, even at the level of the small manor, seem to have dealt only with the unfree, the court which was only a court of custom must have been a comparative rarity even then. After the Black Death, as land changed hands rapidly and social and geographical mobility became more common, the proportion of surviving purely customary courts seems likely to have been small.[46]

Despite the frequency with which the custom of the city was contrasted with the common law, usually meaning the usages of the Court of the Common Bench, therefore, the city's courts heard cases not just according to its own law and custom, but also to the national law and custom of England. Its own customs were

[43] *Ibid.*, p. 181. [44] *CalPMR 1381–1412*, p. 94.

[45] For medieval comments on the custom(s) of the central courts, see Doe, *Fundamental Authority*, pp. 22–6.

[46] Brooks, *Pettyfoggers and Vipers of the Commonwealth*, pp. 35–6; Poos, Bonfield, *Select Cases in Manorial Courts*, 'Introduction'.

not entirely separate from the common law (if recognised and 'allowed' by royal justices from time to time), but a local variant of it. As a justice of the Common Bench and former recorder of London put it in 1527, '[t]he right to hold pleas in London was by the common law', the difference in process being explained by the fact that 'all their exercise is trade, which must have speedy remedy'.[47]

One consequence was that the city's courts did not know any main categories of action which were entirely unfamiliar to the common law. There were, as at common law, public prosecutions, pursued by the king or the city authorities or others on the king's behalf, on the one hand; on the other, there were private or civil suits. The vocabulary, of felony and trespass 'with force and arms' (crimes and violent offences) on the one hand, and of non-forcible trespass (non-violent injury), debt, detinue (unlawful retention of assets), account (liability to account for and repay moneys received on another's behalf), covenant (breach of an agreement) and so forth on the other, was the same in London as it was at Westminster. There were a few terms which suggest that the city did indeed know some actions or procedures unfamiliar to the common law, but these turn out merely to be alternative names for the procedures or actions available at common law: for example, 'shartfort' (in all its variant spellings) for 'foreclosed, forever precluded from further action'. Similarly, a 'plea of naam' (correctly, a 'plea concerning a naam [distress, assets seized to enforce compliance] unjustly taken') was the plaint- or bill-initiated action for the recovery, pending litigation, of assets taken, for example, by a landlord from a tenant who was allegedly in arrears with his rent in order to try to force the tenant to pay up, and which did work similar to the common-law action of replevin.

Limitations upon the city's jurisdiction

Another consequence of the fact that medieval London was part of the national administration of the law was that its jurisdiction and legal privileges (collectively, its 'liberties') were not only delegated, but were also conditional on the king's favour for their continuance. The city's liberties were acquired over time, and not

[47] Baker, *Reports of Cases ... of Henry VIII*, I, p. 63.

everything that had been acquired before 1300 was held thereafter. Not even Magna Carta, granting London all its 'ancient liberties', could guarantee that they would not be restricted or taken away altogether. The most obvious and dramatic way in which its jurisdiction was interfered with was when the city lost self-government ('was taken into the king's hand'), as happened between 1285 and 1298 and again in 1392.[48] Even when the city basked in the king's favour, there were limits to its jurisdiction. Above the level at which they could be dealt with by the Sheriffs' Court, offences and crimes (the 'pleas of the crown') were supposed to be heard by royal justices at sessions of gaol delivery. The same justices also sat at the church of St Martin le Grand at intervals, in order to hear cases in which the superior courts of the city were alleged to have erred in law.

Throughout our period London remained subject to *ad hoc* amendment of its custom and practices, initially by royal decree and subsequently by parliamentary legislation. Although most of these interventions appear to have been designed to adjust the balance of advantage between citizens and foreigns so that it was less favourable to the former, both royal decrees and national legislation had the potential to destroy the distinctiveness, not simply to amend the detail, of city custom. Henry III's reign saw important procedural changes with regard to the treatment of foreigns and aliens litigating in the city courts. When in 1268 the king ordered the city to allow non-freemen, both as plaintiffs and as defendants, to appoint attorneys, his aim was, no doubt, to ensure that the city did not tilt the balance too strongly in favour of its citizens.[49] Over time, kings also ensured that aliens had the right to request a jury consisting half of Englishmen and half of their fellow-countrymen. In the 1380s, the provision was said specifically to be 'in accordance with the statute [of 1365] to that effect'.[50] But the right to a half-alien jury can be traced back much further than that, in each instance to an earlier, royal statute or decree. The 1365 statute itself reflected the provisions of the *Carta Mercatoria* or 'Statute of New Customs' of 1303, which prescribed a jury half of local men and half of foreigners in all

[48] Holt, *Magna Carta*, pp. 454–5 (Clause 13); *CalLBA*, p. xi, *CalLBH*, pp. lii–liv.
[49] Stapleton, *De Antiquis Legibus Liber*, p. 104.
[50] CLRO, HR CP110, m. 20v, referring to 28 Edw. III, c. 13.

actions, and whether the case was between an Englishman and an alien or between two aliens.[51] Even this provision was not a complete novelty. In the ordinances promulgated when the city was under the king's direct control in the 1280s, it was decreed that in cases involving an Englishman and an alien merchant the jury should be composed half of foreigners, at least in cases of debt or covenant and when the foreign merchants might be expected to have knowledge of the matter.[52] These developments were almost certainly not ones that the city initially sought or wanted. Even instances in which the city claimed to have influenced the form of a national statute, as with the Statute of Gloucester which was amended at the city's behest, reveal the subordination of city custom to the common law.[53]

Although there were few alterations to city custom produced directly by royal decree after the accession of Edward III in 1327, parliamentary legislation replaced it and remained, potentially, a significant factor in the development of custom throughout our period. There are numerous examples of acts which were aimed largely or entirely at London and its administration of the law. In 1363/4, for example, a parliamentary statute established that debtors who had been arrested in London on the evidence of 'papers', there being no deed or tally to prove the debt, should be permitted to wage their law if they did not want to submit to the decision of a jury.[54] This provision was clearly designed to protect strangers against London freemen, and is most unlikely to have been sought by the city. It also seems improbable that the common petition of 1495/6, which alleged that London jurors were 'persons of litill substaunce discrecion and reputacion' and that 'perjurye [was] muche and customably used within the Citie', was promoted by the city's governors.[55] Like the 1363/4 provision, it was evidently intended to protect non-citizens, particularly non-Londoners, who tended to be less keen than Londoners on city juries.

[51] *CalPMR 1381–1412*, p. xxvii; Riley, *Munimenta Gildhallae*, II, i, pp. 207–8.

[52] *CalPMR 1381–1412*, p. xxvii; Riley, *Munimenta Gildhallae*, I, p. 292.

[53] Riley, *Munimenta Gildhallae*, II, i, pp. 169–77. For a discussion of the problems caused to the city by this statute, see Sayles, 'Revisions to the Statute of Gloucester, 1278', esp. pp. 470–1.

[54] *Statutes of the Realm*, I, p. 384. [55] *Statutes of the Realm*, II, p. 584.

Sometimes, too, city custom may have been affected by national legislation that was not specifically directed at London. Chapter 2 gives a number of examples of the belated adoption by the city of some of the provisions contained in national statutes. In addition, a city ordinance of 1393 requiring that the sheriffs provide the names of those empanelled in possessory assizes to the litigants several days in advance, if asked to do so, could have been influenced by a parliamentary statute enacted thirty years previously, which ordered sheriffs to array the panels at *nisi prius* four days in advance of the sessions and to let the parties know the names of the jurors, if they wanted to.[56] It certainly seems probable that there was some connection between the parliamentary common petition of 1393 which sought to prevent those central court clerks who were responsible for recording pleas from acting as attorneys, and the steps taken by the city from that year onwards to achieve similar ends in the Sheriffs' Court.[57] And there seems to be no reason to doubt that the use of the action of trespass in the city to protect owners and occupiers of property from the 1400s onwards was a product of the later fourteenth- and early fifteenth-century statutes against forcible entries (violent disseisins).[58]

Decisions made by the central court justices had the potential to be even more destructive of city custom. The powers of the justices were not by any means confined to ensuring that the city administered the law and its custom justly. By 1300, generous if unspecific early grants of jurisdiction to the city had been followed by more cautious re-grants. The 'Henry I' charter of *circa* 1135 allowed the city to administer justice to its citizens in respect of their lands, tenures, securities, debts, and so on, 'according to the law of the city'.[59] This provision was repeated in the first charter of King John.[60] His final one granted them 'all their liberties which they have hitherto enjoyed, as well within the city of London as without'.[61] The city, however, in its support for the rebellious barons in the 1250s and 1260s, gave Henry III cause to be careful about allowing it too much independence. Consequently, while his charter of 1268 granted the citizens 'all their

56 *Statutes of the Realm*, I, p. 390; Riley, *Munimenta Gildhallae*, I, pp. 519–20.
57 *Rotuli Parliamentorum*, III, p. 306; Riley, *Munimenta Gildhallae*, I, p. 519.
58 See pp. 123–8. 59 Riley, *Munimenta Gildhallae*, I, p. 129.
60 *Ibid.*, I, p. 132. 61 *Ibid.*, I, p. 134.

liberties and free customs, etc., as well as to the form and manner of pleading as to all other cases whatsoever', it added, 'provided always, that such customs are not contrary to justice and rightful law.'[62]

This caveat might well have proved to be the trojan horse which permitted the destruction of city custom. In the Middle Ages city custom was usually accepted by the central court justices; normally the only question at issue was whether an alleged custom genuinely was a custom.[63] Sometimes, however, these same justices demonstrated a reluctance to accept that an acknowledged custom ought to continue simply because it had existed, allegedly, since time immemorial. And when they turned a critical eye upon London's customs, they used as their criterion precisely the test mentioned in Henry III's final charter: did these customs conflict with justice and 'rightful' law? In the eyre of 1321, the proviso was employed to good effect by the justices.[64] At times they and the serjeants who worked with them argued that local customs, if they offended against their notions of what was right and reasonable, were void – or, if not automatically void, should be abolished. 'Malus usus abolendus est' was similarly Serjeant Thomas Littleton's view in the fifteenth century. Since central court justices were inclined to believe that justice and reason were largely identical with the custom of their own court, the inevitable tendency of these challenges to local custom was to bring practice in the local courts ever more into alignment with that of the central ones.[65]

Judicial decisions appear, nevertheless, to have had rather less impact on city custom after about 1350 than they had had before that date. There is one report (of [Alderman] 'Simon [or Simpkin] Eyre's Case') from the middle of the fifteenth century in which it appears that city custom was rejected in the Common Bench on the grounds of unreasonableness. Even so, the matter is not entirely clear-cut. In the first place, the assets in dispute were jewels belonging to the king, which might well have affected the

[62] *Ibid.*, I, p. 139.

[63] See *CalLBK*, p. 88, for examples of fourteenth- and fifteenth-century writs ordering the central court justices to allow the city its customs.

[64] Cam, *Eyre 1321*, I, pp. lxi–lxxii, II, p. 255.

[65] *Littleton's Tenures*, Book II, ch. 11, s. 212; Doe, *Fundamental Authority*, pp. 78–83.

outcome. More importantly, perhaps, it is not certain that the alleged custom *was* a custom: the case concerned jewels held in pawn which had been seized by the creditor from his own debtor (and Eyre claimed that he had not known that they were pawned when he arranged for their arrest). While there is no doubt that city custom allowed the seizure of the assets of a debtor's debtor if the debtor's own goods were insufficient, pawned goods were in a rather different category.[66]

The defence and extent of the city's jurisdiction

A number of factors helped to preserve city custom against erosion, at least for a while. In the first place, London enjoyed a number of important concessions with regard to city juries and to the correction of errors allegedly made by the city's highest courts. Until the 1490s, it was not possible to bring an action of attaint against perjured jurors, even those who acted in the assizes and even in the city itself.[67] The privilege was important for two main reasons, leaving aside its prestige value: first, it kept under the city's own supervision one type of failure of justice; and, secondly, it permitted the city's governors to decide how seriously to take jury defaults and how to treat them. At first sight, it appears that the result was relatively lenient treatment of city jurors: the worst they might expect was a period of imprisonment and, in rare cases, apparently, exposure to public humiliation by being paraded through the streets and pilloried.[68] Corrupt jurors in the central courts could in theory face worse penalties than these: even in *Glanvill*'s day, not only imprisonment and obloquy, but the loss of their moveable property as well.[69] In practice, it may be that the less draconian but nonetheless disagreeable punishments inflicted by the city on corrupt jurors were more effective than those notionally employed in the central courts (and

[66] *Les Reports de les Cases ... in temps del roy Henry le siz*, 35 Hen. VI, fo. 25, pl. 33; Baker, *Reports of Cases from the Time of Henry VIII*, II, p. 301.

[67] Riley, *Munimenta Gildhallae*, I, pp. 437–44; also, e.g., TNA (PRO), Early Chancery Proceedings, C1/46, item 433.

[68] *CalEMCR*, p. 13, *CalPMR 1323–64*, p. 267, *CalPMR 1364–81*, p. 145, CLRO, Jor. 7, fos. 129–30, 148 (1460s), CLRO Rep. 9, fo. 280 (1490s). John Stow tells of jurors being paraded and pilloried in 1468 (it may well be one of the cases included above) and 1509: [Stow], *Survey*, p. 208.

[69] Pollock, Maitland, *History of the English Law*, II, pp. 541–2.

than the fines which were sometimes employed in practice), even if London jurors did not commonly die of mortification, as those punished in 1509 supposedly did.[70]

Even more importantly, from an early date, disregarding the claim made in the 1321 eyre that error ought not to be redressed other than by writ 'in the King's [meaning the central] Court', the Husting had been acting as a court of appeal from the Sheriffs' Court.[71] Its right to do so had been conceded tacitly by 1315, when the king granted a petition allowing the goods of defendants in the original case to be seized pending the determination of any writ-initiated action of error brought by them either in the Husting or before the central court justices.[72] Moreover, the Mayor's Court had also started to hear Sheriffs' Court cases in which error was alleged. It was certainly hearing allegations of error by 1298 and continued to do so until 1307 if not later.[73] By the time the plea and memoranda rolls begin, in 1323, however, this particular practice appears to have been abandoned; allegations of error (as opposed to those relating to corruption or 'maintenance' – supporting a plaintiff in litigation in which one had no proper interest) in the Sheriffs' Court from then onwards were only brought by writ, in the Husting. Probably an attack by the royal justices and serjeants in the 1321 eyre on the practice of hearing cases of error in the Husting, which was defended as being done by authority of the king's writs, had persuaded the city to abandon its less defensible practices in the Mayor's Court.[74]

Error in the Husting itself could only be corrected by a special commission of royal justices sitting at St Martin le Grand. It required some effort to establish this privilege.[75] Even once it had been achieved, the city continued to try to evade the oversight of the central court justices. In 1345, it applied pressure to two aldermen, one of whom had already bought a writ alleging error, to accept arbitration. This was done 'in view of the damage which might be done to the city's liberties if the action came to a hearing'. When one of the aldermen, dissatisfied with the arbitrators' decision, refused to accept it, a deputation was despatched to threaten him into

[70] *Great Chronicle*, p. 339. [71] Cam, *Eyre 1321*, II, pp. 254–5.
[72] Riley, *Munimenta Gildhallae*, I, pp. 408–10, CLRO, HR36, m. 29v.
[73] Cam, *Law-Finders and Lawmakers*, pp. 88–9, *CalEMCR*, pp. 15, 254–5.
[74] Cam, *Eyre 1321*, II, pp. 253–5. [75] *CalLBE*, p. 55 (1305).

compliance.[76] Theoretically, too, only the specially commissioned royal justices could correct errors in the Mayor's Court. Again, the city occasionally tried to evade the rules (or plaintiffs in error did so, for some reason): there are a couple of Mayor's Court cases recorded as having been brought on error in the Husting rolls in the 1320s. Curiously, perhaps, this practice survived the 1321 eyre; at least, one instance is recorded in the early 1350s.[77]

Although the city was unable to evade the supervision of the royal justices entirely, it did interpose itself between the Sheriffs' Court, the most active of the city's courts, and the penalties that might otherwise have been imposed upon the sheriffs in cases involving the incorrect application of procedures or careless record-keeping. If the city itself fined the sheriffs when error was found or penalised the court in other ways, none of its records say so. All that appears to have happened was that the original Sheriffs' Court record and judgment were annulled.[78]

Being able to clean up its act in this way was a valuable privilege, considerably reducing the opportunities for external intervention and criticism. At least as valuable, however, was the privilege which applied in every case of error which came before the royal justices: that of having the record 'recorded orally' by the city's recorder, its senior law officer.[79] The inability of the justices physically to inspect (or to have read out to them verbatim) the records of any city court in cases of alleged error made it difficult for them to ascertain whether they did indeed contain errors. There seems little doubt that the city could and did use this provision obstructively, and, in so doing, restricted external supervision of its judicial activities.[80]

However, it is doubtful whether these defences would have counted for much had the relationship between the city and

[76] *CalPMR 1323–64*, pp. 158–9.

[77] CLRO, HR CP45, m. 7 (1320/1), HR CP49, m. 32 (1324/5), HR PL47 [*recte* CP'49A'], m. 3 (1325/6); HR CP75, m. 12v (1351/2).

[78] Of 18 cases brought on error in the Mayor's Court, 1298 to 1307, the record or process was annulled in two instances (although no outcome is recorded in a further five cases): *CalEMCR*, pp. 139, 181–4. In 10 cases, the record was affirmed. The pattern seems to have been similar in the Husting: e.g. CLRO, HR CP53, mm. 21v–22.

[79] Riley, *Munimenta Gildhallae*, II, i, p. 173; for a full statement of the developed practice in error, see *CalPMR 1323–64*, p. 247 (1355).

[80] See, e.g., *CalPMR 1381–1412*, pp. 267–70 (*Aleyn* v. *Bosano*).

English kings between 1327 and 1470 not been generally less prickly than it had been before and would be afterwards, with the exception of the final decade or so of Richard II's reign.[81] A more important factor in the fifteenth century may have been the greater integration of city law offices and the wider legal profession which occurred in the century after about 1390. Partly as a result of this and partly of a more nationalistic sentiment which attributed value to supposedly ancient 'Saxon' customs as against more recent 'Norman' usages, the attitudes of the common lawyers towards city custom began to change in the course of the later fourteenth and fifteenth centuries. Challenges to local custom generally on the grounds of unreasonableness began themselves to be challenged in the central courts. Even as he articulated it, Serjeant Littleton's viewpoint was starting to go into retreat. In a case from the 1450s we find Serjeants Billyng and Nedeham arguing that a city custom might be good despite being contrary to common law (that is, to the common law of the central courts), having, presumably, been granted by the king or in Parliament so long before that no record of the fact remained.[82] Eventually the notion took hold among common lawyers that London customs could prevail against common law simply because, by definition, they *must* have the authority of an act of Parliament behind them, whether or not there was any evidence for the existence of such an act.[83] Even without the invention of these creation myths for London custom, changes in attitudes towards judicial law-making and law-breaking over the course of the Middle Ages would probably have been enough to protect it from the central court justices' notions of what was or was not acceptable. By the sixteenth century it was felt desirable to pass an act of Parliament in order to void a city ordinance: a declaration of 'unreasonableness' in the central courts was not enough.[84]

[81] *CalLBE*, p. 218, Riley, *Munimenta Gildhallae*, I, pp. 438–9, a copy of a writ of 1328 ordering the royal justices to allow 'without demur, the customs of the City recorded by the Mayor and citizens in any plea or plaint', used successfully to secure the same end a century later: *CalLBL*, p. 88.

[82] *Les Reports de les Cases . . . , The Seconde part of Henry the Sixt . . .* , Mich. 35 Henry VI, fo. 35, pl. 25.

[83] *Coke's Reports, Parts 7 and 8*, fo. 126.

[84] Derrett, 'Thomas More and the Legislation of the Corporation of London', p. 177, fn. 12.

It is worth bearing in mind, too, that both royal decrees and statutes and parliamentary legislation were sometimes sought by the city itself.[85] Not all of these attempts to influence national legislation were concerned purely with the city and its affairs, and sometimes the influence was indirect.[86] In the case of parliamentary legislation, even when it was prompted by a common petition, it is often not possible to tell for sure who or what initiated it. Moreover, it seems that the medieval city, while happy to promote the petitions of its constituent organisations, such as the trade companies, did not regard the common petition as an appropriate vehicle for its own concerns, preferring to petition the king, his Council and the chancellor directly. The city records occasionally mention the discussion or preparation of submissions to be made during the course of a Parliament, but the content can usually only be deduced from any legislation passed at that Parliament and the city's known concerns at the period.[87] For example, although the city required that English be used in the Sheriffs' Court in 1356, and a like provision was enacted in Parliament in respect of other English lay courts six years later, it is not possible to show any direct link between the two.[88] It could be that the two provisions were entirely independent of one another (although this seems unlikely), or that the successful introduction of English in a London court encouraged someone unconnected with the city to urge its adoption in other courts. On the other hand, it is quite possible that the city governors, responding to complaints by its freemen who were increasingly using the central courts by this date, took advantage of the invitation on the back of 'the bill for cities and boroughs in Parliament' (as an entry in Letterbook G has it) which asked 'those ... who feel themselves aggrieved [to come] and show specially their grievance, and right shall be done them', to press the case for using English in other courts.[89] Worse, the city's own records can mislead, giving the impression that it had been subjected to royal intervention when it

[85] *CalLBA*, p. 222.

[86] A letter of 1660 describes a petition drawn up 'with good advise & deliberacion of divers Cittizens of London ... & by them intended to be exhibited to the Commonshouse of Parliament' and then forwarded to Kent, where 'the inhabitants ... generally gave good approbacion therto': BL, Add. MS 26785, Sir Edward Dearing's LB, fo. 23.

[87] CLRO, Rep. 1, fo. 10v, CLRO, Jor. 6, photo. 539, Jor. 9, fo. 12, Jor. 8, fo. 163.

[88] Ormrod, 'The Use of English', p. 760. [89] *CalLBG*, p. 145.

had in fact solicited it. Again in Letterbook G, for example, there is recorded under 1363 what is described briefly in the *Calendar* as a [royal] '[w]rit to the Mayor and Sheriffs to cause certain ordinances for preserving the peace, &c, to be proclaimed in the City'.[90] Unlike the writ entered immediately after it (encouraging the practice of archery instead of football in the city), and contrary to what one might suppose, this is not yet another example of a king making new statutes for the city. As is made clear in 'Liber Albus', these ordinances were 'nadgars ordeignez et establis par assent dez Maire et Aldermans, Viscontz, et Comunialte; et apres par nostre Seignour le Roy et soun graunt Conseil affermez, lan de soun regne trent-septisme'.[91] And the city did not often, let alone always, seek royal endorsement of changes to its customs, which, even after they had been altered by royal decree or legislation, could continue to evolve independently.

Arguably one of the greatest limitations to the city's jurisdiction on a day-to-day basis was not the fact that it was subject to supervision and interference by the king and his servants but that it was local and that its authorities controlled neither its suburbs to their fullest extent nor the entirety of its hinterland (the rural region from which it drew its food). Indeed, for most of our period it did not control certain privileged areas, such as ecclesiastical sanctuaries, within its own walls. It does not appear to be the case that the city's governors were able to bring much pressure to bear on the authorities in these areas, presumably because of the profits to be made from craftsmen, tradesmen, prostitutes and others who wanted to live or work close to or in London, but outside its jurisdiction. And although its sheriffs were jointly sheriffs of the county of Middlesex as well as of London, and had possibly once held joint sessions for the two counties, they had certainly ceased to do so by 1300.[92] Moreover, the fact that King's Bench was more-or-less settled in Middlesex by the end of the fourteenth century clearly had an impact on the sheriffs' activities there.[93]

[90] *CalLBG*, p. 154, CLRO, MS LBG, fo. 111.
[91] Riley, *Munimenta Gildhallae*, I, p. 390.
[92] Tait, *Medieval English Borough*, p. 14, Palmer, *County Courts of Medieval England*, pp. 9–10.
[93] Blatcher, *Court of King's Bench*, p. 125.

The city did nevertheless have jurisdiction over a physically large area. The city controlled almost everything within its walls and substantial suburbs beyond, particularly to the west, where the large ward of Farringdon spread along the banks of the Thames as far as Temple Bar. In the early 1550s, after a protracted struggle, it also acquired jurisdiction over the manor of Southwark on the southern bank of the river. Southwark, like the liberty of Blanchappleton, a small manor in the north-west of the city which London eventually managed to acquire from the crown in the 1470s, had long been a source of irritation to the city authorities.[94] And within its boundaries, the charters that London obtained from a succession of medieval kings granted the city privileges and exemptions which gave it a semi-autonomous status in legal matters. During the course of the fourteenth century, moreover, the city's governors came to play an increasingly important part in the administration of 'royal' justice. One valuable privilege was the fact that, uniquely among early medieval English towns and counties, London was treated as a county and could from the first half of the twelfth century elect its own sheriff.[95] Not until 1373 was another English city (Bristol) granted county status and the right to elect its sheriff. At the same time as it obtained county status, or had its status confirmed, London was also granted the privilege of choosing a 'justiciar' to hold the pleas of the crown. These two early provisions, included in 'Henry I's' charter of *circa* 1135, gave the city the right to deal with all routine criminal cases, up to and including the serious crimes which would later be known as felonies.[96] The second provision was not repeated in later charters; and in the charter granted to the city in 1268 by Henry III, the liability of citizens to be summoned into external royal courts to answer for offences done against the king's peace was specifically mentioned.[97] In 1281, however, after the accession of Edward I, the city was empowered to try and to punish peacebreakers; in 1327 the mayor acquired responsibility for acting as a justice of gaol delivery within the city, a grant which specifically gave the right of dealing

[94] [Stow], *Survey*, pp. 442, 160; Lobel, *City of London*, p. 52.

[95] The city itself believed that it had acquired county status by virtue of William the Conqueror's charter: *CalLBK*, p. 153.

[96] Riley, *Munimenta Gildhallae*, I, p. 128.

[97] Riley, *Munimenta Gildhallae*, I, p. 128.

with felonies; and in 1361 London benefited from the general provision that justices of the peace were able to deal with felonies as well as minor offences.[98] By these means, much of what had earlier been taken away with one hand was granted back with the other.

The city's jurisdiction over classes of person and types of cases was also extensive. Royal charters allowed that no city freeman could sue (or be sued) in any court outside the city except in actions involving property held elsewhere and 'moneyers and royal officers'.[99] The city's own ordinances forbade any freeman to sue another elsewhere over some matter arising in the city if he could do so in a city court, the penalty being loss of the freedom, imprisonment and fine. Only if he could satisfy the mayor and aldermen that city officers had failed to do him justice could he escape the penalties.[100] This privilege was insisted upon, even when, as happened in a Husting case brought between 1388 and 1390, the defendant was the 'mayor and commonalty' itself and the two attorneys acting for the city sought to argue that the plaintiff ought to sue at Westminster. The plaintiff, surprisingly perhaps, objected, and responded to protests about the impropriety of the mayor being both judge and litigant in the same case by citing the city's charters. The city's exception failed, and it was eventually forced to proceed with the case.[101] Throughout our period, examples of citizens asking for permission to litigate outside the city, or being punished for doing so without permission, testify to the continuing enforcement of this provision. The city's governors were alert for infringements and not only paid senior clerks in the central courts to act as the city's attorneys, partly in order to claim its rights in such cases, but were also physically well-placed in relation to the central courts to spot any that the attorneys failed to identify, perhaps as a result of some conflict of interest.[102] It was therefore not too difficult for London

[98] *Ibid.*, I, pp. 137, 145; *CalEMCR*, p. xii; *CalPMR 1323–64*, pp. xv–xvi, xxvii; *CalPMR 1364–81*, pp. 44–5, *CalPMR 1323–64*, pp. 48–9 on.

[99] Riley, *Munimenta Gildhallae*, I, p. 131.

[100] *Ibid.*, I, pp. 433–7, and see also p. 147, for the provision that no citizen 'shall be troubled at the Exchequer or elsewhere by bill' save for matters relating to the king or his heirs.

[101] CLRO, HR PL110, m. 15, and see also HR CP24, m. 25b (for 1298 discussion about one freeman suing another in the central courts).

[102] CLRO, Jor. 8, fos. 173, 187, 211v, 212 (licences to sue at common law, 1468–70); *CalPMR 1364–81*, p. 89 (imprisonment of a freeman who admitted

to keep within its jurisdiction any case to which it could sensibly assert a claim.

In practice, moreover, its authority was not confined within its own walls. Actions in debt and account arising from transactions entered into outside the city could be brought in the city courts if the payment, delivery or hearing of the account was due to take place there.[103] Similarly, actions involving London property could be claimed from another court, even if the owner lived elsewhere and was therefore almost certainly not a citizen.[104] In addition, its jurisdiction was not restricted by the 'forty shilling rule', the upper limit on the value of assets in cases which certain inferior courts could entertain.[105] The 'rule' apparently had the long-term effect of taking out of many local courts cases in which the goods or damages claimed were worth more than £2. None of the London courts, however, were affected by this limitation between 1300 and 1550; indeed, in the sixteenth century the city set up its own court for 'petyt matters' under the value of 40*s*, the Court of Requests.[106] The city's exemption was to prove important, particularly in the fourteenth century when even rural county courts are said to have been losing valuable and prestigious business to the central courts.[107]

In summary, the boundaries between the common law and city custom, although generally clear enough at any one time to contemporaries, were like the jurisdictional boundaries which separated the area under the city's authority from those which were not. They were at once capable of being undermined, sometimes surprisingly easily, and yet defensible and well-defended. These facts had considerable implications for the history of the administration of the law by medieval and early-modern London.

suing another at Westminster) Jor. 6, photo. 536, Jor. 7, fo. 22v (punishment for/order to cease suing in an external court, 1461, 1463).

103 Riley, *Munimenta Gildhallae*, I, pp. 215–16.

104 CLRO, HR PL165, mm. 1, 1v.

105 Beckerman, 'The Forty-Shilling Jurisdictional Limit'.

106 CLRO, Rep. 10, fo. 137.

107 Palmer, *County Courts of Medieval England*, pp. 254–62.

2

THE DISTINCTIVENESS OF CITY LAW AND CUSTOM

INTRODUCTION

As we have just seen, London's customs were throughout our period liable to be changed to bring them more in line with nationally applicable principles and procedures. That being so, one might ask whether there really was such a thing as 'city law and custom', even in 1300, let alone by 1550, by which time the common law had for some four centuries been subject to much thought by men experienced in its application and keen to create of it a coherent body of law.

At first sight, it seems doubtful. By 1300, city law and custom was being described, not as an even semi-coherent body of substantive legal principles and procedural practices, but in terms of its departures from the common law. The impression one gets from the London custumals is that these departures were numerous but often minor, and mainly concerned with procedures: relating, for example, to the opportunities for litigants to essoin themselves (excuse their non-attendance). Differences of this type might well be accounted for by the differing frequencies with which particular law courts met and the need, in the case of courts which met weekly or more often, to allow defendants adequate time in which to respond to a summons and prepare their case. One might ask whether a collection of even a thousand such procedural variations deserved to be called 'custom', let alone, 'law'.

But to deny the status of law and custom to those collections of legal rules largely concerned with procedure would be to refuse to acknowledge a great deal of early law. Primitive law does seem to be chiefly concerned, in terms of explicit statements of rules, with procedure rather than principle. If city law and custom had had its development arrested by the growth of the nationally applicable common law, the focus on procedure would not be surprising. So we may be dealing, not with a mishmash of 'sub-laws', but with a genuine but comparatively simple and underdeveloped type of law.

Even this, however, may be ungenerous to city law and custom. City custumals were generally compiled by and for administrators, and they were designed to assist the governors and officers in the administration of the city generally. Administrators, then as now, tended to be more concerned to ensure that things were done correctly, and less concerned with why they were done at all. London's custumals are consequently not books of city law and custom in the sense that *Glanvill* and *Bracton* are books of the laws and customs of England. One would not expect statements of and justifications for substantive law and custom to be found as a matter of course in the custumals. Indeed, if the city's law courts were mainly the province of men who were not legal professionals, one would not necessarily expect to find them anywhere. As we shall see, that does indeed seem to be the case for the first century or so of our period – precisely that period when the majority of the custumals were written. As a result, the best measure of the distinctiveness of the law and custom of London is the nature of the remedies provided by, and the procedures and practices employed in, the city.

DISTINCTIVE LEGAL REMEDIES

Remedies relating to real property

There is no doubt that, in 1300, city law and custom differed from the nationally applied common law in at least one important respect. This related to rules about the tenure and disposal of city property. Sometime before the beginning of our period, possibly quite shortly before, the various forms of property-holding which had doubtless existed in London immediately after the Conquest had been resolved in favour of the simple doctrine that all were freeholds for which the king 'had one penny for socage a year' (that is, the king received a token annual quitrent, or payment in lieu of services, which was subsumed in the fixed sum paid by the city sheriffs to the Exchequer each year); or, as the writs by 1300 invariably put it, were free tenements 'held [directly] of the lord king by the service of one penny a year'.[1] (Socage was the general term for a wide range of tenures, defined by what they were not: not held by military service, by sergeanty or in free alms; and was the city's preferred description in the early fourteenth century of what was otherwise and elsewhere known as burgage tenure, that is, tenure according to borough custom.)[2]

The principle consequence, for our purposes, was that owners of city property could dispose of it freely by will, so long as any widow and dependent children were provided for. According to the plaintiffs in a Husting case of 1303, 'any citizen could bequeath any city tenement which he had acquired as though it was a chattel [personal possession] in his last will'.[3] This point had been reached by the middle of the thirteenth century, when *Bracton* was written; but there appear to have been further developments. According to an interpolation in this section of *Bracton*, it was 'laid down by the barons of London and the burgesses of Oxford [who, from 1156 onwards, shared London's custom] that one may bequeath as a chattel land inherited as well as acquired'.[4] As the interpolator went on to state that, for this reason, 'in boroughs an assize of mort d'ancestor does not lie', and it is clear that assizes, if not of mort d'ancestor itself, at least *in natura mortis antecessoris*, certainly were being brought in London throughout our period, the obvious conclusion is that this was either an error or a reflection of a much earlier rather than a later situation.[5] On the other hand, the very use of the phrase 'in the nature of mort d'ancestor' shows that this was not the national assize. *Glanvill*, who shared the *Bracton* interpolator's belief that the assize proper was not available in cities and boroughs, said that this was because another assize had been established or approved ('constitutam') for that purpose.[6] It looks, in fact, as though the *Bracton* interpolation may be correct, and the assertion

[1] For pre-1300 references, see CLRO, HR PL1, m. 1 (1273, e.g., *le Chelmestere and Others* v. *Lodeham*), HR PL16, m. 2v (1288, *Stratford* v. *Suthbery*); see also *CalLBA*, p. 158 (1284); Tait, *Medieval English Borough*, pp. 96–108, esp. p. 107, fn. 2; Chew, *Eyre 1321*, I, p. lxx, II, p. 119; Bateson, *Borough Customs*, II, p. 160.

[2] Pollock, Maitland, *History of the English Law*, I, pp. 291–3.

[3] CLRO, HR CP29, m. 1v (*Execs. Parson of Bromley* v. *fitzPerine*).

[4] Woodbine, Thorne, *Bracton*, III, p. 295.

[5] CLRO, HR PL1, m. 1, HR PL134, m. 6.

[6] Hall, *Glanvill*, p. 155.

in the Husting rolls in 1303 was only true as far as it went: a testator could bequeath, not only property he had acquired, but also any he had inherited. Certainly when the city was being ruled directly for Edward I in the 1280s and a remedy was provided for the problem which arose when a landowner sold all his real property in the city, with the consequence that purchasers had no way of obtaining from him lands of equivalent value within the city's jurisdiction should his title prove defective, it was envisaged that his heirs might not have inherited any lands at all from him.[7] The *Bracton* interpolator's error, if error there was, lay in assuming that, because London freeholders could sell or give away all their lands in the city if they chose, city freeholds never descended in line with the normal rules of inheritance. Clearly they did; and the particular form of mort d'ancestor in the city reflected the possibility that lands could be inherited according to the usual common-law rules, but might not be.[8]

In the case of the city assize 'in the nature of mort d'ancestor', there appears to be no way of discovering whether it already existed when the assize was introduced nationally, and its continued use was simply approved, or whether it was established as a variant at the same time; the city's records throw no light upon the question. The city did however claim to have offered a legal remedy for unlawful disseisins before the assize of novel disseisin was made available nationally. According to a compilation of city laws which M. Bateson dated to *circa* 1215, the sheriffs had long been empowered to act in cases of alleged 'disseisin without judgment'. The remedy, although it involved an inquest by the alderman and men of the neighbourhood, was not the same as the assize of novel disseisin (or even the city's version, the assize of freshforce): the sheriff, having been informed of the disseisin, was required to initiate the inquiry himself. The person disseised did

[7] Riley, *Munimenta Gildhallae*, I, pp. 292–3.

[8] '[I]f anyone dies in the City seised of any tenement as of fee, and has not devised that tenement..., his heir shall immediately succeed him': Chew, Weinbaum, *Eyre 1244*, pp. 104–5; and see the mayor's statement at p. 121 that 'many foreigns have always been accustomed like us up to the present to sell, assign or even devise their lands to whomsoever they would'; the claim was again made in 1491: *CalLBL*, p. 280. See also *CalPMR 1323–64*, pp. 7–8, for the explanation given by London to Oxford in 1325 of the action taken in circumstances when part of a deceased's property, left by his will, is claimed by one person as 'his right and fee'.

not apparently have to bring a formal plaint of intrusion in the Husting or before the mayor. Having ascertained by the sworn inquest that an unjust disseisin had indeed occurred, the sheriff simply put the plaintiff back in possession and placed the disseisor under sureties 'usque ad placita coronae'.[9] The procedure was explained to the royal justices in eyre in 1244 and was approved by them.[10]

It is possible that the city exaggerated the antiquity of this remedy when it claimed that it predated the introduction nationwide of the assize of novel disseisin in or around 1166. For example, the editors of the city's rolls of assizes of nuisance believed that the London assize of buildings, which city tradition ascribed to 1189, was more probably compiled in 1265–70.[11] On the other hand, the 'lex de assisa' contained in the London collection of *circa* 1215 is very similar to part of the assize of buildings, and may be of twelfth century origin.[12] D. W. Sutherland identified other examples of early procedures for dealing with illegal disseisins, including a very similar one, the 'commonest of all, and ... at least as old as the reign of William the Conqueror', namely 'the practice of empanelling a group of peers and neighbours as a jury to tell the investigator [who might indeed be the sheriff] what he needed to know'.[13] So London could well have had such a procedure even in the eleventh century, one that was subsequently adapted to fit with the system of visitations by royal justices. It was, however, certainly not alone among local courts at the time in offering it.[14]

Next, we have a more certain difference, although it is debatable whether it constitutes a 'distinctive remedy'. For the first seventy or eighty years of our period the city continued to offer in its possessory assizes remedies for disseisins which differed in important respects from the nationally available assizes. First, the assizes were commonly sought informally, by oral or written complaint, not by writ. This was a difference shared with a good

[9] Bateson, 'A Municipal Collection', pp. 482, 708; *idem*, *Borough Customs*, I, pp. xxxvii, 231 (city custom, together with what may be notices of its existence in charters of William I and Henry II); Riley, *Munimenta Gildhallae*, I, p. 114.
[10] Chew, Weinbaum, *Eyre 1244*, pp. 103–4.
[11] Chew, Kellaway, *London Assize of Nuisance*, p. xi.
[12] *Ibid.*, pp. x–xi.
[13] Sutherland, *Assize of Novel Disseisin*, pp. 24–5.
[14] Bateson, *Borough Customs*, I, pp. 240–2.

many other towns, and even with county courts, at least in outlying regions at the beginning of our period.[15] Secondly, and again like other boroughs although the exact limitation varied, there were relative as opposed to absolute time limits within which the assize had to be sought. Beyond that limit, the plaintiff was required to obtain a royal writ (of right).[16] In the case of the national assizes of novel disseisin there was a 'period of limitation' (the date after which the alleged disseisin had to have occurred) which was initially fixed and reset periodically at the date of the king's latest departure overseas, and was eventually (so far as the Middle Ages are concerned) left at 1242.[17] In London, by contrast, the assizes of freshforce had to be sought within forty weeks of the alleged disseisin, and assizes in the form of mort d'ancestor, within a year and a day of the ancestor's death.[18] A short period of limitation helped to avoid doubt and confusion in the potentially less than straightforward circumstances that obtained in cities and towns in which real property was both heritable and alienable at will. In London, these differences were maintained until, probably, the 1380s in the case of the former and until the 1370s in the case of the latter. Thereafter, the period of limitation reduced from forty weeks to forty days in assizes of freshforce, and assizes of mort d'ancestor could be brought, provided that the ancestor had died after the coronation of Henry III. These changes were seen by H. M. Chew as evidence of a fictionalising of the limitation, not a further restriction, and suggested to her that the city assizes had finally joined the national assizes in shedding their original character as a summary, 'stopgap' solution to an immediate problem.[19] For over two centuries after the introduction of the assizes of novel disseisin and mort d'ancestor, therefore, London offered remedies for disseisins which were genuinely quite *novel* and which differed both from those available in the central courts, where the time limit was often many years in

15 Sutherland, *Assize of Novel Disseisin*, p. 63; Bateson, *Borough Customs*, I, pp. 310, 233–4, 235–6, 237, 235; Morris, *Early English County Court*, p. 120.
16 Bateson, *Borough Customs*, I, pp. 235, 236–7, 238–9.
17 Sutherland, *Assize of Novel Disseisin*, p. 55.
18 Chew, Weinbaum, *Eyre 1244*, pp. 104–5.
19 Chew, *London Possessory Assizes*, pp. xxiv–xxv; *ibid.*, item 140 *et seq.*; Sutherland, *Assize of Novel Disseisin*, p. 216, Note C. 8.

the past, and in most contemporary local courts, where time limits in freshforce tended to be set at forty days or less.

Still in relation to unlawful disseisins, it is also possible that the city abandoned 'the entire doctrine that a feoffment over should toll entry' (the common-law rule that an enfeoffment or grant by a disseisor to a third party who had no knowledge of or involvement in the disseisin deprived the ousted person of his right simply to enter or re-enter the property) earlier than was done at Westminster, where the change seems to have been accepted in about 1385. There is no doubt that a sale or gift to a third party sufficed in earlier years to prevent an heir bringing an assize in the form of mort d'ancestor in the city (and so, one might assume, also deprived him of the right to re-enter 'justly'); that point was made in 1244; and the same might well have been true of the assize of freshforce, even though it is not specifically mentioned.[20]

Professor Sutherland noted two cases in the London assizes of freshforce, from 1380 and 1381, in which he detected the earliest recorded sign that the doctrine had been abandoned.[21] In the first case, three of the four defendants claimed that they had been disseised by relatives of the original owner, who had enfeoffed the plaintiffs, and that the first defendant, the true heir, had then re-entered and enfeoffed them; on this basis, they said that 'the assize did not lie'. Evidently they did not believe that the initial enfeoffment had deprived their own grantor of any right of entry he might otherwise have had. The plaintiffs seem likewise to have felt that the first enfeoffment was irrelevant. They stated simply that the relatives of the owner had entered after his death, as his true heirs, and had transmitted their rights to the plaintiffs, before going on to deny one of the statements on which the first defendant's claim to be the true heir depended. They then defaulted, but the case was reopened for some reason seven months later and the jury found for the plaintiffs.[22] In the other case, the defendant, a wife permitted to plead on her own behalf as her husband had conceded, again alleged that she had been in possession of the property until disseised by someone who had granted it to the plaintiff, and that she had promptly re-entered and ejected him.

[20] Chew, Weinbaum, *Eyre 1244*, pp. 105, 104.
[21] Sutherland, *Assize of Novel Disseisin*, p. 162, fn. 6.
[22] Chew, *London Possessory Assizes*, items 151, 161.

The plaintiff did not attempt to argue that the enfeoffment to him deprived her of any right of entry she might otherwise have had, but instead said that her admission to plead by the court had occurred too late, after the different pleas entered by the defendants' representative had already been referred to the assize and most of the jurors had been sworn. The court agreed, and the jurors found for the plaintiff.[23] These cases predate equivalent ones in the central courts, or, rather, in the yearbooks, by several years. On this evidence, the older rule appears to have been being followed in the central courts at least until 1383.[24] Given the nearness in time of these developments, however, it would arguably be unsafe to make much of the apparent precocity of the city assizes in this respect.

On the other hand, there are a couple of London cases from the 1340s in which defendants claimed that they had ejected the plaintiff 'justly' or had re-entered 'as [they were] entitled to do' after an alleged disseisor had enfeoffed the plaintiff. Collusion was alleged in one of these cases, but not in the other, and in neither case was the defendant's claim challenged (indeed, in the second case – in which collusion was not alleged – the plaintiff failed to prosecute his complaint).[25] So conceivably the rule that someone who had been dispossessed could not simply reoccupy the property if it had subsequently been sold or given away by the disseisor was abandoned in relation to the assize of freshforce at an early date, or, perhaps, had never obtained in London.

Conversely, it is also possible that city custom was much slower than the common law in permitting the use of the assize of freshforce to recover rents which were in arrears. Since about 1190, it had been allowed at common law if the plaintiff was not able to distrain for the rent, or if the tenant resisted or 'rescued' (recovered) the distress.[26] Not until 1345 did the city pass a 'new statute' which permitted plaintiffs seeking to recover rents which were in arrears to use the assize of freshforce to do so, in precisely the circumstances permitted by the national assize.[27] As assizes of novel disseisin for rent had been brought in the London eyres of

23 *Ibid.*, item 272. 24 Sutherland, *Assize of Novel Disseisin*, p. 162.
25 Chew, *London Possessory Assizes*, items 14 (1341), 21 (1343).
26 Sutherland, *Assize of Novel Disseisin*, p. 50.
27 CLRO, LBF, fo. 105, Riley, *Munimenta Gildhallae*, I, p. 472; plaintiffs in 1347 referred to this recent ordinance: Chew, *London Possessory Assizes*, items 47 and 48.

1321 and 1341, Dr Chew suggested that the 1345 ordinance was 'intended merely to define or tighten up an established procedure'. Perhaps it was; perhaps the alleged city custom was itself a novelty or the result of some confusion which arose in the 1340s. It remains possible, however, that the city did not allow the use of the assizes for the recovery of rents, even in the circumstances allowed by statute, until 1345, whatever the justices in eyre in 1321 and 1341 may have permitted. Certainly its use to recover rents generally (rather than in cases where the tenant refused to allow the landlord to distrain) was, according to a defendant in a city assize in 1340, contrary to city custom.[28]

It may also be the case that the city was slower to offer a remedy to termors (those who occupied properties for a limited period, or 'term of years'), who were unable to use the national assize of novel disseisin because, not being the freeholder, their right in the property was treated as personal rather than real.[29] The earliest evidence of protection specifically for London termors is a provision allowing those ousted by new landlords after the properties had been sold during the term of their tenancy to bring a writ of *quare ejecit* in the Husting, which was included in the articles promulgated on the king's behalf in the 1280s. If this was indeed the first time termors were offered a remedy in the city courts, they may have remained without one for some fifty years after remedies began to be developed for them nationally.[30]

None of this is particularly impressive. It shows that the city was sometimes out of step with the central common-law courts in terms of the precise nature of the remedy offered, but one might well disagree that any of it amounted to 'distinctive remedies'. Despite what was said in the previous chapter about the similarity of city custom to the common law, however, there were more differences than appear at first sight. The two actions of replevin and naam, for instance, may have done similar work, but they may

[28] Chew, *London Possessory Assizes*, item 4.

[29] Baker, *Introduction to English Legal History*, p. 299.

[30] Riley, *Munimenta Gildhallae*, I, pp. 293–4; Pollock, Maitland, *History of the English Law*, II, pp. 37, 107, 116. It is however just conceivable that the city's early remedy against disseisin, described to the justices in eyre in 1244, being trespassory in nature, was available to anyone who was disseised, regardless of the nature of their tenure. If so, London termors may in fact have enjoyed more protection, earlier, than was available in the central courts.

not have developed in exactly the same way or have been available in exactly the same circumstances. In replevin, the plaintiff 'alleged two separate but connected wrongs: that he had been unjustly distrained, and that the distresses so taken had then been detained "against gage and pledge" (despite the offer of security)'.[31] On one view, the double allegation is to be explained by the fact that the action developed in the rural county courts 'out of a great process called vee de nam (refusal of security)' into a means of reviewing distraints which were not duly authorised by the landlord's court.[32] It may, however, be that the second allegation, that the landlord had refused an offer of security, was simply a fiction designed to create an offence which justified bringing the case in the county court (rather as the allegation that a trespass involved violence later justified bringing it in King's Bench).[33] There is one example in the early Husting of Common Pleas rolls, *Smith* v. *Prior of Holy Trinity*, where it was said that the defendant refused to return the distress against gage and pledge until [it was secured] by pledges given to the sheriffs. As the prior of Holy Trinity was a sokeholder (a landlord with a private court), this could be the explanation for the allegation that he had refused the offer of security: in other words, had the plaintiff not made the allegation, the Court of Husting, the city's equivalent to a county court, could not have entertained the plea.[34] On the other hand, Husting plaintiffs were no more likely to make this second allegation in cases involving city sokeholders than other types of defendants.[35] The initial complaint as well as subsequent pleadings normally related solely to the first allegation, the question of the justice of the distraint: whether, for example, rent was owed by the plaintiff, owed to the individual who had taken the distress, or owed at all. Due authorisation by a private court also seems never to have been at issue. Whatever may have been true of

[31] Brand, *Making of the Common Law*, pp. 308–13, esp. 309.

[32] Pollock, Maitland, *History of English Law*, II, pp. 577–8; Baker, *Introduction to English Legal History*, p. 237; Milsom, *Historical Foundations of the Common Law*, pp. 104–5, 114.

[33] Brand, *Making of the Common Law*, pp. 309–10.

[34] CLRO, HR CP3, m. 3.

[35] Compare, for example, *Smith* v. *Prior of Holy Trinity* with *Uggele* v. *Vicar of St Botolph without Aldersgate* (the vicar was not a sokeholder) and *le Tannere* v. *Master of St Bartholomew West Smithfield* (the master was): HR CP2, m. 1, HR CP12, m. 3v.

replevin in other courts, therefore, it looks as though in London by the early 1270s pleas of naam could be brought freely by any tenant against any landlord. How long this had been the case is, however, uncertain. Practice in London may have been quite recently altered by the emergent theory that city freeholds were all held directly of the king and (or) the belief that any dispute which 'touched a freehold' (for example, because the tenant alleged that the landlord was not entitled to rent from the property because it belonged to someone else) should be litigated in the Husting, the king's court.

Although it is not possible to demonstrate that the city plea of naam existed before the action of replevin was developed in the central courts, the city's own records contain two examples which should warn us not to assume the reverse: that remedies known by common-law names were introduced from the central courts. Whereas naam was the name by which the action to recover distresses was apparently invariably known in London in the fourteenth century, in the fifteenth century it was far more common to describe these cases as 'plaints [*querelae*] of replevin'.[36] And whereas throughout our period city plaintiffs had been able to sue defendants who had allegedly harmed them by performing badly something they had undertaken to do, using the action of trespass, by the 1550s they were describing actions brought for the same purpose as 'upon the case', the term used for the remedy which had only become available in the central courts in the course of the fourteenth century.[37]

Remedies relating to personal property and torts

It is clear from other evidence that the city did at some periods offer remedies which, although most of them fell under the generic headings familiar to the common law, were not contemporaneously available in practice in the central common-law courts. Some involved principles which were never, during our period, accepted in the central common-law courts. Local courts in general were certainly prepared to allow compensation for harm

[36] Compare, e.g., CLRO, HR CP26, m. 1 with Riley, *Munimenta Gildhallae*, I, pp. 188–9 and CLRO, HB1, fo. 28v.

[37] CLRO, Sheriffs' Court Roll [*recte*, *Querela Levata*] 1554 (for further discussion of this, see Chapter 3).

done even when the defendant was not personally culpable. For instance, they allowed plaintiffs to sue the owners of dogs which bit them and theirs even when there was no suggestion that the owner either encouraged the dog or knew that it was aggressive.[38] In a similar vein, they were prepared to allow plaintiffs whose goods had been lost or stolen to reclaim them from whoever held them without having to accuse the holder of having stolen them: as in the case of the 'abdiracionis unius equi', brought in the Sheriffs' Court in August 1320.[39] This action, normally known as *de re addirata*, was not unique to London, being found in a number of local courts and, consequently, in the eyres, but was not otherwise available in the central courts.[40] What is more, these differences were neither modest variants on remedies offered at Westminster nor entirely distinct but unimportant remedies. Possibly a few of them were unique to London.

That some of these London remedies were significant is demonstrated by the fact that they are of precisely the type that R. C. Palmer, in his discussion of the radical changes introduced to the common law in the aftermath of the Black Death, believed were important novelties when they first appeared in the central courts in the second half of the fourteenth century: actions designed to oblige individuals and certain occupational groups to act responsibly and maintain high standards.[41] Among a number of groups he identified as having become subject to legally enforced and punitive controls only after the first onset of the Black Death were physicians and surgeons, innkeepers, and careless householders who failed to keep their fires under control and consequently allowed them to damage neighbouring properties. These developments in the central courts, he thought, quite rapidly affected and altered practice in local courts. For example, the successful prosecution in 1377 of a defendant in the Mayor's Court for having undertaken to cure a patient and failing to do so suggested to him that the city's courts were by then beginning to assimilate the language of and, more importantly, the principles

[38] Palmer, *English Law in the Age of the Black Death*, pp. 246–8.
[39] CLRO, Sheriffs' Court Roll (1320), m. 12.
[40] Milsom, *Historical Foundations of the English Law*, p. 271; Kaye, '*Res Addiratae*', especially Section 4, pp. 379–401 (I am grateful to Sir John Baker for these references).
[41] Palmer, *English Law in the Age of the Black Death*, summarised at pp. 296–306.

underlying what he calls the 'doctor liability' writs that Chancery was then issuing, with their reliance, or partial reliance, on promises to cure.[42]

Both beliefs appear to be mistaken, however. Although Professor Palmer examined local records, including London's, the focus of his study was 1348–1381, and the sources he apparently used for London, the central records apart, were the letterbooks, some early Mayor's Court rolls, and the plea and memoranda rolls. Bearing in mind what has been said about the city's courts and the survival rates of their records in the Introduction, it is not hard to see why he might have been led into misinterpreting an absence of evidence as an absence of activity. Given that the plea and memoranda rolls contain only a small proportion of the personal pleas brought in that court; that even in the 1380s the Mayor's Court was almost certainly still not much involved in private litigation; and that its main function throughout our period was regulatory, it is not surprising that what little evidence its records contain between 1348 and 1381 relating to professional incompetence and negligence is regulatory in nature. If London litigants were prosecuting incompetent doctors and the like in the fourteenth century, they would have been doing so mainly in the Sheriffs' Court.

These were almost certainly unusual cases; there are very few recorded after 1348, and one would not expect them to have been any more common before that date. Nevertheless, by great good fortune the pleadings in a case alleging incompetence by a surgeon do happen to have been recorded in the surviving part of the Sheriffs' Court roll for 1320. In *Stockyng* v. *Cornhull*, a woman brought an action of trespass against a surgeon who, on hearing that she had a diseased foot, approached her and bound himself to cure it completely within a fortnight in return for a payment of half a mark (6*s* 8*d*). The treatment allegedly resulted in permanent lameness. Although the surgeon was also accused of breaking into her house and removing some of her goods, there is no doubt that the incompetent treatment was also a trespass; the jury found against the defendant specifically on this point.[43] And the

[42] *Ibid.*, p. 342, citing *CalPMR 1364–81*, p. 236; and see CLRO, Mayor's Court File of Original Bills, MC1/3A, m. 63.

[43] CLRO, Sheriffs' Court Roll (1320), m. 17v.

existence of a trespass case brought in the 1321 eyre against another surgeon suggests that *Stockyng* v. *Cornhull* may not have been unique among Sheriffs' Court cases at this period; but for the eyre, that court is no doubt where the plea would have been heard.[44] Incompetent or negligent surgeons evidently did face the possibility of being prosecuted in the Sheriffs' Court before 1348. There seems to be no reason to suppose that individuals could not also prosecute physicians in that court, since physicians were prosecuted there at a later date.[45] Such as it is, the evidence suggests that, both before and after 1348, the city regulated the medical professions in much the same way. The only difference was that, after 1423 when the physicians and surgeons were permitted to set up a college to control and educate practitioners, it was normally in their court that questions of professional competence were addressed.[46]

Secondly, the ever-present risk of fire led the city at a relatively early date to punish people who were negligent or reckless in tending fires. If Professor Palmer's statement that 'fire liability for damage to a neighbor's property did not exist prior to 1371' was meant to extend to London (as appears to be the case, since he went on to discuss the 'first pleaded case' in London in 1377), it is also incorrect.[47] In 1302 a case was brought in the Mayor's Court against a woman whose alleged carelessness had resulted in a fire started in her house damaging a neighbour's. Unfortunately it is not clear whether she was being prosecuted by the neighbour or by the city authorities. Either way, she was evidently liable for that damage.[48]

Whether actions for negligence involving fires were confined to the local courts before 1348 is however uncertain: Professor Milsom found a case from 1290 in which the defendants were prosecuted in King's Bench for failing to put out a candle on

[44] Cam, *Eyre 1321*, II, p. 353; see also Weinbaum, *Eyre 1276*, p. 77 (appeal of wounds and battery against Master Robert le Fizicion le Petit and his son; unfortunately no further details are given).

[45] CLRO, HR CP43, m. 17v; and see, for an action brought against a physician in the Sheriffs' Court in the late 1460s/early 1470s: TNA (PRO), Early Chancery Proceedings, C1/46, item 55.

[46] *CalPMR 1413–37*, pp. 174–5.

[47] Palmer, *English Law in the Age of the Black Death*, pp. 276–7.

[48] *CalEMCR*, p. 139. Other towns were equally concerned at an early date to reduce the risk of fires: Bateson, *Borough Customs*, I, pp. 81–2.

going to bed, with the result that their host's house burned down.[49] Indeed, it is a question whether cases of trespass for detrimental performance ('misfeasance') were in reality only available in the local courts until the Black Death struck. Professor Milsom found that by about the middle of the thirteenth century cases of 'civil' trespass, that is ones in which he believed that the allegation of violence, necessary to bring the matter within the purview of the central common-law courts, was fictitious, 'begin to appear on the Common Pleas section of an eyre roll'. This was presumably because plaintiffs who would normally have brought these cases locally were unable to do so for the duration of the eyre, and so they were forced to find ways of arranging for them to be heard by the royal justices. At that time, trespass for misfeasance may indeed normally have been confined to the local courts. Professor Milsom's interpretation of the later evidence, however, is that fictitiously violent trespasses which were really misfeasance cases soon came to be brought directly in the central courts, not just in the eyres, despite an attempt in 1278 to return them to the county courts. On this view, the only change which occurred in the second half of the fourteenth century was that the fiction was abandoned.[50] If so, although it would be correct to say that the practice of prosecuting misfeasance using the action of trespass may well have spread from the local courts, perhaps through the mechanism of the eyre, it had happened before 1300.

The only difference between the remedies offered by the local and central courts by the early 1300s may therefore have concerned misfeasances which involved no physical act at all on the part of the defendant which could be fictitiously described as violent. It was the defendant's negligent inactivity or insufficient performance which was the cause of the harm. These actions can be viewed as falling between misfeasance (harmful performance) and nonfeasance (non-performance). Professor Milsom, like Professor Palmer, saw the use of the action of trespass to prosecute negligent innkeepers as a relatively late, post-1348, introduction into the central courts.[51] The city gave travellers and

[49] Milsom, *Historical Foundations of English* Law, p. 297.
[50] *Ibid.*, p. 287; *ibid.*, pp. 288–90.
[51] Milsom, *Historical Foundations of the Common Law*, p. 287; *ibid.*, p. 292.

lodgers remedies against negligent innkeepers before the Black Death struck, though not perhaps quite as early as Professor Palmer believed. He found an 'innkeepers' oath' which he assigned to 1318; it required that those who owned hostels in which foreign merchants lodged should take responsibility for safeguarding the goods of their guests. However, the entry is apparently a much later (probably fifteenth-century) insertion in an early fourteenth-century letterbook. And in any event the oath probably reflected concern to ensure that the 'hosting' arrangements for alien merchants worked properly, rather than about innkeeping (hosts to foreign merchants apparently often warehoused their guests' merchandise).[52] Innkeepers had undoubtedly, however, long been responsible for their guests' good behaviour and were (by 1342, not 1363) also required to warn their guests not to carry arms.[53] While it is not possible to demonstrate that these particular responsibilities produced litigation in the Sheriffs' Court before 1348, it is likely that they could have done so. A case cited by Professor Palmer, which was heard before the mayor and sheriffs, apparently outside the Husting, does indicate that by 1345 innkeepers in London were held responsible for losses to their guests' goods, and could be prosecuted if their servants stole the guests' belongings.[54] It is also doubtful whether innkeepers who undertook to safeguard their guests' effects and who failed to secure their premises adequately could defend themselves simply by claiming that an intruder had damaged or stolen the guests' belongings. Robbery proved to be an inadequate defence in *Rothinge* v. *Staunford*, a detinue case from 1311, when a Sheriffs' Court defendant who offered to prove the robbery by jury was adjudged undefended, having admitted receipt of a double-sealed purse, contents unknown, and undertaking to keep it safe.[55] The rule may have

[52] Palmer, *English Law in the Age of the Black Death*, pp. 253, 377, referring to *CalLBD*, p. 194 (and see comment at *ibid*., p. 192); Riley, *Liber Albus*, p. 198, fn. 1.

[53] Palmer, *English Law in the Age of the Black Death*, pp. 377–8; *CalPMR 1323–64*, pp. 154, 164. The ordinances of 1363 repeat a good deal of earlier matter: Riley, *Munimenta Gildhallae*, I, pp. 386–91, esp. comments on p. 391.

[54] Palmer, *English Law in the Age of the Black Death*, p. 254; *CalPMR 1323–64*, pp. 220–1. The jury found against the innkeeper, even though it was unable to say which of his servants had (as the jurors believed) stolen the guest's goods.

[55] CLRO, HR CP36, m. 18.

been 'potentially very stringent', as Professor Palmer said of the central courts' interpretation of innkeeper liability after the Black Death, but it reflected the ease with which innkeepers and bailees alike could appropriate other people's goods and the importance of ensuring that they neither did so nor were negligent in discharging their responsibilities.

There are a number of other early cases which seem to show a degree of precocity in the remedies offered by the city courts. A. R. Kiralfy identified one from 1267, in which an official who borrowed armour to protect himself against robbers was apparently sued for 'converting it to his own use'.[56] Debt could also be used fairly inventively (though perfectly logically) by the early fourteenth century to sue for what could be viewed as non-performance or breach of contract which, strictly speaking, ought probably to have been sued in covenant. In another Sheriffs' Court case from 1320, *atte Taye* v. *atte Waye*, a married couple sued a man in debt for failing to honour his promise to give them 100*s* 'in auxilium maritagii', after which – or on the strength of which – they got married.[57] Not surprisingly, the defendant claimed that this was a matter for the church courts.

A feature of the innkeeper's case from 1345 was that the defendant allegedly 'undertook that any goods which [the plaintiff] deposited should be safely guarded'. An undertaking of this sort may have been necessary before the innkeeper could be held liable for the criminal acts of his servants. It was clearly no less important in *Stokkyng* v. *Cornhull* that the surgeon had supposedly 'bound himself to cure [Mrs Stokkyng] within a fortnight'. The voluntary undertaking to keep safe or cure seemed to Professor Palmer to be a significant element in similar cases brought in the central courts after 1348. There, certainly, it was vital that the defendant 'assumpsit se' to do whatever it was he was alleged to have done badly: so important that the phrase gave the action of assumpsit its name. It was also crucial in what was probably the most important of the differences between the central and city courts. This was the readiness of the latter to provide remedies in cases in which an individual had allegedly agreed to pay or render ('concessit solvere/reddere') a certain sum at a

56 Kiralfy, 'Custom in Mediaeval English Law', p. 36.
57 CLRO, Sheriffs Court Rolls (1320), m. 20v.

future date without entering into a written agreement to do so. This formula appears at the time to have been used both of agreements as originally made between the parties and of total liabilities acknowledged by the debtor after the balance had been ascertained by some form of reckoning-up or audit. (Where the agreement was written down, the formula seems to have differed again: an example being a defendant who allegedly 'obligasset se teneri', where the plaintiffs offered a signed, but not sealed, obligation in proof of the debt).[58] A Sheriffs' Court case from 1320, *Executors of le Botiller* v. *la Barbiere*, is an example of a suit brought on the basis of the original interparty agreement, and another from the same roll, *Zemesere* v. *Executors of Bolyngton*, is an example of one based on an acknowledgement after an audit. In the former case, the dead man's executors sued the defendant after she failed to pay for 30*s*-worth of cloth within a fortnight, as she had allegedly agreed to do.[59] In the latter, the dead man was said to have purchased fish from the plaintiff and then, after an audit of his account, to have conceded that he owed the sum for which his executors were now being sued.[60] Professor Milsom evidently thought that it was the allegation that the defendant had agreed to pay the overall sum that was not only the basis of the action which allowed plaintiffs to sue for the total owed to them rather than for each debt separately, but also the reason why the wager of law was precluded in such cases.[61] It seems more likely, however, that it was the additional allegation that the undertaking had been made before two witnesses which precluded wager of law in this type of debt case.[62]

The rule that the testimony of two witnesses who were present at a reckoning of the overall account allowed creditors to sue for the balance on the account in the city courts came to be another,

[58] CLRO, Sheriffs' Court Roll (1320), m. 6v (*Heigne* v. *Execs. of Heigne*).

[59] CLRO, Sheriffs' Court Roll (1320), m. 3v; see also mm. 4 (*Hendeman* v. *Borgeis*, *Wrotcham* v. *le Rede*), 7 (*le Barbier* v. *le Chandeler*), 7v (*Trugge* v. *Cook of Westminster*).

[60] CLRO, Sheriffs' Court Roll (1320), m. 15v.

[61] Milsom, *Historical Foundations of the English Law*, p. 260 and fn. 1.

[62] For the testimony of two witnesses to the original agreement precluding wager of law, see CLRO, HR CP43, m. 4 (*Jannoie* v. *Brunlesge*, 1318), HR PL47, m. 5 (*le Barbier* v. *le Keu*, but rule subsequently challenged, 1325); CLRO, Jor. 6, fo. 67v (statement of the rule, 1473). In 1358, however, the use of two sworn witnesses in this way was prohibited in the Sheriffs' Court, on the grounds that witnesses of this type were easily and commonly bribed: CLRO, LBG, fo. 92.

quite significant, difference between the remedies offered by London and by the Common Bench. After 1403, when an act of Parliament appears to have prohibited the suing of consolidated debts in the Common Bench, plaintiffs had to describe and plead each debt individually.[63] Not only was suing on a balanced account or *eque* a much simpler method of dealing with debts arising from multiple business transactions, but it allowed for the way that commerce worked, with servants and partners both owing and being owed money. Not until just before the end of our period did King's Bench offer a remedy in the form of the action of debt *sur concessit solvere* to settle a balanced account. Even then, a defendant was not barred from waging his law in King's Bench by the plaintiff's proffer of the defendant's own signed deed, if unsealed, or of two witnesses to the original transaction, as was the case in the city courts. Likewise, specialty was required in King's Bench, but not the city, in order to sue in covenant or to sue executors in debt.[64]

At much the same time as the action of assumpsit came into use for misfeasance cases in the central courts, it was also being used against defendants who had allegedly undertaken to perform something and had then entirely failed to do so, although this particular remedy ceased to be available for a period in the mid-fifteenth century, and thereafter could be used only in specific circumstances.[65] There is no evidence that straightforward cases of alleged nonfeasance were being prosecuted as trespasses in the Sheriffs' Court in the first few decades of the fourteenth century (non-performance of an undertaking in *Jannoie* v. *Brunlesge* was, it will be recollected, sued in covenant, and the couple in *atte Taye* v. *atte Waye* who married on the promise of a gift of money which was never honoured sued in debt). What little evidence there is, however, suggests that, in London as in the central courts, it was the conjunction of a failure to perform an undertaking with a claim of deceitfulness on the part of the defendant which eventually persuaded the courts to accept that nonfeasance (and partial performance) could be prosecuted as trespass or sued as covenant.[66] It may have been accepted in London before 1348 that it

63 Milsom, *Historical Foundations of the English Law*, pp. 260–1.
64 Baker, *Oxford History of the Laws of England*, VI, p. 283.
65 *Ibid.*, pp. 316–20, 322–3. 66 *Ibid.*, pp. 323–32, esp. 328–9.

was a trespass to undertake to do something, knowing that one could not do it, to the other person's damage. In 1345 a city attorney, Christian de Bury, was prosecuted by his clients in deceit and trespass for failing to plead in a Sheriffs' Court debt case.[67] The jury found for Bury; it is unfortunately not clear why. It is possible, however, that the jurors would have found for the plaintiffs had they been persuaded that Bury had deliberately failed to appear for them. If so, by the 1340s the city courts did offer an alternative, trespassory, remedy for nonfeasance in certain circumstances. And, if it did, this was at a time when an equivalent remedy was apparently not available in the Common Bench. It was however still some way from using trespass to sue for compensation for non-performance which was not deliberate, but which nevertheless caused harm or loss. Such cases continued to be sued in covenant in London throughout our period.[68]

A third formulaic phrase that occurs in the 1320 Sheriffs' Court part-roll is the allegation that the defendant did something, 'usurpando sibi officium X'. In the surgeon's case the plaintiff claimed that the defendant had approached her, 'usurpando sibi officium surgici'. In another trespass case, *Drayton* v. [*Roger de*] *Mymmes*, the defendant, a chandler, was said to have attached the plaintiff's horse and cart, 'usurpando sibi officium ballivi domini Regis'.[69] The obvious implication of the phrase, given that 'usurpare' had long since acquired its modern meaning of 'to appropriate unlawfully', is that Cornhull and Mymmes were passing themselves off as something they were not.[70] If so, however, it seems surprising that Cornhull was described, presumably at the plaintiff's instance, as 'John de Cornhull surgeon'. And while there is no evidence that Roger de Mymmes held any sort of city or external office, it is perfectly possible that he did. He seems, from his appearance as a witness in several documents relating to properties in the Wood Street area between 1317 and 1347, to have been a man of some standing in his ward.[71] What the

[67] *CalPMR 1323–64*, p. 218.

[68] CLRO, MS 'Precedents & Pleadings in the Mayor's Court London', p. 300 (1478).

[69] CLRO, Sheriffs' Court Roll (1320), m. 15v.

[70] Here as elsewhere, comments about the contemporary meaning of Latin words are based on Latham, *Revised Medieval Latin Word-List*.

[71] *CalLBE*, pp. 79, 162, *CalLBF*, pp. 91, 162.

phrase may signify, therefore, is not that the two men had appropriated offices or occupations to which they had no claim, but that they had abused or misused them. That is very probably true of the two trespass cases on the same roll involving defendants who were (city) rent-collectors, and who are alleged to have taken the plaintiffs' goods (on one occasion, at least, as a distress), having entered the premises 'vi et armis'.[72] In all four cases the plaintiffs may have been using exaggerated language in order to create a trespass out of some objectionable but not necessarily unlawful official act. As with the 'conversion' case from 1267, they might well have been asking the court to take a view on whether the officials had conducted themselves appropriately in the discharge of their office.

Fifteenth-century legal devices

In a rather different category are the developments of the fifteenth century. Even then, however, the city was developing and employing legal devices and actions known to the common law either before they were employed in that way elsewhere or for purposes that appear to have differed from the purposes for which they were employed contemporaneously in the central courts. The effect was to offer, if not different remedies, at least remedies for different problems.

The earliest of these fifteenth-century remedies was the legal device known as the 'gift of goods and chattels'. Such gifts were recorded in the London plea and memoranda rolls, among other places, from the 1370s onwards. By these gifts the donors, ostensibly, granted all their personal property to the donees. In some cases, that may indeed have been either the intention or result of the gift; but clearly this was not always so. Before the 1430s, the gift was comparatively uncommon and was merely one of the number of devices by which men and women of all conditions from all parts of the country might achieve a variety of ends. Where the gift was not genuinely an outright one, the aim might be illicit (to defraud creditors or to protect the assets of someone

[72] CLRO, Sheriffs' Court Roll (1320), mm. 7 (*Russeles* v. *le Chapeleyn*), 21v (*le Glovere* v. *Newmarket*); for a similar case brought by a writ of trespass against the St Paul's rent-collector in about 1340, see *CalPMR 1323–64*, p. 121.

accused of felony). In the 1460s, for instance, a London freeman was said to have granted all his goods and chattels to two men while seriously ill; one of his creditors was able to persuade a city jury that this was done by collusion, to defraud the other creditors.[73] Equally, however, the 'gift' might serve as a means of granting power of attorney (commonly, when the donor planned to travel overseas), of raising large sums of money or of paying off a debt.[74]

From 1430 on, however, the device began to be used much more frequently. Totals of Chancery enrolments rose from 25 in the period 1422–29 to 156 in 1429–35, more than doubled in 1435–41, and eventually reached 938 in 1454–61. Over the same period, enrolments in the city's plea and memoranda rolls rose from 6 to 166.[75] Having compared developments in Chancery and in the city, P. E. Jones, the editor of the later volumes of the plea and memoranda rolls, concluded that the device was first popularised in London and that this popularity was transmitted by contacts between Londoners and others to the Home Counties before eventually spreading almost nationwide. The annual totals of gifts recorded in the plea and memoranda rolls and in the Chancery close rolls started to rise significantly at precisely the same time (regnal year 1429/30). Bearing in mind, however, that seven times as many gifts were being recorded in the close rolls as in the plea and memoranda rolls by the 1450s, it is the relationship of these increases to the peak years in the early period of growth which is most revealing. In London, the peak years were in the second half of the 1450s, after which there was a modest decline. Plea and memoranda roll enrolments shot up from just over one per cent to over 81 per cent of the peak at a very early stage, between 1429 and 1434. In Chancery, the pattern was different. From 1429 enrolments began to rise only gradually towards the high levels obtaining in the second half of the 1450s, and the rise may have

[73] TNA (PRO), Early Chancery Proceedings, C1/31, item 1.

[74] *CalPMR 1437–57*; for non-London examples, see, e.g., *CalCR 1422–9*, pp. 267, 272, 388.

[75] For an extensive discussion of this development, see *CalPMR 1413–37*, pp. xix–xxiii, esp. xxiii, and *CalPMR 1437–57*, pp. xxii–xxviii, where the totals for 1435–61 are tabulated (additional calculations from *CalsCR 1422[-]35* and *CalPMR 1413–37*).

continued thereafter.[76] In other words, the rise was much slower and reached a peak later in Chancery than was the case in London.

Moreover, not only were the great majority of the early Chancery-enrolled deeds made by London donors, but many of those made by non-London donors were grants to Londoners.[77] A good many gifts to or by Londoners were enrolled only in the plea and memoranda rolls: even in 1437–57, less than 11 per cent of the deeds enrolled in the plea and memoranda rolls had a counterpart in Chancery, for example.[78] Nevertheless, as time went on there clearly was a move on the part of Londoners towards recording their gifts in Chancery, with or without a duplicate enrolment in the Mayor's Court. In 1429–35, almost as many London donors recorded their gifts in the plea and memoranda rolls as in the close rolls, but by the later 1450s, nearly four times as many Londoners' gifts were recorded in Chancery as in the city records. That change in recording practices, and the fact that Londoners from the outset used Chancery as well as the Mayor's Court, does not alter the probability that the popularity of the device itself had its roots in London and the commercial needs of Londoners. In the case of those recorded in the Mayor's Court rolls, gifts tended to be made to an individual who was the principal 'beneficiary', together with a small number of others; about one in five involved co-grantees who were city clerks, law officers, and other lawyers with connections to the city.[79] It seems likely that some, perhaps the majority, of these post-1430s gifts were made in order to secure loans or advances of credit at a period when creditors were in a position to insist on arrangements which enabled them to recover their assets as easily and certainly as possible.[80] In this

[76] Increasing from around 1% of the late 1450s' total in 1421/2–1428/9 to about 20% in 1429/30–1434/5; thence to *c.* 60%, 1441/2–1446/7; and finally reaching *c.* 90%, 1447/8–1453/4.

[77] Starting at 68% in 1422–29, rising to 79% in 1429–35, 81% percent in 1435–41, reducing back to 67% in 1454–61, by which time the total number of enrolments in Chancery each year had gone up enormously.

[78] *CalPMR 1437–57*, pp. xxii–xxviii, esp. xxiii.

[79] Based on plea and memoranda rolls for 1437/8 and 1457/8 (A65 and A82).

[80] This was probably always one of the uses to which they were put, certainly in London; see *CalPMR 1382–1412*, pp. 198, 197. That Nicholas Brembre, in 1387, acknowledged a deed of grant to various fellow-citizens 'to do and dispose thereof as their own goods, without any reclamation or condition whatsoever' suggests that even then 'reclamations and conditions' were familiar adjuncts of these 'gifts': *ibid.*, p. 134.

case, because the grantee(s) 'owned' the assets, either they could avoid litigation altogether, or could be certain of winning their case if forced to litigate in order to obtain them, should the grantor default on the debt. On the other hand, what secured the creditor, rendered the debtor extremely vulnerable. One motive for recording gifts of goods and chattels in the records of Chancery (as with those of the Mayor's Court) was almost certainly to enable private individuals who had no other connection with the court to take advantage of its equitable jurisdiction, should creditors attempt to help themselves to more of the debtors' goods than was fair and reasonable.

The second fifteenth-century remedy to show some distinctive features was the collusive recovery. This legal device had deep roots. Men and women who held land for their lifetime or for some other period of time but had no right to sell it outright had long sought ways of doing so. In particular, the development of the rules of inheritance at common law which enabled owners of land to grant it in 'fee tail' (generally, to the grantee and his lineal descendants only, the land reverting to the grantor/grantor's heir (the reversioner) or to another grantee (the remainderman) for failure of lineal heirs), and which subsequently enforced the doctrine that such entails were perpetual, meant that those who received or inherited entailed land could not dispose of or resettle it as they pleased. If they attempted to do so, the heir in tail, the reversioner and the remainderman would usually, by 1300, seek to protect their rights by bringing a legal action against them.[81]

Clearly, while owners of entailed land might well be able to find purchasers willing to pay something for their short-term interest, it would normally be impossible to realise its full market value under such circumstances. So these owners tried to find ways of 'barring the entail', or preventing the heir in tail *et cetera* from recovering the land at law. A warranty by the original grantor that he would defend the purchaser's rights at law or recompense him if the land was lost might do the trick in certain circumstances. Or the would-be seller (the 'tenant') might arrange to 'lose' the land to his would-be purchaser, using a feigned action at law, the

[81] Plucknett, *Legislation of Edward I*, pp. 122–5. For the development of entails and perpetual entails, see Biancalana, *Common Recovery*, Chapters 1 and 2; for the development of protections for the reversioner and remainderman, see *ibid.*, pp. 69–82.

collusive recovery. In certain circumstances, a judgment against the tenant would bar the entail.[82] A further refinement was the 'common recovery', which seems to have developed in the Court of the Common Bench from the 1440s onwards. The tenant would grant the land to the would-be purchaser, who would then bring an action against him to 'recover' the land. The tenant would vouch to warranty a third party whom he claimed had originally granted the land to him and had promised to protect that grant in any subsequent legal proceedings by defending the case himself. Despite the fact that this was untrue, the third party, the vouchee, would admit that he was bound to fight the case on his behalf. The vouchee would then ask for an adjournment; and, when the court reconvened, would default. The would-be purchaser would therefore 'recover' the property as a result of the vouchee's failure to defend the action. The attraction of employing the writ of right in this way was that, '[w]hether or not the land was entailed, a recovery on a writ of right had the greatest preclusive effect'.[83] A number of the early cases of common recovery in the Common Bench involved lawyers and court clerks, who appear to have been using them, not only to sell or resettle land, but to end long-lasting disputes and to avoid future litigation.[84] So acceptable did this legal device become that, by the early 1470s, fictitious vouchees in the Common Bench had transmuted into 'common vouchees' or paid court officials.[85] Such were the characteristics of the common recovery, as it had developed out of the collusive recovery in the Common Bench by the 1490s.

The relevance of this to London is that most of the recoveries of lands and tenements initiated by writ of right in the Husting of Pleas of Land from the mid-1450s onwards have the hallmarks of the common recovery, the 'acceptable' collusive recovery: a cooperative court, prepared to maintain a record specifically of this type of action; immediate acknowledgement of his obligation to warrant by a vouchee who just happened to be standing by, ready to be summoned, and who immediately defaulted after a token adjournment; consequently, a very rapid resolution; and, in

[82] *Ibid.*, p. 195. [83] *Ibid.*, pp. 251–61, 265–6. [84] *Ibid.*, pp. 254–5, 258–9.

[85] A court official, Robert Kyng, was sufficiently active from the early 1460s onwards to justify viewing him as the first common vouchee: Baker, *Introduction to English Legal History*, p. 282, fn. 10.

a few cases, vouchees who may have been hired hands.[86] It is probably significant, given the involvement of court officials and lawyers in the Common Bench cases, that the first London example of this type of action to be recorded in a separate plea roll is (Undersheriff) *Rigby and Others* v. *(Thomas) Pynchon*, a case from May 1455.[87]

So the obvious conclusion is that these Husting cases were simply, in the main, a way of passing title securely: and a very appropriate use of the Husting that would have been, too. The obvious conclusion may not, however, be the correct one. It certainly leaves some questions unanswered. Why, if owners of city properties really could sell, give or bequeath them as they pleased, did they use the collusive recovery at all? Presumably because these were a special type of inherited properties, those subject to entails. That entails are so rarely mentioned in the city records is not proof that entailed property itself was a rarity in the city.[88] It is a possible explanation; but, given what is known about some of the properties concerned, it seems unlikely.

As with gifts of deeds and chattels, it is not normally possible to tell from the record what lay behind these developments in the city. In the few cases of collusive recoveries where more information is available, however, the evidence reveals that the tenants (defendants) were probably not intending to transfer the title to the relevant properties on a permanent basis. The use made of the collusive recovery by the Pynchon family (the tenants in the first recorded city example) is a case in point. A further action involving Thomas Pynchon and Rigby, together with one of Rigby's earlier associates, Thomas Elys, was brought in 1460, exactly five years later.[89] The precise nature of this gap is worth noting. Although the number of the properties is different (eight in 1455, six in 1460), they are all described as lying in Birchin Lane, in the parish of St Michael, Cornhill. Two years later Pynchon's heir, Baptist, quitclaimed five properties in the same locality to Elys and Rigby.[90] Baptist Pynchon was involved in a further collusive

[86] Jones, Smith, *Guide to the Records in the CLRO*, p. 64 (but incorrect to say that this type of action occurred 'after 1461').
[87] CLRO, HB1, fo. 27, CLRO, HR PL167, m. 1.
[88] See below for provision made by the Mayor's Court to protect it from creditors.
[89] CLRO, HB1, fos. 43v, 44, HR PL167, mm. 11, 11v.
[90] CLRO, HR W&D192, m. 4.

recovery in the 1470s. When he transferred five properties to Gilbert Bellamy, he bound himself to 'suffer the said Gilbert . . . to recover the property by writ of right in the next Husting of Pleas of Land'.[91] Bellamy did indeed successfully recover the properties by an action begun in June and determined in November 1477.[92] In this case, however, Pynchon took the additional precaution of having an indenture enrolled in the Mayor's Court plea and memoranda rolls. It explained the exact nature of the bargain that he had struck with Bellamy. Pynchon was using the properties to raise £300. Bellamy retained the properties until he was repaid, at which point he undertook, on pain of losing £600, to reconvey them to Pynchon. If however Pynchon failed to repay the debt within eight years, Bellamy obtained the properties outright.

The question is, was Baptist Pynchon's use of the collusive recovery unique? That he went to the trouble to have the indenture publicly recorded suggests that it might have been. It is difficult to be sure: neither the absence of other indentures, nor the fact that some of the collusively recovered properties remained in the demandants' hands in the long term, proves that the original intention was to transfer them. After all, once the transfer had taken effect or the properties had been reconveyed, indentures would normally have been destroyed. And potential creditors would no doubt be keenest to obtain the security of a collusive recovery in cases where they doubted the debtor's capacity to repay, and wanted to avoid litigation when they foreclosed.

It seems unlikely, however, that Baptist Pynchon's 1470s transaction was the first example of a collusive recovery being used to secure a debt. Unless the Pynchons had very substantial property holdings in one area of London, the five properties involved, described as being 'in Cornhill in the parish of St. Michael', were probably the ones Baptist had quitclaimed in 1462.[93] In other words, he had regained possession of the properties in the interim. It seems quite possible, too, that these

[91] *CalPMR 1458–82*, pp. 111–12.

[92] CLRO, HB1, fos. 121, 121v; CLRO, HR PL168, mm. 41–41v.

[93] The properties concerned could well be the same as certain shops in Birchin Lane, the reversion of which was granted to Pynchon and others by the executors of John More, brewer, in 1416, and which Pynchon and his wife were granted in 1422 and again five years later: CLRO, HR W&D144, m. 7 (*bis*), HR W&D152, m. 1v, HR W&D156, m. 3.

five properties were parcel of the eight recovered against Thomas Pynchon in 1455 and of the six recovered against him in 1460. Nor was this use of the recovery peculiar to the Pynchons. On 27 February 1473 the two principal demandants in a collusive recovery effected in the Husting five days previously agreed in the mayor's presence that, if within a year of the death of both of them the tenants paid £100 to their executors, 'the said recovery and quitclaim should be void and of no effect'.[94] While this could be a case of a childless couple (the demandants were man and wife) allowing the former owners an opportunity to repurchase, the fact that a fixed sum is mentioned suggests rather that it was a repayment.

A final reason for suspecting that the collusive recovery was not employed in London in the second half of the fifteenth century primarily as a way of transferring title securely, as it was in the Common Bench, is the failure of the so-called 'common vouchee', the court officer who came to monopolise the role in the Common Bench from the 1460s on, to establish himself in the city courts at the same time. No such development occurred in the city's Court of Husting until, probably, around 1500.[95] Thirty-nine different men appeared as vouchees in collusive recoveries between the 1450s and 1480s. Moreover, to protect himself against the possibility of being sued by the former tenant for compensation, at least in the early days when his position was a trifle uncertain, the fictitious vouchee needed to be a landless man.[96] It is clear from the fact that some of the vouchees who appeared in the Husting also served there as jurors that they at least were fairly substantial property-owners. Probably what protected them was the real nature of the arrangement, the existence of documents which proved what it was, and the willingness of another city court to enforce the true, rather than the apparent, agreement. So, while it would be unsafe to assume that the same type of financial or commercial transactions underlay all the earlier collusive recoveries effected in the city, from Thomas Pynchon's 1455 case

[94] *CalPMR 1458–82*, p. 76, referring to CLRO, HR PL168, m. 27.

[95] By 1507, Geoffrey Bocher was appearing regularly as a vouchee, and was almost certainly a hired hand, although there seems to be no evidence to show whether he held any city office: CLRO, HB2, fos. 5, 8v, 9, 12, 15 (*bis*).

[96] Milsom, *Historical Foundations of the Common Law*, p. 187; Baker, *Introduction to English Legal History*, pp. 319–20.

onwards, it would clearly be no less unwise to take it for granted that all these recoveries resulted in a permanent transfer of property, or, at least, were intended to do so.

It looks as though this use of collusive recoveries was genuinely a new development in London. At the very least, something had occurred which led the clerks to take the trouble to record them separately from the mid-1450s onwards. It was very probably a deliberate introduction, and it might well, as J. Biancalana suggested, have spread from the Common Bench to the city. Thomas Rigby was well-placed as undersheriff to encourage and exploit the opportunities offered, and Thomas Pynchon's own legal connections included no less a personage than the future justice of King's Bench, Thomas Young, who was his brother-in-law and feoffee (and Alderman John Young's brother).[97] On the other hand, although Professor Biancalana identified three possible instances of a Common Bench common recovery being used to secure mortgages or debts, none was straightforward and none predated the earliest of the city cases.[98] So perhaps the development of the collusive recovery in the city, though very probably prompted by developments in the Common Bench, thereafter went its own way.

DISTINCTIVE PROCEDURES

It is also clearly the case that London's courts employed some distinctive procedures. Again, however, some of the differences were probably of little consequence. For example, the city custom in real actions, which required the service of summonses at the property in dispute and gave a routine allowance of three summonses and three essoins to the tenant, was different from the practice of the Court of the Common Bench.[99] That difference, however, may simply have reflected the differences between the central and city courts in terms of jurisdiction and routine. It probably did not greatly affect such things as the speed or frequency with which such actions were determined.

[97] CLRO, Jor. 8, fo. 133v.

[98] Biancalana, *Common Recovery*, pp. 388–9: cases of 1458 and 1502 (*bis*); and see also *ibid.*, p. 318, fn. 10.

[99] Riley, *Munimenta Gildhallae*, I, p. 181.

More interesting, at first sight, is the availability of the process by which a court authorised the arrest of the defendant and his imprisonment if he was not able to provide adequate sureties for his appearance in court or if he seemed likely to abscond. It was being awarded by the 1410s at the latest in actions of covenant brought in the Sheriffs' Court, but was not made available in such actions in the central courts until 1531.[100] That covenant was in this respect an anomaly by the later fourteenth century[101] might however have led the city to extend the process to covenant by mistake.[102] Moreover, the availability of this more rigorous process in covenant does not seem to have made much difference to the action's popularity, or, rather, lack of it. In 1320, covenant, detinue and account constituted respectively three, three-and-a-half and eight per cent of all cases recorded on the surviving Sheriffs' Court part-roll. By the 1460s, if the Chancery writs *corpus cum causa* and *certiorari* are representative, these three actions seem still to have been being brought only rarely in the Sheriffs' and Mayor's Courts. There are respectively no actions of covenant, five of detinue and three of account among almost 150 actions mentioned in the file for 1464, which seems to be fairly typical.[103]

There were however some procedural differences which are worthy of note. One of them concerned the use of arrest in actions other than covenant. In the city, it was probably available in all the other personal actions by, or close to, the beginning of our period. Account seems in 1320 to have been the type of case in which it was most commonly ordered, presumably because receivers, rent-gatherers and bailiffs tended to be men of limited resources compared to the plaintiffs, and business partners (another common class of defendant in account) were not necessarily Londoners. What is also clear, however, is that the Sheriffs' Court at that date was ordering the arrest of defendants in account

[100] *Ibid.*, I, pp. 199, 213; Baker, Milsom, *Sources of English Legal History*, p. 342, fn. 7.

[101] See below.

[102] Defendants at common law had been liable to arrest in actions of trespass since the middle of the thirteenth century: Sutherland, 'Mesne Process', p. 487. The process was made available by statute in 1267 in account against certain classes of defendant and in debt and detinue against defendants generally in 1351: Baker, Milsom, *Sources of English Legal History*, p. 342, fn. 7.

[103] TNA (PRO), Chancery *Corpus Cum Causa* Writ Files, C244/99.

before auditors had been appointed. This was in line with one of the clauses of the Provisions of Westminster (1259), incorporated in the Statute of Marlborough eight years later, which allowed for the arrest in account of bailiffs or receivers (and only bailiffs and receivers) who had absconded, if they had nothing within the court's jurisdiction by which they could be distrained. In this respect, it was more rigorous than the Statute of Westminster II (1285), according to which defendants could be imprisoned by the auditors only after it had been established that they did indeed owe money to the plaintiff, pending payment of the sums owed. On the other hand, under the 1259/1267 provisions, it was still necessary for the plaintiff to take two bites of the cherry: first, by proving in account that the defendant was liable to him as his accountant (that is, as his bailiff or receiver), after which the plaintiff appointed auditors who determined, out of court, whether he was indeed owed money, and, if so, how much; secondly, by suing for that money in debt.[104] There is no evidence that a two-stage process was necessary in the London Sheriffs' Court in the 1320s. Moreover, that court would also order the arrest of defendants in debt cases, some thirty years before this was made available in debt nationally.[105] Given the large numbers of actions of debt brought in the Sheriffs' Court, that was, for the period before 1351, an important difference.

There seems to be no way of knowing exactly how old was the city practice of arresting defendants in non-trespassory personal pleas. The overall impression is, nevertheless, that the city process had either rapidly diverged from the practice of the central courts or preserved earlier practice which had been rejected for a time by the Common Bench.[106] Whatever its origin, it offered a practical

[104] Plucknett, *Legislation of Edward I*, pp. 151–6. For the first appearance, in 1260, of the writ, *monstravit de computo*, which authorised the arrest of landless bailiffs in account, see Brand, *Kings, Barons and Justices*, pp. 117–18. This particular writ was in the non-returnable form (that is, in the form intended to initiate litigation in a local court rather than in a central court) and related to a London case; for the continuing use of the non-returnable form of the writ, probably uniquely, in the London Husting until the early 1300s, see *ibid.*, pp. 316–20, 313.

[105] See, for example, CLRO, Sheriffs' Court Roll (1320), mm. 5 (*Dunmowe* v. *Execs. of Farneham*), 5v (*Execs. of Servat* v. *Hudde of St Albans, chaplain*).

[106] According to one source, from Henry I's reign (1100–35) to Henry III's (1216–72), landless defendants in personal actions were liable to arrest or, if

solution to a problem that was acute in all local jurisdictions, with their limited ability to recover absconding defendants.

The process, it should be said, was only available in personal pleas brought informally. In the thirteenth and early fourteenth century (until the 1310s) this meant that it could not be used against precisely that class of persons covered by the statutory provisions which permitted arrest: receivers, bailiffs and, under the Statute of Merchants, business partners.[107] By 1320, however, it had ceased to be normal practice to bring personal pleas in the Husting, and it was becoming ever less common to initiate personal pleas by writ in any city court. The result was that the city custom came to apply, not only to the full range of personal actions, but also to the full range of defendants, including receivers, bailiffs and business partners.[108]

The ability to arrest defendants who had nothing by which they could be distrained within the city potentially solved one problem. It was obviously of no use, however, in those cases where the defendant did have property, real or personal, in the city. Such defendants might still default despite being distrained or attached, and regardless of any fines imposed. In disputes over realty, if the defendant persistently defaulted, the property could be 'taken into the city's hands' and given to the plaintiff. In these cases, since the common law offered an adequate solution to the problem, the city largely followed suit (except that the property was handed over to the plaintiff initially for a year and day, and only thereafter, if the defendant still failed to appear, permanently).[109] But that was not true of disputes over personalty rather than over rights in land. The defendant who persistently refused to appear to answer an allegation in such cases remained throughout our period a serious problem at common law. One solution was suggested by *Bracton* in the 1250s: 'it would be well to adjudge to the plaintiff seisin of enough chattels to satisfy the debt and damages, and also summon

they evaded arrest, were outlawed within the jurisdiction concerned: Whittaker, *Mirror of Justices*, pp. 127, 126.

107 CLRO, HR CP28, m. 4v (*Wrotham* v. *Haveryng & Campes*).

108 It seems likely that the defendant in the 1320 Sheriffs' Court case, *Beauflour* v. *Arnald of Castelion*, was a business partner; his arrest was ordered at an early stage. As far as one can tell, this case was not begun by writ: CLRO, Sheriffs' Court Roll (1320), m. 5v.

109 Pollock, Maitland, *History of the English Law*, II, pp. 592–3; Woodbine, Thorne, *Bracton*, IV, p. 150.

the defendant; and then, if he appeared, his chattels would be restored to him and he would answer to the action, and if he did not appear the plaintiff would become their owner'. The common law of the Common Bench, however, 'would not give judgment [in personal actions] against one who had not appeared.'[110] From the start of our period, the city had no such inhibitions in informally initiated cases.[111] In the Sheriffs' Court it was standard practice by 1320 at the latest to give attached goods to the plaintiff once the defendant had defaulted four times, although the plaintiff or his attorney had to take an oath that he was owed the sum concerned and to provide security that he would return the goods should the defendant appear within a year and day and show that he owed nothing.[112]

Even this procedure was not always enough to protect a plaintiff against a determinedly uncooperative defendant. It was in the nature of moveable property that it could be removed. The city, like other local jurisdictions, adopted a number of measures to prevent defendants evading justice in debt cases by removing themselves from the city, together with their personal property. It managed at quite an early stage to plug one loophole. In the early fourteenth century, defendants in the Sheriffs' Court and Mayor's Court were apparently bringing writs of error in the Husting or before the royal justices in order to introduce a delay which they used to remove their goods from the city. In 1315, the city petitioned successfully that the process in such cases (which were heard according to common law, not city custom) should be altered to permit the arrest of the goods of plaintiffs in error.[113]

Even more effective or useful, to judge by the frequency of references to it, was the procedure of foreign attachment. The practical implications of foreign attachment were that not only assets held by family, friends, servants and agents of the defendant on his behalf, but also those belonging to partners and independent buyers, sellers and borrowers, were at risk of arrest.

[110] Pollock, Maitland, *History of the English Law*, II, pp. 594–5.

[111] See, for example, *Nony* v. *Waledene* (1303), a Mayor's Court case where goods were handed over to the plaintiff after valuation when the defendant failed to appear: *CalEMCR*, pp. 147–8.

[112] *Dunmowe* v. *Execs. of Farneham*: CLRO, Sheriffs' Court Roll (1320), mm. 5, 8, 11, 14v, 17, 19.

[113] CLRO, HR PL36, m. 29v, Riley, *Munimenta Gildhallae*, I, pp. 408–9.

Although there was an opportunity for third parties to recover mistakenly arrested assets – where they were not the defendant's and where the third party himself owed nothing to the defendant – this would not have been of much use to a buyer who had bought goods from the defendant on credit or someone who had simply borrowed money from him, certainly once the repayment date had passed.[114] Given that some debts with short repayment dates were allowed to run on for years and yet were not considered 'hopeless' (in other words, they were probably long-term loans which could be called in at the will of the lender), this provision potentially had quite serious consequences for those who borrowed money: though not much more so, admittedly, than is the case nowadays for those who borrow using a bank overdraft. Again, this went beyond the normal common-law procedure of attachment of a defendant's moveable property, wherever it was, in order to deal with the defendant who might try to remove himself and his goods beyond the city's reach (or beyond the notice of the sheriffs' sergeants, at least). As Miss Bateson pointed out many years ago, apart from creditors litigating in borough courts, the only medieval Englishman to enjoy the privilege of recovering the sums owed to him from his debtor's debtor was the king.[115] Moreover, whereas the debtor of a royal debtor could expect to be sued in the Exchequer by the normal course of the law, in borough courts the goods of the debtor's debtor were liable to immediate arrest, with the onus being on him to appear and to show that he did not in fact owe the original defendant the sums allegedly due.

The procedure in execution of a judgment in debt whereby, if all else failed, the Sheriffs' Court would authorise the valuation of any lands and tenements an absconding debtor held in the city and allow the plaintiff to recoup the sums due from them also varied from, and in some ways went beyond, the procedures then offered by the central courts, in that it was available in all debt cases and extended to all the real property held by the debtor in the city.

[114] See *CalPMR 1458–81*, p. 52, where a broker (business intermediary) attempted to contest a foreign attachment made in September 1443 on the grounds that the sum he admittedly owed the defendant was not due to be repaid until the following Christmas and Easter. The court ordered that the lesser sum due at Christmas be paid to the plaintiff at once, under mainprise (security), and that the greater sum be paid to him at Easter.

[115] Bateson, *Borough Customs*, II, pp. lvii–lviii.

The Statutes of Merchants and the Staple had permitted recovery of duly registered debts from the whole of a debtor's lands since 1285 and 1353 respectively.[116] But although the procedure offered by the Sheriffs' Court is explained in 'Liber Albus' immediately after two sections describing pleas between merchants, there is no indication that it applied only to inter-merchant pleas, let alone only to debts registered under the arrangements set up by the statutes. Indeed, to the contrary: the process with regard to recognizances recorded in the Sheriffs' Court specifically excluded the recovery of debts from real property.[117]

As Common Clerk Carpenter's account of process in the city courts is almost always accurate, where it can be compared to the practice in particular cases, there seems to be no reason to doubt that this procedure was followed in his day. Unfortunately, there do not appear to be any surviving examples of its employment at an earlier period. How well-established it was in the 1410s is therefore impossible to tell. In 1345 'new statutes in amendment of the law of the city' were passed, in which the article providing for damages in [Sheriffs' Court] cases where the debtor failed to acknowledge and repay the debt immediately mentioned only 'biens et chateux' as being taken in execution. This is probably not significant, however, since it is not discussing absconding debtors, but merely dilatory or impoverished ones.[118]

If it was the case that there were periods in which London offered plaintiffs comparatively rigorous procedures which were not available in the central courts, it also offered defendants protection which may not have been available in the central courts either. By the 1410s, a defendant in a London action of debt on a conditioned bond, or where there was a double penalty in the event of default of payment, could 'confesse ye dede, and pray that it may be enqueryde of ye dutye [ask that the court assess what was justly due, including any damages]'. This applied equally, whether the entire sum or only part of it was allegedly outstanding, and regardless of whether the defendant denied the debt or acknowledged it immediately.[119] Even Chancery may not have

[116] Plucknett, *Legislation of Edward I*, pp. 138–43.

[117] Riley, *Munimenta Gildhallae*, I, pp. 215–16, 216, 216–17; *ibid.*, I, p. 215.

[118] *Ibid.*, I, p. 471, based on CLRO, MS LBF, fos. 105–5v.

[119] Guy, *St German on Chancery and Statute*, p. 111; Riley, *Munimenta Gildhallae*, I, pp. 211–12.

offered relief against penalties as a matter of course in the first half of the sixteenth century.[120] How and when the custom became established in London is impossible to say. The city had since 1345 permitted the award of damages, assessed either by the court or by a jury, in those debt cases in which a defendant failed to acknowledge the debt in court at the first opportunity and thus delayed the judgment. Possibly defendants were able to take advantage of this provision in order to challenge excessive penalties on debts secured by bonds. Additionally, it may well be that, throughout our period, the mayor and aldermen or sheriff were prepared to question the plaintiff about the loss actually suffered by him, where the defendant claimed that the penalty was disproportionate. It would not be surprising if they were willing to do so. The city authorities had long had a duty to prevent 'unlawful' (probably meaning excessive rather than any) profit-taking on loans, which was regarded as usurious, and excessive penalties for default in payment could well have been viewed in a similar light.[121]

What these examples also demonstrate is that the city could be as slow to adopt procedures and other measures available nationally as to adopt nationally available remedies; and, once again, that it did not necessarily apply them in exactly the same way and circumstances. The award of damages in dower cases, allowed for the first time in 1345, came very late indeed: the Statute of Merton (1236) had contained such a provision. In its 1345 statutes the city also sought to protect the plaintiff in debt cases against overvaluation of assets seized in lieu of unpaid debts by allowing him to refuse to accept the assets concerned. The valuers would be obliged to take them instead, reimbursing the plaintiff from their own goods. This echoed a provision included over sixty years previously in the Statute of Acton Burnell, the precursor of the Statute of Merchants.[122]

120 Baker, *Oxford History of the Laws of England*, VI, p. 823. It would however be surprising if Chancery had not provided relief against penalties in the fifteenth century (note Cardinal Morton's opinion, as chancellor, in 1494); and for the possibility that the central courts achieved similar ends informally, by encouraging or obliging the plaintiff to remit part of the penalty, see *ibid.*, pp. 381–3.

121 Riley, *Munimenta Gildhallae*, I, pp. 368–71, CLRO, MS LBH, fo. 260; Seabourne, *Royal Regulation of Loans and Sales*, pp. 35, 38–40, 48–55, 65–7, and *idem*, 'Controlling Commercial Morality in Late Medieval London'.

122 Plucknett, *Legislation of Edward I*, p. 138.

Finally, there is the procedure adopted in the Mayor's Court, which is somewhat different again. Here, all debtors were liable to have their goods and chattels and, if they did not suffice, half their lands adjudged to their creditors in satisfaction of the debt. This provision did not apply, however, if the land was entailed; presumably plaintiffs in such cases had to sue by writ.[123] Its form is the same as that employed when the procedure was initiated by a writ of *elegit*, which from 1285 onwards offered creditors who had successfully sued in debt, or whose debtors had acknowledged their indebtedness by entering into a recognizance, a swifter way of attempting to recover the sums owed.[124] The difference is that there is nothing to suggest that in the Mayor's Court the cases had normally to be brought by writ, although the same procedure applied in the Husting, where in the early fourteenth century the few debt cases usually were begun formally. So it seems likely that in this instance the city had simply adopted a particular nationally available procedure for use in cases brought informally. Probably Common Clerk Carpenter's decision to describe one procedure in relation to the Sheriffs' Court and the other in relation to the Mayor's Court reflects a difference in the way that the courts were used. Recognizances could be employed for many purposes, but it looks as though the Mayor's Court, in and out of session, continued to be the place where important financial transactions were normally registered.

[123] *CalPMR 1323–64*, pp. 226–7.
[124] Plucknett, *Legislation of Edward I*, pp. 148–50.

3

THE CITY LAW COURTS

'CITY COURTS' AND 'COURTS IN THE CITY'

This study focuses on the main city law courts. There were other city courts, but not every court held in London was a city court in the sense employed here: that is, a court which 'belonged' to the city, was peculiar to it, and over which it had control. There were, moreover, quite a few courts which have claims to be considered as city courts but which, for the reasons explained below, are either not discussed at all, or are discussed only to a limited extent.

In the second category, courts which were held in the city but which were not courts of the city, are the church courts and private jurisdictions which coexisted with courts administered by or on behalf of the city.[1] Church courts remained a significant element in the administration of the law in, rather than by, London until the end of our period. This was not true of private courts, also known as sokes, but some of them were still functioning effectively (as far as one can tell) throughout the first half of the fourteenth century. Until the 1350s one still finds the sokereeves, or court-holders, of churchmen being appointed to claim their masters' courts in the Husting of Common Pleas.[2] There is even an example, from 1300, of a detinue case being removed from the prior of St Bartholomew's soke into the Sheriffs' Court and from there, on error, into the Mayor's Court.[3] While this indicates that

1 Cam, *Law-Finders and Lawmakers*, pp. 85–94, Jones, 'City Courts of Law', pp. 301–2.

2 CLRO, HR CP1, m. 2, CP5, m. 4, HR CP1, m.2, HR CP10, m. 15. The last appointments of sokereeves are recorded in the mid-1350s: HR PL74, m. 4v, HR CP79, m. 27v.

3 *CalEMCR*, pp. 89–91.

by this date these courts were in certain circumstances subject to city supervision or interference, they were not the city's courts.[4]

In addition, there were the sessions of the peace, gaol delivery, *oyer et terminer*, and so on, which were held in the city from time to time. In such cases, city governors could be, and by the later fourteenth century were, commissioned to act for the king. Those courts and sessions which existed mainly in order to identify and deal with serious offences and crimes do not seem, from the limited available evidence, to have exhibited many distinctive characteristics when sitting in London.[5] They are thus best studied as examples of their type, not as city courts, and hereafter are mentioned, if at all, only in passing.

There are also sessions which were quite closely associated with the city (assizes of freshforce and nuisance and coroner's and escheator's courts) but which were not 'city courts' in the sense employed here. The assizes of freshforce and nuisance were held before the sheriffs and coroner and the mayor and aldermen respectively, and, from 1327 on, the mayor was permanently escheator *ex officio*. Until 1478, however, the coroner was not a city officer, although his deputy, who usually performed his duties for him, seems not uncommonly to have held another city office, and this was also true of the coroner himself after 1478.[6] Over and above what is about to be said, these courts are not a major focus of attention. This is because, where records survive, they have been edited and discussed already, and there is not much more that can usefully be added, except in relation to the activities of the main city courts. In the case of the coroner's and escheator's courts, this means that there is virtually nothing to add, save that the fact that the majority of city tenements were held by burgage rather than feudal tenures resulted in relatively few properties escheating to the king (being taken into the king's hands) either temporarily, until the heir made fine with the king for possession, or for a longer period because no heir could be identified.[7]

[4] *CalPMR 1364–81*, pp. xv–xviii.

[5] Introduction to *CalEMCR*.

[6] Chew, 'Office of Escheator', p. 324; Introductions to Chew, *London Possessory Assizes*; Chew, Kellaway, *London Assize of Nuisance*; Sharpe, *Calendar of Coroners' Rolls, CalLBB*, esp. pp. vi–xvi; and Kellaway, 'The Coroner in Medieval London'.

[7] Chew, 'Office of Escheator', p. 325.

With the assizes of nuisance, however, there was some potential overlap between these sessions and the administration of the law in the city courts. This is for two reasons: first, although the local regulations known as the 'lex de assisa' which began to be recorded in London custumals from the later twelfth century onwards were primarily concerned with preventing fire and with hygiene, they offered a means for litigating disputes over such things as party walls and shared privies; and damage done to property might alternatively be treated as a case of trespass and brought in one of the city courts.[8] Secondly, other aspects of 'nuisance', such as obstructing or failing to maintain highways and bridges, were presented by the wardmote inquest juries and were prosecuted in the Mayor's General Court (see below) as well as being litigated in the assizes.[9] As the number of private complaints of nuisance evidently decreased sharply after the late 1370s, it seems likely that plaintiffs were choosing for some reason to initiate their cases by other means and in other forums.[10]

The possessory assizes designed to deal with disseisins (in practice, the city's versions of the assizes of novel disseisin and mort d'ancestor) have already been discussed at some length. This is partly because, although the city's surviving assize records have been published and fully discussed elsewhere, the rules governing these assizes in London differed somewhat from the rules governing them elsewhere; partly because the capital may have offered similar but distinct remedies; and partly because the possessory assizes were even more likely than the assizes of nuisance to be employed for the types of cases which could have been brought in the city courts, depending on the way that the alleged facts were interpreted. There was a tendency, on the one hand, to blur the boundaries between a remedy designed to restore immediate possession to the ousted occupier, regardless of any right he might or might not have to occupy the property, and remedies which would test questions of right; and on the other hand, the obvious implication of violence in 'freshforce' at least

8 Chew, Kellaway, *London Assize of Nuisance*, pp. ix–xii; *ibid.*, item 55, *CalEMCR*, pp. 104, 230.

9 Chew, Kellaway, *London Assize of Nuisance*, pp. xxvi–xxviii, items 449–50, 453–9, and *CalPMR 1364–81*, pp. 156–7.

10 Chew, Kellaway, *London Assize of Nuisance*, p. xxx.

made an action of trespass a possible alternative in certain circumstances.

So, if none of the courts discussed above were, what was a 'city court'?

When the historiographer and antiquarian John Stow was at work on his *Survey of London* in the later sixteenth century, he stated that the city kept no fewer than nine courts at its Guildhall. Of these, one was purely governmental and legislative (the Common Council); one related to the control of particular city companies (the Hallmote); two were largely administrative, and specialised (the Court of Orphans and the Chamberlain's Court for apprentices); and four were what we would recognise as law courts, although two of them had other functions (the Husting, the Mayor's Court and its sixteenth-century offshoot, the Court of Requests, and the Sheriffs' Court). In addition, there was what Stow calls *the* Wardmote (my emphasis), known earlier as the [Mayor's] General Court, at which returns from individual wardmotes were dealt with.[11]

As far as the wardmotes and the Mayor's General Court or Wardmote are concerned, there is no doubt that the latter was a court of law; indeed, it was a specialised session of the main Mayor's Court. It is not clear, however, that even in 1300 the individual wardmotes were genuinely courts of law. They were, as their name suggests, the courts of the administrative divisions known as wards, over which the aldermen presided and at which, among other things, nuisances and other infringements of city ordinances were presented. They appear to have been the equivalent of the rural hundreds and were well-established in terms of their routines and activities by 1300. Their routine meetings were however infrequent (four times a year in the early 1300s, in theory at least, and annual by the early 1400s, although they could be summoned by the mayor on an *ad hoc* basis at any time).[12] Presentments and individual complaints made before an alderman or his deputy, in or out of the wardmote, evidently played a fairly important part in the maintenance of civic law and order. Fifteenth-century Chancery petitions frequently

[11] [Stow] *Survey of London*, p. 282.

[12] Barron, 'Lay Solidarities: the Wards of Medieval London'; *CalPMR 1413–37*, pp. xxiv–xxx, *CalEMCR*, p. 218.

complained that the petitioner had been imprisoned by the sheriffs at an alderman's instance, awaiting an appearance in court.[13] It may well be that a good deal of lesser business was dealt with by the aldermen in an administrative or quasi-judicial fashion: minor or first-time offenders may simply have been ordered to amend their property or ways. The powers of aldermen and city officers were considerable but often of uncertain extent and nature: it would, for example, be hard to say precisely whence Thomas More derived the authority which enabled him, almost certainly while he was an undersheriff, to order the beating of a lunatic who was making a nuisance of himself.[14] However, although wardmotes were part of the overall judicial system they had by this date no formal power to determine cases, even of the most minor kind (the fact that wrongdoers were regularly presented for offences, and nothing was done about it, was a source of irritation to the wardmote inquest jurors).[15] The individual aldermen and the wardmotes formed at most the preliminary stage of legal proceedings, and they are not discussed further here.

There were also some minor courts which were undoubtedly city courts but were of so informal a nature, at any rate for most of our period, that they too are not discussed at length. Characteristic of medieval London's administration of the law – and indeed of the administration of the law generally at this period – was the blurring of the boundaries between formal court-holding, background examinations of evidence, and informal dispute resolution. This reflected a general absence of clear distinctions between judicial and governmental or administrative functions. The medieval reality was that much 'legal' work involved the enforcement of civic and company regulations, which is arguably an administrative activity rather than legal one. Indeed, such distinctions are anachronistic. In addition, there seems even at the end of our period to have been a lingering sense that jurisdiction and administrative authority resided in the functionary and did not necessarily, at least in normal circumstances, have to be exercised in specific locations, at specific times and or according to

13 E.g., TNA (PRO), Early Chancery Proceedings, C1/32, mm. 53, 79, 371, 377, 413, 433, 434.

14 Trapp, *Complete Works of Sir Thomas More*, IX, p. 118.

15 *CalPMR 1413–37*, pp. xxviii–xxix.

specific procedures, despite the general trend towards more rigidity and formality (and hence, more certainty).

The tendency to regard as a court any situation in which a judgment of some sort was being rendered is observable in the embryo Court of the Chamberlain in the fifteenth century and in much earlier sessions of indeterminate character, conducted by either the mayor or the recorder with perhaps just one or two aldermen present, or by a few aldermen, which dealt with judicial business. There are, for example, references to the mayor and aldermen 'assembled as a Court of Scavengers', to the mayor and recorder 'sitting as a tribunal on the bench in Guildhall', to the mayor apparently sitting alone to hear a case, and to the Court of the Mayor and Chamberlain, which dealt with apprenticeship cases; and the auditors appointed in orphanage and account cases were referred to as the 'Court' (and conducted themselves as one).[16] A later example is provided by the sheriff's counter or compter, a combination, for most of our period, of his office and a lock-up or prison. In 1421, a plaintiff in error objected that the record stated, in a typical preamble of the period, that the plea had been brought in the counter of Sheriff X, 'which counter' (said the plaintiff) 'is neither a place nor a court of record for the holding of any plea'.[17] Just over a hundred years later, nevertheless, the city itself was in no doubt that the session held in the 'hall of the counter' was a session of the Sheriffs' Court. Probably the same was true in 1421, whatever litigants might allege.[18] That such courts are barely discussed in this book does not mean that they were unimportant. It is just that what can hardly be seen can hardly be described.

Over time, the city also delegated jurisdiction to new courts, many of which it created without reference to anyone else. Among these were the courts of the various city trade companies. The importance of these formalised subordinate jurisdictions can easily be underrated. Given that by the fifteenth century it appears to have been normal even for men who entered the city freedom by patrimony or purchase to do so via a city company, that consequently at some periods perhaps one in seven adults

[16] *CalLBC*, pp. 150, 196; *CalPMR 1364–81*, p. 138; *CalPMR 1458–82*, p. 53; CLRO, HR CP31, m. 4v; *CalLBC*, p. 197.

[17] CLRO, HR CP147, m. 5v. [18] CLRO, Rep. 8, fo. 277.

living in the city were members of a company, and that a good many disputes must have involved masters and their men or rival traders, it is probable that the contribution made by the companies as a whole to the resolution of commercial and even personal disputes was significant.[19] This is particularly likely to have been true from the 1470s onwards, when many companies which had not previously held courts received charters granting them this privilege.

Likewise, after the establishment of the city's great reformatory, Bridewell, in the late 1540s, its court came to deal with a wide range of offences, from minor nuisances to criminal acts which would presumably have attracted quite severe punishments had they been dealt with at the sessions of the peace. While a study of these subordinate jurisdictions is beyond the scope of this book (chronologically so, in the case of Bridewell), their existence and its potential impact on the administration of justice within the city should not be forgotten.

THE EARLY HISTORY OF THE MAIN CITY COURTS

Introduction

The main city courts in 1300 were therefore the Court of Husting, the Mayor's Court and the Sheriffs' Court. The situation a hundred years earlier had, however, been very different. The 'birth' of the common law in about 1200 and the emergence of the two main central common-law courts at Westminster seem to have led to considerable changes in the city law courts themselves and in the types of legal remedies they offered. As these changes help to explain both the situation in 1300 and developments thereafter, they are discussed in detail below even though they are outside the period covered by this book.

Before examining their early history, it should be said that by 1300 the city's main courts were clearly regarded, both within the city and outside, as the king's (or royal) courts. Historians, including city historians, do not always recognise this, however, writing of 'king's courts' and 'local courts' in the Middle Ages as if

[19] E.g., Davies, *Merchant Taylors' Court Minutes*, pp. 131, 149, 189, 192; 132, 138, 141, 143; 188, 197–8, 205.

the latter were not also royal courts. Although sometimes 'king's courts' is simply being used as a shorthand for 'central Westminster courts', at other times this is clearly not so. It could well be, of course, that in the century following the Conquest jurisdiction was widely perceived as a personal possession: the king's, a bishop's, a baron's, a town's, just as surely as a piece of land was theirs. The immediate descendants of William I's followers probably did consider that their fathers and grandfathers had won whatever properties and privileges the heirs now enjoyed with their own trusty sword. The development of feudal theory by royal lawyers, however, encouraged the king at least to believe that almost all rights were held from him. No man and no entity such as a town possessed his or its lands, properties, privileges or jurisdiction absolutely. Before the end of the twelfth century kings were requiring their subjects to show by what royal grant or warrant they exercised some privilege.

This process reached its zenith late in the thirteenth century, with Edward I's *quo warranto* proceedings. But even a hundred years earlier, royal servants and others associated or familiar with the king's court do not seem to have believed in entirely private jurisdictions, save over unfree tenants. This is despite the fact that they wrote as though they did regard the majority of secular courts as not being the king's courts. *Glanvill* refers to 'the court of the lord king' and to 'the courts of the sheriffs of the counties' as though the latter were not the king's courts. He also says that it was not 'the custom of the court of the lord king to protect [agreements made] in courts other than that of the lord king'. This seems decisive. Later, however, the author remarks, 'I am considering only the custom and law of the chief court of the lord king'.[20] He was almost certainly using 'court of the lord king' as a form of shorthand; he meant, throughout, the king's chief court.[21]

It seems likely that by the end of the thirteenth century kings and their advisers took the view that secular jurisdiction over free men and women was delegated jurisdiction. That belief was implicit in their assertion of the right of the king's representatives to regulate and correct inferior secular courts. Sometimes, too, the belief was made explicit. When in 1268 Henry III decreed that in

[20] Hall, *Glanvill*, pp. 4, 124, 147.
[21] A point made in Finlason, *Reeves' History of English Law*, I, pp. 457–8, fn. a.

future attorneys were to be allowed to foreigns as well as citizens in real actions, both as plaintiffs and as defendants, he said that this was to be 'sicut *alibi* in curia nostra' (my emphasis), not 'sicut in curia nostra', which suggests that he viewed city courts, too, as being part of 'our court'.[22] In 1374, a Common Bench record referred to 'husteng regis london'.[23] Just like *Glanvill*, London's governors, or their clerks at least, sometimes referred to 'the king's court', meaning a Westminster court. They did this in a 1357 Husting case which, because of a bastardy allegation, was referred to 'the king's court'.[24] Like *Glanvill*, too, they did not mean to suggest that the city courts were not the king's courts. The city itself was insistent on the royal nature of its courts: both the Sheriffs' and the Mayor's Courts were described as 'courtz nostre Seignur le Roy' and the like.[25] Nor does the evidence suggest that the city was significantly slower than royal officials to accept that the city's courts were the king's courts. An early thirteenth-century description of the city's laws refers to a plea sued 'en la curt le rei, co est a saueir en husteng'.[26] London's courts were the king's courts.

The Husting

The Husting was apparently in existence by the tenth century; by 1300, therefore, it had over three hundred years of development behind it. It was in origin much more than a law court, and, once the city's status as a county in its own right was recognised, appears to have been the equivalent of a rural county court. It continued to discharge its ancient role as a forum for administrative and governmental business throughout our period, although the governmental element was, by 1300, limited to the election of aldermen, city officers, and, from 1409 on, members for Parliament.[27] The administrative side related almost entirely

22 Stapleton, *De Antiquis Legibus Liber*, p. 104. 23 CLRO, HR CP98, m. 4v.

24 Riley, *Munimenta Gildhallae*, I, p. 196, CLRO, HR PL78, m. 17v.

25 Riley, *Munimenta Gildhallae*, I, p. 199; CLRO HR CP63, m. 20 (Sheriffs' Court is 'Curia domini Regis' (1339)); Mayor's Court File of Original Bills, MC1/2A, m. 57, TNA (PRO), Early Chancery Proceedings, C1/46, item 40 (1467–73?) (Mayor's Court is 'the King's Court before the Mayor and Aldermen').

26 Bateson, 'London Municipal Collection', p. 493.

27 The previously variable practices used when electing representatives for parliaments and other national assemblies (for which, see *CalLBB*, pp. 33,

to proclamations requiring individuals to appear before the central courts, leading eventually to the outlawing of defaulters, and to the publication of important documents, in particular, those relating to city freeholds. It was in the Husting that (if they were wise) citizens had their deeds, wills and testaments read, approved and recorded. Its importance as a registry, along with the other city courts, was reinforced in 1320, when the city's governors decreed that in debt cases and others involving contracts no document drawn up outside its jurisdiction would be accepted in evidence, and that anyone refusing to produce other evidence would be judged undefended.[28]

Until perhaps the final decades of the twelfth century, it is likely that private litigation in the Husting was conducted extremely informally by later standards. This is suggested by the fact that the twelfth-century charter probably granted either by Henry I or Stephen spared Londoners the penalties for 'miskenning', or not pleading in the correct form; that in 1259 they are said to have obtained from Henry III a provision that litigants would only be required to appoint advocates in pleas of the crown and writ-initiated actions over real property; and that seven years later they had to be ordered to allow all litigants to appoint attorneys in actions over realty.[29]

What these articles and provisions also show is that the way in which the city conducted legal proceedings in the Husting was changing, and that the changes were probably not entirely to its liking. The eventual result was a considerable formalisation of procedures, the introduction of written court records (rather later than one might expect, suggesting, again, some preference for the traditional way of handling legal disputes) and attempts to control and discipline legal representatives. These changes almost certainly occurred because the legal workload itself changed considerably in the hundred years or so before 1300. Dr Thomas found evidence which he believed showed that the Husting had, in the early part of the thirteenth century, exercised jurisdiction over all pleas save those of the crown, including breaches of city

214–15, *CalLBC*, pp. 24, 36, 59–60, *CalLBD*, pp. 33, 289, et seq.) were regulated by royal writ in 1409: *CalLBI*, p. 181.

[28] *CalLBE*, p. 133.

[29] Riley, *Munimenta Gildhallae*, I, p. 129; Stapleton, *De Antiquis Legibus Liber*, pp. 42–3; Riley, *Munimenta Gildhallae*, I, p. 138.

ordinances and personal actions such as debt, as well as actions fought over land or rights in land.[30] That would be what one would expect of a county court. If so, however, all but one of these types of business had largely been lost by 1300.

The records of the city and of the central courts reveal a succession of alterations to the organisation of the Husting during the thirteenth century which help to explain how and why this happened. By 1300, the court had two separate sides or sessions, known as the Pleas of Land and the Common Pleas. The division appears to have been established in 1244. During the course of the eyre of that year, the justices ordered or confirmed an arrangement whereby the Husting of Pleas of Land would be held fortnightly. As the Husting was then being held (or could be held) weekly, this meant that other types of pleas, known as 'Common Pleas', could be heard in the intervening week, with the probable result that a Husting of Common Pleas developed.[31] (At this period 'Pleas of Land' appear to have encompassed all or almost all actions relating to rights in real property, which, by this date, had to be initiated by purchasing a royal writ ordering the court concerned to hear the case. 'Common Pleas' probably meant all types of actions over personal property, whether begun formally, by writ, or informally, by bill or plaint.) In 1260, a further reorganisation occurred when it was decided that certain of the actions over rights in realty, those for the recovery of dower and of rents and services, should in future be brought 'in the Common Pleas'.[32]

The reason for these changes is apparently that the court's workload rose sharply sometime in the course of the late twelfth and early thirteenth centuries. According to a late thirteenth-century London chronicler, a city alderman, 'pleas initiated by many types of royal writ' flooded the court.[33] Unfortunately, there were problems about expanding the court's sessions to meet rising demand. Most charters since that supposedly granted by Henry I in the first half of the twelfth century specified that it was to be held once a week. Overspill sessions were permitted on Tuesdays from Henry III's reign on, presumably because by the middle of

[30] *CalEMCR*, pp. xiii–xiv, xxi–xxiii.
[31] *CalEMCR*, pp. xiii–xiv; Chew, Weinbaum, *Eyre 1244*, p. 95.
[32] *CalEMCR*, p. xiv; Stapleton, *De Antiquis Legibus Liber*, p. 46.
[33] Stapleton, *De Antiquis Legibus Liber*, p. 45.

the thirteenth century the pressure on the court had become intolerable.[34] Beyond this, however, no increase was permitted. Thereafter, '[a] meeting on Wednesday, though it might be held in full Husting, could not be described as a Court of Husting without offence to the [city's] charters'.[35]

The insistence that the Husting sit for no more than two days a week meant that there was a limit to the amount of additional work it could absorb. Dr Thomas concluded that the Husting gradually became specialised, and other city courts took over the remainder of its work. It was his belief that the writ-initiated cases relating to realty eventually squeezed out the personal actions, the original 'common pleas'.[36] It is certainly the case that the Husting was by the end of the thirteenth century a court which was concerned almost entirely with rights to or arising from freeholds.

By 1300, then, the Husting of Pleas of Land entertained almost nothing except actions brought by a writ of right, in which the demandant claimed that he was the rightful heir to the property. This action could also be pleaded either 'in the manner of a writ of entry' or 'in the manner of a writ of *formedon*'; that is, the demandant alleged additionally that the tenant's occupation arose from a lease or grant (an entry) made unlawfully, for example, by a minor or by someone who had no long-term right in it, or that, for example, it had been a gift made to person X and his lineal heirs with the condition that the property should return to the grantor and his heirs if X's line failed, which it had. The Husting of Common Pleas handled an array of other property-related or 'mixed' actions: actions begun by writs of dower, to enable widows to gain possession of the rents and properties to which they were entitled; *ex gravi querela* or of partition, to force executors and co-heirs to hand over or share out inheritances in property or its sale value; of customs and services (alias gavelet, occasionally also described as *cessavit* [*per biennium*]), for the recovery of services and rents, where the landlord had no means of forcing compliance by seizing some of the defaulter's goods, or of the property itself where the arrears were irrecoverable; of mesne, to make a landlord or former owner meet an obligation to a third party with which the property was burdened, and which the third

34 Riley, *Munimenta Gildhallae*, I, pp. 129–35, 140.
35 *CalEMCR*, pp. xiii, xvi. 36 *Ibid.*, pp. xix–xx, xii.

party had recovered from the tenant; and of waste, to prevent depredations and damage by tenants. Although occasional actions of account, covenant, debt and trespass, including a few initiated by plaint rather than writ, were still being brought in the Husting in the early 1300s, by 1330 the only personal pleas begun informally were those which resulted in possessory assizes or assizes of nuisance (which were not of course heard in the Husting) or which initiated a plea of naam.[37] Pleas of naam were however the most frequently brought actions of all: two-thirds of essoins (excuses for non-attendance) entered in the Common Pleas roll for 1300–1 were in cases of naam, for example.[38]

The Sheriffs' Court

The Sheriffs' Court, if it did benefit from the overspill from the Husting, as Dr Thomas thought, was not the only beneficiary. There is, for example, early evidence of a court presided over by the mayor and sheriffs (like the Husting, but not the Husting) which, though primarily concerned with punishing minor lawlessness and enforcing city ordinances, did occasionally involve itself with personal pleas. This it continued to do until at least the 1320s, despite the claim by a defendant in error in 1318 that 'the mayor and sheriffs are not judges in any plea of the city except in the Husting'.[39] As it had been provided in the 1221 eyre that the mayor and sheriffs, together with two or three aldermen, could hear plaints by travelling merchants if the Husting was not sitting that day, the city may have had some authority for its 'court' (the parties in the 1318 case were Florentine merchants). However, the fact that the few later sessions held before the mayor, sheriffs and aldermen seem to have confined themselves mainly to dealing with offences against the city rather than actions between individuals suggests that the practice of hearing personal pleas between travelling merchants in this tribunal had been abandoned by about 1330. In the form envisaged in 1221, it may well, therefore, not have lasted much more than a century.[40]

[37] E.g., CLRO, HR CP28, m. 12v, HR CP29, m. 15, HR CP30, m. 3.
[38] CLRO, HR CP27; *CalEMCR*, pp. xviii–xx (Thomas does not seem to have realised that pleas of naam were not normally initiated by writ).
[39] CLRO, HR CP43, mm. 4–4v, HR CP46, m. 4v. [40] *CalEMCR*, p. xvi.

By the early fourteenth century, the tide seems to have been turning against the use of *ad hoc* sessions for formal litigation, no doubt precisely because of uncertainty over their legal status. The Sheriffs' Court offered an obvious forum for hearing cases which could no longer be handled so informally. Dr Thomas was surprised by the number of personal pleas being brought in the Sheriffs' Court in the early fourteenth century. He believed that the court, though of ancient origin, in its early days possessed a jurisdiction of unusually minor character.[41] There appears to be no definite evidence for a separate shrieval court until at least 1230, even if Dr Thomas's dating is correct, however, when there is a reference to the sheriffs holding pleas in their 'hostiels'; and in fact Dr Thomas's dating may not be correct.[42] The only earlier evidence for a shrieval court, possibly, is an article in the 'Henry I' charter, which said that there should be no miskenning in the Husting, the Folkmoot and 'other pleas within the city'.[43] As there were certainly other courts in the city at this period – the charter itself mentions the sokes – that is hardly conclusive. For a number of reasons, including the importance of some early London sheriffs and the high sum paid for the farm of the city, it would be surprising if the judicial powers of this officeholder were significantly less than those of other contemporary sheriffs.[44] It seems more likely that the only 'Sheriffs' Court' in 1200 was the Husting, given that this court performed so many of the functions of a county court; that, like the rural county courts, it was presided over by the sheriffs; and that the thirteenth-century sessions held before the sheriffs 'outside the Husting' had an informal quality.[45]

[41] As Dr Thomas seems to have believed that the part-roll for 1320 covered a whole year, he presumably did not realise just how busy the court in fact then was: CalPMR 1381–1412, p. xiii.

[42] CalEMCR, pp. xiv–xv, referring to CLRO, MS Liber Ordinacionum, fo. 173. Miss Bateson thought the entry as a whole was of *c.* 1300; as it is evidently a compilation of quite diverse material, Dr Thomas's arguments for the earlier date, which depend largely on a reference later in the entry to sheriffs who served in the early thirteenth century, are not compelling.

[43] Riley, *Munimenta Gildhallae*, I, p. 129.

[44] Brooke, Keir, *London 800–1216*, pp. 185–92, 371–4.

[45] Morris, *Medieval English Sheriff*, pp. 193–200; and see Brooke, Keir, *London 800–1216*, 'Index', *sub* 'London, Courts', where the Sheriffs' Court is not mentioned at all.

Dr Thomas's explanation for the emergence of the court as a major legal forum was that it was the sheriffs who initially dealt with the old 'common pleas' shed by the Husting during the course of the thirteenth century. If his dating is correct, they were hearing pleas of debt brought by citizens by the 1230s. Less doubtfully, in 1259 it was decreed that all inter-citizen debt cases should be heard before them.[46] That certain writ-initiated Husting cases were transferred to the Husting of Common Pleas the following year suggests that this might have been the point at which the Husting largely ceased to entertain any case which did not relate to freehold property; and that the Sheriffs' Court emerged as a distinct, formal entity at or shortly before this date. Despite the fact that the justices in eyre ignored it in 1276, it was without doubt a distinct court, and referred to as such, by the final quarter of the thirteenth century (the references being to 'the Court of the Sheriffs', not to pleas heard or persons appearing before the sheriffs).[47]

By 1300, the Sheriffs' Court was the city court of first resort for most individuals and most kinds of minor criminal and civil cases. Whatever may have been the case in theory (or in other local courts), it is clear that the London Sheriffs' Court did at this date hear private cases which allegedly involved quite serious violence.[48] Personal actions of debt, trespass, detinue, covenant and account were routinely being brought there. Even at this date, each sheriff held his own side of the court separately (a practice which was questioned during, but which survived, the 1321 eyre).[49] Like the Husting, therefore, the 'Sheriffs' Court' was effectively two courts, although in this case there was no difference between the types of cases handled by each side of the court. By this stage, each sheriff was also hearing personal actions

[46] Stapleton, *De Antiquis Legibus Liber*, p. 41.

[47] Weinbaum, *Eyre 1276*, p. xxiii; TNA (PRO), Gaol Delivery Rolls, JUST3/35B, m. 53 (1276/7).

[48] Milsom, *Historical Foundations of the English Law*, pp. 287–8, for the statement in the *Registrum Omnium Brevium* that viscontiel trespass writs should not contain the phrases 'vi et armis' or 'contra pacem [domini Regis]' 'because the sheriff cannot deal with those'. For examples of trespasses allegedly committed *vi et armis*, see CLRO, Sheriffs' Court Roll (1320), mm. 7 (*Russeles* v. *le Chapeleyn*), 21v (*le Glovere* v. *Newmarket*) (it is probably relevant that they were not, as far as one can tell, brought by writ).

[49] Cam, *Eyre 1321*, II, pp. 254–5.

brought by or against foreigns, with the earliest evidence of a specific shrieval *curia de forinsecis* (which served both non-citizen denizens and alien merchants) dating from 1300.[50]

The Mayor's Court

In 1300, the workload of the Mayor's Court embraced a wide range of activities which were mainly regulatory in nature. Those people whom the wardmote inquest jurors considered to have offended against civic ordinances, 'the correction of which pertains to the city', found themselves the object of the attention of the Mayor's Court. Aldermen produced a duplicate of the wardmote inquest presentments to the next Mayor's General Court – Stow's Court of the Wardmote – so that matters which came under that court's jurisdiction could be identified. The Mayor's Court also dealt with the results of the occasional crown-instigated purges of vagrants, prostitutes and the like.[51] Major city disturbances, insubordination to the city's governors and officers, and misconduct by city officers were dealt with by this court. It enforced various ordinances controlling prices, weights and measures. It also regulated apprenticeships and the guardianship and inheritances of fatherless minor heirs (known as city orphans), although increasingly these tasks were delegated to the chamberlain and common serjeant respectively. This trend led eventually to the establishment of the formal Courts of the Chamberlain and of Orphans. In addition, the mayor was empowered to take recognizances of debt, which the city did after its own fashion, and he and the aldermen supervised the conduct of the city's officers, including its sheriffs and their staffs.

In relation to personal pleas, the role of the Mayor's Court before 1300 is almost always referred to as though it were ancillary to the other courts: for example, the ordinance which Dr Thomas dated to about 1230 decreed that, if an action of debt brought against a city freeman before the sheriffs was being unduly delayed, it could be heard before the mayor or his deputies.[52]

50 *CalEMCR*, p. 69.

51 *CalPMR 1381–1412*, pp. xiv, xix; *CalEMCR*, pp. xx–xxiii; Riley, *Munimenta Gildhallae*, I, pp. 37–8; and e.g., CLRO, Jor. 6, photos. 511, 512–19; Jor. 8, fos. 49–9v, 47–50v.

52 *CalEMCR*, p. xvii, citing CLRO, MS Liber Ordinacionum, fo. 173.

Conversely, in 1319 a set of articles granted by Edward II forbade the mayor to summon before himself or to hear in the Mayor's Court any shrieval pleas or any other pleas except those which were traditionally his to hear.[53] The 1319 articles reflect the contemporary view that, as far as personal pleas were concerned, the Mayor's Court was not a court of first instance except where the cases involved foreign merchants (and perhaps non-citizens generally), breaches of city regulations or national legislation, assaults on city officials, and the like.[54]

Two streams contributed to the development of the Mayor's Court in its first hundred years. One was the overspill from the Husting. The city's mayors were probably holding sessions for various administrative and governmental purposes from the time of the first mayoralty in the late twelfth century. It was natural enough that, once the Husting became too busy to cope, the mayor and aldermen should expand their sessions to include those aspects of the Husting's workload which were designed to ensure general orderliness within the city and conformity to any aspects of its life which were covered by its own laws. The same logic saw them holding assizes of nuisance, which regulated new building, encroachments, failures to repair properties, obstructions of passageways, and other similar hazards and inconveniences, while the sheriffs held the assizes which dealt with trespass-like disseisins and other wrongs.

The other stream which contributed to the development of the Mayor's Court was simply the existence of the mayor himself from the late twelfth century onwards. It was also natural that the poor, the weak, and the wronged who had no other remedy – or those who claimed to be so – should ask him to help them.[55] Contrariwise, great men might ask him to intervene in a dispute with a city freeman: as in a trespass case brought by Sir John Botetourte, where the cask of wine promised by the defendant in compensation was given by the plaintiff to the chamber officials, presumably because he felt that the city had done him a favour.[56]

53 Riley, *Munimenta Gildhallae*, II, i, p. 269, *ibid.*, I, p. 142.
54 *CalEMCR*, pp. xvii, 3, 29, 76; see also pp. 28–9 for examples of 'appropriate' mayoral cases.
55 For a session held in 1305 'concerning plaints and petitions' see *CalEMCR*, p. 196.
56 *CalEMCR*, p. 53.

The mayor also had a general responsibility for ensuring that alien merchants and other merchants visiting the city were treated fairly and their cases dealt with expeditiously. The desire of those with power to exercise it, whether out of a genuine wish to help the unfortunate or from vainglory, would tend to ensure that mayors responded. This response was, however, evidently regarded as a matter of grace, not of right. Even in the early fifteenth century, by which time the prohibition on acting as a court of first instance was no longer enforced, the common-law bills which initiated personal pleas in the Mayor's Court continued to be couched in the language of petitions, soliciting help rather than assuming that it would be made available. This may well have been a result of the lingering sense that it was a concession to the private individual to allow him to initiate an action before the mayor and aldermen, instead of in the Sheriffs' Court.[57]

What this does not explain is why, by the 1290s, the Mayor's Court was, at least occasionally, entertaining personal pleas between citizens. The late thirteenth- and early fourteenth-century mayors' rolls show that their court was then hearing actions of account, covenant, debt, detinue and trespass. True, there are relatively few such cases, and in many instances it is clear that special factors influenced their treatment, as in the 1299 debt case which was eventually remitted to the Court of the Steward and Marshal; and it is very likely that a number of covenant cases brought in the wake of a royal writ which attempted to regulate the value of coins known as pollards and crocards came into the Mayor's Court because disputes arising out of disagreements over the currency in which the payment was to be made were then regarded as regulatory matters (the court clearly enforced royal orders and national statutes on much the same basis as it enforced the city's own ordinances).[58] The same may be true of a trespass case, in which the plaintiff alleged that the defendant had substituted inferior-quality lead for that given to him with which to cover a roof, since the jury consisted partly of the defendant's fellow-craftsmen.[59] Nevertheless, the very fact that the articles

[57] The ordinance of *c.* 1230 or *c.* 1300, which permitted freemen who were experiencing delays when suing before the sheriffs to bring their cases before the mayor, had reserved any profits arising from such cases to the sheriffs: *CalEMCR*, p. xvii.

[58] *CalEMCR*, p. 48; *ibid.*, pp. 55–6, 56.

[59] *Ibid.*, p. 82.

granted by the king in 1319 sought to prevent mayors from hearing pleas which were not traditionally theirs to hear demonstrates that at least one of them was doing just that.

Given that personal pleas had apparently been successfully redistributed from the Husting to the Sheriffs' Court, Dr Thomas wondered why and how the Mayor's Court started to hear ordinary personal pleas. It is possible that the mayor and aldermen were hearing a few inter-personal disputes, just like those brought in the Sheriffs' Court, well before 1300. But, if so, their involvement in private litigation was at first probably casual in nature. If asked to arbitrate or adjudicate, then they did so. The case brought by Sir John Botetourte may be an example of one which, though apparently a normal common-law action, was in fact being dealt with informally. But Dr Thomas suspected that there was more to it than this; that the answer lay in the fact that the city's 'system' of law courts was not very systematic in 1300. Considerable jurisdictional overlap existed. And wherever there is jurisdictional overlap, there may be competition between courts. This was particularly likely to be so at periods when the profits of justice and fees were valuable both to the holders and staffs of courts and when the right to hold courts was an important indicator of social status.

The various ordinances and articles of 1230 or 1300 and 1259 as well as those of 1319 led Dr Thomas to conclude that there had been a tussle over jurisdiction between the two courts during that period. If so, it culminated in a decisive victory for the Sheriffs' Court in 1319. In the late thirteenth century and early fourteenth the mayor and aldermen were dealing with what look like a few ordinary personal pleas between citizens. By contrast, all the personal pleas in the surviving Mayor's Court plea and memoranda rolls of the twenty-odd years after 1319 are between merchants, usually aliens, and others.[60]

Appearances are somewhat deceptive, however. It certainly was the case that there was an attempt in 1319 to limit the mayor's jurisdiction. And it is no doubt true to say that the 1259 enactment ordering that inter-citizen debt cases should be heard before the sheriffs could well have provided the justification for later resistance, by the Sheriffs' Court or by the citizenry at large, to

[60] *CalPMR 1323–64*, pp. 113, 131, 217, 258–9, 261, 262, 263, 267.

the reception by the Mayor's Court of inter-citizen debt cases. However, this particular enactment, like that of 1230 or 1300, is only suggestive of a conflict over jurisdiction between the two courts if the Mayor's Court was already sufficiently formalised and active to present an alternative to the Sheriffs' Court – and that is by no means certain. In 1259, the aim may merely have been either to enforce the transfer out of an increasingly overloaded Husting of one of the largest classes of personal actions or to ensure that the increasing numbers of debt cases did not start to affect that court's work adversely: the Mayor's Court is not mentioned.

Moreover, the 1319 articles could well have been a response to a temporary problem created by the legal expertise or personal preferences of the then mayor, John de Wengrave, a former city recorder. He had, perhaps, been abusing the right given to his predecessors to intervene when cases which were being heard before the sheriffs were delayed, or simply taking an excessively generous view of the types of cases that the Mayor's Court could properly hear, as a court of first instance.

In addition, and probably even more importantly, there is the question of the political climate of 1319, both nationally (where the unresolved power-struggle between the king, Edward II, and the baronial 'Ordainers' continued to bubble under, awaiting the outbreak of 1321/2) and within the city, where inter-party rivalries were intense. The fact that John de Wengrave's regime ended in serious allegations of misconduct against him and his supporters in the 1321 eyre, and that the royal letters patent mention that the articles were issued in response to letters sent to the king under both the city's and the new mayor's seals, make it seem unlikely that the city was primarily concerned about straightforward jurisdictional rivalry between the Mayor's and Sheriffs' Court. This was a wide-ranging and very political set of articles.[61] The probability is that, apart from in the 1310s, there was no battle over jurisdiction in personal pleas. Litigants might very occasionally try to bring inappropriate cases into the Mayor's Court but, if they did so, the sheriffs reclaimed them.

As a result, although the Mayor's Court clearly could and did entertain some personal pleas by 1300, they almost all fitted into

[61] Riley, *Munimenta Gildhallae*, II, i, pp. 268–73.

the categories that the mayor was allowed to hear. Moreover, the total was very low. The rarity of references to the court outside its own records also indicates that it was still not recognised as a court of law for the hearing of personal pleas at the beginning of our period. Indeed, its status as a court of record was still being challenged in the fifteenth century.[62] The most one can say with certainty about this court, therefore, is that it began to emerge as a court of law for the hearing of personal pleas sometime during the course of the thirteenth century. Even in the early fourteenth century, however, its formal jurisdiction was strictly limited and there was still some uncertainty about its status in this respect. The period of its greatest growth lay sometime in the future.

POST-1300 DEVELOPMENTS IN THE MAIN CITY COURTS

The Husting

There seems to have been nothing between 1300 and 1550 to match the scale or frequency of the reorganisations of the Husting that occurred during the thirteenth century. On the other hand, there were a few innovations, one of which, at least, has some interesting features.

A novelty which did not in the event take root was an action brought by bill in 1382, involving an alleged enfeoffment to uses (creation of a trust for the creator's benefit). The plaintiff complained that he had been defrauded of the reversion of properties worth £20 a year, for which he had paid £200. He claimed to have made the purchase through two friends, who had 'taken the estate of the reversion by the owner's grant to the plaintiff's use and profit', and that he had subsequently been persuaded by one of his friends, the first defendant, to release the other, the second defendant, from his obligations. The first defendant had then refused to honour his agreement with the plaintiff. The plaintiff's

[62] *CalEMCR*, pp. xxiv–xxv; CLRO, Jor. 7, fo. 72. Common Clerk Carpenter, writing in the 1410s, had very little to say about the Mayor's Court: Riley, *Munimenta Gildhallae*, I, pp. 390–1. Indeed, he omitted the description of the court from a lost (probably early fourteenth-century) London source which is preserved in a Bristol custumal, although he used information about the Husting and the Sheriffs' Court from the same source: *CalEMCR*, pp. xxv–xxvii.

problem was that, on the face of it, he had no right in the properties concerned. As the first defendant pointed out, the plaintiff had granted him the tenements by deed, with no conditions specified, and the deed had been duly enrolled and was good both according to city custom and the common law.[63] The case was eventually abandoned some three years later. Given that there is no evidence that this was done as a result of some compromise between the parties, it may be that the complaint was heard elsewhere (most obviously, in the Mayor's Court). Alternatively, the plaintiff may simply have despaired of success and the disputed properties may have ended up among 'all [the first defendant's] lands and tenements in the city and suburbs' which he quitclaimed in 1388.[64] If so, it is hardly surprising that no more such cases were brought in the Husting. This isolated action is nevertheless of interest both as, perhaps, an example of the inflexibility of the Husting compared to other city courts, and as evidence of the types of pressures which were to lead to the development of the Mayor's Court as a court of conscience.

Rather more important was the change which occurred in the second half of the fifteenth century. From the mid-1450s, the number of lawsuits brought in the Husting began to rise slightly as the action of right took on a new lease of life. The reason for this is that it began to be employed in the Husting in order to effect collusive recoveries. This fictitious action came to be the mainstay of the Court.

Valuable though no doubt the collusive recovery was, its development did not prevent the Husting, which may have been the city's only law court in 1200 and which was its premier court throughout our period, becoming almost moribund as a court of law by 1550.[65] The Husting rolls themselves offer one possible explanation for the court's decline. From the early 1340s onwards, it became common to record in the main rolls requests for assizes of freshforce, in the form of mort d'ancestor and of nuisance. Assizes were of course being held long before then: the majority of the assizes of nuisance for which entries on the separate assize

[63] *Lambe* v. *Badby/Newenton*: CLRO, HR CP105, m. 1v. The first defendant, William Badby, may have been the future alderman of that name.

[64] CLRO, MS Calendar of Husting W&D, vol. IV, p. 135 (HR W&D117, m. 12 (item 105)).

[65] See Chapter 4 for details of the changing workload of the city's courts.

rolls survive were brought before 1350 and, although the record of only one early possessory assize, for 1317, now apparently exists among the city records and the surviving series of assize rolls begins in 1340, much earlier records are mentioned.[66] Indeed, bringing 'plaints [*queremoniae*] of intrusion' (requesting possessory assizes), as opposed to writs of right, was stated in the early 1250s to be one of the alternatives open to those who wished to claim city properties, and the only surviving Husting rolls of *interlocutoriae* (notes – unfortunately very brief – referring to interim discussions and decisions by the bench), from 1298, list seventy-four requests for assizes, including two 'in natura mortis antecessoris'.[67]

Administrative change seems the likeliest explanation both for the appearance of these entries in the 1340s and its timing. It is probable that the city used to record the requests in the rolls of *interlocutoriae*, and, when the clerks ceased making these records, they had to find another home for them. Nevertheless, that the surviving possessory assize rolls and the first entries in the Husting rolls relating to requests for possessory assizes come from the 1340s suggests the possibility that the assizes were by then being used in ways which affected the main business of the Husting more than had been the case in the past. Although over seventy requests for possessory assizes were recorded in 1298, this may have been a quite exceptional number (1298 was the year the city recovered self-government). When they start to appear in the main Husting rolls in the 1340s the numbers were initially low: just one in 1343/4, for example. Nevertheless the decennial total for 1341 to 1350 was more than 100, and, for the rest of the century, decennial totals were well over 200. This contrasts with what happened to actions brought by the writ of right. Indeed, the

[66] CLRO, HR CP60, m. 1v; HR CP65, mm. 2, 11, 14v, HR PL64, mm. 2v, 3, 7v, 12, 21; Chew, Kellaway, *London Assizes of Nuisance*, p. xxx, Chew, *London Possessory Assizes*, pp. xi–xii (noting the 1303 ordinance relating to the delivery of the rolls of assize at the end of a sheriff's term of office, and also a reference to the mort d'ancestor rolls in 1294).

[67] CLRO, HR CP23, mm. 25–8 (or 25a–d). The numbers of cases in the surviving assize rolls, which are plea rolls, are seriously misleading: e.g. the assize rolls contain nine entries which definitely relate to regnal year July 1381 to July 1382, whereas the Husting rolls record thirty-four: compare Chew, *London Possessory Assizes*, pp. 56–61 with CLRO, HR PL105, mm. 1, 4, 8, 12, 16, 20v, HR CP107, mm. 1, 5v, 10, 15, 19, 22, 26, 29, 31.

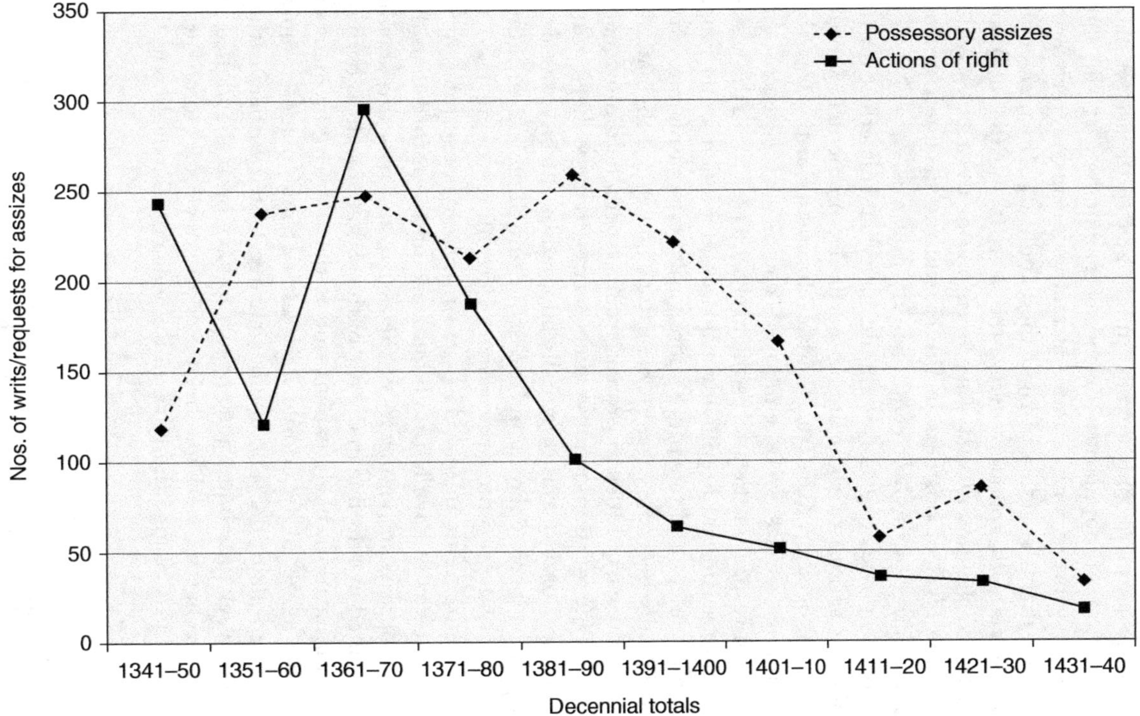

Figure 3.1 Comparison of right actions and possessory assizes

profiles of decennial totals of actions of right and of recorded possessory assizes roughly mirror one another (see Figure 3.1).

If this is not mere coincidence, it might be that the assizes had a second burst of popularity, providing Londoners of the later fourteenth century with a more attractive means of recovering properties than the action of right then could do. If so, since the assizes were held separately before the sheriffs and (deputy) coroner, this development may have been one of the factors which caused the level of business in the Husting to decline from the second quarter of the fourteenth century onwards.

Why the possessory assizes should have had this effect on the number of actions of right at this particular moment is another question altogether. It is true that developments in the way that the national assizes were employed could have affected city practice in respect of the assizes themselves. Over time, the assize of novel disseisin had been made available in a much wider range of circumstances and to a much more varied type of plaintiff than had originally been the case. Perhaps the extension of the national assize by the early 1300s to protect creditors who held mortgaged lands, a type of transaction which seems to have been quite common in London, was eventually adopted by the city, but only after having been delayed by the same unwillingness to admit change as had prevented the assize of freshforce being used to protect annual rents until 1345.[68] If so, the city's capitulation in this case seems to have left no other trace on the record than the eventual increase in popularity of the assize; and why this should have resulted in a decline in the use of the action of right is hard to say. A rather more likely explanation is that the employment of the city's assize of freshforce itself altered and made it more attractive to plaintiffs. The obvious change, noted earlier, is that the forty-week time limitation appears to have been abandoned in the 1380s, having perhaps been under attack for some little while.[69] If this change did have an influence on the decline in the

[68] Sutherland, *Assize of Novel Disseisin*, 'New Tasks for the Assize', especially p. 138.

[69] Chew, *London Possessory Assizes*, pp. xxiv–xxv. The fact that there was an attempt in 1384 to prevent the bringing of assizes of freshforce outside forty weeks, and that the assize was described as 'now abused in the court of the Sheriff', makes it seem likely that there were problems with enforcing the limit by this date: *CalLBH*, p. 242.

use of the action of right, however, the city was clearly very slow indeed to respond to the 'abuse' of the assizes. The case for linking the decline of the action of right with the increasing popularity of the assizes between about 1340 and about 1400 is not a strong one, therefore.

Another possibility is that plaintiffs simply came to prefer not to initiate actions for the recovery of lands by writ. The action of right was by the second quarter of the fourteenth century an extremely old-fashioned action with distinct procedural drawbacks.[70] Or (and) it could be that the whole 'writ system' was a victim of its own success. Courts which had once been closed to all but those in some privileged relationship to them had been forced by writs to open their doors wider. Having once done so, they realised the financial and other advantages of increased litigation, and it ceased to be necessary to buy a writ in order to get them to entertain it. Or (and), again, there were developments during the course of the fourteenth century which made it easier to bring disputes over rights to real property informally, as though they were disputes over personalty.[71]

Whatever the reasons, given the procedural drawbacks of the action of right and the widespread availability of even more attractive alternatives by the time the possessory assizes themselves started to go out of favour, it is not surprising that the action of right never recovered the ground it had lost in the 1330s.[72]

None of this helps to explain the later but even steeper decline in the overall number of writs brought in the Husting of Common Pleas. The obvious answer is that it reflected the drop in population. The profile for individual years supports this, with annual totals for the 1350s at their highest in the two years immediately after the Black Death first struck, in 1348/9, and thereafter struggling to reach half the earlier levels. This change was so sudden and so marked that it seems unlikely to have resulted from, for example, legal developments elsewhere within or outside the city. The onset of the Black Death may also partly explain relative increases in the use of writs to enforce the execution of testaments and against waste. Possibly executors were becoming

[70] See Chapter 5. [71] See below p. 123.
[72] Sutherland, *Assize of Novel Disseisin*, pp. 170–6.

more lax or dishonest, but it may well be that the Husting was being used as a way of confirming that the executors could proceed as planned. The evidence is not good, but it looks as though the majority of the testaments involved, from the 1350s onwards, had not been enrolled in the Husting: of twelve cases between that date and 1457, six definitely were not enrolled, two either were not enrolled or related to testaments enrolled in the 1330s, two definitely were enrolled, and two more probably were.[73] This reflects a change in practice: from the second half of the fourteenth century onwards, city freemen were decreasingly likely to have their wills and testaments enrolled in the Husting. In the cases in which no enrolment had taken place, at least, the court may in effect have been granting probate.

Both the action to oblige the executors to execute testaments and the action of waste involved matters of peculiar concern to a city in which property could be bequeathed and there were ordinances controlling what tenants could do with fixtures and fittings as well as with the produce of a particular property. It is not surprising, given the disruption to normal tenure and inheritance created by successive outbreaks of the Black Death, that they should have become more popular from 1350 onwards. So these developments served a useful purpose at a time of considerable social upheaval. They appear however to have been almost entirely a response to the Black Death. Eventually, other mechanisms were found, with executors who failed to discharge their responsibilities being obliged 'in conscience' to do so by the mayor and aldermen and those tenants who damaged or removed property being sued in the Mayor's Court for breach of the city's ordinances.[74]

Despite the importance of the cases brought in the Husting throughout our period, therefore, the changes which had occurred in the thirteenth century had a detrimental long-term effect on the court, judged as one in which genuine disputes were resolved by

[73] Riley, *Munimenta Gildhallae*, I, pp. 184–5; CLRO, HR CP74, m. 10 (Coudres), HR CP77, mm. 1 (Asshwy?), 4 (Hegham?), 12 (Tayllur), HR CP78, m. 3 (Bosenho, Burdeyn), HR CP79, mm. 1 (Mareschal), 10 (Chayham), 21 (atte Sloo), 24 (Abyndon), HR CP80, mm. 12 (Hornere), 26 (Lincoln), and *CalHW&D*, I, pp. 214 (Asshwy), 255 (Hegham), 677 (Mareschal), 503 (Chayham), 413 (Abyndon, 1336?), 426 (Hornere, 1337?).

[74] See Chapter 4.

the course of the law. Perhaps precisely because the system of writs was so successful in opening up courts to litigants who would not previously have had access to them, or because litigation itself had become much more commonplace and routine by 1300, or for some other reason or combination of reasons, the popularity of the writ as a means of initiating a lawsuit declined in the main local courts in the first half of the fourteenth century. This was almost as true of disputes over rights in and to real property as of personal actions, as ways were found to litigate over them without having to have recourse to the old real and mixed actions which had formerly to be brought by writ. Any court which had 'specialised' in writ-initiated actions was potentially an endangered species, occupying an evolutionary dead end (this was certainly true of local courts, and arguably it was no less true of the central courts). In the case of the London Court of the Husting, the gains of the previous century or so were lost; indeed, the Husting may well have been less active as a court of law by 1400 than it had been two hundred years previously. These losses proved irreversible.

The Mayor's Court

In view of what has been said about the pre-1300 history of the Mayor's Court, the most remarkable as well as the earliest post-1300 development is that, by the fifteenth century, personal pleas of debt, covenant, detinue, account and so on figured regularly in the plea and memoranda rolls and other Mayor's Court records. These cases evidently originated in the Mayor's Court: there is nothing to suggest that they were brought on error or because of complaints about delays in or the conduct of the Sheriffs' Court.

By the 1440s the Mayor's Court was entertaining several hundred personal pleas a year, the great majority of which did not fit the traditional mayoral categories. Because the plea and memoranda rolls of this period clearly record only a fraction of the personal pleas brought, and the same may have been true of many or even all of the earlier rolls, it is not possible to tell from them when the change occurred. That the reappearance of certain types of actions did not occur until the 1360s does, however, suggest that the change began in the second half of the fourteenth century. It is also to the 1360s that the first dateable examples of the surviving Mayor's Court bills belong. This decade and the next witnessed the beginning of a surge in litigation in a number of borough courts. It is by no means unlikely that the Mayor's Court was one of the beneficiaries.

The reappearance of personal actions is probably roughly contemporary with the introduction of a procedure which came to be known as *querela levata*. This permitted either party to obtain a mayoral writ authorising the removal of the case from the Sheriffs' Court to the Mayor's Court. The procedure may initially have been intended to regularise and place a check upon arrangements for the removal of cases which were being delayed in the lower court. In due course, however, any restrictions on the circumstances in which cases could be removed were lifted, and Mayor de Wengrave's successors were eventually able to do with impunity what he himself had been attacked for doing: remove before themselves undetermined Sheriffs' Court cases at will and hear them in the Mayor's Court.

The procedure in its fully developed form (allowing any case to be removed, regardless of whether it was being delayed or not) was probably introduced shortly before the end of the fourteenth century. It was then that the mayor and aldermen on several occasions explained in considerable detail the supposedly immemorial custom by which they could, if they pleased and one of the parties asked them to, summon before them any Sheriffs' Court case which was still pending.[75] The dearth of earlier references to removals for reasons other than delay, error or misconduct (after 1319, at least), the growth in numbers subsequently, and the fact that after a short while the procedure seems to have been taken for granted, all point to it being a novelty in the 1390s. Providing someone was prepared to pay for it, there no longer had to be any justification for the removal of Sheriffs' Court cases into the Mayor's Court. The number of *querelae levatae* never seems to have been very high, however. The importance of the procedure lay in the fact that it may have established the principle that any sort of personal plea could be heard in the Mayor's Court, whether or not the Sheriffs' Court was overloaded. The probable

[75] *CalPMR 1364–81*, pp. 250–1, 251–3, 265 (containing references to 'immemorial' custom), 262–3, 285, 292–3, 294, 296, 300–1, 303–4, 317 (other *querelae levatae*, without such references).

consequence of these changes, moreover, was that it eventually became accepted that ordinary personal pleas could not only be transferred to the Mayor's Court, but could be initiated there. The old distinctions between 'mayoral' and 'shrieval' types of cases had been erased.

Another major development in the Mayor's Court occurred at much the same time and in a similar way. In 1378 an entry in the plea and memoranda rolls noted that 'because the plaint concerned merchandise, the mayor fixed a day for the hearing in a private room in the Guildhall before himself and other aldermen, who were merchants, so that the action might be terminated according to the law merchant'.[76] By the 1390s, the mayor and aldermen were insisting that any case which was to be determined according to the merchant law could only be heard before them, a claim they rationalised on the grounds that, being merchants themselves, they were peculiarly competent to try such matters.[77]

A further significant development which seems to be have been substantially a product of the later fourteenth century was the fact that the mayor came formally to enjoy a power to remedy injustices 'in conscience' (later, in equity) where strict law or custom could not do so. In some shape or form, this power had no doubt been in existence for as long as the mayoralty had been. Once formalised, however, it was extended beyond attempts to settle a dispute *ab initio* in private and without recourse to law, and by the fifteenth century enabled any litigant who claimed that, because of the limitations of the common law and city custom, a case could not be justly determined in the Mayor's Court proper or Sheriffs' Court, to ask the mayor and aldermen to hear it informally. (Having said that these informally adjudicated cases related to matters which could not be resolved in the common-law courts, this is true of the majority, but not all. Six of the petitions (bills requesting the resolution of disputes informally) contained in the first of the early files of Mayor's Court bills are appropriate matters for a court of conscience.[78] Four others involved

[76] *CalPMR 1364–81*, p. 248.

[77] CLRO, MS Liber Dunthorne, fo. 68 (1390), *CalPMR 1381–1412*, pp. 251–3 (1398).

[78] CLRO, Mayor's Court Files of Original Bills, MC1/1, items 19, 32, 24, 17, 18, 122.

the enforcement of company regulations, rights and discipline.[79] The final two, however, seem at least possibly to have been capable of remedy at common law; these involved a refusal to honour bequests and to repay a debt in full.)[80] Despite the fact that the number of such cases, too, was probably initially very low, they encouraged the growth of the equitable side of the Mayor's Court.[81]

The long-term result of these developments of the later fourteenth century was a separation of the Mayor's Court into two distinct sides: one, sitting in the main Chamber or Outer Chamber, which handled both the traditional 'mayoral' cases and the former 'shrieval' types of personal pleas according to law and custom; the other, sitting in a private room known as the Inner Chamber, which dealt with matters informally, through arbitration or adjudication according to conscience. As Dr Thomas remarked, informal adjudication in due course became so separate from the Mayor's Court proper as 'not to preclude proceedings elsewhere', including in the Mayor's Court itself. This point had certainly been reached by 1407. That year, an alien merchant was described as coming before the mayor and aldermen to lay his complaint (*querimonia*); the mayor and aldermen then proceeded, according to the law merchant and the custom of the city, to summon a witness and question him on oath before giving their judgment. A month later, when the respondent failed to deliver goods as ordered, the complainant had to sue him by an action of detinue. This involved full pleadings and a jury; it was not simply an attempt to enforce the previous judgment.[82] The inability to preclude action at common law was a feature of all the various forms of complementary or informal dispute resolution available at the time, including disputes determined according to conscience and merchant law.[83] As the later thirteenth-century treatise *Lex Mercatoria* put it, 'if the ... parties would rather withdraw and prosecute pleas ... at common law, and refuse mercantile law, they certainly can'.[84]

[79] *Ibid.*, items 29, 30, 72, 16. [80] *Ibid.*, items 62, 4.

[81] For Sheriffs' Court and Mayor's Court cases removed into the Inner Chamber before juries had rendered their verdicts, see TNA (PRO), Chancery *Corpus Cum Causa* Writ Files, C244/104, item 91 (1466), C244/112, item 9 (1471).

[82] *CalPMR 1381–1412*, pp. xvii–xviii, referring to 285–6, 287–8.

[83] Post, 'Equitable Resorts before 1450', pp. 76–7.

[84] Basile *et al.*, *Lex Mercatoria*, p. 2. This treatise was possibly itself of London origin.

It should be emphasised, however, that this was not in fact a feature of all cases heard by the London mayor and aldermen according to merchant law. The critical point was that the case should be determined according to merchant law. An example is the 1475 case *Wood* v. *Eton*, in which the mayor and aldermen decided that Eton should pay Wood £391 7*s* 8*d* which Eton had received from Wood's former factor 'pro respectu habendo in partibus transmarinis'.[85] Sometimes cases which were described as being heard according to merchant law were heard formally, in open court, and, as far as one can tell, determined according to city custom and the common law.[86] Moreover, hearing a case 'according to merchant law' was a phrase that might mean several things. It might mean that the court adopted certain procedures which differed from those adopted at common law: the three differences noted in the treatise *Lex Mercatoria* were that the court would sit from day to day and hour to hour if necessary, to accommodate passing merchants; that individuals who acted as sureties for the defendant were liable for the whole of the sum owed, costs and damages if the defendant could or would not pay; and that defendants were not permitted to 'wage their law' (offer to swear) that they were not liable if the plaintiff proffered a tally (a wooden stick, notched to record the sums owed and then split across the notches to produce two identical halves) or 'suit' (witnesses).[87] These procedural variations appear to have been absorbed into the normal workings of the Mayor's Court, and to have been available as an alternative in appropriate cases.[88] Their adoption did not make the session any less formal or its judgments any less final than they normally were in cases heard according to common law and custom. Hearing a case according to merchant law could also mean 'taking into account the current practices and customs of merchants'; and this seems to have been the usual meaning by the fifteenth century, by which time the origin of the procedural variations had been half-forgotten. Again, even though any examinations of witnesses or discussions to establish what these mercantile usages were might well take place privately in the Inner Chamber, that fact alone no more rendered the overall

[85] CLRO, Jor. 8, fo. 96. [86] *CalPMR 1437–57*, pp. 105–6.

[87] Basile *et al.*, *Lex Mercatoria*, pp. 2–3.

[88] CLRO, HR CP43, m. 4 (*Brunlesge/Bromleske* v. *Janniore*), HR CP49, m. 16 (*Blank'* v. *Bromleske*, another case from the 1320s, which was initiated by writ).

hearing informal than did the use of juries composed of merchants.[89]

Although fundamental alterations in the workload and structure of the Mayor's Court were achieved by the 1440s at the latest, change continued long after that date. Even in the mid-fifteenth century, the boundaries between the administrative and judicial activities of the mayor and aldermen when sitting in the Inner Chamber were not clear-cut, and it was not until the second half of the century that the clerks started to note at certain points in the journals that the mayor and aldermen were 'iudicialiter sedentes'.[90] By the 1470s, what was done in the Inner Chamber of the Guildhall was being treated as the work, not of the Mayor's Court, but of the Court of Aldermen. The clerks were choosing their words advisedly when they wrote of parties consenting to 'abide the judgment of the mayor and aldermen' rather than 'of the court'.

On the 'Outer Chamber' side of the court, the eventual outcome (certainly by the 1440s) was a more formal approach: the mayor and aldermen were presumably anxious to avoid errors which might lead to an appeal; the clerks became, and were obliged to become, familiar with the common-law forms and generally more legally experienced; and litigants tended to take it for granted that, in the Chamber at least, their cases would be handled very much as they would have been, had they been heard before one of the sheriffs. Once it became common and simple to use the Mayor's Court for civil actions, other factors, such as a desire for the speediest possible resolution, would have come into play. Some plaintiffs may well have preferred to pay extra for the privilege of having their case heard in the superior court.

As the scope and activity levels of the Mayor's Court grew, its jurisdiction in conscience started to attract criticism. (This is no doubt one reason why the Mayor's Court clerks became more punctilious as the fifteenth century progressed.) Until the middle of the century, the mayor and aldermen took it for granted that cases which were being heard according to law and custom could be transferred into the Inner Chamber for informal resolution in conscience while they were still pending in either the Mayor's or

89 Baker, 'The Law Merchant and the Common Law before 1700', esp. pp. 345–52.
90 E.g., CLRO, Jor. 7, fos. 226v, 227, 228v.

the Sheriffs' Courts. In a Chancery petition of the 1460s or 1470s, however, it was claimed that the mayor and aldermen had stayed an action on the common-law side of the Mayor's Court, perceiving (according to the petitioner) that the 'great embracery' or corruption of the jury would lead it to find for the original plaintiffs, even though a deed being used in evidence was sealed with a forged seal. The mayor and aldermen were said to have acted as they did 'out of pity and consideration of the verdict', knowing that the petitioner could have no remedy except by conscience. Apparently their aim was to allow the petitioner time to appeal to Chancery; there is no suggestion that there was any attempt to transfer the case to the Inner Chamber.[91] This petition may well date to after 1475, for in that year, as part of an ordinance designed both to prevent abuse of the mayor's jurisdiction in conscience and to protect it from external interference, it was decreed that the mayor was not to accept any dispute for resolution in conscience until the case had run its course at common law.[92] In 1528, the Court of Aldermen again insisted that such cases should not be removed before judgment had been rendered, requiring in addition that all bills relating to matters in conscience should be (checked and) signed either by one of the city's law officers, the recorder or the common serjeant, or by the common clerk.[93] After the 1475 decision, the only recourse for a litigant who was reluctant to take the risk of losing his case at common law was, it seems, Chancery.

Increases in private litigation meant, almost inevitably, increases in the demand for juries. The burden imposed on leading Londoners by jury-service was the reason given for the establishment in 1518 of the Court of Requests.[94] It was initially envisaged as a temporary measure; the act enabling its establishment was for a period of two years. However, the act was renewed, seven months after it had expired, for a further seven years, and the court eventually became a permanent institution.[95] By Stow's

[91] TNA (PRO), Early Chancery Proceedings, C1/46, item 9.

[92] *CalLBL*, pp. 134–5, CLRO, Jor. 8, fos. 113v-4.

[93] CLRO, Rep. 8, fo. 59. This arrangement was subsequently formalised, with the recorder and common clerk (or other city 'counsellor') being required to sit in the Outer Chamber every Saturday to hear these 'bills of Equity': CLRO, Rep. 9, fos. 225–6.

[94] CLRO, MS LBN, fo. 71, Rep. 10, fo. 137.

[95] CLRO, MS LBN, fo. 141v.

day it was 'commonly called the Court of Conscience', but at its inception the aim was not to provide an additional forum for the equitable determination of poor men's causes (as was the case with the national Court of Requests, established thirty-five years earlier, from which the city no doubt took the name) but rather to reduce the number of cases involving relatively small claims, under 40*s*, for which juries were summoned.[96] Until 1550 at least, the city's real 'court of conscience' remained the informal side of the Mayor's Court. And here, as in the national Court of Requests, although petitioners to the mayor did as a matter of course describe themselves in the most wretched terms, it was the inability of the common law to provide a remedy that justified recourse to the court, not the small size of the claim or the alleged poverty of the petitioner.

The story of the Mayor's Court during the century after 1350 appears to have been one of growth and expansion. Given that by 1300 the city already had two courts capable of handling the full range of actions that could be brought in the city, one might well wonder why the Mayor's Court developed in the way that it did, and why that expansion was eventually stopped in its tracks, if perhaps only temporarily. One possible explanation of its expansion as a court of common law and city law and custom in the early days is the role played by the mayor and the common clerk in the registering of debts under the Statutes of Merchants and the Staple.[97] It might well have seemed logical and reasonable to permit creditors to make use of the enforcement powers of the Mayor's Court in the event of defaults, and, by extension, to use the court itself to enforce any agreement, not just debts acknowledged and recorded according to the provisions of the statutes, registered at Guildhall. As was mentioned earlier, in 1320 the city's governors decreed that in debt cases and others involving contracts no document drawn up outside its jurisdiction would be accepted in evidence, and that anyone refusing to

[96] Although the national Court of Requests was apparently not formally known as such until the 1520s, it seems the title was in common use by the 1480s: Hill, *Ancient State, Authorities and Proceedings of the Court of Requests*, pp. xv, xxxviii, Pollard, 'Growth of the Court of Requests', p. 301.

[97] London was a staple town from 1326 until 1353, when the Staple was transferred to Westminster.

produce other evidence would be judged undefended.[98] This decree was probably one of the things which encouraged parties entering into agreements or wishing to have some other fact publicly recorded increasingly to pay to have them entered in the Mayor's Court memoranda rolls.[99]

Another possibility is that, if the Sheriffs' Court got busier as the fourteenth century advanced, cases brought there will have suffered delays.[100] The more cases suffered delays, the more cases could, perfectly legitimately, be removed into the Mayor's Court. If so, the continuing presence of even modest numbers of private pleas which had overflowed from the lower court will have helped to accustom Londoners to the idea that the Mayor's Court could deal with ordinary private pleas of the 'shrieval' type.

There are however other factors which might have contributed to the development of the Mayor's Court in the last quarter of the fourteenth century. It was then that the city first began, apparently as a matter of policy, to prefer to employ men as its recorders whose primary expertise was in the common law.[101] The occasional presence of well-qualified common lawyers in the later fourteenth century might perhaps of itself be enough to encourage a more professional approach on the part of the court and a desire to state clearly where and before whom cases being heard according to different 'laws' could be brought. Secondly, and probably more importantly, the city was at loggerheads with the king, Richard II, and his uncle, John of Gaunt, in the late 1380s and early 1390s. This may be what lay behind a number of fierce challenges to the city's jurisdiction at this period (one disgruntled plaintiff appealed to Gaunt's council).[102] These challenges might

[98] *CalLBE*, p. 133. This rule was enforced: see e.g. TNA (PRO), Early Chancery Proceedings, C1/64, items 467, 914. It was justified on the grounds that London jurors had no means of knowing whether or not such documents were genuine: Riley, *Munimenta Gildhallae*, I, pp. 209–10.

[99] E.g., the Indexes to *CalsPMR 1323[–]1437* list no bonds (excluding non-voluntary undertakings, e.g. for keeping the peace, appearance in court and good behaviour), 3 recognizances (1323–64); no bonds, 5 recognizances (1364–81); 32 bonds, 8 recognizances (1381–1412); 60 bonds, 27 recognizances (1413–37).

[100] See further p. 125.

[101] See Chapter 7.

[102] *Walpole* v. *Botlesham*: *CalPMR 1381–1412*, pp. 156–7, 158–60, 161, *CalLBH*, pp. 368, 374, 392–3, 395–6. The bridge masters also spent exceptionally heavily on legal costs (nearly £50) between 1388 and 1391, which may be evidence of a more general resistance to, or vulnerability of, city organisations at the period:

well have acted as a stimulus to some serious thinking about the role of the Mayor's Court in the closing years of the fourteenth century. Finally, it might be argued, and Professor Palmer has indeed argued, that the late-fourteenth-century developments in the Mayor's Court should be regarded more broadly as part of a thrust by the city, prompted by central government, to reassert the proper order of things in the wake of the Black Death.

The expansion in and formalisation of work on the 'Inner Chamber' side of the Court had other origins. The first hint that the informal aspect of the mayor's jurisdiction was beginning to be more than just an occasional element in the Court of Aldermen's work comes from the 1350s, when we have indirect evidence of the existence of an 'Inner Chamber'. Dr Thomas suggested that it was the peculiar demands of cases heard according to merchant law, involving examinations of accounts and of witnesses, that prompted the move to a more intimate and private setting.[103] He also thought that claims that only the mayor and aldermen should hear cases according to merchant law was a response to the 1353 Statute of the Staple which required, among other things, that mayors of staple towns should hear disputes between staple merchants and their associates according to merchant law and not common law or borough custom (not that London was, after 1353, a staple town).[104] These explanations fitted well with his general view of the Mayor's Court. They do not, however, seem to fit all that well with the known chronology of developments in the Mayor's Court relating to the merchant law, which occurred some decades later. The division of the Mayor's Court into an Outer and an Inner Chamber sometime in or before the 1350s (if that is indeed what happened) may simply have been the product of that general trend towards more privacy, even secrecy, which characterised social life in the later Middle Ages. Having acquired such a private room, it is natural enough the mayor and aldermen should start to use it for the resolution of those cases which did not have to be heard in public; and having started to use it for those cases, it is not surprising that they

CLRO, MS (trans.) Bridge Masters' Annual Account Rolls 1381–9, pp. 257, 266, 275; *ibid*., 1390–1405, pp. 30, 74, 93.

[103] *CalPMR 1381–1412*, p. xviii. [104] *Ibid*., pp. xvi–xvii.

should eventually come to see the Inner Chamber as the proper forum for them.

Overall, the developments which occurred in the Mayor's Court between about 1350 and about 1450 were very important: immediately, because they further enhanced the prestige of the court and increased the professionalism of its staff; and for the future, as they laid foundations which have enabled it to last to the present day. But even in 1450 the Mayor's Court seems still to have been above all a regulatory court. Things changed thereafter. Beginning in the late 1470s and 1480s, the court shed many interpersonal disputes which it would once have handled on behalf of city companies to the companies' own courts; a formal Court of Orphans and Chamberlain's Court for apprentices relieved the mayor and aldermen of direct responsibility for these matters, too; and in the sixteenth century the Court of Requests mopped up minor cases. Although much of this related to personal pleas, in sum these changes represented a retreat from the close regulation of citizens' affairs by the mayor and aldermen which had been a characteristic of the earlier period. The constraints on the mayor's exercise of his jurisdiction in conscience might also have had consequences beyond the specific cases involved, because, for instance, creditors and debtors saw less advantage in enrolling their agreements under the court's auspices. As we shall see in Chapter 4, it does look as though a good deal of what had been gained a hundred years earlier in terms of private litigation may have been lost by the 1530s, if only temporarily. Had the population not begun to rise sharply at much the same time, history might, perhaps, have repeated itself. Just as the Husting, which had shed much of its workload to other courts by 1300, found itself without enough to do once writ-initiated actions lost popularity, so, by delegating jurisdiction over a whole range of offences and inter-citizen disputes to other courts at a time when business was brisk, the Mayor's Court may subsequently have found itself vulnerable to any subsequent downturn in litigation. As the profits of the two main central common-law courts reached their lowest point for some two centuries in the 1520s, it could well be that some of factors that depressed their workload then depressed that of the Mayor's Court likewise.[105]

[105] Blatcher, *Court of King's Bench*, p. 21.

The Sheriffs' Court

In consequence, presumably, of his belief that the Sheriffs' Court was largely eclipsed by the Mayor's Court during the course of the fourteenth century, Dr Thomas had little to say of its post-1300 development. But not only was it not eclipsed, there were probably some positive developments in terms of its workload and of the type of case it heard.

In relation to the types of litigation entertained by the Sheriffs' Court, however, one post-1300 change must have affected it adversely. This was the effective elimination of cases which could only be determined according to merchant law.[106] Although the 1378 case which was heard in the Inner Chamber before the mayor and aldermen 'because the plaint concerned merchandise' was not a Sheriffs' Court case, it reflects what appears to have been a change of attitude towards such lawsuits during the final quarter of the fourteenth century. As a result, a whole class of business had passed from the Sheriffs' Court to the Mayor's Court by the end of the century.

It did not mean that the Sheriffs' Court could not hear cases brought between merchants, including foreign ones. But such cases had not only to be determinable according to common law and to city law and custom but could not, apparently, require the court to take into account the commercial practices peculiar to merchants. Thus, a case involving a sum which one merchant had undertaken by written obligation to pay another in a London parish would be entertained by the Sheriffs' Court, because these merchants had done nothing, and sought to use no evidence, that any other Sheriffs' Court litigant might not do or use. However, a case in which a merchant undertook to repay another for payments made between the parties' factors, or involving questions of 'usance' (the time customarily allowed for transit between commercial centres), or letters of credit in favour of an unnamed bearer, concerned specifically mercantile practices and therefore, by 1400, came within the ambit of the mayor.

[106] The Sheriffs' Court was still hearing cases according to merchant law in the 1370s, since such a case is mentioned in a Mayor's Court petition which cannot be earlier than 1372/3 (it relates to events that occurred during John Philpot's shrievalty), and perhaps even up to the time when the mayor and aldermen made their pronouncement against the practice in 1390: CLRO, Mayor's Court Files of Original Bills, MC1/1, item 122, *CalLBG*, p. 297.

Another development of note, a positive one in this case, concerned the use of trespass in realty-related actions. If, as seems to be the case, property-owners during our period were increasingly using their lands and tenements in order to secure loans, one might perhaps expect proportionately more cases to be brought by short-term holders of property against their tenants in the Sheriffs' Court and rather fewer by freeholders against their tenants in the Husting. What one would not expect to see in the Sheriffs' Court would be cases which turned on disputes over the ownership of real property; and, indeed, there is no evidence that cases of this type were being heard there during the fourteenth century. The demarcation between cases involving rights to freehold property and those which involved other types of assets had, however, become blurred by the fifteenth century. The plea and memoranda rolls of the 1420s include details of two Sheriffs' Court cases which alleged unlawful entry for the purpose of taking possession, out of a total of eight Sheriffs' Court cases mentioned in this source for the same period. The allegations were brought as actions of trespass or of trespass and contempt (the terminology employed when the trespass was prohibited by national or city statute), and the defendants were ordinary private persons.[107] This is in marked contrast to the situation a hundred years earlier. In the first half of the fourteenth century, property-related trespass seems to have been quite commonly aimed against city chamber rent-gatherers (and possibly, therefore, renters and other officials in general).[108]

What is not in evidence is any innovation by the Sheriffs' Court itself which can definitely be said to have been introduced after 1300. Such as it is, the surviving evidence suggests that during our period the court became more strictly a court of law and custom, discouraged both from applying other 'laws' and from introducing novel remedies and procedures of its own. Equally, however, there is also no evidence, except possibly towards the end of our period, of the adoption by the Sheriffs' Court of the legal remedies which had appeared in the central courts in the fourteenth and fifteenth centuries. This is probably because most if not all

[107] *CalPMR 1413–37*, pp. 191–3, 214–15.

[108] CLRO, Sheriffs Court Roll (1320), mm. 7, 21v; see also *CalPMR 1323–64*, p. 121.

Sheriffs' Court cases were by this time brought by plaint or bill and therefore did not have to be shaped to fit the 'forms of action' recognised by Chancery. As a result, litigants and their legal advisers had a fairly free hand in deciding who to sue for what, and how. If litigants thought they had a case, they were allowed to try to persuade the court of its merits. In consequence, there was no need either for the extension of remedies by analogy with those which already existed, something which was provided for in the 1285 statute which permitted Chancery to provide writs 'in consimili casu', nor for the later 'action on the case'. As was mentioned earlier, it was not until just after the end of our period that a Sheriffs' Court action undoubtedly described by the court itself as 'trespass on the case' made its appearance in the records.[109] Although it is impossible to be sure how recent this change of terminology was, it certainly occurred after 1480, and quite possibly after the first decade of the sixteenth century, since there is no mention of it in either the surviving plea and memoranda rolls or in a fragment of a Sheriffs' Court record of summons and attachments dated to 1511.[110] Possibly a Chancery petition in which a London tailor complained about a London grocer who was suing him in an action of 'trespass upon his case' sometime between 1504 and 1515 refers to a Sheriffs' Court case; but even this is not certain.[111] As Winchester's City Court knew an action described in its records as 'trespass on the case' by the 1520s, however, it is by no means impossible that this was also true of London's Sheriffs' Court by this date.[112]

Given that that there is so little evidence available to show what happened to the Sheriffs' Court during our period, it is, naturally, very difficult to say why it happened. It is, however, probably the

[109] CLRO, 'Sheriffs' Court Rolls' [*Querela Levata*], 1554. There are slightly earlier examples of cases which appear, in the records of the central courts, as assumpsit and action on the case, but it is not certain that they would have been so described in the Sheriffs' Court: Baker, *Oxford History of the Laws of England*, VI, p. 282, fns. 62 (assumpsit, 1485), 63 (action on the case, 1533–44).

[110] CLRO, Fragments of Sheriffs' Court Roll 1501–11 (photocopies of Bodleian MS. Latin Misc. b. 17. no. 161).

[111] *Early Chancery Proceedings, Vol. IV,* List & Index Soc., XXI, p. 242 (TNA (PRO), Early Chancery Proceedings, C1/316, item 59).

[112] HRO, Winchester City Court Rolls, W/D1/71, mm. 4, 4v; for the appearance of the equally superfluous action of assumpsit in other local courts by the 1520s, see Baker, 'Law Merchant and the Common Law before 1700' in Baker, *Legal Profession and the Common Law*, pp. 340–68, esp. p. 352, fn. 46.

lack of surviving records which creates the impression that any changes in its workload were the result of developments in other courts: the shedding of its surplus litigation by the Husting in the thirteenth century, the appropriation by the Mayor's Court of cases heard according to the merchant law in the fourteenth. But for much of the fourteenth century, the reverse may be the case. Arguably, it was the attractiveness of the Sheriffs' Court to litigants which drew the remaining personal pleas away from the Husting in the early 1300s, and it was the continuing rise in its workload which subsequently obliged the Mayor's Court to start entertaining these lawsuits once again. It was suggested earlier that one possible explanation for the reappearance in the Mayor's Court of 'shrieval' types of pleas is that the Sheriffs' Court was by the 1360s so busy that it could not cope expeditiously with them. There is no direct evidence of delays in the Sheriffs' Court in the 1360s and 1370s, and indeed in 1356 the sheriffs were ordered to hold a single joint counter and to share their staff.[113] This was, however, almost certainly a response to a sharp but short-lived drop in litigation in the immediate aftermath of the Black Death. A mere two years later, the sheriffs were ordered to revert to two separate counters, presumably because their workload had by then largely recovered; the order was given specifically on the grounds that lawsuits were being delayed.[114] This in turn suggests that litigation may have risen disproportionately in the late 1350s, as social and economic circumstances changed (in other words, as much litigation was being undertaken by the reduced population as had been undertaken before 1348). If so, it could explain why neither the sheriffs nor their staffs complained about the reappearance of 'their' type of pleas in the Mayor's Court and the disappearance from their own court of cases heard and determined according to the merchant law.

Like the Mayor's Court, however, the Sheriffs' Court experienced a very sharp decline in its workload in or by 1550. Why it occurred at all, and why it seems to have occurred later than in the Mayor's Court, is equally uncertain. The sheriffs' clerks themselves said it was 'by reason for povertie privilege and such other like thing', suggesting a mix of economic problems and

[113] *CalLBG*, p. 72. [114] CLRO, HR PL80, m. 11.

competition or jurisdictional overlap with other courts.[115] In theory, the establishment of the Court of Requests should have affected the Sheriffs' Court more than the Mayor's Court, since the former seems to have entertained more disputes over assets of low value than the latter.[116] But although there is evidence of hostility to the Court of Requests among the attorneys working in the Sheriffs' Court, it comes from the 1540s.[117] That suggests that it was the much later and unrelated decline in the workload of the Sheriffs' Court, or some other factor altogether, that generated tension, rather than that the establishment of the Court of Requests in 1518 caused a significant decline in the workload. Conversely, the establishment of Bridewell in 1548 happened too late to explain an apparently catastrophic decline in the workload of the Sheriffs' Court by 1550. For reasons discussed in Chapter 10, competition from the central courts also seems to be an unlikely explanation: certainly the recovery of the Common Pleas and King's Bench from the 1550s onwards appears to have occurred too late to have had any adverse effect on the Sheriffs' Court by 1550.[118]

The likeliest explanation for its decline, therefore, is that it too was part of a general recession in litigation at the period, with different courts experiencing a nadir at different times, depending upon such factors as their attractiveness to litigants and the volume and types of cases they entertained. If that is the case, one would expect both the Mayor's and the Sheriffs' Courts to have recovered the lost ground within a decade or two; that was certainly true of some other borough courts, which experienced a surge of litigation during the second half of the sixteenth century.[119] Because the Sheriffs' Court had not lost its jurisdiction over private litigation except where it was of modest value (and there were days of roaring inflation ahead), its difficulties were unlikely to be permanent. As we shall see, the court was still entertaining several thousand civil cases in the later eighteenth century. While there can be no certainty on this point, the complaints made from the 1570s onwards about foreign pleaders

[115] CLRO, Rep 12/2, fo. 263; see Chapter 10 for a discussion of the possible impact of privileges of court.

[116] See pp. 236, 238–9. [117] CLRO, Rep. 12/1, fos. 14, 29v.

[118] Brooks, *Pettyfoggers and Vipers of the Commonwealth*, Chapter 4 and pp. 51, 56.

[119] Champion, 'Litigation in the Boroughs', pp. 205, 207.

(advocates) practising in the city's courts does suggest that they were by then not only providing enough work for legal representatives based in them but were able to offer a happy hunting-ground for hungry lawyers.[120] It is true that the city authorities were also exercised by the fact that some Elizabethan Sheriffs' Court attorneys were working in external courts, which might suggest that there was fierce competition for a limited amount of work. At this time, however, the anxiety was probably still about the threat to the city's 'secrets' rather than external competition, since the foreign pleaders were said to 'brynge in question and dowbte the customes and usages of this Cytie'. The situation had clearly changed by the early seventeenth century, when foreign attorneys were accused of causing suits begun in the city courts to be removed to Westminster.[121]

As far as the appearance of cases alleging forcible entries is concerned, it was almost certainly a response to national legislation of the late fourteenth and early fifteenth centuries.[122] It was suggested earlier, in relation to the decline in the use of the action of right, that fourteenth-century litigants might have begun to employ the possessory assizes as a way of disputing ownership of property. That cannot, however, explain the continuing very sharp decline in Husting business from 1400 onwards. Recorded requests for assizes too fell off rapidly at this point, to well below 100 per decade from 1411 onwards, almost vanishing after 1440. (This, incidentally, appears to have been part of a national trend, judging by the rapid shrinkage of the surviving rolls of the justices of assize after 1400.) It may be no coincidence that from 1381 onwards there was an alternative mechanism available in the statutory action of trespass, aimed against unjust or violent 'forcible entries'.[123]

And yet, if it was the statutory provisions alone which prompted litigants to use the action of trespass and contempt to recover possession of their properties, one might have expected the proportion of trespass actions brought in the Sheriffs' Court to have risen shortly after 1381. The evidence is however ambiguous. There could possibly have been a proportional

[120] CLRO, Rep. 17, fo. 212, Rep. 18, fo. 280.
[121] CLRO, 'Remarks Submitted to Authority for Reform', p. 2; CLRO, Rep. 19, fo. 271v; 'Remarks Submitted to Authority for Reform', p. 2.
[122] Milsom, *Historical Foundations of the Common Law*, p. 445. [123] *Ibid.*, p. 161.

increase in trespass over the period, perhaps within the context of a general increase in Sheriffs' Court litigation. However, all the trespasses for which details are given in the pre-1410 *querelae levatae* involved alleged forcible entries for the purpose of carrying off goods (in reality, many of these were probably, as in the 1320s, actions of naam); there is only one 'contempt and trespass', about which, unfortunately, no further details are provided.[124] One case out of thirty-nine, two to three per cent, and that one not definitely connected with a forcible entry for the purpose of occupation, hardly seems to offer even a partial explanation for the reduction in both actions of right brought and requests for possessory assizes made in the Husting from 1380 onwards. On the other hand, as we shall see, the fifteenth-century Sheriffs' Court was probably entertaining thousands of cases each year in the fifteenth century. Even two-and-a-half per cent of a relatively modest 2,000 personal actions would give fifty cases a year; and there was no year after 1325 when the Husting of Pleas of Land entertained as many as fifty actions of right – indeed, there was no decade after 1410 when it entertained so many. Moreover, litigants' habits are unlikely to have changed overnight. Not until the early 1400s did the number of plaints of intrusion start to decline noticeably; not until after 1410 did the drop become a sharp one. Perhaps the high profile of 'forcible entry' cases in the plea and memoranda rolls of the 1420s is not mere coincidence but reflects the fact that proportionately many more of them were being brought by then.

A possible difficulty with this explanation of events is that the reasons given for the switch nationally from the assizes to actions of trespass and contempt after 1381 do not seem all that convincing in relation to London. Professor Milsom suggested that trespass had a superior appeal because, by limiting its penalties either to those who had no right of entry, however they intruded themselves, or to those who had such a right, but exercised it violently or in a threatening manner, it allowed for peaceable possession by those who did have a right of entry. (This is precisely how the action of trespass brought against chamber rent-gatherers in the 1320s appears to have been used: if the distraint

124 CLRO, MS Sheriffs' Court Rolls [*Querelae Levatae*] 1406/7, 1407/8, especially Sheriff Pomfreyt's Roll, 1407/8, item 3.

was unjust – taken before the rent was due, for example – the renter was found guilty; if not, he was acquitted.) Professor Milsom thought that novel disseisin, conversely, might have lost ground because litigants disliked the 'laxity of pleading in the assize' or were worried by the fact that the justices of assize were part of a criminal administration.[125] Neither of these explanations seems particularly satisfactory in relation to the possessory assizes held before the London sheriffs, since they also heard trespass cases, admittedly in separate sessions, and do not seem ever to have been overly concerned about strict pleading. And the fact is that the city had forbidden forcible entries for many years if not many centuries by the time that litigants in its courts seem to have taken to using trespass in place of the assize, as opposed to alongside it. (In a case from 1417, the plaintiff in fact cited both the statutes and city custom.)[126] Neither is it likely that the appeal of the trespass allegedly *vi et armis* was the penalties inflicted, since losing defendants in the city courts were merely fined. Nor, indeed, does it seem to be the case that the increasing use of the assizes to establish title, and consequent tendency to delve deeply into the facts in order to prevent fraud, led to them becoming as protracted and complicated as the old actions of right. Even in the middle of the fifteenth century, verdicts in the city assizes were commonly reached within a couple of months, and the city courts soon took to checking the parties' title in trespass, too.

It may well be the case, however, that the assizes had suffered the usual fate of elderly actions, and had ossified and become unfashionable. Disseisins in the city were evidently no longer very *novel* by the fifteenth century, the time limitation, by then reduced from forty weeks to forty days, having become a fiction. In this case, alignment with the standard common-law practice seems to have been detrimental. Moreover, bringing an action of trespass in the city's courts, rather than through the assizes, may simply have come to be seen as the appropriate mechanism for discouraging anti-social behaviour, which was of course very much the concern of the city authorities. As the mayor and aldermen said in the 1417 case just mentioned, forcible entries of this kind 'were an injustice to the public'.

[125] Milsom, *Historical Foundations of the Common Law*, p. 161.
[126] *CalPMR 1413–37*, pp. 56–8, 57, fn. 1.

Overall, such changes as the Sheriffs' Court experienced between 1300 and 1500 do not appear to have affected the nature of its activities or its workload to anything like the same extent as the developments of the thirteenth century. Although the late fourteenth-century restriction on determining cases according to merchant law obviously affected what the court could do, the number of such cases was probably never very great. The range of Sheriffs' Court actions may have decreased somewhat, but it remained the city's principal court for the litigation of personal pleas well into the sixteenth century. What it may have begun to lose at this period was its dominant position in terms of being the city court to which the vast majority of private litigants automatically turned and in which the vast majority of offences and minor crimes were dealt with. Moreover, by 1550 its character may have changed significantly. The appearance of 'trespass on the case' probably represents the culmination of a lengthy process of alignment with the practice of the central common-law courts. Because this was a court which proceeded by bill, process remained relatively flexible compared to the central courts until the written bill also achieved popularity there. Concern for correctness of form, however, may well have been established by the middle of the fifteenth century. If so, the days of genuine experimentation and toleration of novelty will have been long gone by the end of our period.

4

THE ADMINISTRATION OF THE LAW IN THE CITY'S COURTS: I

INTRODUCTION

This chapter and the next examine the practical aspects of the administration of the law in the main city courts: in the case of this chapter, where they sat, when they sat, how flexible or inflexible their programmes were, and how much of each type of 'legal business', particularly private litigation, they dealt with.

LOCATION OF THE COURTS

We know that the Husting was in session at Guildhall in 1252. Indeed, it may well have been held there from the second quarter of the twelfth century, when a city guildhall is first recorded.[1] Sessions of the Mayor's Court were from its earliest days doubtless held somewhere in Guildhall, too. In 1298, a man complained that he had been attacked by another man, in the presence of the mayor and alderman, when he 'was attending Guildhall ... in order to receive the judgment of right adjudged to him' in an earlier case.[2] This incident might have occurred in either the Mayor's Court or the Husting; but the fact that the sheriffs, who were the mayor's co-judges in the Husting, are not mentioned suggests that it was the former. In contrast, for most of the thirteenth century sessions before the sheriffs outside the Husting were apparently held 'en hostiel des Viscontes' (which could mean either the sheriffs' own houses or their counters),

[1] Barron, *Medieval Guildhall of London*, p. 15; Nightingale, 'Origins of the Court of Husting', pp. 559–78.
[2] *CalEMCR*, p. 15.

presumably because of their informal character.[3] But by the early 1300s some of its sessions were being held at Guildhall, for in 1303 one of the sheriffs brought an action against a man for an assault which had occurred 'in his Court in the Guildhall'.[4] Indeed, the account given by Common Clerk Carpenter in 'Liber Albus' of early fifteenth-century practice suggests that at this date all sessions of the Sheriffs' Court were being held at Guildhall.[5] By the 1530s, however, it is clear that two of the four weekly sittings only were held at Guildhall and the others in the sheriffs' counters.[6] This may have been the case throughout our period, although the fact that in the fourteenth and early fifteenth centuries pleadings could occur and judgments be rendered on either of the sheriff's two court days suggests otherwise.[7] Later on, certainly, 'courts' held in the counters very probably dealt with routine business, such as the initiation of pleas, whereas those at Guildhall were the formal sessions of the court ('full' courts) during which litigants pleaded, juries rendered their verdicts, and judgments were given.[8]

In the early 1300s, the Husting was held at the west end of the main hall, and the Sheriffs' Court may have sat opposite it, at the east end. There they evidently remained throughout the fourteenth and into the early fifteenth century. Between 1411 and *circa* 1430, however, Guildhall was rebuilt. At that time, the arrangement of the main hall appears to have been reversed, so that the Husting was held at the east end and the Sheriffs' Court at the west end, where they stayed for the rest of our period.[9] How courts of this period were physically arranged is uncertain: in 1291, when an advocate was accused of disrespect towards a Sheriffs' Court clerk who had refused to let him work in that court while he was under suspension, he 'put himself upon the record of the four benches of the court'.[10] This might suggest that the 'courtroom' then consisted of a square, the four benches creating its sides. There is also a reference to a bar in regulations of the

[3] Riley, *Munimenta Gildhallae*, II, i, p. 280. [4] *CalEMCR*, p. 152.
[5] Riley, *Munimenta Gildhallae*, I, p. 199. [6] CLRO, Rep. 8, fo. 277.
[7] *CalEMCR*, pp. 133–4, 134–5 (1302); CLRO, HR CP38, m. 11 (1311), HR CP147, m. 5 (1421).
[8] Riley, *Memorials*, p. 27; *idem*, *Munimenta Gildhallae*, I, p. 181.
[9] Barron, *Medieval Guildhall of London*, p. 30; Riley, *Munimenta Gildhallae*, I, p. 20.
[10] Riley, *Memorials*, pp. 27–8.

1280s covering the duties of advocates, and, as in a reference from 1321, it was clearly the barrier which separated the area occupied by the judges and their clerks and legal advisers from the body of the court in which the litigants or accused, their legal advisers and friends and any onlookers stood.[11] It is certainly likely that the 'court' consisted of more men in the earlier period than the later: on one of the rare occasions when we are told who assessed damages when the 'court' did so, the list includes, not only five aldermen, who were at the time required to attend sessions of the Sheriffs' Court, but also the common clerk, two pleaders (advocates) and two attorneys.[12]

By the 1290s there was also a room at Guildhall known as the Chamber, possibly on the upper floor of a wing at the east end of the main hall.[13] This may have been where the Mayor's Court was sometimes held, as it was in the following century.[14] In the 1330s the Mayor's Court apparently sat either in the Chamber or in the same place as the Husting.[15] It would not be surprising if at first formal business (prosecutions for breaches of city ordinances, for example) tended to be conducted in the hall of Guildhall and more private matters – though not necessarily less important ones – were dealt with in the Chamber. From the 1370s on, this room was sometimes known as the Upper Chamber; whether it had been relocated or whether this was merely an alternative name for the original Chamber is not clear. Either way, by this time the Mayor's Court seems normally to have sat there.[16] In the later fourteenth century it was probably only held in the main hall of Guildhall when it was sitting as the General Court, the future Wardmote Court, or, perhaps, as what became known as a 'congregation of the mayor and aldermen', to enact ordinances and discuss city business in the presence of other leading citizens.[17]

11 Riley, *Munimenta Gildhallae*, I, p. 596; *idem*, *Munimenta Gildhallae*, II, p. 295.

12 *CalEMCR*, pp. 264 (1305), 102 (1300); by 1321, aldermen were no longer required to attend: see Cam, *Eyre 1321*, II, pp. 254–5.

13 Barron, *Medieval Guildhall of London*, pp. 19–20, 22.

14 Riley, *Munimenta Gildhallae*, I, p. 20; *CalLBB*, p. 216.

15 *CalEMCR*, p. xxvi. Unfortunately session headings only begin to mention the place where the court was held in the 1360s.

16 *CalPMR 1323–64*, p. 261 (1363), *CalPMR 1364–81*, pp. 1, 39, 41, 54 *et seq*. ('the Chamber' and 'the Upper Chamber' were clearly synonyms: see *CalLBH*, pp. 108, 109).

17 Barron, *Medieval Guildhall of London*, p. 22; *CalLBB*, pp. 216–17. For congregations held in [the main hall of] Guildhall, see, e.g., *CalEMCR*,

This change may well be related to the fact that the Chamber had evidently been divided or extended by then to produce a private inner room, since the 'Outer Chamber' is mentioned in 1352.[18] When in the 1420s a new building was begun to the north-west of the main hall, the Mayor's Court and Court of Aldermen were housed in two separate, though connected, second-floor rooms; what relationship this building had to the one which had previously housed the [Outer] Chamber and Inner Chamber is unknown.[19]

Fluid though the distribution of work in the Mayor's Court long remained, the major reorganisation of the early fifteenth century did eventually see formal process in litigation heard according to common law and city custom firmly consigned to the public forum and other disputes equally firmly consigned to the private one. In 1409 the Court of Aldermen decreed that it should thenceforth sit 'on the usual days in the principal chamber of the Guildhall, and there hold openly the Mayoralty Court between parties desirous of bringing plaints as of old accustomed, and not in the Inner Chamber as has been done some few years past'.[20] Thereafter, although detailed investigations relating to common-law actions (such as the examination of witnesses or documentary evidence) continued to take place in the Inner Chamber, formal process was conducted in the Chamber. It may well be, of course, given the somewhat contradictory evidence for the later fourteenth century, that before 1409 no particular significance attached to the venue, as far as the relatively few private cases were concerned. The mayor and aldermen heard them wherever it was convenient to do so; in the Outer Chamber when the court was in session anyway, and in the Inner Chamber on days and at times when it was not. But whatever was the reality of the situation before 1409, thereafter there clearly was an intimate connection between the Inner Chamber and cases tried according to non-common-law principles and practices.[21] It is not the case,

pp. 131–7, 141, *CalPMR 1323–64*, p. 229; although they were sometimes held in the Chamber: *CalPMR 1364–81*, p. 39.

18 *CalLBG*, p. 3.

19 Barron, *Medieval Guildhall of London*, p. 22 (suggesting that the original Chamber(s) might have lain in a 'north-south crosswing at the eastern end of the [main hall]'), 30–1.

20 *CalLBI*, p. 80.

21 TNA (PRO), Chancery *Corpus cum Causa* Writs Files, C244/108, m. 170; TNA (PRO), King's Bench Plea Rolls, KB27/827, m. 104.

however, that the work done in the Inner Chamber was solely concerned with private disputes. Given that the city journals were, until the end of the fifteenth century, primarily the recordbooks of the Court of Aldermen, it is probable that all the fifteenth-century entries in them relating to legal actions concern work done in private.[22] From these entries it is evident that the Inner Chamber was as likely to be used if a case arose out of pure criminality as out of commercial transactions. Even once the city's governors were acting as justices of the peace and were sitting on commissions of gaol delivery and *oyer et terminer*, there seems to have been a tendency to try to deal with civic disturbances internally. In 1468, for example, when national political tensions produced turbulence within the city, a number of furriers, tailors and cordwainers were examined in the Inner Chamber in connection with an abortive raid on Flemish workers living in Southwark.[23] Indeed, using the Inner Chamber may have seemed especially attractive when the criminality had political overtones.

SESSIONS AND ROUTINES

The Husting

Once established, the two sides of the Husting had distinct identities. It came to be accepted doctrine that the process leading to outlawry had to take place in successive sessions of one type of Husting or the other, and the reversal of an outlawry could be obtained at least partly on the grounds that the sheriff's return to the initiating writ did not specify the side of the Husting at which the outlawed individual had been warned to appear.[24] Writs alleging error in the Sheriffs' Court seem always to have been brought in the Husting of Common Pleas, as, in later years, were writs ordering the election of members for Parliament. Wills and

[22] E.g., CLRO, Jor. 7, fo. 114v; *CalPMR 1458–82*, pp. 24–7, 57–64, relating to CLRO, Jor. 6, photo. 545, Jor. 8, fo. 9.

[23] CLRO, Jor. 7, fos. 178–8v; and see *CalPMR 1323–64*, p. xiv, for the city's hostile reaction to the way that the justices of gaol delivery had dealt with rioters in 1267.

[24] Riley, *Munimenta Gildhallae*, I, p. 190; TNA (PRO), King's Bench Plea Rolls, KB27/860, m. 62v (*Donn* v. *Walsh*).

testaments, however, could be enrolled on either side of the court, the freedom of the city could be granted on either side, and both sides could receive requests for an assize.[25]

The replies given by the city to the royal justices in the 1321 eyre and the account in 'Liber Albus' a hundred years later give the impression that there was a well-established routine governing the Husting programme during our period, at least when it was sitting. On the other hand, it was far from clear from either source when it did and did not sit. According to 'Liber Albus', one or other side of the court sat (on Mondays, with an overspill to Tuesdays if necessary) every week, 'except for certain festival times and days and other reasonable causes'.[26] The city's reply to the justices in eyre in 1321 was along the same lines: the Husting was then held fortnightly, 'except at certain times of the year, as in August, and at other specified times of the year'.[27] By the eighteenth century, the weeks in which the court did not sit, in addition to the summer break and the major religious festivals, could potentially number fifteen (the rule then was that the court did not sit if a specific saint's day fell on the Tuesday of the week concerned). The 'August' break by then lasted from 1 August to 29 September and the Christmas vacation from 16 December to 6 January.[28] These rules were clearly not fully developed in our period: for example, a session was held on 11 June 1274, St Barnabas' Day, a day on which the court was not held in the eighteenth century.[29] Indeed, although there clearly were rules about when the court did and did not sit, they appear to have been different.[30] Nevertheless, even in the early 1300s the court seems commonly not to have sat at all between late July (sometimes even late June) and mid-October or even November. As it rarely sat in December either, the second half of the year tended to be a quiet period.[31]

[25] Sharpe, *CalHW&D*, I, pp. xxiv–xxv; CLRO, HR PL1 m. 3, HR CP39, m. 17, *CalPMR 1364–81*, pp. 143, 255; Riley, *Munimenta Gildhallae*, I, p. 142.

[26] Riley, *Munimenta Gildhallae*, I, p. 181. [27] Cam, *Eyre 1321*, I, p. 32.

[28] Emerson, *Concise Treatise*, pp. 13–15. [29] CLRO, HR CP2, m. 8.

[30] See CLRO, HB2, 1506–37, fo. 42v, for the note that the court was not held 'because the Feast of St Mary Magdalene was Monday 22 July this year' (i.e., the feast was a non-court day in the early sixteenth century, though it was not in the eighteenth century, and Monday, rather than Tuesday, was the critical day at that time).

[31] E.g., no sittings, 30 July–19 November 1302 or 26 November 1302–5 February 1303; no sittings, 6 July–19 October 1461, 14 December 1461–19 January 1462,

Moreover, at no stage after 1272, from which point rolls survive, was the 'rule' about holding Hustings of Pleas of Land and of Common Pleas alternately strictly adhered to. Indeed, it was comparatively uncommon for a session of one side of the Husting to follow a session of the other at a week's interval. Conversely, there were times when a session of one side of the court followed another of the same side a week later.[32] As a result, the rolls record a very variable number of sessions each year. In 1302, for example, there were eight sessions of the Pleas of Land and seven of the Common Pleas.[33] After 1305 the number of sessions per year declined for a while, with three or four sessions on each side of the court being most common from 1306 onwards instead of six or more before. The aggressive questioning of city practices by the royal justices in 1321 appears to have had a salutary effect, however. From 1322 onwards, it was rare for the annual total of sessions even of the Common Pleas to be below half a dozen.

This pattern, or, rather, lack of one, continued into the fifteenth century. A consequence of the irregularity and hence unpredictability of Husting sessions was that it was easy to miss a court. In 1321 it was argued that the court's programme ought to be fixed, a view which was probably held by most of the royal justices and serjeants present, although it did not prevail.[34] It is not surprising, therefore, that the court's own judges were required to be summoned to the Husting.[35]

The Mayor's Court

The belated separation of common-law litigation from informal dispute resolution probably helps to explain why merchants' requirements, and thus merchant law, had a considerable impact on the routines and procedures of the Mayor's Court. Whenever the court entertained cases involving travelling merchants, it was obliged to sit on a daily basis if necessary so as not to delay them.

23 February–10 May 1462, 12 July–10 October 1462, or 8 November 1462: CLRO, HR PL24, PL25, HR CP27, CP28; CLRO, HB1, fos. 45v-8.

[32] E.g., sessions of the Common Pleas held on 19 and 26 February 1330; thereafter alternate weekly sessions of Pleas of Land and Common Pleas were held until 19 March: CLRO, HR CP53, HR PL52.

[33] CLRO, HR PL24, HR CP27, CP28.

[34] Cam, *Eyre 1321*, I, p. 32.

[35] CLRO, HB1, fo. 33v (1457).

'Liber Albus' implies that this flexibility had been extended to all cases before the court.[36] In practice this does seem to have been the case, judging by the fifteenth-century plea and memoranda rolls. In the years around 1300 it seems to have sat, if required, on every day except Sunday, though with a bias towards the end of the week.[37] By the later fifteenth century, the plea and memoranda rolls show that it would even open its doors on Sundays.[38] Despite the reference in the 1409 decree to the court's 'usual days', and the fact that by the late eighteenth century it would not sit on over twenty individual saints' days in addition to the Christmas and Easter/Whitsun periods and the summer vacation, in our period it was effectively almost permanently open even to plaintiffs who were city freemen. Examples are to be found of sessions being held on almost all the days which would, in the eighteenth century, be non-court days, including days during what would later be the summer and Christmas vacations.[39] Clearly the medieval court did not take fixed vacations. From the beginning to the end of our period, it was active during all the months of the year.

The Sheriffs' Court

As we have seen, 'Sheriffs' Court' is a somewhat misleading title: by 1300, and probably for some years before that, there were two quite distinct courts, held on different days. Thus the first Sheriffs' Court session mentioned in the early Mayor's Court rolls, from February 1300, is the 'Court of Henry de Fingrie, Sheriff of London'.[40] Cases begun on one side of the court stayed on that side and were recorded solely in the roll of the sheriff

[36] Riley, *Munimenta Gildhallae*, I, p. 390.

[37] Compare *CalEMCR*, pp. 89–91 (rolls for 1298, 1299, and 1299/1300, where the only court recorded as sitting on Sundays was the Prior of St Bartholomew's soke) with *CalPMR 1458–82*, pp. 16–30 (rolls for mayoral years 1460/1 and 1461/2).

[38] *CalPMR 1458–82*, p. 17, recording the entering of a bond on Sunday 12 July 1461.

[39] Emerson, *Concise Treatise*, pp. 39–43. In our period, the Court was open, not only on individual saints' days (such as 2 February, the Purification of the Blessed Virgin Mary) which were non-court days in the eighteenth century, but also on occasion during the later vacation periods, between 1 and 24 August and 16 December to 6 January: *CalPMR 1458–82*, p. 31; *ibid.*, pp. 10, 20, 22, *CalEMCR*, pp. 210, 214, 246; *ibid.*, p. 232, *CalPMR 1458–82*, pp. 40, 46, 50.

[40] *CalEMCR*, p. 91.

concerned. Although there appears to be no statement in the surviving material of a rule forbidding the hearing of later stages of a case begun on one side of the court on the other, it is certain that this was no more allowed than it was permissible to make the various proclamations leading to outlawry on different sides of the Husting. The potential for administrative confusion alone, given that each sheriff was, for most of our period, served by separate staffs, would have made such flexibility undesirable, and it would also greatly have increased the opportunities for trickery.[41]

Each sheriff held, in principle, two 'common' or 'general' courts (courts for city freemen, also known, by analogy with the *curiae de forinsecis*, as *curiae de intrinsecis*) a week. In addition, there were the courts for foreigns (non-freemen, both denizen and alien).[42] In dealing with general inter-citizen cases, the Sheriffs' Court was by the seventeenth century sitting on Wednesdays to Saturdays, each sheriff taking two of the four days.[43] Since a case from 1304 was heard before Sheriff Combemartin on a succession of Thursdays and Saturdays, and Wednesdays to Saturdays were said to be the court's 'dies juridici' in 1385, the obvious conclusion is that these four days remained the normal days of the Sheriffs' Court throughout our period.[44] In fact, practice varied over time: in 1300, Sheriff de Armenters apparently sat on a Thursday, a Saturday and a Tuesday, and in 1358, the sheriffs were not alternating at all, but were 'holding a single counter and court in common'.[45] This period apart, however, some alternating arrangement prevailed. In 1320, one of the sheriffs sat routinely on Tuesdays and Thursdays; as he presided over courts for foreigns on Mondays and Saturdays, his colleague must at that period have been holding his normal sessions on Wednesdays and Fridays.[46] Tuesdays to Fridays were also the standard days for the sheriffs' common courts in the early sixteenth century.[47] The one weekday on which common courts were not held was Monday, presumably because the sheriffs had in theory to be available to

[41] *CalEMCR*, pp. 117–18. [42] *CalPMR 1381–1412*, pp. 114–15.
[43] CLRO, *Practise of the Sheriffs Court London*, p. 3.
[44] CLRO, HR CP29, m. 17; *CalPMR 1381–1412*, p. 114.
[45] *CalEMCR*, pp. 102, 101; CLRO, HR PL80, m. 11 (as they had been ordered to do two years previously: *CalLBG*, p. 72).
[46] CLRO, Sheriffs' Court Roll (1320). [47] CLRO, Rep. 5, fo. 82.

attend the Husting.[48] Courts for foreigns had to be held whenever business required, because of the well-established principle that travelling merchants should have 'hastif remedie', and – presumably – the assumption that any 'foreign' was by definition at least potentially a travelling merchant. In practice these cases were heard in or after the common courts when they were sitting, and on intervening days when they were not. Monday, presumably because the sheriffs were in reality not often required to hold a session of the Husting on that day, was a popular day for these particular courts.[49]

In view of the misleading statements made about the routine in the Husting, it is also worth asking whether, between them, the sheriffs really did hold their common court four times a week. The answer seems to be that, on the whole, they did. The dates given in the record of a particular action in the Sheriffs' Court in 1304 shows that the case was dealt with on 1, 15, 20 and 22 February, and then on 12 and 21 April.[50] Partial details of another case record sessions on Wednesday 26 September [*recte* Thursday 27?], Saturday 6, Thursday 11, Saturday 20, Thursday 25 and Saturday 27 October 1302.[51] The surviving membranes of the sheriff's roll for 1320 list common courts on 1, 10, 31 July (plus courts for foreigns on 14 and 17 July), 12 (and 28) August, 2 and 18 September (and 20 and 25 September). Even for the three months concerned, the roll looks to be incomplete and, in any event, covers what was probably a quiet period. Among the errors alleged in a Sheriffs' Court case initiated on 22 May 1399 was the failure to note in the record the common courts held between the session at which the jury was summoned, on Wednesday 28 May, and the one when it appeared and gave its verdict, on 30 July. The plaintiff in error, who seems to have been confused in his chronology, listed seven 'intervening' courts (two of these were in fact said to have been held on Wednesday 14 and Friday 16 May). Despite this confusion, apparently at least five courts were held in the last three weeks of May 1399.[52] It looks, therefore, as though there were usually two sessions a week on each side of the court during the busier periods and at least three a month even in high

[48] CLRO, HR CP147, m. 5v.
[49] For the handling of 'foreign' cases, see, e.g., CLRO, HR CP43, mm. 4–4v.
[50] CLRO, HR CP29, m. 17. [51] *CalEMCR*, pp. 134–5.
[52] CLRO, HR CP125, m. 7v.

summer when the more substantial citizens tended to leave town for the pleasanter surroundings of the countryside.

By the eighteenth century, the Sheriffs' Court took slightly different summer and Christmas vacations from the Husting and the Mayor's Court. In addition, it did not sit on the same specific feast and saints' days as the Mayor's Court.[53] There is no definite evidence that any similar programme of non-court days existed in our period. Some of the gaps between sessions recorded in individual cases may well reflect, however, not the fact that no process occurred that week in the case concerned, but that no court sat because the day on which it was due to be held was one of the main saints' days of the period. In 1302, for example, a case was adjourned from Thursday 11 to Saturday 20 October, perhaps because Thursday 18 October was St Luke's Day.[54]

Conversely, Common Clerk Carpenter thought it worth mentioning that the Sheriffs' Courts did not observe the law terms kept by the central courts. This was undoubtedly the case for most and quite probably all our period. In 1320 the Sheriffs' Court was sitting between 1 July, which is about a fortnight before the Trinity term normally ended, and 25 September, shortly before the Michaelmas term began.[55] The records of Sheriffs' Court cases brought on error in the later fourteenth and early fifteenth century show no change of practice: between them, they mention every month of the year, including the summer vacation months.[56] And it is clear, from the fact that several Chancery petitions of the late fifteenth century complained that petitioners had been subjected to actions brought in the Sheriffs' Court 'in this vacation' or while 'the chancellor is away from London and the king's courts are closed', that this continued to be the case in the later fifteenth century and, presumably, into the sixteenth.[57] On the other hand, the London Sheriffs' Court did not observe 'county days', as courts presided over by other sheriffs did, no doubt precisely because it was not a county court. (The York Sheriffs' Court, set up after that city became a county in 1396, adopted many aspects of London practice but, unlike the London

[53] Emerson, *Concise Treatise*, pp. 91–3. [54] *CalEMCR*, pp. 134–5.

[55] Riley, *Munimenta Gildhallae*, I, p. 199.

[56] CLRO, HR CP79, mm. 18, 18v, CP110, mm. 20v, 21, CP122, mm. 6, 11v, CP125, m. 3v, CP147, m. 5v.

[57] TNA (PRO), Early Chancery Proceedings, C1/64, items 672, 454, 478.

Sheriffs' Court, it held monthly 'county days', which were distinguished from the more frequent 'Sheriffs' Courts of Pleas'.)[58]

LEVELS OF LITIGATION

The Husting

Despite its venerability, in 1300 the Husting was still quite a lively court. Even in the mid- to late-fifteenth century, the average number of deeds and wills enrolled each regnal year was over thirty. The importance and ponderous nature of some legal actions in the Husting meant that it was never likely, given the restrictions on its sessions, to entertain vast numbers of them. Nevertheless, at the beginning of our period some seventy-five writ-initiated cases were being brought each year on average, together with, probably, similar numbers of pleas of naam and a few writs of error. Taking both sides together, the court's workload appears to have reached its zenith in the 1310s, but it remained at what was, for this court, a relatively high level for many years thereafter. Excluding writs of error, the annual totals of writs on both sides of the court for the period 1300 to 1350 always exceeded seventy.

Perhaps surprisingly, the first onset of the Black Death did not immediately produce a sharp drop in the overall numbers of writs brought in the Husting. Average annual totals were still over fifty between 1361 and 1370. Indeed, there was an increase in two types of action in the second half of the fourteenth century. Writs *ex gravi querela* brought to enforce the execution of testamentary bequests of properties and rents enrolled in the Husting rose from an average of some 13 a year in 1300–49 to 18.5 a year in 1350–99. Having constituted just over 7 per cent of the total of writs brought before 1350, they made up a quarter of those brought between 1350 and 1399.[59] From the 1350s onwards, too, significantly more

[58] Alexander, 'Dates of County Courts'; Palmer, *County Courts of Medieval England*, pp. 4–6; Stell, *Sheriffs' Court Books*, pp. 5, 7, 449–68, esp. 452–68, 266, 355.

[59] For examples of actions relating to testamentary bequests of tenements and rents see CLRO, HR CP109, m. 8v (*Badby & Badby* v. *fitzNichol*), HR CP63, m. 11v (*le Treyere* v. *Abbot of Waltham Holy Cross*).

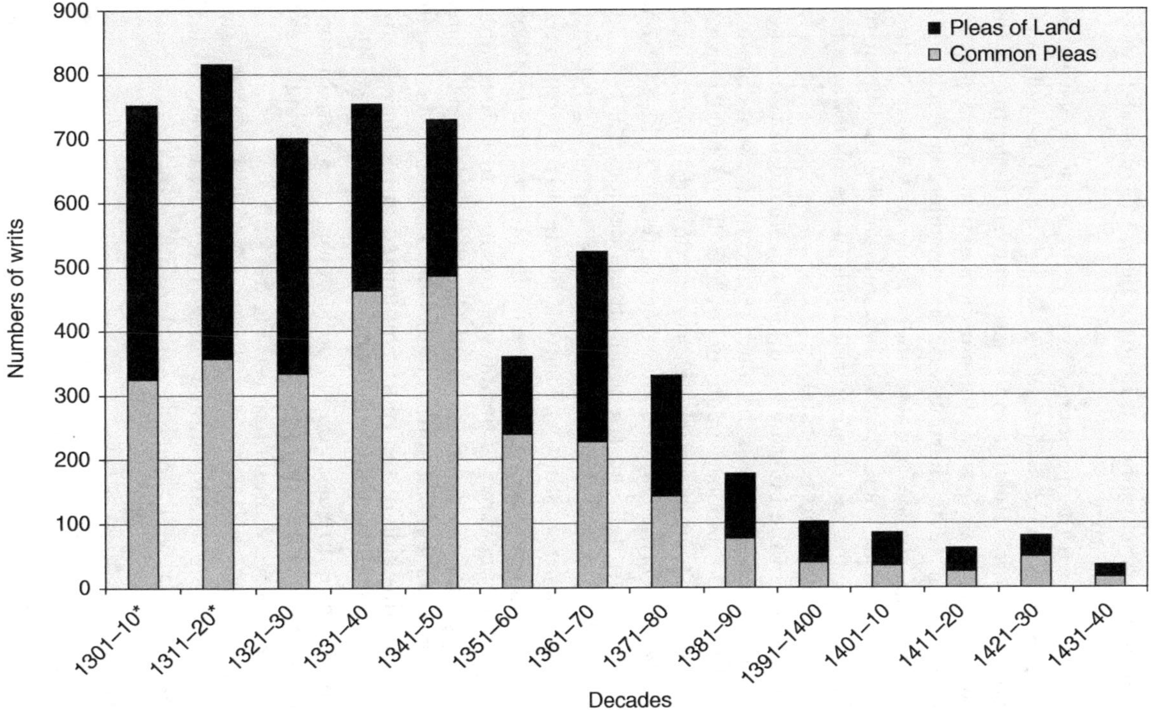

Figure 4.1 Decennial totals of Husting writs, 1301–1440

* Some figures are estimated from nearest year where rolls are missing. Writs of error and pleas of naam are excluded from the calculations.

actions of waste were begun by writ, to prevent damage to or over-exploitation of property by tenants and other occupiers with only short-term rights in it: one was brought before 1350, and 29 in the following half-century (see Figure 4.1).

The increase in the number of such actions was however low. The reason why they constituted such a significant proportion of the workload of the Husting in the later fourteenth century is that they increased at a time when the numbers of other types of action decreased. After 1370, there was a very considerable decline. By the early 1430s, the average was under four writs a year on both sides of the court. There was a minor rally in the middle of the century, but for the rest of our period under a dozen new actions a year seems to have been normal.[60]

The decline in the Husting's workload occurred in two stages. In the first three decades of the fourteenth century, writs brought in the Pleas of Land had made up over half the total of writs brought in the Husting as a whole, between 35 and 45 writs a year. After 1320, nevertheless, their number started to reduce. If one ignores the sharp fall and rise again in the decades 1351–60 and 1361–70, which was very probably a reaction to the Black Death, the decline was steady but substantial. By the 1370s, the annual totals averaged less than 30, and were under 10 from the 1390s on.

The relative buoyancy of overall writ totals up to 1370 resulted from the fact that the workload of the Common Pleas peaked later than that of the Pleas of Land, in the 1340s. The numbers of writs brought on this side of the court plummeted in the decade after 1350, stabilised briefly in the 1360s, and then continued their descent. In the entire decade 1391–1400, fewer writs were brought in the Common Pleas than had been brought in the single year, 1359, when 43 were presented (see Figure 4.2).[61]

Even once the Pleas of Land began to be used for collusive recoveries in the 1450s, annual totals rarely exceeded 10 and decennial totals were generally around 50.[62] In the sixteenth

[60] Excluding writs of error and pleas of naam, the average for the 1460s and 1470s was 4.5 writs *p.a.*; 12 writs were brought in 1507, the first year after 1483 for which full details are available, and 10 in 1550: CLRO, HB2, fos. 4v–15, HB3, fos. 163–92.

[61] And 1359 was nothing exceptional, judged by the previous decade: in 1343, 93 writs had been brought in the Common Pleas.

[62] 45 in the decade 1461–70, for example; in the following decade, the total was 44: CLRO, HB1, fos. 46–86, 86v–[135].

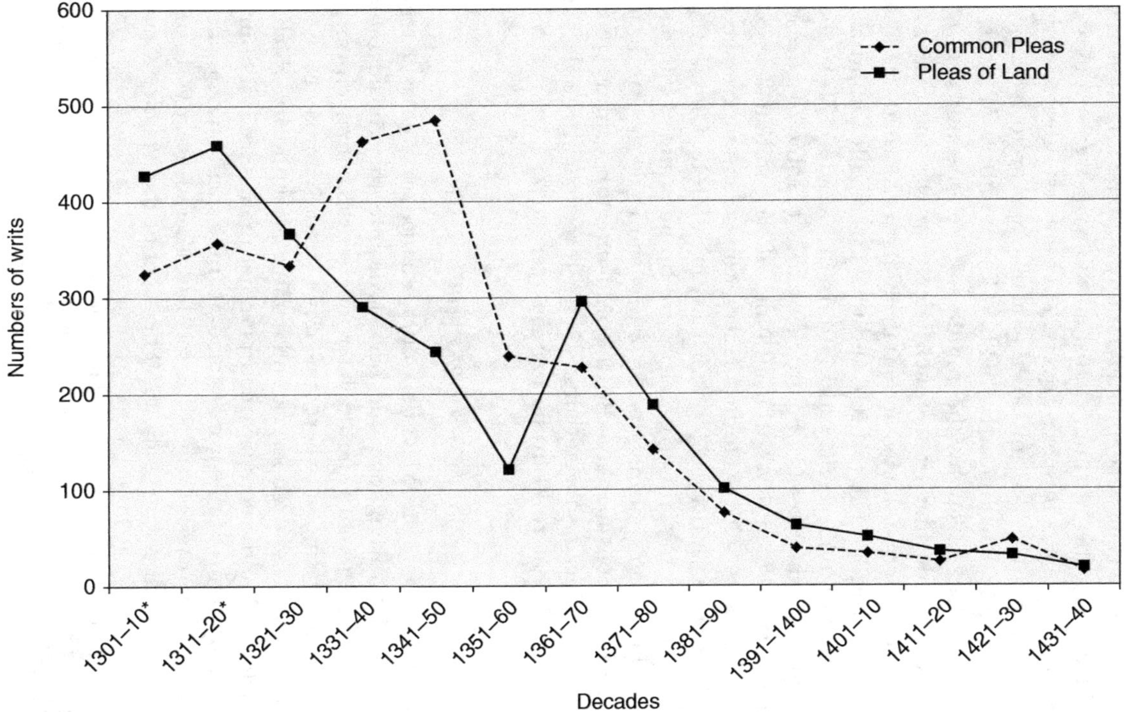

Figure 4.2 Comparison of numbers of writs brought in the Common Pleas and Pleas of Land

century, although the decennial totals of all types of writ excluding error were higher than they had been in the 1450s, it appears to have been very unusual for any genuine litigation at all to take place in the Husting; almost all the writs were brought in order to initiate a collusive recovery.[63] The worst affected action was mesne: no writs to initiate this action appear to have been brought in the Husting after 1342.[64] The numbers of writs of error, too, had fallen by the middle of the fifteenth century. However, the decline set in much later than was the case with other types of writ-initiated action: the highest recorded total (37) was in the decade 1391 to 1400, and totals were still comfortably in the twenties in the 1420s and 1430s. In the decade 1471–80 they reached an all-time low (3), before rising back to some 20 a decade in the sixteenth century.[65] But all types of writ-initiated actions reduced greatly, with even dower decreasing from an average of over 5 actions a year, 1380–99, to 1.5 a year, 1400–48. Only 7 writs of customs and services or gavelet were brought after 1400, and, unless changes in recording habits or procedures deceive us, naam also suffered considerably. By the mid-fifteenth century these pleas had reduced substantially: 21 are recorded in the decade 1471–80, and a mere 14 in the previous decade.[66]

The Mayor's Court

As we have seen, the Mayor's Court retained its role as a regulatory court throughout our period despite the considerable changes it underwent from the later fourteenth century onwards, although increasingly, where the city's trade companies were concerned, it acted to supervise and enforce the authority which it had delegated to the company courts rather than as a court of first instance. In terms of the proportion of its time spent on regulatory activities, nevertheless, the situation had altered greatly. In the early fourteenth century, about 60 per cent of the Mayor's Court

[63] In 1507, the first full year after 1482 for which a complete record survives, 12 writs of right and one of waste were brought; in 1550, there were 9 writs of right and one of waste: CLRO, HB2, fos. 4v–15, HB3, fos. 163–92.

[64] CLRO, HR CP66, m. 26, *Lyndesseye* v. *Fouk*, seems to have been the last case.

[65] CLRO, HR CP115-HR CP124; CLRO, HB1, fos. 86v–[135]. In both 1507 and 1550, a mere two writs of error were brought, suggesting a further decline by or after 1500: CLRO, HB2, fos. 4v-15, HB3, fos. 163–92.

[66] CLRO, HB1, fos. 46–86, 86v–[135].

business, as recorded in its rolls, appears to have involved the enforcement of city regulations or the disciplining of city officers. Judging by the entries in the later fifteenth-century journals, this kind of Mayor's Court business, together with other forms of activity relating to the enforcement of the court's authority, such as recognizances or bindings over to abide by an arbitration, to await an informal adjudication – not to go to law, in other words – and to appear in court, constituted a much lower proportion of the court's business by this date. Supervision of the sheriffs, whether it took the form of removing cases from the Sheriffs' Court into the Mayor's Court because of some alleged malpractice or disciplining shrieval staff, contributed very little to the totals: nothing at all in over half the years. On average, the journals of the 1460s and 1470s contain three entries a month relating to law and order problems, in addition to the occasional binding-over and recognizance to keep the peace. The proportion could nevertheless vary considerably from year to year. Nearly 60 per cent of the journal entries were of this type in 1478, when, among other things, the political situation was fraught and a fight between some Londoners and the king's servants caused the Court of Aldermen much work, whereas the proportion was a mere two-and-a-half percent in 1471. To these activities we should add, at all periods, the work generated by the wardmote inquest presentments. Although these are occasionally recorded in full in the plea and memoranda rolls, and individual cases sometimes found their way into the journals, it looks as though both the presentments and any Mayor's Court records relating to them were normally kept separately.[67] Most have not survived.

Informal adjudications and arbitrations may never have absorbed a great deal of the mayor and aldermen's time. Only two arbitrations are mentioned in the early Mayor's Court rolls, one of which might have been arranged under the aegis of the Mayor's Court, the other being noted, apparently, merely because one of the parties to the arbitration wanted to force the arbitrators to give their award.[68] It is, however, far from certain that these types of proceedings would normally have been entered in the court rolls, and the true total may well have been higher. If the evidence from

[67] *CalPMR 1413–37*, pp. 150–9, CLRO, Jor. 6, pp. 511, 512, 513, 519.
[68] *CalEMCR*, pp. 43, 50.

the city's journals can be trusted, informal dispute resolution seems to have contributed rather more to the workload of the court in the middle of the fifteenth century, with an annual average of over 20 arbitrations a year recorded in the early 1460s, and over 35 a year in the second half of that decade. Thereafter, however, there seems to have been a sharp decline. Recorded arbitrations were running at an average of 5.5 a year in the first half of the 1470s. Between late 1475 and mid-1478, not a single arbitration seems to have been arranged under the aegis of the Mayor's Court; there were apparently 8 in the next five years.

Petitions also seem to have contributed only modestly to the workload of the Mayor's Court. There are two pleas noted as having been begun by petition in the early Mayor's Court rolls.[69] Petitions constitute about 6 per cent of the surviving bills of the 1360s and 1370s. The evidence for later periods is far from satisfactory, but, such as it is, it supports the impression given by the surviving bill files of the first half of the fifteenth century, which is that petitions became even less common after 1400, and formed an even lower proportion of the total workload of the court, than they had been and done in the second half of the fourteenth century. There are, for example, seven petitions out of 377 items in the surviving bill file covering 1443 to 1457 (less than 2 per cent), four of them relating to apprentices, the rest to failures to execute testaments properly.[70] Similarly, three petitions by apprentices were enrolled in the plea and memoranda rolls for 1437 to 1457.[71] These sources may well underestimate the original number of petitions, however: the latest bill file, because it excluded 'inner chamber' business, and the plea and memoranda rolls, because petitioners were probably less likely than litigants to ask (and pay) to have the details enrolled.

As far as private litigation is concerned, the situation had naturally changed a great deal over the same period. It was not simply that the court was hearing more private litigation, although it undoubtedly was. The early Mayor's Court rolls record a good many cases of trespass involving assaults but fewer than 30 actions of debt for the period 1298 to 1307, and about double this number

[69] *Ibid.*, pp. 176, 185.
[70] CLRO, Mayor's Court Files of Original Bills, MC1/3, items 1, 171, 231, 290, 339; *ibid.*, items 232, 294, 295.
[71] *CalPMR 1437–57*, pp. 50, 65, 114.

of actions of detinue, account and covenant combined. By the middle of the fifteenth century, the position had apparently changed dramatically. Over 90 per cent of all the common-law bills surviving for the later 1450s relate to actions of debt; trespasses, even including a number of undertakings to keep the peace, contribute a mere 5 per cent.[72] However, 90 per cent may be an abnormally high proportion. Debt certainly had increased enormously as a proportion of Mayor's Court business since the early fourteenth century, but the considerable economic difficulties of the 1440s and 1450s probably produced atypically high levels of debt cases at this period. (They were also at an unusually high level in 1471, 1474 and 1475. All three years were ones in which creditors might have been unusually concerned to recover debts: the first reflecting the disruptions of civil war in 1469–71, the latter two, the economic dislocation created by the French expedition of 1475, as creditors called in debts in order to pay the enormous sums granted to Edward IV in taxes and gifts. Similarly, large numbers of debt cases were brought in the early 1480s when Londoners were called upon to support weakened royal finances at a time when the country became involved in a war with Scotland.)[73] Once the Mayor's Court began routinely to entertain private litigation, debt probably normally constituted between 50 and 60 per cent of all personal pleas, with trespass constituting about 15 per cent. The proportion of other types of actions seems to have remained low throughout, varying between about 10 and 20 per cent. Even so, in the fifteenth century the variety of types of action was probably greater than in the Sheriffs' Court. It was, for instance, possible throughout our period to bring actions of waste in the Mayor's Court, because there were both statutory and customary prohibitions on waste and the court would enforce them, as it would other national statutes and city ordinances.[74] By

[72] Based on CLRO, Mayor's Court Files of Original Bills, MC1/3A. By this stage, the Mayor's Court was also entertaining a few actions of trespass involving forcible entries: *CalPMR 1381–1412*, pp. 256–7 (1397), *CalPMR 1413–37*, pp. 56–8, *CalPMR 1437–57*, pp. 12–13, 117–18, *CalPMR 1458–82*, pp. 81–2, 94–5, 104–5.

[73] Based on TNA (PRO), Chancery *Corpus Cum Causa* Writ Files, C244/91–/128.

[74] *CalPMR 1364–81*, p. 172. Cases of this type were brought in the Mayor's Court, as were instances in which the waste was committed while litigation over proprietary rights in the property was under way in the Husting: *CalPMR 1323–64*, p. 185, *CalPMR 1364–81*, pp. 172, 179, 210, *CalPMR 1381–1412*,

the fifteenth century, the court would also respond to 'bills of complaint' against executors who had allegedly failed to discharge their responsibilities; and, although this phraseology suggests that the cases were brought in the Inner Chamber, it looks in fact as though they were heard according to law and custom.[75]

Because the surviving enrolments of Mayor's Court cases in the plea and memoranda rolls are to some unknown extent and according to some uncertain criteria selective, precisely how much private legal business the Mayor's Court was handling cannot be determined accurately after 1307. Some idea of how much is missing can be got by comparing plea and memoranda roll entries of the 1450s with a file of bills of the same date. It is clear that it is a composite file, made up from at least two others; several bills bear the same contemporary numeration, the highest duplicate being 285. The original files seem to be for the years 1456/7 and 1457/8, and must once have contained no fewer than 374 and 285 bills (the highest individual and highest duplicate numerations respectively). The plea and memoranda roll for 1456/7 records the presentation of just three bills, that for 1457/8, two, which suggests that less than one per cent of cases were eventually entered in these rolls.[76] If the Mayor's Court could entertain approaching 400 bills a year relating to private common-law litigation by the later 1450s, it had probably at least quadrupled this aspect of its workload in 150 years. One of the fullest of the surviving Mayor's Court rolls, for 1304/5, probably contains notices of all the actions brought in the court. This records around 100 individual cases, a good many of which involved complaints against or by city officers or by apprentices, which would probably not have resulted in a personal action on the common-law side of the court a hundred years later.

Unfortunately, no further bill files survive for the fifteenth and early sixteenth centuries. It is tempting, therefore, to try to squeeze something out of the plea and memoranda rolls, despite their obvious limitations. An analysis of legal records entered on

pp. 129–30; *CalPMR 1323–64*, p. 261 (1363, referring to the prohibition of waste pending litigation).

75 *CalPMR 1413–37*, p. 6, *CalPMR 1437–57*, p. 11.

76 CLRO, Mayor's Court Files of Original Bills, MC1/3A, esp. items 186/188, 235/254, 223/230, 228/232, 227/233, 50/240, 131/132; *CalPMR 1437–57*, pp. 151–7 (Roll A81), *CalPMR 1458–82*, pp. 1–3 (Roll A82).

them between 1437 and 1482 suggests a decline both in the volume of business, with over half the legal entries being contained in the nine rolls covering the period November 1437 to October 1445, and of the numbers of cases begun by plaint (down from nearly 40 per cent to 2 per cent of the total by the early 1480s).[77]

In the absence of other evidence, this might reflect nothing more than a decreasing willingness on the part of poorer litigants to pay for having the outcome of their cases recorded in the memoranda rolls (assuming that it was poorer litigants who tended to make their plaints orally). It is therefore of interest that the journals of the common council, which probably provide a fairly reliable indicator of 'inner chamber' work, suggest that informal legal business also declined, in this instance in the 1470s. The annual average for 1461–71 was 107 entries relating to this aspect of the mayor and aldermen's work; for 1472–82, it was 60.

The evidence from Chancery, however, gives a rather different picture as far as common-law cases are concerned. The average number of references to Mayor's Court cases in the surviving *corpus cum causa* or *certiorari* writs for November 1461 to October 1471 was about 12 a year; between November 1471 and October 1481, it was over 18.[78] In 1456/7, the number of Chancery references to Mayor's Court cases was also 12.[79] 1456/7 was a year during which, it will be remembered, at least 374 personal actions were initiated in that court. This gives a probable maximum ratio of one case in 31 resulting in a reference in a Chancery writ. If a similar ratio obtained on average during the two subsequent decades, the Mayor's Court would have been entertaining 465 private common-law cases a year, on average, between 1460 and 1480, with about 370 cases a year on average in the 1460s and about 560 in the 1470s. So the workload of the common-law side of the court could have increased substantially after 1470, especially bearing in mind that the survival-rate of writs was going down at the same time. But it is of course possible that the increase was in the proportion of Mayor's Court litigants who

[77] As a number of rolls are missing, especially after 1460, the analysis covers four periods consisting of nine, nine, ten and nine years respectively.

[78] TNA (PRO), Chancery *Corpus cum Causa* Writ Files, C244/91–/112 (part of), C244/111–/129.

[79] TNA (PRO), Chancery *Corpus cum Causa* Writ Files, C244/82–/84.

petitioned Chancery in the 1470s. What happened to the workload of the common-law side of the Mayor's Court from the late 1450s onwards is unclear, therefore. Possibly it continued to rise for a time; but the evidence from the city's own records suggests that the number of 'inner chamber' cases, at least, declined.

Whatever may have been the case in the fifty years after 1480, by 1540 the Mayor's Court clerks were complaining that their court, once so remunerative, had lost so much business that their traditional fees and emoluments were no longer sufficient to support them, and were asking to be granted clerical posts on the sheriffs' staffs and elsewhere as these became available.[80] This clearly did not resolve matters, for in 1550 they joined with the sheriffs' clerks to petition for 'some aid and augmentation' of their fees and procedures.[81] How great the reduction in the court's workload was, and how long it lasted beyond 1550, there seems unfortunately to be no way of telling.

The Sheriffs' Court

The effect of the changes which the Sheriffs' Court underwent in the later fourteenth and early fifteenth centuries appears to have been to alter the proportion of different types of action brought before it. Quite what form that change took, however, is more difficult to say, since the various surviving sources disagree. What is fairly certain is that, in the summer of 1320, debt cases made up about 56 per cent of the court's workload; trespass, about 25 per cent; account, about 8 per cent; and detinue and covenant, most of the rest.[82] By contrast, about 35 per cent of the surviving *querelae levatae* in 1406–8 and about 44 per cent of the writs of error brought in the Husting, 1401–10, involved actions of trespass.[83] In the period 1459 to 1480, 75 to 80 per cent of the surviving Chancery petitions relating to the London Sheriffs' Court refer to actions of debt or trespass, in almost equal proportions.[84] Judging

[80] CLRO, Rep. 10, fo. 173v. [81] CLRO, Rep. 12/2, fos. 262–2v, 263v.

[82] CLRO, Sheriffs' Court Roll (1320).

[83] CLRO, Sheriffs' Court Rolls [*Querelae Levatae*], Box 1.

[84] TNA (PRO), Early Chancery Proceedings (*List & Index Society* vols. XII and XVI), C1/46 (1467–73, plus 1433–43?): 153 London petitions, 59 involving trespass and 62, debt; C1/67 (1475–80, 1483–5?): 44 petitions, 17 involving trespass and 17, debt; C1/31 (1465–70, plus 1480–3?): 25 petitions, 10 involving trespass and 10, debt.

by these three sources of evidence, therefore, trespass formed a higher proportion of the Sheriffs' Court workload in the early 1400s than it had done in 1320, and the proportion of trespass cases continued to increase during the course of the fifteenth century.

On the other hand, in the Chancery files of writs *corpus cum causa* of the later fifteenth century, debt clearly predominates. Until the 1480s or thereabouts, these writs are a better guide to the types of cases referred to in petitions brought in Chancery than the petitions themselves because so many have been lost. In some years, it is true, trespass cases in these Chancery writs were within ten per cent of debt: indeed, in 1467/8, trespass cases outstripped those in debt by some way. However, at other periods there were between a third and half as many debt cases again as trespass. On average, about half were debt cases and about a third were cases of trespass.[85]

There is a possibility that other types of action might have been less likely to result in an appeal to the chancellor. In the later fourteenth and fifteenth centuries, petitioners to Chancery requesting a writ *corpus cum causa* quite often complained that they had been imprisoned pending their appearance in court.[86] Such complaints were perhaps more likely to be provoked by the procedures adopted in dealing with trespass cases than with any other type of personal plea, because defendants in trespass were obliged to offer security for their appearance in court immediately. That meant that the inability of some to do so inevitably became an issue and at an early stage. It is also possible that defendants in trespass cases, many of which involved alleged physical or verbal assaults, tended to be poorer or rougher than defendants generally, and more liable to imprisonment. That, too, would have exaggerated the proportion of trespass cases. Another factor which might have resulted in relatively few non-trespass cases figuring in Chancery petitions was local partiality, or suspicion of it. If there was a general suspicion among non-Londoners that city jurors were prejudiced against them, there would be a disproportionate number of petitions relating to cases

[85] Based on TNA (PRO), Chancery *Corpus Cum Causa* Writ Files, C244/91–C244/129.

[86] Tucker, 'Early History of the Court of Chancery', pp. 800–1.

in which one of the parties was either not a Londoner or a foreigner.[87] And although foreigns were more likely than London residents to be imprisoned pending trial in non-trespass cases for fear that they or their goods might leave the city, that would not result in more cases of covenant or account appearing in the Chancery records, if Londoners did not commonly employ non-Londoners to do work for them or to act as their partners, receivers and agents. There may be some under-representation of these types of cases, therefore.

Overall, the evidence suggests that the proportion of the two main types of civil action changed, but not greatly, over the course of the fourteenth and fifteenth centuries, staying at around 50 per cent for debt and rising from about 25 to about 33 per cent for trespass. The likeliest explanation for the tendency of peaks in trespass cases to coincide with peaks in the overall number of Sheriffs' Court cases referred to in Chancery writs is that they coincided with disturbed periods in the city's history. That coincidence is hidden from us in the Chancery petitions, which are not closely dateable. Even so, trespass appears to have prospered, relatively speaking, while other forms of action did not. That is not to say that the absolute number of other types of actions declined. It might well be that, as the workload of the Sheriffs' Court rose after 1320,[88] trespass contributed more than its fair share to that increase.

Exactly how busy the Sheriffs' Court was, it is quite impossible to tell. In the fifteenth century, the number of more serious criminal cases which began life as presentments in the Sheriffs' Court and ended up in King's Bench was certainly low: details of five survive in the King's Bench indictment files for 1465, for example, less than a tenth of the total for Middlesex.[89] That may have been because the city was relatively untroubled by crime at this period. A number of coroners' rolls survive from the first half of the fourteenth century. They record 20 unlawful killings a year, excluding suicides, in London in 1300/1, 1321/2 and

87 TNA (PRO), Chancery Ancient Proceedings, C1/32, item 439 ('jury promised that they will credit no Lombard'), C1/46, item 438 (a yeoman from Ware complaining about the partiality of a London jury).

88 See below.

89 TNA (PRO), KB Indictment Files, KB9/308–KB9/311, especially KB9/309, item 46, KB9/310, items 27, 60, KB9/311, items 99 and 102; KB9/309, item 32.

1339/40.[90] Although we cannot entirely rely on the jury verdicts, let alone be sure that all suspicious deaths were reported, this evidence in combination with the King's Bench records does suggest that unlawful killings were at a much higher level in the first half of the fourteenth century than was normal even in similarly disturbed times during the fifteenth century. (It should be said, however, that the recorded murder rate in the first half of the fourteenth century was, at between 11 and 19 a year out of a population which is unlikely to have exceeded 80,000, probably between five and ten times that experienced by London in the late twentieth century).

The prosecutions of petty offenders – nightwalkers, drunkards, prostitutes, gamblers, not to mention footballers and tennis-players, whose antisocial activities so exercised the minds of the royal and city authorities – left little mark on the records until just after the end of our period, when they started to appear in the surviving records of the Bridewell Court. There is a marked contrast between the number and variety of Middlesex returns into King's Bench from the 1460s, which cover a wide range of crimes and offences, and the few London returns, which relate almost entirely to the most serious crimes: treason, murder and robbery. It seems likely, therefore, that the less serious crimes and offences were being dealt with by the London Sheriffs' Court.[91] As one would not expect that there would be fewer of these in London than there were in Middlesex, in the middle of the fifteenth century the Sheriffs' Court was probably handling at the very least 50, and more likely 100, such cases a year as well as trespass cases initiated by private individuals. When the city's population was at its height for our period, in the early fourteenth century and mid-sixteenth century, the total of prosecutions and private suits concerning alleged offences was almost certainly higher, and perhaps disproportionately so because of the effects of overcrowding, poverty and the difficulties of policing in such

[90] *CalCorR*, pp. 1–32, 33–69, 234–71; Hunnisett, 'Reliability of Inquisitions'; Smith, 'Medieval Coroners' Records'.

[91] Although some cases clearly started life as presentments in the Sheriffs' Court and were then prosecuted in King's Bench, e.g. the alleged rape of seven-year-old Margery Hamer by Thomas Aubreyson (TNA (PRO), KB Plea Rolls, KB27/836, m. 180v and CLRO, Jor. 7, fos. 188v-9), this may not be true of all, e.g. Jor. 7, fo. 148v (*White* v. *Cope*, on an allegation of 'felonious rape') and Jor. 8, fos. 14, 16, 18 (*Scovile* v. *Jordan*, rape of or sexual assault on a minor).

circumstances. The evidence of the surviving part-roll for 1320 suggests that up to 500 trespass cases were prosecuted privately in the Sheriffs' Court in the year 1319/20, with perhaps 400 of these alleging violence. In addition, there will have been cases which were prosecuted by the city authorities as a result of arrests by officers or jury presentments. We also have an indication in the early Bridewell records of the levels of minor disorderliness in the city at the end of our period. These list 445 offenders of various types ('prostitutes, adulterers, bigamists, drunks, thieves, swearers, slanders, dice-players, runaway servants and apprentices') in 1560/1, together with 69 vagrants.[92] Sexual misdemeanours were usually dealt with in the Mayor's Court, even when the mayor and aldermen were not conducting one of their periodic purges of the city, but some of the other types of offence would have been the province of the sheriffs, if they came to court at all. Aggregating these figures suggests that the Sheriffs' Court might have handled up to 1,000 public prosecutions a year at peak periods in the fourteenth century, ranging from the mildly antisocial to the criminal, but perhaps only a few hundred a year in the late fourteenth and fifteenth centuries.

In just three months during the summer and early autumn of 1320, well over 200 cases were recorded on one sheriff's roll.[93] Assuming the late summer of 1320 to have been fairly representative, and that both sides of the court were equally busy, the Sheriffs' Court in the first decades of the fourteenth century was entertaining between 1,500 and 2,000 actions a year. Moreover, as the surviving membranes do not appear to include all courts held during this quarter, and the summer months were probably relatively quiet, the true figure could well be significantly higher.

What happened to activity levels in the Sheriffs' Court in relation to private litigation between 1320 and 1550, there is no way of knowing. Indeed, not until the later eighteenth century does a reasonably full picture emerge, when, for example, in 1769/70 over 1,700 civil pleas a year were levied in a single counter, giving a probable total of around 3,500 such actions on both sides of the court.[94] Unfortunately, comparisons between 1320 and

[92] Beier, 'Social Problems in Elizabethan London'.

[93] 209 cases in six common courts, 18 in four courts for foreigns: CLRO, Sheriffs' Court Roll (1320).

[94] CLRO, Sheriffs' Court (Poultry Counter) Minute Books A and B.

1770 are meaningless. What we do know, however, is that several other borough courts saw a doubling or more in the activity-levels of their courts in the later fourteenth and early fifteenth centuries.[95]

The fact remains, nevertheless, that we cannot demonstrate that there was a similar increase in the Sheriffs' Court in the late fourteenth and early fifteenth centuries, or even in that court in conjunction with the Mayor's Court. The few surviving city records give no more than a glimpse of the work of the Sheriffs' Court between 1320 and 1550. The evidence from the plea and memoranda rolls even appears to show that there was a decline in the Sheriffs' Court activities after the 1450s: excluding the records of the Court for Foreigns, 14 Sheriffs' Court cases were recorded between 1381 and 1412, 25 between 1413 and 1437, 25 between 1437 and 1457, but only 7 between 1458 and 1482.[96] That would not necessarily be incompatible with what we know of developments in other boroughs, where litigation levels had fallen from their earlier peak by the 1450s. Indeed, there may very well have been a general slump in litigation in the middle of the fifteenth century, when economic and political factors were adverse. Nevertheless, the *querelae levatae* are an extremely unreliable guide to the activity levels of the Sheriffs' Court. Only a small proportion were enrolled in the plea and memoranda rolls; two are recorded there for 1406–8, although over 40 bills survive from the same period.[97] As it is very unlikely that the proportion of Sheriffs' Court cases which found their way onto the plea and memoranda rolls remained constant between 1381 and 1482, the most one can say confidently is that the *querelae levatae* recorded there represent no more than a fraction, possibly no more than 5 per cent, of the original total of *querelae levatae*; and the original total of *querelae levatae* can itself have been no more than a fraction of the total of Sheriffs' Court cases.

[95] Britnell, 'Colchester Courts and Court Records', Table 1, p. 134, and HRO, Winchester City Court Rolls, W1/D1/7–12, /37, /56 plus W1/D2/1 (court of piepowder roll) (up from the 200s in the 1350s to over 400 in 1400 and (probably) to around 450 in the mid-1420s).

[96] *CalsPMR 1381[–]1482*, Indexes, *sub* 'Sheriffs' Court' and 'Undersheriffs'.

[97] *CalPMR 1381–1412*, pp. 285, 287; CLRO, 'Sheriffs' Court Rolls' (*Querelae Levatae*), Box 1.

A better guide, at least for most of the fifteenth century, can be obtained from the Chancery files of *corpus cum causa* and other judicial writs. The *corpus cum causa* writ files were examined from 1461 to the early 1480s, when levels of litigation might well have been lower than they had been prior to 1450. Even within these twenty-odd years, there was very considerable variation in the number surviving in any one year, from a low of around 90 in 1476/7 to a high of over 200 ten years before. And what survives may well be only a small part of what once existed. The only files now existing for 1458/9 contain 5 writs of privilege, together with 59 writs of *corpus cum causa* and 9 writs of *certiorari* relating to London Sheriffs' or Mayor's Court cases.[98] The sheriff's register for the same year contains at least 40 writs of privilege (probably in fact 44), and it is possible that the survivors of the other types of writ represent a similarly low proportion of the original totals for this year.

In the circumstances, all that one can say for certain is that it was relatively uncommon in the 1460s and 1470s for Chancery to receive petitions relating to fewer than 100 or more than 200 Sheriffs' Court actions a year: the lower limit was only breached in five years during those two decades. The average for the 1460s and 1470s is some 116 cases *per annum*. This suggests (possibly, all other things being equal) a modest decline in the Sheriffs' Court cases in the 1470s. Even the 1470s average was probably not much lower than those achieved in the decades before 1450, however. The number of earlier Chancery writs which mention Sheriffs' Court cases (which is not quite the same thing, since one writ could refer to several cases) was, for example, 68 in 1436/7 and 71 in 1440/1, with a quite exceptional 106 writs in 1441/2.[99] If one adds 50 per cent to these totals to allow for multiple references (there are on average around half as many cases again as there are writs) but takes into account the better survival rates of the earlier writs, any difference between the 1430s or 1440s and the 1460s or 1470s would seem to be small.

In the absence of a single Sheriffs' Court roll for these years, or even part of a roll, there is no way of knowing for sure even

[98] TNA (PRO), Chancery *Corpus cum Causa* Writ Files, C244/86, C244/87; CLRO, MS 205C/15, Sheriff's Register of Writs.

[99] TNA (PRO), Chancery *Corpus cum Causa* Writ Files, C244/16–18, /29–31, /32 Parts I and II, /33 (C244/16, /29 and /32 are original files).

roughly what proportion of all cases resulted in a Chancery petition. However, it may be indicative that in the later 1450s the proportion of Mayor's Court cases which resulted in Chancery petitions appears, from the surviving writs for a single year, to have been no more than 3 per cent. If a similar proportion applied to Sheriffs' Court cases, the average number of actions levied between 1461 and 1483 would have been around 3,800 *per annum*.

By contemporary standards, this would be a high level of activity. It is certainly not unlikely, given that, even after nearly thirty years of declining population, the city of York Sheriffs' Court was in the late 1470s entertaining 800–900 cases each year, and that London's population was at this period probably more than ten times that of York.[100] The number of commercial actions brought in London's courts might even have risen disproportionately as economic activity increasingly centred on the city in the later fourteenth and fifteenth centuries.

In fact, the only reason why it might occasion surprise is if it is assumed that no local court, not even the capital's, could possibly come within spitting-distance of the central courts in terms of the amount of private litigation entertained. There are no reliable figures for the central common-law courts at the same period, so it is difficult on two counts to make a comparison between the workloads of the Sheriffs' Court and the two main central courts. M. Hastings' count of all entries (not cases) in the plea rolls of the Common Bench for Easter 1472 and Michaelmas 1482 suggested that the Common Bench entertained something over 5,000 actions a year in both 1472 and 1482. C. Brooks, working on the assumption that about twice as many actions were initiated in the two main Westminster courts as resulted in the appearance of the defendant in court, reckoned that they were entertaining some 4,000 cases between them in 1490 and about twice as many in 1450; and, perhaps, about 6,000 in the decade 1470–80, when the profits the court made from sealing fees in private litigation fell about halfway between the 1450 and the 1490 figures. Since King's Bench seems then to have been earning around 12 per cent of the profit made from sealing fees by both courts, that would suggest that some 5,300 actions a year were being initiated in the Common Bench in the 1470s, and 700 private cases a year in

[100] Stell, *Sheriffs' Court Books of York*, pp. 114–264.

King's Bench.[101] These calculations depend on correctly identifying the ratio of initiating activity to subsequent process. All that can therefore be said is that a figure for the Common Bench of 5,000–6,000 new cases a year in the 1470s and 1480s appears to represent a popular 'guesstimate'. If so, the Common Bench may have been entertaining half as much litigation again as the contemporary London Sheriffs' Court.

Even that, however, might underestimate the activity levels of the latter court. In the first place, the survival rate of writs was declining in the 1460s and 1470s. Secondly, the ratio of surviving writs *corpus cum causa* to the numeration on the surviving Mayor's Courts bills for 1456/7 is based on three Chancery writ files, two of which were unreconstituted (and all the references to Mayor's Court cases came from these two files).[102] If, for the sake of argument, the number of references to London cases in the unreconstituted files is a better guide to the totals once contained by all the files than are the annual averages for the 1460s onwards, we would be looking at some 230 references a year to Sheriffs' Court cases in the 1460s and a ratio of Chancery references to cases – based now on an assumed 18 rather than 12 references to Mayor's Court cases in 1456/7 – of about 1 to 21. That would suggest that the Sheriffs' Court was entertaining some 4,700 personal pleas a year in the 1460s, at a time when the Court of the Common Bench was handling, perhaps, 6,000–7,000 a year.

All this is of course highly speculative. But certainly there is nothing to suggest that the Sheriffs' Court was in anything other than rude health for most of our period, or that it was less busy in the fifteenth century, even in the 1440s and 1450s, than it had been in the early fourteenth; on the contrary. By the middle of the sixteenth century, however, its workload does appear to have reduced sharply, if one may trust the claims of its clerical staff. According to their petition of 1550, their records showed that the courts of both counters were then handling less than half as many cases as they had previously done.[103] Moreover, there are a

[101] Based on Hastings, *Court of Common Pleas*, p. 27, fn. 47; Brooks, *Pettyfoggers and Vipers of the Commonwealth*, pp. 86–7; Blatcher, *Court of King's Bench*, p. 21.
[102] TNA (PRO), Chancery *Corpus cum Causa* Writ Files, C244/82 (writs dated between 25 July 1456 and 13 August 1457), /84 (dated between 26 June and 5 December 1457).
[103] CLRO, Jor. 12/2, fos. 262v-3.

number of things which suggest that, even if there was a sudden drop in or shortly before 1550, it came after a long period of gradual decline.[104] It seems clear from the evidence discussed in Chapter 7, for instance, that the undersheriffs' workload had reduced considerably by the early sixteenth century (although this could be because someone else was doing most of their work). More impressive, at least at first sight, is the reduction in the number of Chancery petitions complaining about the activities of the city's courts. Of over 1,000 surviving petitions presented in 1500 and 1501, only 64 were directed against the sheriffs and (or) the mayor and aldermen ('anti-official' petitions being the type most likely to concern cases brought in, or arrests ordered by, the London courts).[105] Between 1547 and 1551, the total was a mere 12 out of nearly 3,500 petitions.[106] It is true that the petitions offer both a much less complete and a less accurate picture of the numbers of London cases involved than do the endorsements on the writs; petitioners not infrequently failed to mention all the cases against them, and seem sometimes not even to have known in which court a particular case had been brought. But they are probably not misleading in the sense that the number of London petitions concerning cases brought or pending in the city's courts declined after 1500: some 60 out of under 200 writs contained in a *corpus cum causa* writ file for 1500/01 were directed to the London sheriffs and (or) mayor and aldermen, whereas, of some 50 surviving writs in the *corpus cum causa* file for 1537/8, only 9 were directed to the city authorities.[107]

Dramatic as this sounds, however, it is unlikely that it reflects an equivalent reduction in the workload of the city's courts. Two things changed about the relationship between Chancery and the city courts in the last few decades of the fifteenth century. First, one of the main reasons why petitioners sought the help of Chancery in London cases in the first half of the fifteenth century was apparently that they wanted that court to arrange bail for

[104] This combination occurred in the case of Winchester's City Court: HRO, Winchester City Court Rolls, W/D1/71, W/D1/80; W/D1/56, W/D1/63.

[105] TNA (PRO), Early Chancery Proceedings, C1/236–46, printed in the *List of Early Chancery Proceedings*, XXIX.

[106] TNA (PRO), Early Chancery Proceedings, C1/1188–267, C1/1269, C1/1316–17, C1/1271–85, printed in the *List of Early Chancery Proceedings*, LIV.

[107] TNA (PRO), Chancery *Corpus Cum Causa* Writ Files, C244/147, C244/175 (the totals for the first five years of Edward VI are too low to be of any use).

them.[108] Indeed, a fifteenth-century entry in the Sandwich town custumal specifically notes that those committed to prison by the Westminster, London or other courts could obtain a writ *corpus cum causa* from Chancery in order to be put to mainprise ('remys a reremayn') until they had satisfied the plaintiff in respect of his claim.[109] Of 59 writs *corpus cum causa* directed to the London sheriffs in the surviving files for 1458/9, only four do not have attached memoranda recording the bail arrangements: and in three of these exceptional cases, it is clear that something which was once attached to the writ has since been detached.[110] From the mid-1470s onwards, however, it seems to have become easier for defendants in the city's courts to obtain bail without involving Chancery, probably because city attorneys, who had long been prepared to act as mainpernors for some of their clients, were increasingly willing and able to provide the majority with the security they needed.[111] The most obvious sign of this change is that, until the 1460s, the *corpus cum causa* files commonly contained seven to ten times as many 'London' writs of *corpus cum causa*, which required the production of a prisoner as well as the record of a case, as writs of *certiorari*, which required production of the record alone. By the mid-1470s, however, writs of *certiorari* were evidently as common as, or more common than, writs of *corpus cum causa*, and by 1481 there were perhaps three times as many of the former as the latter.[112]

Secondly, at some point in the later fifteenth century Chancery began to confine itself to matters which could genuinely only be

108 Introduction to TNA (PRO) Class List C250; Tucker, 'Early History of the Court of Chancery', pp. 800–1.

109 East Kent Archives, Sandwich Town Custumal, SA/LC2, fo. 67v.

110 TNA (PRO), Chancery *Corpus cum Causa* Writ Files, C244/86, /87.

111 TNA (PRO), Chancery *Habeas Corpus Cum Causa* Writ File C250/14, item 11 (1423/4, Common Attorney Robert Threlkelde, together with Thomas Basset, for whom, see Chapter 7), CLRO, Mayor's Court File of Original Bills MC1/3A, item 16 (1457, mainpernor, Common Attorney Hugh Warter), CLRO, Sheriffs' Court Roll (*Querela Levata*) 1554 (Mayor's Court Clerk and attorney Roger Coys). This practice was (allegedly unsuccessfully) forbidden by the early seventeenth century: CLRO, 'Remarks Submitted to Authority for Reform', p. 3.

112 TNA (PRO), Chancery *Corpus Cum Causa* Writ Files, C244/95 (1462/3, 68 *corpus cum causa*: 8 *certiorari*), C244/116 (1473/4, 25:29), C244/118 (Feb/Sep 1474, 27:32), C244/130 (1481, 17:51). As late as 1474/5 31 of 44 petitioners who asked for a writ *corpus cum causa* aspparently obtained bail by so doing: Introduction to TNA (PRO) Class List C250.

resolved equitably.[113] There seems also to have been a growing reluctance in Chancery, as there was in the Mayor's Court, and probably for much the same reasons, to interfere with cases before they had run their course at common law, even if the petitioner claimed that a just determination could not be achieved. The evidence relating to London suggests that the reason may be that cases like this were considered too open to abuse. In the twenty years after 1460, an increasing proportion of Chancery writ endorsements made by the clerks of the Sheriffs' Court and Mayor's Court noted that one of the cases against the petitioner was awaiting either a verdict by jury or law, or judgment. By the 1480s, about half seem to have had such an endorsement.[114] The increase in both absolute and relative numbers suggests that recourse to Chancery might have been becoming almost a routine way of delaying or disrupting litigation in the city courts once it was clear that the petitioner was likely to lose. The elimination of this abuse and a reduction in the number of petitions designed merely to secure bail in cases in the city courts could well have reduced 'anti-official' London petitions to a small fraction of their former totals. It is therefore unsafe to use Chancery petitions, even in the sixteenth century, as a way of gauging increases and decreases in the activity levels of the city courts.

What one can say, unless one disbelieves the sheriffs' clerks, is that the decline in the workload of the Sheriffs' Court was a very considerable one. If we take the two extremes of the estimates for its activity levels in the fifteenth century, this could mean that it was entertaining between 1,500 and 2,400 personal pleas a year in 1550: in other words, probably no more than it had handled in the 1320s.

[113] Baildon, *Select Cases in Chancery*, p. xxi.

[114] In 1462, 22–23%, in 1467/8, 30%, in 1474, 25–26%, and in 1481, 47% of writs were so endorsed (cases which were described merely as 'pending' are excluded): TNA (PRO), Chancery *Corpus Cum Causa* Writ Files, C244/95 (14 out of 62 writs), C244/104 (23/77), C244/118 (15/59), C244/130 (32/68).

5

THE ADMINISTRATION OF THE LAW IN THE CITY'S COURTS: II

INTRODUCTION

This chapter is about the nature of the process employed in the main city courts (process being the stages by which a case progressed) in civil lawsuits, the evidence used, the methods of trial available and most commonly employed, and the penalties imposed on losing or recalcitrant litigants. In our period, process differed considerably in different situations. In the most informal, it barely existed: the mayor and perhaps one of his fellow-governors or an official would make themselves available at particular times and in particular places, a complainant would approach them with an oral complaint, the other party might be summoned to put his or her case, either party might be questioned and any evidences examined as the judge or tribunal saw fit, and adjudication would follow. No special rules governed, for example, who summoned the person complained about, whether that summons had to be witnessed or testified to, how long before the hearing it had to be delivered, and whether the person complained about was entitled to any respites. When courts were in formal session, however, the failure to follow strict rules (which varied according to the type of action being heard), that is a failure of 'due process', would result in the case having to be abandoned or the judgment annulled. On the whole, cases heard according to common law and custom followed some form of formal process, whereas those heard according to conscience (and, sometimes, according to merchant law) were handled informally.

REAL AND MIXED ACTIONS

Originating and mesne process

In real and mixed actions (mainly cases brought in the Husting, in other words), process followed a similar course to that found in the central common-law courts, although city custom introduced some variation even then. To begin with, there was the originating or initiating activity which had to take place before the court could entertain the case. In most types of case brought in the Husting, this involved the purchase of a writ from Chancery. As Westminster was only a mile or two from the centre of London and standard writs (writs 'of course') cost 4*d*, this was of itself not much of an obstacle. In pleas of naam, even when they concerned freeholds and were heard in the Husting, demandants did not need to get a writ. They could simply submit their complaint at a sheriff's counter and, if practicable, the distrained goods would be returned to them after valuation.[1]

The Husting had cognizance of the case once the demandant (as plaintiffs were known in real and most mixed actions) had appeared with his writ, found pledges (financial sureties) to pursue his action, and the contents of the writ had been read to, understood and 'recorded' by the court. By the 1450s, it had ceased to be necessary, even in the Husting, to find genuine pledges to prosecute, presumably because it was felt that the fines imposed on demandants who failed to prosecute their suit were sufficient to deter time-wasters.[2]

What followed was mesne or intermediate process, designed to get the tenant (as the defendant was known in realty and most mixed cases) to appear and to return whenever the court required him to do so. The tenant was simply summoned, 'two or three days ... or the Sunday' beforehand, to appear in court at the next session of the appropriate Husting.[3] According to 'Liber Albus', the custom was (in right cases, at least) for the summons to be made at the property in dispute rather, than, say, the tenant's main residence or wherever he happened to be living, if that was not the disputed property.[4] There seems to be nothing in the surviving records to prove or disprove this statement, but it is unlikely that Common Clerk Carpenter misreported the practice of his time in a matter with which he should have been very familiar. The short notice apparently given in the summons is doubtless explained by the fact that the tenant was not required to

[1] Riley, *Munimenta Gildhallae*, I, p. 188.

[2] E.g., *Aleyn* v. *Neudigate*, pledges, Richard Chepe, William Street ('Cheap Street'): CP168, m. 1.

[3] Riley, *Munimenta Gildhallae*, I, p. 184. [4] *Ibid.*, I, p. 181.

turn up immediately. In some real and mixed actions, he was entitled to be summoned three times by the sheriffs' sergeants and could choose not to appear until the third occasion. This applied to cases begun by writs of right, dower, customs and services and mesne.[5]

The exceptions were actions begun by writs of waste, partition, *ex gravi querela* and pleas of naam (in terms of intermediate process, the latter were treated more like personal than real actions). In these actions, only one summons was allowed, the provisions in the case of waste being governed by statute.[6] As if to emphasise this difference in treatment, the entry recording the first stage of process in these cases was normally recorded separately, between entries relating to the first and second summons in other types of action. At first sight, partition appears to have been somewhat different again. Tenants were simply warned to appear at the next court 'to show, do and receive whatever the court should decide' in relation to the division of the property.[7] In practice, however, attachment seems routinely to have been employed if the tenant failed to appear, having been warned to do so; it does not appear to have been the case that the court would simply proceed to divide up the disputed property or assets without further attempts to secure his presence.[8] In naam, a failure to cooperate with the court (by refusing to allow the return or even sight of the distrained goods, for example) also resulted in distraint, or, rather, counter-distraint, the awarding of what was known as a withernaam against the landlord.[9] It seems to have been normal practice for the demandants in mesne to bring a plea of naam at the same time: in other words, they simultaneously tried to recover the distress and to force the intermediate 'landlord' to provide the service or

[5] Although there is no mention of the action of mesne in 'Liber Albus', no doubt because it was nearly 80 years since one had last been brought, it is clear that 3 summons were allowed: e.g., CLRO, HR CP43, mm. 1, 5, 8 (*Gunthorp* v. *Mazeliner & Another*).

[6] Riley, *Munimenta Gildhallae*, I, pp. 184–5, 186–7, 189; CLRO, HR CP73, mm. 17, 18 ([daughter of Margery, daughter of Walter de] *Finchyngfeld* v. *Gargrave*), HR CP168, mm. 3v, 3 (*Prior of St Bartholomew, West Smithfield* v. *Trevilian*, waste), HR CP29, m. 1 (*fitzPeter* v. *le Mareschal*, naam).

[7] Riley, *Munimenta Gildhallae*, I, p. 189, CLRO, HR CP51, m. 1 (*Fournyval & Others* v. *Essex*), HR CP151, 5 (*Acre* v. *Otle*).

[8] See CLRO, HR CP71, mm. 3, 5, 7 (*Bole* v. *Harewold*), 12, 14, 15 (*Pyk* v. *Pyk*).

[9] CLRO, CP48, m. 15 (*Rys* v. *Leyre*).

payment which had been demanded from them. For example, Common Clerk Hugh de Waltham and his wife brought a writ of mesne against Isabel de Bray concerning a property which she had granted them and for which they were obliged to pay 50*s* a year to St James's Hospital, and from which the Prioress of St Helen's was demanding a quitrent of 18*s* a year. At the court following the reading of the writ, the prioress and the Walthams both essoined and thereafter the plea of naam was held in abeyance pending resolution of the primary action.[10]

Once a tenant had been duly summoned and had failed to appear, the next stage was, theoretically, to order his attachment 'by gage and pledge' (that is, he was required to find security that he would appear at the next session of the court). In the action of mesne, however, default by the mesne (intermediate) landlord then, or at at any stage in the process, seems in practice to have led to the order to distrain him.[11] Distraint was not necessarily much of a sanction. Although the court could order distraint of increasing severity, culminating in distraint 'ita quod de exitibus' (when the sheriff arrested and became responsible for the profits of the disputed property), often it simply repeated the order to distrain; and even successful distraints might involve derisory sums. In a case of waste from the early 1460s, *Prior of St Bartholomew, West Smithfield* v. *Trevilian*, the defendant was attached by genuine pledges, but when this failed to secure his appearance and the sheriffs were ordered to distrain him 'by all his goods and chattels', they managed a mere 6*d* and obtained sureties for his appearance from clearly fictitious characters.[12] The demandant who was obliged to sue two or more tenants was in an even worse predicament. In *Gunthorp* v. *Mazeliner and Another*, for example, a case of mesne, first one defendant would default, distraint would

[10] A case complicated by Isabel's claim that it was her co-parcener to property allocated to her in an earlier partition case who was obliged to pay the quitrent: CLRO, HR CP49, mm. 21v, 23; CLRO, HR PL47 (*sic*; this is the CP roll for 1290/1, which should come between HR CP49 and HR CP50), m. 1v, referring to an action brought in July 1284 (the membranes covering this session are missing).

[11] E.g., CLRO, HR CP42, mm. 15, 22 (*Secheford* v. *Rys*); HR CP43, m. 17, HR CP44, m. 4 (*Mynggi* v. *St Edmunds*); HR CP54, m. 12v, HR CP55, m. 2v (*Ispania* v. *fitzJohn le Conestable of Guildford*); HR CP58, mm. 11, 13, HR CP59, m. 1 (*Amys* v. *Hardel & Hardel*).

[12] CLRO, HR CP168, mm. 3v, 3, 2, HB1, fos. 44v–6.

be ordered against him, and he would then appear; at which court, the other defendant would default, distraint would be ordered against him, and so on. This kept the case going for years.[13] It was not normally possible to proceed against one tenant (or defendant) in the absence of another, unless the court was ordered to do so by writ, because, say, one tenant was abroad, or unless the court itself licensed someone to replace a tenant named in the writ: for example, a third party who claimed that the disputed right was at risk of being lost by the 'wrong' tenant, perhaps collusively.[14]

Delays and deferrals

There will always be occasions when one of the parties is genuinely unable to appear in court when required to do so, and the city courts were no exception to the general rule that a litigant who was too ill, in childbed or not in his or her right mind could be excused either temporarily or permanently (with alternative arrangements made in the latter case). In addition, both parties were allowed to essoin (excuse their non-attendance) after each court appearance, unless specifically told otherwise, and certain other essoins were either automatically available or were almost certain to be allowed in appropriate circumstances. No reason or excuse was required.

In actions begun by writs of right or of customs and services, tenants were permitted a 'common' (routine) essoin on three occasions, in addition to their three summonses.[15] In all other types of action, including, it appears, naam, only one common essoin was normally permitted, although exceptions did occur.[16]

[13] CLRO, HR CP43, mm. 1 *et seq.*, HR CP44, mm. 5v, 8, 17, 21, HR CP45, mm. 1, 10, HR CP46, mm. 1, 6, 12, 13v, 17.

[14] CLRO, HR CP29, m. 8v (*Grascherche* v. *Wylemyn & Others*); HR PL23, m. 3v (*Sutton* v. *Essex*).

[15] Riley, *Munimenta Gildhallae*, I, pp. 181, 186; CLRO, HB1, fos. 49, 51v (*Porthaleyn & Porthaleyn & Others* v. *Friston*, right), HR CP39, m. 11 (*Prior of St Mary's, Southwark* v. *Hakeneye*, customs and services).

[16] E.g., for single essoins in dower, CLRO, HB1, fos. 103v, 106 [*bis*] (*Hall* v. *Wynn & Others*), 136v, 139v, 140 (*Sutton* v. *Brice & Others*), but HR CP29, m. 2 (*Longesstone* v. *Punge*, tenant essoined three times); for *ex gravi querela*, HR CP109, m. 8 (*Badby & Badby* v. *fitzNichol*); for mesne, HR CP44, mm. 5v, 8, 17, 21 (*Gunthorp* v. *Mazeliner and Another*); HR CP168, mm. 3v, 3 [*sic*] (*Prior of St Bartholomew, West Smithfield* v. *Trevilian*, waste); HR CP70, mm. 7, 11, 14 (*Hunnesdon & Hunnesdon* v. *Banham & Others*, partition); Riley, *Munimenta*

Having appeared, or at each additional stage in the case, the tenants could absent themselves from the next session before being required to answer the plaintiff further.[17] All tenants could obtain a 'licence to imparl' (an extension of time to consider their response, normally until the next session of court) or could be granted a 'loveday' (a delay in proceedings, which might be continued over many sessions, to allow time to negotiate an agreement), providing both parties wanted it.

Tenants summoned to answer writs of right, customs and services, dower, and *ex gravi querela* could also request a 'view', that is, an adjournment so that the location and exact extent of the property in dispute could be confirmed.[18] As far as can be determined, a view was invariably granted if requested in these actions: there is no evidence that the court would only allow it under certain conditions or for certain purposes.[19] Certainly an attempt in 1290 by a demandant, who claimed statutory authority, to preclude the tenant from having a view in a dower case was successfully countered by the tenant, who said that it was contrary to city custom to deny a view in such cases.[20] The view gave the tenants a further opportunity to essoin themselves, as did the right, in these actions, to vouch to warranty in the Common Bench whoever had granted the property to the tenants, if the vouchee (grantor) lived elsewhere. Despite doubts expressed in 1314, from 1316 onwards it was settled that this process involved the suspension of activity in the Husting until – and only until – such time as the central court had determined whether or not the alleged vouchee was indeed obliged to warrant the tenants.[21]

Finally, tenants could defer matters for the longer term if they were able to produce a royal writ certifying that they were

Gildhallae, I, p. 188 (naam, see p. 176, under 'Personal Actions', for the reasons for relying on 'Liber Albus' in this case).

[17] E.g., CLRO, HR PL168, m. 12v (*Joy & Joy* v. *Langton & Langton*).

[18] Riley, *Munimenta Gildhallae*, I, pp. 182, 185 (*bis*), 186, CLRO, HR PL168, 12v, HB1, fos. 70–4 (*Joy & Joy* v. *Langton & Langton*).

[19] *Pace* Finlason, *Reeves' History of English Law*, I, pp. 420–2, citing *Bracton*.

[20] CLRO, CP18, m. 12v (*Suffolk* v. *Cosin*).

[21] CLRO, HR CP40, mm. 20–20v, Riley, *Munimenta Gildhallae*, II, i, pp. 169–70, 170–7.

required elsewhere on the king's service or, in actions brought by writ of right, to show that they were under age.[22]

Judgment in default

It was not of course just the tenant who might default: a great many demandants failed, for one reason or another, to prosecute their suit. In all types of formal action, regardless of their nature and how they were initiated, the demandant's failure to essoin himself or to appear in person or by attorney resulted in him being 'non-suited', that is, his action was terminated and the tenant went quit 'without a day' (was not required to appear again). This outcome did not, however, necessarily prevent the demandant bringing the action again and again, providing it had not gone too far. The one exception was the plea of naam, at least after 1307: in this action, if the demandant failed to pursue the case, on the first or second occasion the distrained goods would simply be returned to the landlord; but on the third occasion that it happened, the return would be permanent and the demandant would not be permitted to make any further attempts to recover these particular assets.[23]

It was, however, with defaults by tenants that courts were chiefly concerned, and particularly with persistent defaults which might defeat justice. In actions of right, customs and services, *ex gravi querela* brought for the execution of testaments and dower, if the tenant failed to appear after any permitted delays, the court would take the disputed lands into its own hands, by a process known (if the tenant had not appeared at all) as *grand cape* and, if he had appeared on at least one occasion, as *petit cape*.[24] If

[22] For a case lost by the tenant, Nicholas de Segrave, who failed to produce [evidence in support of] his essoin, see CLRO, HR PL98, 14–14v. For examples of demandants being told to await the defendant's minority, see HR PL23, mm. 1 (*Hatfeld* v. *Gut*), 2v (*St Martin* v. *fitzPerine*).

[23] CLRO, HR CP32, m. 17. This provision had been enacted in the Statute of Westminster II twenty-two years previously, but was probably intended to apply solely to the central courts: Brand, *Making of the Common Law*, p. 319, Riley, *Munimenta Gildhallae*, I, p. 188.

[24] Riley, *Munimenta Gildhallae*, I, pp. 181, 186, 185, 185–6; CLRO, HR CP5, m. 1v (*Herang* v. *Abbot of Wardon*), HR CP66, m. 14v (*Offington* v. *Parson of St Mary Wolnoth*), CLRO, HR CP54, m. 9v (*Bondon* v. *Corp & Others*), CLRO, HB1, fo. 93v (*Hall* v. *Galyon & Others*).

the tenant defaulted again, the court would adjudge the property to the demandant in the tenant's absence.[25] In actions of customs and services, there was a further stage: the tenant had a year and a day after the initial judgment to appear and to satisfy the demandant for any arrears and to provide security for future payments.[26] If the demandant was the head of a religious house or similar 'incorporeal body' and the judgment in default would result in the transfer of the property to him in perpetuity, the sheriff would also be ordered, in compliance with provisions introduced by statute in 1285, to conduct an enquiry to confirm that there was no collusion between the demandant and the tenant (this was because the action could be used fraudulently to evade the restrictions on giving or selling property to corporations).[27] Even this did not necessarily end the matter, in that the demandant would very probably need to seek the court's help in executing the judgment. This he did by bringing a bill of *scire facias* once the year and a day had elapsed, which required the tenant to appear and to show, if he could, why the judgment should not be executed.[28] If he again failed to appear, or appeared but could not show any reason why execution should be stayed, the property was the demandant's in perpetuity and, to use the phrase generally employed in actions of customs and services, the tenant was thereafter 'shartfort' (precluded from any further action in relation to it).

In dower cases, the sheriff would be required to summon a jury of the neighbourhood for a different purpose: to confirm that the plaintiff's husband had died in possession of it, that his possession was of a type to give rise to a claim for dower, to ascertain its value and sometimes, from 1345 on, to assess any damages due in compensation because the court considered that the litigation had been unduly prolonged in order to deny the widow the use or profits of her property.[29]

[25] Riley, *Munimenta Gildhallae*, I, pp. 181, 186. [26] *Ibid.*, I, p. 186.

[27] CLRO, HB1, fo. 55 (*Keeper of St Giles, Cripplegate* v. *Wydeslade*).

[28] Riley, *Munimenta Gildhallae*, p. 184; for ways of 'curing' the default, see *Bracton*, IV, pp. 154–5.

[29] Riley, *Munimenta Gildhallae*, I, pp. 184–5, and e.g. CLRO, HR CP79, mm. 8, 26 (*Bedel & Bedel* v. *atte Pye*).

Actions of waste, partition and mesne were again different. In none of these actions was the process of *cape* available.[30] In partition, if the tenant persistently defaulted, the court would itself proceed to assign a portion of the property to the demandant in the tenant's absence. In mesne, a single jury was required to establish what loss the plaintiff had suffered by having been distrained by or forced to pay rent to the 'superior landlord' and whether the defendant was the mesne, that is, responsible for paying the rent or performing the services.[31] In waste, it was normally necessary to summon two juries: the one, to confirm that waste had been committed and to assess the damages, the other, to confirm that there was no fraud or collusion in those cases where the demandant was head of a corporation.[32]

As we have seen, distraint could be ordered repeatedly, and without any increase in severity. Possibly this was not quite such an unavoidably frustrating a process for the demandant as it appears, since more rigorous process was certainly sometimes awarded, and a token distraint could be followed by an immediate order to begin the process which would lead to the recovery of the property or assets, as happened in *Prior of St Bartholomew, West Smithfield* v. *Trevilian.*[33] It may therefore be that some demandants preferred to apply only mild pressure, perhaps while negotiating with the tenant. Moreover, in mesne, where the defendant had no property in the city, as was quite possibly the case in *Ispania* v. *fitzJohn le Conestable [the Constable] of Guildford*, or where repeated distraints of Londoners proved ineffective, it could even be the case that the defendant's failure to respond after process had reached a certain stage entitled the plaintiff to withhold sufficient rent to recover the distress.[34]

Finally, as was said earlier, in naam, if, having been told to appear on a specific date, the defendant failed to do so, the

[30] Riley, *Munimenta Gildhallae*, p. 189, CLRO, HB1, fos. 23, 23v, 24, 25 (*Neudigate* v. *fitzSimond & fitzSimond*, partition; CLRO, HB1, fo. 45v (*Prior of St Bartholomew, West Smithfield* v. *Trevilian*, waste).

[31] For example, CLRO, HR CP9, m. 1v, *le Cotiller* v. *Abel.*

[32] CLRO, HB1, fos. 45v, 46.

[33] See also CLRO, HR CP3, m. 3 (*Meryene* v. *Cous*).

[34] CLRO, HR 54, m. 12, HR CP55, mm. 2v, 3v; see also CLRO, HR CP58, mm. 11, 13, HR CP59, mm. 1, 4v, 6, 9v, 10v, 12v, (*Amys* v. *Hardel & Hardel*, tenants, a city freeman and his wife, amerced); there seem to be no further references to this case.

plaintiff retained the distrained goods and the defendant had no further claim on them (although he could still seek to recover the rent using either the action of customs and services or, after 1345, the assize of freshforce).

Pleadings

Once the opposing parties had been got to court on the same day and were ready to proceed, the demandant would make his count (statement of complaint) as the first stage in the pleadings (putting the parties' cases and arguing the legal points). Demandants in city courts were, under the terms of the city's charters from the 1130s onwards, spared fines for 'miskenning' (failing to employ the correct legal phrases and terminology).[35] In real and mixed actions begun by writ the case was nevertheless as vulnerable in London as anywhere to being thrown out if the count and the writ did not agree or if either failed to include all the details required by law. It was vital, for example, to name all the tenants whose rights were being challenged, including any husband (or wife, if the property concerned were hers) to whom a tenant was married at the relevant date and excluding any spouse from whom the tenant had then been separated or divorced. The only way to amend the details once the case was under way was to allow the writ to 'fall' and to purchase another.[36] It was also vital to mention all other material facts which could affect the outcome. In 1292, the demandants in a right case lost for 'counting badly': they had failed to mention, when describing the descent of the property, that a previous heir had entered a religious order.[37]

On the other hand, even in actions begun by writ, the city seems to have been reluctant to limit the types of argument that litigants could put to the jury. As was mentioned earlier, actions described indifferently in the Husting rolls as being brought by writs of right could be pleaded 'in the form of' (as though they

[35] Riley, *Munimenta Gildhallae*, I, p. 295 (Edward I's ordinances, *c.* 1285). According to the author of *Leges Henrici Primi*, writing some 170 years earlier, miskenning then 'magis inhorruit in Londonia': Downer, *Leges Henrici Primi*, p. 124.

[36] CLRO, HR PL4, m. 3v; HR PL11, m. 5.

[37] CLRO, HR PL18, m. 10v.

were brought by) writs of entry and of formedon.[38] Of this, Common Clerk Carpenter commented that 'demandants shall declare against [the tenants] in the nature of whatever writ they shall please ... without protestation being made that they will sue in the nature of any writ [in particular]'; or, as William Fletewode put it in the following century, 'I doo thinke that by the lawe a formedon dothe not lye in London ... but their remedie ys to sue a writt of right & then to declare in what nature of accion they will.'[39] In 1334, a tenant argued that she did not need to answer the plaintiff's writ of right, since he claimed to have inherited a property as (third) heir after his brother, describing his right, which derived from a gift 'in free marriage' to their grandparents, as being 'per formam donacionis'.[40] The court rejected her argument. It also resisted attempts to use the form of the pleading to limit how the case could be determined. In 1300, the demandant in another right action, *Sutton* v. *Essex*, argued that 'all writs, as well of entry as of formedon, ... ought to be determined according to the form in which they had been pleaded'. Since the tenant had failed to deny her assertion that he 'only had entry through her former husband, whom she could not contradict before her divorce', and she had provided the necessary evidence of that divorce, she asked that he be judged undefended. The tenant, however, argued that the issue of whether or not she was divorced should be put to the jury, as part of the general question of who had 'the greater right' to the property. The court hesitated, presumably feeling that, since the central question of the divorce was contested, it ought indeed to be put to the jury; and it appears that, after several adjournments and *loquelae*, it was.[41]

The 'form of the pleadings' changed physically during our period. It is clear that, by the early sixteenth century, it was quite common, perhaps even standard practice, for Husting litigants to present their declarations and responses to the court in written form, although this did not prevent them or their legal

38 For an early statement to this effect (referring to writs of entry only, since the earliest known writ of formedon dates from 1257), see Chew, Weinbaum, *Eyre 1244*, p. 105, and Brand, *Making of the Common Law*, pp. 227–32, esp. 228–9. On the rules which developed around the writs of entry and formedon, see Biancalana, *Fee Tail and the Common Recovery*.

39 Riley, *Munimenta Gildhallae*, I, p. 182; BL, Harleian MS 5156, fo. 2.

40 CLRO, HR PL65, m. 23 (*Wilenhale* v. *Wilenhale*).

41 CLRO, HR PL24, mm. 3v, 17.

representatives also doing so orally.[42] It was certainly not a recent development, since in the late 1450s there is an example of a Hustings demandant being given a day to put in his declaration, and we are told that the tenant put in his 'advocacio' the following Monday.[43] While we cannot be certain that written pleadings were not in use in the Husting much before this, the first sign of them occurs very shortly after (within a decade of) the abandonment of formal 'session-and-plea' rolls and the introduction in their place of a session book and of rolls which recorded determined pleas in collated form, often, though not always, with a separate membrane for each case.[44] It is also noteworthy that, while the session book from the outset normally records merely that 'X declared against Y in such-and-such an action', just as it records merely that a 'writ of Z &c [was read] against Y', jury verdicts were given in detail, sometimes considerable detail.[45] In other words, either there were additional rough papers in which the clerks wrote up those details which were not given in the session books but which later appeared in the record of determined cases, or they were by the late 1440s using not only the writs but also written pleadings in order to provide that detail. It is by no means inconceivable that they made rough notes during the court sessions. The session book itself does, however, look like a record in which session headings were entered in advance and brief notes of process and pleadings were recorded, often rather untidily, as they occurred. There is one other piece of evidence which suggests that the division of the Hustings records into a session book and plea rolls was associated with the introduction of written pleadings. The first mention of the latter in the Hustings records only just predates the first reference to paper pleadings in the yearbooks. Since these had 'probably become the rule' in the Common Bench by the 1520s and appear to have been quite common in the London Husting a decade or so earlier, it seems reasonable to suppose that developments in the Husting and the

42 CLRO, HB2, fos. 11v, 39v, 47, 40v, 162, 188 and 306, 198v and 189.

43 CLRO, HB1, fo. 28v.

44 CLRO, HB1, CLRO, HR PL168, HR CP168 on. A tendency to collate pleas which had been or were expected to be determined, by extending the entry recording the initial pleadings with notes of subsequent process, is evident by the middle of the previous century: HR CP74, m. 14v (*Deynes* v. *Aylward*).

45 CLRO, HB1, fo. 8v, *Lawys* v. *Sudbury*.

central courts were roughly coincident, in this respect at least. If so, the middle of the fifteenth century is probably when the practice first emerged in both.[46]

PERSONAL ACTIONS

Without the account contained in 'Liber Albus', it would be difficult to be sure about the exact process in pleas of naam, even when they were heard in the Husting, with its plentiful surviving records. The reason is that naam was normally begun informally and process in informally initiated cases (those begun by oral plaint or by bill) was not normally entered on the court roll until at least some of the routine stages were over.[47]

There is another difficulty with personal actions, even those which were begun by writ. Although the part-roll of the Sheriffs' Court for 1320 is in certain respects the best evidence we have for practice in that court, it is impossible to tell for sure how most of the actions recorded in it were initiated. This is because the tendency not to enter details of cases on the court roll at the outset applied to all types of personal actions, regardless of the way in which they were initiated and regardless of which court heard them. Since the clerks who wrote up the roll did note writs *de minis* (ordering the court to take sureties from the person named in the writ for keeping the peace against the plaintiff), the probability is that they would have noted that a plea was begun by writ whenever that was the case. Indeed, there is an example of a writ of trespass, albeit one returnable in the central courts, on the roll.[48] No other types of writ are recorded on that roll; so it could well be that none of the pleas were begun by writ. We cannot be entirely certain of that, however, since it has been suggested that one of the actions of account entered there was in fact initiated by a writ *monstravit de computo*, the assumption being that the action, *Odi* v. *Amyigi*, discussed in the 1321 eyre, was the same as the

[46] Hastings, *Court of the Common Pleas*, p. 13.

[47] Although there are a few examples of Husting cases being noticed only once, on determination (see CLRO, HR CP40, mm. 3, 4), it was probably not normal in the city courts for these actions to be entered only once they had been determined or abandoned, as apparently happened with bill-initiated cases in the 1321 eyre: Cam, *Eyre 1321*, I, pp. xciii–xciv.

[48] CLRO, Sheriffs' Court Roll (1320), m. 15v.

action of account between the same parties recorded in the Sheriffs' Court roll in the summer of 1320. It is certainly true that some of the records produced by the Sheriffs' Court were misleading in this respect. There is an example of a return of a Sheriffs' Court case included in the Mayor's Court rolls (a consolidated summary, however, not an exact copy of the original entries in the court roll) which describes the case as a 'plea [of] account', with no mention of a writ, to which a writ *de computo inter mercatores* is attached. On the other hand, in the eyre it was said that, as one would expect, the defendant had been arrested, whereas there is no evidence in the Sheriffs' Court roll to suggest that this occurred; so perhaps the plaintiff took several bites at this particular cherry.[49]

In these circumstances, all that can be said for sure is that, despite the apparent absence of cases initiated by writ in the summer of 1320, such cases were still being brought occasionally in the fourteenth century.[50] The writs of error brought in the Husting during the later fourteenth and fifteenth centuries, however, invariably referred to the original Sheriffs' Court action as a 'plea (*loquela*) brought without the king's writ', and writ-initiated actions can at most have formed a tiny proportion of the workload of the Sheriffs' Court after 1350.[51]

In the first half of the fourteenth century, initiating procedures in the Mayor's Court were probably even more informal than they were in the Sheriffs' Court. Very occasionally, actions were initiated by writ, almost always when the city's governors had allegedly failed to do justice to whoever had obtained the writ.[52] It was certainly not the normal way of initiating a personal action: not one of those recorded in the plea and memoranda rolls appears to have been begun by writ. Plaintiffs and petitioners alike either stated their case orally or presented a written bill. And even the

[49] Cam, *Eyre 1321*, II, pp. 218–19 and 219 fn. 1, referring to CLRO, Sheriffs' Court Roll (1320), mm. 18, 22v, 25v; CalEMCR, pp. 132–3 (1302).

[50] CLRO, HR CP40, m. 23 (1315, writ of account), HR CP49, m. 16 (writ *ex gravi querela*, 1324–5); *CalEMCR*, pp. 69, 99, 132–3,140–1; *CalPMR 1323–64*, p. 213 (1344).

[51] E.g. CLRO, HR CP53 (1329/30), m. 22, HR CP79 (1355/6), mm. 18, 22, HR CP110 (1385/6), m. 20v, HR CP122 (1397/8), m. 4. The last reference in the plea and memoranda rolls to a Sheriffs' Court case involving a writ (of *justicies*) is from 1385: *CalPMR 1381–1412*, p. 93.

[52] *CalEMCR*, pp. 164, 43, 42.

'common-law' bills were, initially, of an informal character. The earliest surviving examples, from the late 1360s, are almost indistinguishable from contemporary non common-law bills or petitions, even when they involved large sums of money and wealthy individuals (such as the Luccan merchant who brought a bill against a London mercer over a detained bond and £8 5*s*).[53] What appear at first sight to be the pitiful supplications of obvious candidates for extra-legal assistance, like the 'poor old mariner' whose ten-year-old daughter had been taken into service without an apprenticeship, and who sought help 'for God and as a work of charity', turn out to be ordinary Mayor's Court bills.[54] The only way to tell fourteenth-century common-law bills from bills which are petitions is that some were at this date marked, in a contemporary hand, 'supplication'.[55]

By the second decade of the following century, administrative practices had altered, almost certainly because of the changes in attitude towards the court's work which had led to its physical reorganisation. From the first quarter of the fifteenth century, as far as one can judge from the poor dating evidence, the Latin bill in standard common-law form began to take over from the petition-like French bill; the latest surviving example of the latter seems to be from the 1440s.[56] French petitions also largely disappear from the plea and memoranda rolls at the end of the 1440s. Thereafter, most petitioners seem either to have made their statement orally (as John Fortescue did in 1457 and several Hanse merchants did in 1466) or to have produced a petition in English, as the scrivener, Richard Claidich, probably did in 1452. The only petitions which continued to be in French were, it seems, those of apprentices.[57]

[53] CLRO, Mayor's Court File of Original Bills, MC1/1, m. 32.

[54] *Ibid.*, MC1/1, m. 13.

[55] *Ibid.*, MC1/1, mm. 30, 31 (to add to the confusion, in some fourteenth-century common-law bills the plaintiff referred to himself as 'supplicating and complaining', whereas by the 1440s this sort of language is precisely what marks out the petition from the common-law bill).

[56] *Ibid.*, MC1/1 (*c.* 1370–*c.* 1390, 174 bills, 24 Latin), MC1/2 (*c.* 1380–*c.* 1410, 224 bills, 90 Latin), MC1/2A (*c.* 1380–*c.* 1440, 70 bills, 36 Latin), MC1/3 (*c.* 1440–*c.* 1460, 375 bills, 303 Latin), MC1/3A (1456–8?, 264 bills, all Latin); *ibid.*, MC1/3, m. 171 (French common-law bill which contains a reference to August 1443).

[57] *CalPMR 1437–57*, pp. 153–5, *CalPMR 1458–82*, p. 46; *CalPMR 1437–57*, pp. 124–5 (the whole entry is in English); and see also *CalPMR 1458–82*, pp. 28–9, 114–16, where the petitions are transcribed in full; *ibid.*, pp. 18, 47, for French elements from apprentices' petitions incorporated in the Latin record.

By this stage, petitions differed in certain important ways from the common-law bills. No cause of action was specified; the document, if not described as a 'supplication', is referred to as 'a [certain] bill', not 'an [original] bill of debt/trespass/detinue' and the like. The clerks were careful to distinguish, not just Inner Chamber cases from those heard in the (Outer) Chamber, but also those which required adjudication by the court from those in which arbitration was the preferred course. The probable reason for the disappearance of petitions from the latest surviving medieval bills is that filing practices had been tightened up by the 1440s, with common-law bills and petitions, if the matter was set down in writing at all, kept separately. For the would-be litigant, the likely effect of this change was to create of the Mayor's Court an alternative forum for litigation which employed very similar initiating procedures to the Sheriffs' Court.

Originating and mesne process

Where personal actions were brought by writ, they were initiated in the same way as real and mixed actions: the plaintiff would obtain a writ from Chancery and bring it to the Husting, the Mayor's Court or the sheriff's counter, as appropriate. In other cases, the fact that Mayor's Court and Sheriffs' Court plaintiffs did not need to buy a writ from Chancery in order to initiate their cases simplified the procedures at the outset. They could set the ball rolling by going to Guildhall to make their complaint orally or to hand over a bill detailing their complaint. Alternatively, as with cases of naam brought in the Husting, they could visit a sheriff's counter and present their bill there. As both counters were in the area of Cheapside (the westernmost one being, for most of our period, in the vicinity of the Cheap Cross, the easternmost, on the north side of Poultry), London residents and visitors never had far to go.[58] They appear to have been able to use whichever counter suited them: convenience, in terms both of the location of the counter and the days on which each side of the court sat, presumably influenced them most if no other considerations did.

[58] The westernmost counter seems to have been relatively mobile: CLRO, HR CP146, m. 2v (1422, Milk Street); Lobel, *City of London*, p. 70 (1429, to the west of Bread Street; 1555 on, Wood Street).

Theoretically, they were required to find pledges to prosecute their complaint, although these were probably often if not always fictitious by the early fifteenth century.[59]

In all personalty-related cases, regardless of which court heard them, what process was then awarded depended partly on the defendant's status (freeman of the city or not, having lands and tenements in the city by which he could be distrained or not) and partly on the nature of the action. All defendants in trespass actions were attached as a first step. As was mentioned in the previous chapter, defendants were often unable to offer such security, particularly, it seems, if they were strangers to the city, in which case they were physically arrested. The usual process in other actions allowed for a single initial summons.

If the defendant could be attached at the first summons, he would be. If he then failed to appear, a 'better attachment' would be ordered, several times if necessary; or if he would or could not be attached, distraint and 'better distraint' would follow – but only, of course, if he had property in the city by which he could be distrained.[60] Speedy process was the aim: if adjournments were required, they were supposed to be to the next full session of the court, not some later date, unless both parties agreed otherwise.[61] As far as it is possible to tell, it was normal to apply steadily increasing pressure to a recalcitrant defendant, with attachment being ordered before distraint; sometimes, however, distraint was ordered immediately upon what was apparently the first default.[62] Either the courts allowed themselves some discretion in the use of these sanctions, or the rules themselves were flexible, allowing a stage to be left out if, for example, a defendant was known to be particularly uncooperative or had previously refused to offer any

59 CLRO, Sheriffs' Court Rolls [*Querelae Levatae*], 1407–8, items 5, 14, 15; CLRO, Mayor's Court File of Original Bills, MC1/2 (*c.* 1380–*c.* 1410), items 222 and 189. They seem however usually to have been genuine until the late fourteenth century: e.g. CLRO, HR CP79, m. 18 (1355/6, Sheriffs' Court case, *Herpesfeld* v. *Prior of St Bartholomew, West Smithfield*); CLRO, Mayor's Court File of Original Bills, MC1/1 (*c.* 1370–*c.* 1390), item 2, MC1/2, item 4.

60 Riley, *Munimenta Gildhallae*, I, pp. 199–203, CLRO, Sheriffs' Court Roll (1320)), mm. 1–2v; for summaries of process, e.g. CLRO, HR CP38, mm. 11, 24, or HR CP125, mm. 3v, 7v.

61 CLRO, HR CP125, m. 7v.

62 E.g. in the Husting cases, *Vyleyn* v. *Greneford* and *Wolleward* v. *Gille*, both covenant: CLRO, HR CP3, mm. 3v, 4, HR CP12, mm. 1, 2.

form of security.[63] On the other hand, the goods attached or distrained as part of the intermediate process were often of modest value, even after several orders to make a better attachment had been issued. This was not invariably so, however: gages in *Walpol* v. *Ponchon*, a Sheriffs' Court case from 1320, were valued at 17*s*.[64] As with trespass, moreover, if it was impossible to attach or distrain the defendant because 'he had nothing within the city', or if the court was persuaded that he would otherwise abscond, his arrest would be ordered.[65]

In trespass and account, once the defendant had been persuaded to appear or had been physically arrested, if there was doubt about his reappearance, he could either be mainprised (a form of bail, in which others – mainpernors – undertook to have the defendant in court on demand either on pain of financial penalties or, occasionally, 'body for body', that is, of imprisonment themselves if they failed) or remanded to prison while the case continued.[66] As with attachment, it tended to be easier for city freemen to find others to act as their mainpernors. For defendants of means, however, being without acquaintance locally may not have been an insuperable obstacle to obtaining bail. As we have seen,[67] there is some evidence to suggest that attorneys and clerks supplemented their fees by acting as mainpernors for their own or other men's clients, presumably for a consideration. Finally, if the appearance of some but not all of the defendants could be secured, the defaulter(s) would be 'separated' and the case would continue against the others in his or their absence.[68]

[63] John Gille, the defendant in *Wolleward* v. *Gille*, above, certainly proved to be a hard nut to crack: see also CLRO, HR CP13, mm. 3, 4, 6v, HR CP14, mm. 1v, 2v, 3v *et seq.*, HR CP15, mm. 3 *et seq.*; and, in *Wolleward (assign of Mathilda Juvenal)* v. *Gille*, HR CP20, m. 1, HR CP22, mm. 2v, 4, 5v, 8 *et seq*. In the first case, process had moved rapidly through the 'grand distress' (m. 3) to 'distress even to the issues' (m. 7).

[64] CLRO, Sheriffs' Court Roll (1320), m. 13.

[65] CLRO, HR CP122, m. 11v, HR CP147, m. 147; HR CP125, m. 3 (arrest apparently ordered immediately).

[66] CLRO, HR CP22, m. 1 (*Elyot* v. *Kent*); *ibid.*, m. 4 (account, defendant remanded to prison, having acknowledged the debt but being unable to pay, until he did so); CLRO, Sheriffs' Court Rolls [*Querelae Levatae*], 1407–08, items 1, 3, 8 and 9 (all trespass; defendants attached, then mainprised).

[67] See p. 162.

[68] CLRO, Sheriffs' Court Roll (1320), m. 8 (*Donmowe* v. *Farneham and Others*).

Delays and deferrals

The plea and memoranda rolls give the impression that initial essoins were not allowed in the Mayor's Court. The rolls may well be misleading, however, since the cases recorded there had generally been determined, and the entries, in cases where the defendant did not simply default, began with his first appearance and possibly simply ignored earlier process. And, contrary to the interpretation of a passage in 'Liber Albus' which appears to deny essoins to defendants at all stages of personal actions in the Sheriffs' Court, the city statutes of 1345 certainly regarded as ancient custom the allowance of a single essoin after the first summons in pleas of debt, covenant 'and the like'.[69] Even in trespass, defendants were usually allowed at least one essoin.[70]

Contrariwise, after 1345 essoins for royal service, which resulted in an adjournment of the case, sometimes for long periods, were not allowed to defendants in the Sheriffs' Court until the point at which the pleadings had been completed.[71] Defendants who were absent on royal service were expected to retain essoiners to 'cast their essoins' for them. Once the case had been pleaded to trial or judgment, the defendant's personal appearance was required and he could obtain an adjournment by claiming that he was unavoidably detained on the king's service. If however he subsequently defaulted, having been given an alternative date for his appearance, or failed to provide the writ proving that he had been on the king's service when essoined, he rendered himself liable to be 'adjudged as the law of the city requires'.[72]

As with real and mixed actions, each stage of the process entitled the defendant (providing he had duly appeared at that

[69] Riley, *Munimenta Gildhallae*, I, p. 474.

[70] Riley, *Munimenta Gildhallae*, I, p. 202 and marginal note: see CLRO HR CP38, mm. 11 (*Franceys* v. *Medelane*), 24 (*Bevere* v. *Basyate*), CLRO, Sheriffs' Court Roll (1320), m. 1 (*Peroun* v. *Botiller*). The passage seems in fact to relate only to restrictions on essoins once the parties had pleaded to judgment or jury, but even these were not invariably prohibited so long as they did not hold up the case: CLRO, HR CP79, m. 18v (*Herpesfeld* v. *Prior of St Bartholomew's, West Smithfield*, plaintiff essoined after jury failed to appear).

[71] There seem to be no essoins for royal service recorded in the part-roll for 1320, so the 1345 'statutes' may have been merely confirmatory of existing practice in this respect. Essoins for royal service were however accepted in the Mayor's Court: *CalEMCR*, pp. 121, 122.

[72] Riley, *Munimenta Gildhallae*, I, p. 471, extracted from CLRO, MS LBF, fo. 105.

stage) to a further essoin before his next appearance. In 1311, for example, a series of respites combined with ten essoins on the part of the defendant in *Rothinge* v. *Staunford* helped to extend proceedings through thirty-one sessions and almost five months.[73] As the respites were the product of uncertainty on the part of the court, however, the defendant's essoins almost certainly only delayed judgment by a single session.

Judgment in default

In debt, and apparently also in account, there was the procedure known, in London as in other boroughs, as 'foreign attachment'.[74] The procedure had two aspects worthy of note. The first permitted plaintiffs, in the common event that the court's officers claimed to be unable to find anything within the city by which a defendant could be attached, to assert that there were in fact assets available and to arrange for their seizure. The second allowed the attachment of assets belonging to the defendant's debtor where the defendant's own goods and chattels were insufficient to cover the amounts claimed by the plaintiff.[75] If the debtor's debtor did not challenge the attachment by swearing that the defendant had no interest in the assets (because the 'debtor' in fact owed him nothing of any substance), and providing that the plaintiff or his attorney swore that the debt was genuinely owed, the assets were valued and handed over to the plaintiff under mainprise to keep for a year and a day. Should the defendant fail to appear to contest the action within that period, the assets were adjudged to the plaintiff.[76]

If all else failed, in debt cases the Sheriffs' Court would eventually authorise the valuation of (rents and other profits arising from) any lands and tenements that the absconding debtor held in the city and allow the plaintiff to recoup the sums due from them. Again, there was a safeguard which permitted the defendant, if he appeared within a year and day and was able to

[73] CLRO, HR CP36, m. 18.
[74] For its use in account, see *CalPMR 1413–37*, p. 35, a Mayor's Court case.
[75] TNA (PRO), Early Chancery Proceedings, C1/31, items 510, 64, 139 and CLRO, Mayor's Court Files of Original Bills, MC1/3A, items 8, 10.
[76] Riley, *Munimenta Gildhallae*, I, pp. 207–9; *Reports de les Cases . . . in temps del roy Henry le siz*, 22 Hen. VI, fo. 47v, pl. 2.

show that he owed nothing, to have the sums returned to him; thereafter, he could not reclaim them.[77]

Pleadings

In personal actions brought by writ, defendants did occasionally try to force the abandonment of the case on the grounds that there was discrepancy between the nature of the writ and the pleading: for example, that a plaintiff (whose writ complained that the defendant, 'plotting to defraud him', had removed abroad evidences relating to a debt owed to the plaintiff, together with both his own and the plaintiff's goods) had counted against the defendant as though this had been an action of debt, whereas 'no action of debt was mentioned in the writ'.[78] On the other hand, it was neither a common nor a successful stratagem in personal pleas even when brought by writ, and was of no use in actions brought informally because, after 1389 at least, the plaintiff could simply amend his bill or plaint up to the time when the issue was to be tried or judgment rendered, if it conflicted with his pleading.[79] Nor, despite the existence of a case from 1300 which the plaintiff lost, apparently, because he called the defendant 'Matthew' on one occasion and 'Maykin' on another, is there much to suggest that cases had to be abandoned and started again if, for example, surnames were misspelt.[80]

It was nevertheless a requirement in all actions brought according to law and custom that the defendant explicitly deny the allegation as a whole or in part.[81] Secondly, he had to offer a defence squarely to the allegation and not some general mitigation. Thus in the Sheriffs' Court detinue case just mentioned, *Rothinge* v. *Staunford*, a defendant who claimed that she had been robbed of a purse containing valuables was judged undefended because she did not deny undertaking to keep the purse safe and failing to do so. Saying that the purse had been sealed and that she

[77] Riley, *Munimenta Gildhallae*, I, pp. 216–17.
[78] CLRO, CP49, m. 16 (*Blank'* v. *Brunlesqe*, 1324); this was brought by a writ *ex gravi querela*, an example of its use in a non-testamentary case.
[79] *CalLBH*, p. 374, *Munimenta Gildhallae*, I, p. 218.
[80] *CalEMCR*, p. 100. The real issue here may have been that the plaintiff was trying to bring the same case twice.
[81] E.g. *CalEMCR*, p. 117.

had no means of knowing what was in it (and therefore could not know what she was supposedly 'detaining'), or offering to prove that she had been robbed, was not answer enough. Nor was it a sufficient answer to add that, as she had been bound and gagged, she had been unable to raise the hue and cry.[82] On the whole, however, the question at issue was whether a particular form of proof offered by one of the parties was appropriate to the type of action, superior to the form of proof offered by the other party, or sufficient to have the case dismissed.[83]

As to how the pleadings were physically presented to the court, the truncated form of most plea and memoranda enrolments, together with the evident tendency of the sheriff's clerks to omit details they considered irrelevant when compiling the return in cases in which error was alleged or the record appealed to, means that it is not possible to be sure when written pleadings were first introduced or became commonplace in the Mayor's or Sheriffs' Court. Certainly it cannot have happened by the beginning of our period. It was precisely because the pleadings were recorded by the sheriffs' clerks that the mayor and aldermen found it necessary in 1304 to set up a mechanism for dealing with Sheriffs' Court enrolments which allegedly omitted aspects of the parties' pleadings or failed to enrol them 'secundum quod allegantur et proponuntur'.[84]

At first sight, the evidence suggests that written pleadings started to become commonplace in the Mayor's and Sheriffs' Courts in the late 1460s or early 1470s, probably as the culmination of a slow process by which the clerks came increasingly to rely on documents supplied to them by the litigants. A 'memorandum' of 1414, which was entered in the plea and memoranda roll, appears to be a slightly modified copy of the plaintiff's original bill, since it is written in French, still the predominant language of Mayor's Court bills at this period, and refers to 'two schedules annexed' (not to the plea and memoranda roll) which recorded the assets of the plaintiff's late father. The rest of the

82 CLRO, HR CP36, mm. 18–18v.

83 CLRO, HR CP38, m. 24 (*Bevere* v. *Basyate*, 1313–4, wager of law allegedly not permitted in trespass); HR CP40, m. 4 (*Brunlesqe* v. *Jannoie*, debt: the plaintiff's production of two witnesses in an earlier plea of account had 'excluded the defendant from [waging] his law').

84 Riley, *Munimenta Gildhallae*, II, p. 90.

record of this case is in Latin, and, though very detailed, might well represent what had been said in court after the defendants (the father's executors) had had a chance to scrutinise a copy of the bill and had appeared in court a month later.[85] Presumably the additional material was written up by the court clerks. This is, moreover, the only evidence even of this limited use of a bill before 1462, when the original bill of Henry Hoggys of Whitchurch was recorded without modification, in English, with the rest of the proceedings recorded in Latin.[86] Additionally, in 1457 the extremely circumstantial testimony of one John Bracy was recorded in English, apparently verbatim. It seems much more likely that the clerk had it in writing than that he copied it down as Bracy spoke.[87] This use of bills and of written testimony to save on clerical effort may have accustomed the clerks to taking advantage of documents supplied by litigants, but, if it suggests anything, it is that written pleadings were not being employed in the Mayor's Court even in the early 1460s.

The situation at about this date would have been favourable to their introduction. By the late 1450s, the Sheriffs' Court (or, rather, no doubt, each side of the court) possessed a *liber causarum*.[88] It is by no means unlikely that the Mayor's Court had something similar, too. There survive from the seventeenth century some Mayor's Court *libri causarum* which were compiled by the clerk-attorneys for their own purposes, as a brief record of clients, their cases and the sums owed by them to the attorneys.[89] The fifteenth-century Sheriffs' Court 'book of causes [or cases]', however, was almost certainly different in form and purpose: it was either like the 'minute book' kept by each counter in the eighteenth century or was the equivalent of the Hustings session book.[90] Either way, by the late 1450s the Sheriffs' Court appears to have had books in which, probably, brief notes of lawsuits and of

[85] *CalPMR 1413–37*, pp. 6–7. [86] *CalPMR 1458–82*, pp. 28–30.

[87] *CalPMR 1437–57*, pp. 153–5 (the record is incomplete).

[88] CLRO, Sheriffs Register of Writs, fo. 26.

[89] CLRO, MS MC2A, vol. I, [Attorney James Gibson's] 'Liber Causarum, anno 3 Junij 1679. usque ad 28 Junij 1684'.

[90] CLRO, MS Sheriffs' Court (Poultry Counter) Minute Book, 1769–70. This listed, almost on a daily basis, the cases and process ordered on them. It is similar to the piepowder court books being kept by Southampton in the 1470s, although the entries in these books are rarely dated: see, e.g, SRO, Southampton Town Court Books, SC7/1/3 (Piepowder Court, 1474/5).

process upon them were kept; and this record, whether it was a court book which listed cases under session headings or a counter book which listed them as they were received at the counter, probably did not give much if anything in the way of detail about pleadings. Given that even some London common councilmen could still barely write their own names, the establishment of the office of writer of bills in the Sheriffs' Court, apparently in the early 1450s, would have made it easier for the court to demand legible documents from litigants, which could have included written pleadings.[91]

On this basis, it looks as though written pleadings were introduced in all the city's courts at much the same time as they appeared at Westminster. Tidy though that conclusion would be, however, it is virtually certain that it is incorrect. A form of written pleadings was probably in use in the Mayor's Court, at least, much earlier than this, by the 1370s or 1380s. In 1382, the Mayor's Court was keeping a separate file of 'bills terminated between Easter and the Feast of St John the Baptist'.[92] The reason for filing determined cases separately is probably that they were more likely than others to be written up in the plea and memoranda rolls, at the successful litigant's request, or for the court's own purposes, as was the case in the Husting after 1448. By the second half of the fourteenth century, bills formed a part of the record which could quite easily be used for later reference. The Mayor's Court bills and petitions of the late 1360s onwards are frequently annotated with details of process and determination, as are the early fifteenth-century *querelae levatae*.[93] Moreover, the earliest surviving file of original bills contains just the sort of ancillary documents needed to supplement a session or counter book. Two of these included notes recording the responses by both parties in two cases brought against the same defendant, John Pecche, sometime after August 1366, and a third containing Pecche's pleadings alone.[94] There is also another example of composite written pleadings in a case brought by William

[91] CLRO, Recognizance Roll 21, mm. 2, 2v, William Basset and John Rympyngdon admitted to the freedom in that office, 1452.

[92] *CalPMR 1381–1412*, pp. 16–17.

[93] E.g. CLRO, Mayor's Court File of Original Bills, MC1/1, item 4, which is annotated at the top and down the left-hand side.

[94] *Ibid.*, MC1/1, items 133, 134 (this refers to Pecche's loss of the freedom in 1366), and 135.

Cressoner against two parsons in 1368.[95] Both the individual and the composite pleadings could possibly have been notes taken in court, although they look rather too neat for that; but it is not clear why a clerk would bother to file them if the court still had a plea roll in which the same information was recorded. So it seems likely that the Mayor's Court had stopped maintaining a plea roll by the third quarter of the fourteenth century, at the very latest. Moreover, it is far from certain that a court clerk *qua* clerk was responsible for producing even the composite pleadings in the cases involving Pecche and Cressoner. For reasons given below in relation to the Sheriffs' Court, there are grounds for thinking that attorneys might have been responsible for producing these documents. Whether that is so or not, written pleadings cannot have been coming into use for the first time by the late 1460s. Not only is there evidence that a decade earlier they were being filed separately from the bills, but even in the 1420s there are references to the common clerk and other clerks working for him being paid 'to enter a plea and replication' and the like, which is strongly suggestive of written pleadings.[96]

Since no original Sheriffs' Court bill appears to survive for our period, we have no means of knowing whether the Mayor's Court, being much less formal in its record-keeping than the Sheriffs' Court was in the late fourteenth century, abandoned a formal plea roll earlier than the Sheriffs' Court did. That a sheriff's sergeant could still, in the 1460s, claim that the Mayor's Court was 'not a court of record' might (perhaps) suggest that there were differences between the record-keeping practices of the two courts even at this date.[97] On the other hand, with the last London eyre having taken place in 1341, and given that personal actions did not normally involve matters which would require the court to keep a formal record of the outcome for year after year, the temptation to

[95] *Ibid.*, MC1/1, item 142, beginning 'A la bille avaundit les ditz Geffrey & Wauter fasont protestacion'. The related bill is item 149, which has proforma elements (gaps left and subsequently filled in with names, for example, 'Et predicti *Galfridus* & *Walter* in propris personis'). This file also contains written notes of summons, attachments, receipts, attorney appointments, and jury and wardmote inquest verdicts.

[96] *Ibid.*, MC1/3A, items 16, 192, which refer to 'X pleading as on the file'; GH Library, Microfilm 297, Merchant Taylors Accounts, I, fo. 146.

[97] CLRO, Jor. 7, fo. 72.

make record-keeping simpler and easier would have been as great in the Sheriffs' Court as in the Mayor's. It may be that we can trace the steps involved. In 1345, attorneys working in the Husting were required to keep proper notes and to confer with the common clerk in order to ensure that their clients' pleas were accurately recorded.[98] Herein, we may have the origin of written pleadings. If the attorneys were not only taking detailed notes of the pleadings, but the clerks were expected to use them when writing up the formal record even in the Husting, it is hardly surprising that the clerks should in due course have ceased to bother to make notes of the pleadings themselves. That would be particularly true, if the attorneys could be trusted to record the pleadings accurately. And, as we shall see in Chapter 8, the relationship between the city's courts and the majority of the attorneys working in them probably was, for much of the fourteenth century, a close one.

So, while the form of the early written pleadings, at least in the Mayor's Court, may have differed from and been more variable than that which was normal by the 1470s, it is likely that these documents were in use occasionally in both the Mayor's and the Sheriffs' Courts well before 1400. By the 1450s, they were probably numerous and commonplace.

USE OF EVIDENCE IN CITY COURTS

If the Husting rolls are any guide, a significant amount of time in contested cases in that court was spent challenging the demandant's writ or either parties' pleadings rather than in examining sources of evidence.[99] Litigants nevertheless certainly offered evidence to support their claims.[100] Deeds, including wills and other documents recorded in the court's own rolls, were one of the main sources of evidence relied upon by litigants in the Husting.

[98] CLRO, MS LBF, fo. 105, printed in Riley, *Munimenta Gildhallae* I, p. 473.

[99] E.g., CLRO, HR PL14, m. 15v (*Passener* v. *Nedding*), HR PL15, m. 11 (*Treyere* v. *Alegate*), HR PL18, m. 10v (*Scardeburgh* v. *Tulesan*), HR PL22, m. 3 (*Wyke* v. *Laufare*). This was despite claims that city custom allowed a certain laxity in pleadings, a claim which, as we have seen, was to some extent justified: CLRO, HR PL15, m. 11 (*Treyere* v. *Alegate*).

[100] E.g., letters testifying that the demandant had been divorced, and letters from the mayor of Lynne testifying that the demandant had been detained by a serious illness rather than in prison: CLRO, HR PL23, m. 3v, PL17, m. 4.

Witnesses were also sometimes referred to. Occasionally they reinforced the jury as an investigative instrument: in two early cases, the issue in one instance was put to a jury and Robert de Arraz, 'together with other witnesses nominated by the Court', and in another the court ordered that the matter should be enquired into by a jury and named witnesses.[101] In two more cases, from 1317 and 1318, both the jury and witnesses (to an allegedly false deed, in the first instance) were summoned to court.[102] More unusually, there is a reference in 1298 to witnesses for the defendant being 'sworn and separately examined'.[103] There are fewer references to witnesses or 'informers' in later years, though they do occur.[104] Whether the clerks simply omitted references of this type later, when the record tends to be more formal and stylised, or whether it became less common for witnesses to appear in the Husting, there seems to be no way of knowing.

In personal actions, city custom accepted a greater variety of forms of evidence, from sealed or signed documents through negotiable instruments (that is, IOUs which were transferable to third parties) to a plaintiff's bare word; although the slighter the evidence of the debt, the easier it was, naturally enough, for the defendant to disclaim it. City courts would accept the sworn or unsworn testimony of witnesses that the debt had been incurred or paid; they would also examine the plaintiff on oath or otherwise if the defendant alleged part-payment.[105] Actions could therefore be brought to recover debts even when the plaintiff was unable to produce physical evidence of the alleged indebtedness.[106] Equally, the absence of physical evidence of the repayment of a debt was not necessarily fatal to the defendant.

101 CLRO, HR PL15, m. 6 (1288), *CalEMCR*, p. 58 (1300), HR PL26, m. 9v (1304).

102 CLRO, HR PL38, m. 29, HR PL39, m. 6v.

103 CLRO, HR PL21, m. 17.

104 CLRO, HR PL73, m. 4 (witnesses failed to agree on, among other things, the hour, day or place of the making of John de Godefeld's testament, and were punished for their evident collusion in an attempted fraud); for a late instance of 'informers' being added to a jury, see *CalPMR 1381–1412*, pp. 41–2 (1383).

105 E.g., CLRO, Jor. 4, fos. 123–4, Jor. 7, fos. 114v, 125v, 130 (witnesses sworn/sworn on the bible), 124v (witnesses merely said to have affirmed/been examined according to conscience).

106 *Munimenta Gildhallae*, I, p. 214.

Another source of information available to the city's courts for most of the fourteenth century was the jury. In 1389, it was the expressed opinion of the city's judges that jurors existed to inform them.[107] Consequently, city juries were subject, not only to selected additions to their ranks, but also to cross-examination, to manipulation of their composition, and even to rejection of their verdict by the bench. That information-giving was originally the purpose of English juries, there is of course no doubt; and the editor of the early Mayor's Court rolls provides a number of examples to demonstrate this, including other instances of juries being questioned to elicit further information, from the end of the thirteenth century and until the end of the fourteenth.[108] The record of the original session in 1389 also shows that the jurors were not simply left to return a general verdict. The plaintiff claimed that his version had been 'abundantly affirmed by the verdict of the jury given in answer to questions by the court'.[109] It is not clear whether the jurors were responding to a set of questions or articles given to them in advance, which is what the phraseology rather suggests, or whether the court questioned them upon their verdict afterwards; but, given the approach taken by the bench in other cases at this period, it is likely enough that the judges were in the habit of asking the jurors whatever they pleased.

It is therefore not surprising that we find witnesses and 'informers' being added to juries in the fourteenth century; their functions were not dissimilar. Indeed, as we shall see shortly, their functions overlapped in other ways. Witnesses as informants appear to have been regarded with favour. Information-giving by, and examination by the court or its deputies of, a whole range of expert and casual informants, including of course the parties themselves, in and out of formal session, seems to have been a normal mode of conduct.[110] Even so exalted a person as Thomas Young, then a justice of King's Bench, appeared as a sworn witness before the mayor, aldermen and recorder in 1476.[111]

[107] *CalPMR 1381–1412*, p. 157. [108] *CalEMCR*, pp. xlii–xliii, 16, 31, 40.
[109] *CalPMR 1381–1412*, p. 157; *ibid.*, p. 160.
[110] *CalPMR 1437–57*, pp. 11–12, 20–1, 26–7 (public testimonies); for references to aldermen examining the parties or witnesses: *CalLBI*, p. 80; Riley, *Munimenta Gildhallae*, I, p. 217; *CalEMCR*, pp. 183–4; *CalPMR 1458–82*, p. 29.
[111] CLRO, Jor. 8, fo. 133v.

When in doubt the court examined as many witnesses as it possibly could, and it would make do with one credible witness if that was all there was.[112] Experts, from the four sworn 'Viewers' or city surveyors, who routinely reported to the court in assizes of nuisance and in other property-related disputes from the early fourteenth century onwards (formerly a committee of aldermen had been required to inspect the alleged nuisance themselves), to medical practitioners of various types and the 'matrons' who examined female victims of alleged sexual offences, were also quite familiar figures in the city courts.[113]

Examination on details, to establish both the quality of the witness's knowledge and the reliability of his memory, seems to have been standard practice. In an early fourteenth-century case, the first witness was prompted to say what colour clothing the defendant was wearing, exactly when he and the plaintiff had had their alleged meeting, and who else was present.[114] Under examination in a Mayor's Court case in 1464, the single witness described a meeting held in the presence of a notary, at which one of the litigants in a court case had sought to find out what evidence the witness had given either during an audit of account or at an earlier hearing, and to persuade him to sign a deed stating that he had not seen a particular account book before.[115] The witness's recollection was clearly cloudy. When another witness testified before the mayor and aldermen in 1461 that he had seen one Jacob Doode going into another man's house on a certain date, he was asked whether he knew Doode; to which he replied, Yes, he had often seen him in Lombard Street.[116] A year later, in *Davy* v. *Brandon* (the keeper of the Fleet prison), the court questioned a witness in ways that threw doubt on Brandon's version of events. This was done at Davy's request, 'so that trought [truth] might be

[112] *CalPMR 1437–57*, pp. 99–100 (many witnesses being 'examined separately in the ... Chamber of the Guildhall'); CLRO, Jor. 7, fo. 87 (single witness). It is, incidentally, not the case, during the later part of our period at least, that churchmen could not testify in the city courts, as was claimed in 1276: Weinbaum, *Eyre 1276*, p. 104, cited in Kiralfy, 'Custom in Medieval English Law', p. 37; see Jor. 6, photo. 500, for the examination of 'W. Kymberley, priest' (1461).

[113] Chew, Kellaway, *Assize of Nuisance*, pp. xix–xx (surveyors); CLRO, Jor. 6, photo. 528, Jor. 8, fo. 19 (doctors and apothecaries); Jor. 7, fos. 188v–9 (matrons).

[114] *CalEMCR*, pp. 242–3. [115] CLRO, Jor. 7, fo. 87.

[116] CLRO, Jor. 6, photo. 500.

knowen'.[117] The case of *Herell* v. *Lambard /Basingthwaite* (1471) also throws light on the methods used. One witness, for example, was asked if he was prepared to swear to the authenticity of an unsealed document, which he claimed was a copy of an indictment for a felony allegedly committed by Mrs Herell's father: he insisted that he was telling the truth but declined to take an oath. Another witness, testifying on oath, was asked whether he knew for a fact that the man he accused of stealing a salt-cellar from him had done so; he replied that he did not, but that 'he supposed by his conscience' that the matter was as he alleged. These examinations were often important for the outcome of the case. *Herell* v. *Lambard /Basingthwaite* turned largely on the credibility of these witnesses (including a ward beadle). The mayor and aldermen eventually declared the accusation that Mrs Herell's father lived a riotous life was 'insufficiently proved'.[118]

The examination of witnesses did not of course eliminate error. The fact that the court accepted the testimony of witnesses as evidence offered scope for abuse, although there is little evidence of its actual occurrence.[119] The real difficulty seems to have lain in the nature of witness evidence itself. In a scandalous case in which John Wetherley, a prisoner, accused Sheriff Simon Smith of extortion, the mayor and aldermen went to considerable lengths to examine the janitor and other staff of the Poultry counter, and indeed the other sheriff, in order to test Wetherley's claims. These examinations convinced them, as they said, that Smith was indeed guilty of wrongdoing. It was only when further witnesses came forward that it became clear that Wetherley had lied.[120] Yet there is no suggestion that the staff at the Poultry counter had deliberately assisted Wetherley. Probably their evidence had failed to convince the Court of Aldermen that the sheriff had acted properly.

METHODS OF DETERMINATION

The penultimate step in all forms of action was for one party to offer to prove his case by an appropriate method. The most

[117] *Ibid.*, Jor. 6, photo. 545.
[118] *CalPMR 1458–82*, pp. 24–7; *ibid.*, pp. 57–64, especially 62–3, CLRO, Jor. 8, fo. 9; also CLRO, HR CP79, m. 22.
[119] For a rare example of a confession of two perjurers, see CLRO, Jor. 8, m. 67.
[120] CLRO, Jor. 7, fos. 187v, 191–1v.

familiar of these in English law today is the jury, the use of which is largely confined to criminal trials. In the Middle Ages, however, the jury was more commonly employed in civil cases than it is today. In such cases, both parties were supposed to agree to 'put themselves on their country' (the jury); in practice, there seem to be no examples of outright refusals. Rather, reluctant litigants continued to offer alternative methods of trial until it became clear that they would have to accept a jury on a specific issue or be judged undefended.[121] The only significant formal restriction on its employment in city courts came in 1518; cases in the Court of Requests could not go to a jury.

While juries were evidently regarded by the city authorities for most of the fourteenth century as sources of information rather than as a method of determination, such attitudes may well not have persisted much beyond the 1390s. Juries certainly continued to give their verdicts in detail, offering the bench the opportunity to query their findings. It is therefore possible that the reason why a case was adjourned in December 1480 to allow the jury to obtain 'fuller advice' was that the court had found its answers to questions inadequate.[122] It seems unlikely, however. It is probably significant that the 1389 case was appealed because of the decision not to accept a jury's verdict. Certainly there do not appear to be any other recorded examples of the court itself deciding on the composition of a jury (although litigants could of course challenge individual jurors and, in some cases, could request specially composed juries) or refusing to accept a verdict. And it is doubtful whether by the later fifteenth century any city court saw a jury as simply a source of evidence. It is therefore much more likely that in the 1480 case the bench was responding to the jurors' sense of their inadequacy for the task; and what prompted that was the fact that the jury no longer controlled its own acquisition of knowledge. 'Fuller advice' was an apt phrase. The role played by juries was an increasingly passive one: rather than being 'self-informing', they were informed by others (if they chose to listen). In 1492 a city jury was accused of refusing 'to hear or give credence to any evidence given to them on the defendant's part'.[123] Fifteenth-century jurors seem to have been expected to behave

[121] E.g. CLRO, HR PL23, m. 3v (*Sutton* v. *Essex*).
[122] *CalPMR 1448–82*, pp. 48, 82, 144. [123] CLRO, Rep. 9, fo. 280.

much like the Aldersgate wardmote inquest jury of Elizabeth I's reign. The wardmote jurors, according to their instructions, simply sat on a bench behind a table in the hall for five hours from eight in the morning on specified days. Anyone who wished to bring some offence or nuisance to the jury's attention had to call on them there. No attempt was made to carry out any further investigations: the jury made its mind up on the basis of the statements given to it by the parties concerned.[124] The probability is that the parties in fifteenth-century personal actions expected their jury, too, to do little more than listen to their version of events and to examine any proofs or witnesses that they might bring along.

Clearly the Elizabethan wardmote jury heard evidence outside court. Yet John Fortescue, writing in the 1470s but presumably with his time as chief justice of King's Bench in the 1440s and 1450s in mind, described the provision of information to the jury as occurring in court. According to him, the jurors were sworn and immediately had the record and the particular issue on which they were to pronounce read out to them. The parties or their representatives then made their declarations and responses, adduced their evidence, including the testimony of sworn witnesses, and explained its significance. Thereupon the jurors withdrew to confer and, returning, gave their verdict.[125] This sounds very much like a truncated version of the procedure employed in modern trials.

If Fortescue was telling the truth, there was little opportunity for the jury to brief itself in advance or out of court, and the process of providing it with information was firmly under the court's control. But perhaps the explanation for the apparent contradiction between his account and what we know of the conduct of city juries is that the procedure adopted differed, depending on whether the case was a civil or criminal one, and, in the case of the latter, whether the jury was a jury of presentment or indictment (roughly equivalent to a modern American grand jury, which considers whether there is any case to answer) or a petty (trial) jury. It may well be that the petty jurors who appeared before Fortescue in King's Bench were indeed expected

[124] GH Library, Aldersgate Wardmote Minutes 1467–1801, fos. 57v, 1.
[125] Chrimes, *Fortescue, De Laudibus Legum Anglie*, p. 61.

to reach their verdict rapidly, on the basis of evidence collected by the presenting jurors (some of whom could be included in the petty jury), information offered by the prosecution and defendant, and any pleadings, whereas civil and presenting juries were allowed time to gather information. There is certainly evidence by the later fifteenth century of delays between the empanelling of London trial juries in civil litigation and the hearing of the case.[126] Alternatively, it is possible that practice changed sometime in the course of the fifteenth century, and that Fortescue's account simply became outdated within a few decades of its creation. The city records of the fourteenth and early fifteenth centuries also give the impression that the jury was empanelled, elected and sworn and gave its verdict, except for a few instances, on the same day.[127] The plea and memoranda rolls note just one example, from 1399, when the jury in a city court asked for a week's respite before giving its verdict.[128] The one exception was the assize jury (which was not, of course, strictly speaking a 'city jury'). In 1393 it was ordered that these juries should be empanelled several days before their verdict was taken, '[i]ssint qe les parties poent avoir la copie et conyssance de les nouns qi passerount en mesme lAssise'.[129] It seems very likely that the aim was to allow two or three days in which the parties could put their side of the argument to the jury. If so, it can hardly have been done in court. From the early 1460s onwards, however, there are a fair number of examples of adjournments to allow the trial jury 'to be better advised' or because it could not agree. In a Sheriffs' Court case from 1461, the delay was of over two months, and in 1475–6, in a Mayor's Court case, the jury was summoned in October and finally returned its verdict in June (although, admittedly, this delay included jury defaults).[130] Clearly, however these juries were

[126] For late fifteenth-century juries of presentment at sessions of the peace, but apparently not petty juries, being routinely given 'an hour or a day for their verdict', see, e.g., the detailed directions contained in SRO, 'Fifteenth Century Formulary', SC2/8, fos. 129–9v.

[127] E.g., CLRO, HR CP110, m. 20v, a Sheriffs' Court case, where it appears that the jury appeared for the first time on 16 November 1385, the day it gave its verdict and taxed the damages; Riley, *Munimenta Gildhallae*, I, pp. 519–20.

[128] *CalPMR 1381–1412*, p. 266.

[129] Riley, *Munimenta Gildhallae*, I, pp. 519–20.

[130] For trial jurors who 'took a day to geve therin their veredite' after being empanelled (1467), see CLRO, Jor. 7, fo. 139v (but note that this could have been in a possessory assize) and *CalPMR 1457–82*, pp. 23–4, 94, 144.

informing themselves in order to reach their verdict, it was not, or not entirely, before their first formal appearance, and it was almost certainly not in court. If practice did alter in this way over time, it might perhaps reflect changes in the way that trial juries were expected to inform themselves and, consequently, how they were regarded by the bench and parties alike.

Information-giving out of court seems to have remained common practice for at least a hundred years after that. It was clearly normal in the 1570s for advocates and counsel to 'give in evydence' to city juries outside court, since the way that the city sought to prevent foreign pleaders doing this alone was to disallow any bill of costs resulting from their activity unless a common pleader was charged for at the same time. (Had this evidence-giving occurred in court, of course, it would have been possible to take direct action against the intruders.)[131] R. Tittler's investigation of the first references to juryrooms in town guildhalls and courtrooms likewise suggests that trial juries in other boroughs were continuing to obtain their information outside court until the second half of the sixteenth century. Indeed, the apparent absence of any reference to a juryroom at Guildhall during the sixteenth century suggests that London may have been slow even compared to much smaller boroughs to segregate juries in court to allow them to consider their verdict in private.[132]

An alternative to the trial by jury in personal actions was a procedure known as 'trial by witnesses'. The phrase is somewhat misleading: then as now, the witnesses were sources of information.[133] Unlike today, however, their testimony could under certain circumstances be determinative. In medieval London, a longstanding city custom permitted one of the parties to offer to prove his case by producing two witnesses. They were then examined under oath by a couple of aldermen, and, if their testimony agreed in every particular, judgment was given accordingly.[134] (Having said that the witnesses failed in the proof

[131] CLRO, Rep 19, fo. 271v.

[132] Tittler, 'Sequestration of Juries in Early Modern England', p. 302.

[133] See comments in Bellamy, *Crime and Public Order in the Later Middle Ages*, p. 148, and fn. 42, citing *CalPR 1381–84*, p. 381, where a London cordwainer is said to have been 'by witnesses sworn and examined adjudged to death', which suggests that judgment lay with the witnesses rather than the examiners.

[134] *CalEMCR*, pp. xxxvii–xxxix; and see pp. 138, 182.

if they did not agree with each other exactly, allowance was made for genuine lapses of memory, if the differences were not critical to the party's case.)[135] The journals contain numerous examples of two witnesses testifying that they were present when a bargain was struck, or that the debtor had confessed his debt in their presence.[136] There was nevertheless a suspicion of sworn witnesses: an ordinance of 1358 forebade their use in the Sheriffs' Court as a way of preventing the defendant from waging his law, on the grounds that witnesses of this type were easily and commonly bribed.[137]

Wager of law, also known as 'proof by oath-helpers', was another alternative to the jury. Initially, it allowed a litigant who was a freeman (or freewoman) to offer to clear himself by swearing to the truth of what he said, either by himself or with the backing of a number of trustworthy neighbours, and sometimes additional freemen, who were prepared to swear 'according to their conscience that the oath was true'; in effect, since they were not expected to know the facts, that they believed that the individual concerned was telling the truth. In civil actions, six oath-helpers were usually required, although fewer or more are to be found.[138] Providing that all got through their oath without hesitation or error, proof had been made. Wager of law was available as a method of trial in all actions, including violent trespass, until the city was taken under the king's direct control in 1285.[139] Thereafter, a defendant who was accused of assault which resulted in bloodshed or moderately serious harm was forced to accept a jury unless the

[135] *CalEMCR*, pp. 182–4 (where it was a difference between the sum claimed by the plaintiff and recollected as owing by the witnesses, rather than that one witness remembered the plaintiff using a 'schedule' during the reckoning whereas the other did not, that was critical) and 242 (where the evidence was merely said to be 'similar').

[136] E.g. CLRO, Jor. 7, fos. 228 (*bis*), 228v–9, 229, 231, 231v–2, 232, 234v (*bis*), 235, 236, 237, 238v (*bis*), 239v, 240 (*bis*), 240v, 241, 241v (*bis*), 242, 242v (*bis*), 243v, 244, 244v (witness depositions, mainly by pairs of witnesses).

[137] CLRO, LBG, fo. 92; the city 'statutes' of 1345 required that witnesses should be reputable, not suspect, and 'ne pas commune seutiers ne proeves devaunt lez Ordinaries au Seint Poule [Paul's] ne aillours': Riley, *Munimenta Gildhallae*, I, p. 475.

[138] *CalEMCR*, pp. 17–18 (two), CLRO, Jor. 7, fo. 209 (twenty-four).

[139] Riley, *Munimenta Gildhallae*, I, p. 204; *CalEMCR*, pp. 105 (wager of law allowed in debt), 113 (in detinue), 121 (in covenant), 132 (in account), 97–8 (in trespass (defamation)), 139 (in trespass (assault)) and see fn. 1.

plaintiff agreed to allow him to wage his law.[140] Contrariwise, it was extended by parliamentary statute in 1363/4 to foreign defendants in debt cases in which the plaintiff relied on 'papers' rather than a sealed document as evidence of the debt.[141]

In the Mayor's and Sheriffs' Courts it was also possible for one party to challenge the other to take an oath immediately, by himself, as to the truth of an otherwise unsupported claim or denial (the 'peremptory oath').[142] Third parties whose assets had been seized in the course of an attachment, foreign or otherwise (that is, in the defendant's hands or not), were also permitted to swear alone that the defendant in the original case had no interest in the goods.[143] In certain circumstances – where, for example, a litigant was prepared to make unsworn claims but not to repeat them on oath, or where the challenger himself was uncertain about the truth of his opponent's claim – it no doubt provided a swift and effective means of deciding the issue.

Finally, an entry in the Husting rolls in the middle of the fourteenth century reminds us of a method of determination which was almost certainly even more common in the Mayor's and Sheriffs' Courts. The mayor and five aldermen, we are told, had a discussion (*colloquium*) in full court and decided that a woman claiming to be the nearer relative to the deceased should have the disputed property.[144] What was said in the early fifteenth century of the sheriffs – that they were 'accustomed to examine the parties in all personal pleas pending before them, each apart, and to proceed to judgment upon their findings' – was probably equally true of the mayor and aldermen throughout our period.[145]

Although only one method of trial (the peremptory oath) was not available in the Husting at the beginning of our period, there was a very strong bias towards two methods. In cases begun by writ which were contested to the end, in practice the only normal methods of determining a real or mixed action after 1300 was either for one of the parties to produce incontrovertible proof that he had the right to the property (for example, a sealed deed which the other litigant could not show was a forgery) or for both of them to put the issue to a jury. Of nearly 1200 Husting cases

140 Riley, *Munimenta Gildhallae*, I, p. 294. 141 *Statutes of the Realm*, I, p. 384.
142 Riley, *Munimenta Gildhallae*, I, p. 521, *CalEMCR*, pp, xxxv–xxxvi.
143 *CalEMCR*, pp. 95, 17–18. 144 CLRO, HR PL71, m. 5.
145 Riley, *Munimenta Gildhallae*, I, p. 217.

brought between 1272 and 1448 (excluding pleas of naam) with an outcome that has been traced, only some two hundred were fought to the end. Of this smaller number, about three-quarters went to a jury and about a fifth were decided by the production of conclusive evidence. (The remainder were either dismissed as having been brought before, or decided by wager of law, which effectively disappeared from the Husting after 1298.)[146]

The jury was less frequently sought in personal than in real and mixed actions. In the summer of 1320 litigants in the Sheriffs' Court put themselves on a jury in 28 per cent of contested cases. In the Mayor's Court in the 1450s, about half of the contested cases were determined by a jury.[147] It was most commonly employed in trespass cases; as the numbers of trespass cases increased, so, probably, did the use of the jury. Nevertheless, it seems never to have been as popular a method of determination in either the Mayor's or the Sheriffs' Court during our period as it was, even in 1300, in the Husting.

Waging one's law remained quite a popular method of determination in both the Mayor's and the Sheriffs' Court. Defendants continued to wage their law in the city courts throughout our period, as far as one can tell: it was the method of trial in over a quarter of determined Sheriffs' Court cases in 1320 and over a third of determined Mayor's Court cases in the late 1450s. By contrast, the peremptory oath was probably never a common way of determining a case. Examples can nevertheless be found throughout the late thirteenth and fourteenth centuries and even into the first half of the fifteenth century, after which it may have fallen out of favour.[148]

FINES, DAMAGES AND COSTS

After the case had been pleaded to issue (the parties had identified the fundamental question in dispute between them which could

[146] An exception occurred in 1332, when a defendant was allowed to wage his law that he had not been summoned to court by the sheriffs, as they claimed; but this was a different matter: CLRO, HR PL53, m. 15.

[147] Based on 157 cases in CLRO, Sheriffs' Court Roll (1320) and 24 cases in CLRO, Mayor's Court Roll MC1/3A (excluding non-prosecutions and persistent defaults by the defendants).

[148] *Munimenta Gildhallae*, I, pp. 217, 521; *CalEMCR*, pp. 13–14, 66–7, 122–3, *CalPMR 1323–64*, pp. 119–20, *CalPMR 1381–1412*, pp. 13, 19, 77, 224, 230, 268–9; *CalPMR 1413–37*, p. 31.

be tried by a method appropriate to that type of action) and had been tried, the awards and penalties for the losing party naturally also varied. As we have seen, whether damages were awarded depended on the specific type of action, not on its nature. As far as real and mixed actions were concerned, they were available in waste, mesne and, in due course, in dower, but not in right, customs and services and partition, where successful demandants merely recovered their property or rents, or in naam.[149] Even then, the way in which damages were assessed varied according to the reason why they were awarded at all. In dower, mesne and waste, one of the tasks of the jury was to assess the value of any profit lost or waste done; but whereas in waste successful demandants got punitive damages (three times the value of the waste), 'according to the statute', and there may well have been a punitive element in some awards of damages in mesne, in dower they merely recovered the profits they had been denied by tenants who prolonged litigation excessively.[150] And even this limited award of damages in dower was an advance on the position before 1345. Until then widows had apparently received nothing in compensation for any part of the income withheld between their husband's death and the judgment in their favour, a situation which might well explain why widows were being 'longement and tortenousment delaies de lour dowere avoire'. Even then, it looks as though damages would only be awarded if, firstly, the tenants continued to deny the demandant's right to dower from the property in dispute after the initial stages of

[149] Pollock, Maitland, *History of English Law*, II, pp. 597; Riley, *Munimenta Gildhallae*, I, pp. 182, 185, 187, 188. Despite the explicit statement in 'Liber Albus' to the contrary, damages certainly were claimed in naam on occasion at the beginning of our period, possibly because it was not yet standard practice to bring cases alleging official wrongdoing in the Sheriffs' Court (see below, p. 204): compare CLRO, HR CP3, m. 1 (*Nedding* v. *Evesham*, no damages awarded) with HR CP2, m. 1 (*Uggele* v. *Vicar of St Botolph without Aldersgate*, damages claimed, the defendant justified the distraint, and the issue went to jury).

[150] Riley, *Munimenta Gildhallae*, I, p. 187; CLRO, HB1, fos. 44v (*Prior of St Bartholomew, West Smithfield* v. *Trevilian*, waste), 104 (*Cook* v. *Waver*, dower). In mesne, the sum claimed sometimes far exceeded the loss sustained by the demandant: e.g., CLRO, HR CP42, m. 26 (*Secheford* v *Rys*, 100*s* damages claimed, distrained to the value of 6*s* 8*d*).

process (up to the view) were over, and, secondly, the demandant asked for them.[151]

Before the fifteenth century, there seems to be no way of knowing whether successful demandants were awarded costs in Husting cases, even in those types of action in which damages were available. By the 1460s, however, costs were definitely being awarded to successful demandants in dower cases: in *Lawys* v. *Sudbury*, a case which lasted for twenty months, damages were assessed by the jury at £10 13*s* 4*d*, with costs of 5 marks (£3 6*s* 8*d*).[152]

One penalty which was always imposed (if sometimes 'condoned' or set aside because, for example, the person concerned was poor, a minor or a city officer) was the amercement or court fine.[153] Litigants who lost, defaulted (on each occasion that they defaulted), failed to prosecute their case or came to an agreement were liable to pay an amercement to the court.[154] Those who acted as pledges were likewise liable to amercement if they failed to do as they had undertaken to do – providing, of course, that they were real people. It was presumably the litigant who actually footed the bill, particularly when the litigant's attorney acted as one of his pledges.

Unfortunately, there seems to be nothing to show how much litigants were normally fined in the Husting, assuming that there was a set level or levels of fine. Although the sixteenth-century Husting books record a number of payments to the city chamber (financial department), they are invariably for enrolments of deeds, indentures, testaments and other documents.[155] All we know is that, certainly at the beginning of our period and possibly still at its end, the sheriffs were entitled to receive those fines. This may explain why receipts of amercements are not also recorded in the Husting books, since by the sixteenth century these were written up by the Mayor's Court clerks.[156]

151 Riley, *Munimenta Gildhallae*, I, p. 470; and see, e.g. *Poures* v. *Bristoll* (1346), where the demandants recovered the dower, but no damages are mentioned, whereas in a case from the next decade, *Bedels* v. *atte Pye*, damages were successfully sought: CLRO, HR CP70, m. 19v; HR CP79, m. 26.

152 CLRO, HB1, fo. 48v.

153 E.g., *CalEMCR*, p. 94 (defendant was poor), CLRO, Hr CP74, m. 14v (defendant was a minor).

154 E.g. CLRO, HB1, fo. 48v (*Lawys* v. *Sudbury*).

155 CLRO, HB3, fos. 7, 19v, 27v, 35, 95, *et seq.*

156 Riley, *Munimenta Gildhallae*, I, p. 190; it was Common Clerk William Blackwell who, in 1551, noted in Husting Book 3 that a sheriff's secondary had paid him for enrolling various documents therein: CLRO, HB3, fo. 183v.

Personal actions brought under the Statutes of Merchants and the Staple could result in the imprisonment of the losing defendant.[157] In personal pleas where the penalties were not prescribed by statute, however, prison as a punishment, as opposed to a way of preventing the defendant from absconding before paying any sums and fines due, appears to have been almost unknown in the early part of our period.[158] This was so even when the trespass of which the defendant had been convicted involved 'beating', 'wounding' and the like (and it is clear from the jury verdicts that some of these assaults, which involved edged weapons, could have been quite dangerous).[159] It was more common for the parties to agree compensation between them than for the case to be determined in court with a judgment against the defendant and imprisonment pending fine.[160] Contempt of court or of the city's governors, on the other hand, was likely to result in imprisonment.[161]

From the beginning of our period, plaintiffs could ask for damages in trespass cases heard in the Sheriffs' Court. These, if the matter went to trial, were usually but not always taxed (assessed) by the jury, generally at a much lower value than the plaintiff had claimed.[162] The only other type of personal action in which damages were awarded in this court in the early 1300s was covenant.[163] In 1345, however, it was decided that in debt cases damages should be awarded to cover the period between the first court to which the defendant had been summoned (assuming that

[157] *CalEMCR*, p. 108.

[158] Although Robert, clerk of St Botolph without Aldgate, was imprisoned, despite having found sureties for bail, because he had carried arms contrary to the king's proclamation; contempt cases such as this did usually result in imprisonment (see below): CLRO, Sheriffs' Court Roll (1320), m. 25.

[159] See *ibid.*, m. 3 (*Toppesfelde* v. *Eye*, *le Rede* v. *atte Marche*) and *CalEMCR* p. 190.

[160] E.g., *CalEMCR*, pp. 94, 95, but, contrariwise, pp. 180, 189–90.

[161] *CalEMCR*, pp. 111, 198.

[162] E.g., in *Muchford* v. *Kersaulton* and *Eppinghethe* v. *Faber*, both plaintiffs claimed 40*s* damages, and were awarded 6*d* (about 1 per cent) and 40*d* (about 8 per cent): CLRO, Sheriffs' Court Roll (1320), m. 7.

[163] For its award in covenant in two cases in 1305, see *CalEMCR*, pp. 243 (but possibly heard and determined according to merchant law) and 263–4 (a dispute over an agreement to sell a house). For the absence of awards in other types of personal action, see CLRO, HR CP43, mm. 4–4v (*Jannoie* v. *Brunlesqe*, 1318, debt), Sheriffs' Court Roll (1320), m. 3v (*Scot* v. *Hopton*, detinue).

he did not immediately acknowledge the debt) and execution of the judgment.[164] There seems to be no evidence from the surviving records to show whether or not damages were in fact awarded in debt cases brought in the Sheriffs' Court immediately after this provision was enacted, but in 1356, it was decreed that successful plaintiffs should be allowed a fixed rate of 4*s* in the pound, and damages were certainly being claimed by the 1390s. Moreover, under the 1356 provisions, defendants in cases – apparently all personal pleas – involving a 'failure of prosecution' could claim unspecified 'reasonable' damages.[165] Damages continued to be unavailable in detinue and account; and there was evidently doubt whether they were available in naam. Thus in a plea of naam heard in the Sheriffs' Court in 1354 (a plea of 'chattels unjustly taken and detained' because rent was in arrears; the plaintiff claimed that he was allowed to effect repairs, recovering his expenses from the rent, and had spent so much that he owed nothing to the defendant), the Sheriffs' Court refused to award damages to the successful plaintiff on the grounds that city custom did not permit it. But when the case was brought on error a year or so later, it was remitted to the court with the order that the original jury should be summoned again, with replacements for those who had died in the meanwhile if necessary, to assess the damages.[166] The reason for the doubt is almost certainly that many of the pleas of naam brought in the Sheriffs' Court were brought there, rather than in the Husting, precisely because the plaintiff was alleging a wrongful act, a trespass, often by an official. It followed that damages could be awarded, just as damages were available in actions brought against sheriffs for wrongful arrest.[167] The 1354 case was unusual, in that it was not obviously trespassory in nature, and it is not surprising that there was doubt about the custom in such circumstances.

In personal actions, where damages went, one might have expected costs to have followed. They were awarded by the

[164] Riley, *Munimenta Gildhallae*, I, p. 471, the rate being 20 per cent *per annum, pro rata*.

[165] *CalLBG*, p. 73; CLRO, HR CP122, mm. 5v–6, 11v (*Sewale* v. *Sewale*, *Lytelyngton* v. *Execs. of Sturmy*, 1397); *CalLBG*, p. 73.

[166] CLRO, HR CP79, mm. 18v, 19.

[167] CLRO, Sheriffs' Court Roll (1320), m. 7 (*Russeles* v. *Chapeleyn*, the chamber renter) and *CalEMCR*, pp. 256–8 (*le Pesshoner* v. *[Sheriff] Bolet*).

Sheriffs' Court on at least one occasion early on in our period, in a trespass case from the 1310s, and also in the case brought against the sheriff, but even these instances may have been exceptional.[168] There seems to be no evidence to show whether or not they were being awarded in other types of personal actions either at this date or later in the century, when damages began to be awarded.[169] Apart from the cases just mentioned, the earliest specific reference to 'costs [*misis*] and expenses' appears to be from 1421, when they were awarded in a debt case.[170] On the other hand, the high rate of damages (20 per cent per annum) allowed to plaintiffs in debt cases in 1356, and the damages allowed to defendants in unprosecuted cases, might have included an element for costs.

Even if the defendant acknowledged the debt, execution would be granted against him unless he immediately offered a day for repayment, and the assets seized would be valued at the next court and delivered to the plaintiff the following day. Moreover, if the plaintiff was not satisfied with [the valuation placed on] the assets, the appraisers were supposed to keep them; the plaintiff would then be entitled to recover the debt from the appraisers' assets.[171] This particular provision may well not have been enforced, however, since there appear to be no recorded cases in which the plaintiff sought to have it applied or the appraisers complained that the plaintiff was being unreasonable in refusing to accept the assets offered.

Practice in the Mayor's Court differed somewhat. Damages certainly were awarded in appropriate cases of trespass, as happened in 1337, when a minor's guardian was found guilty of taking from him a book called 'Legends of the Saints', written in English, worth 30*s* (40*s*, according to the plaintiff). The jury assessed damages in this case at 6*s* 8*d* (the plaintiff had asked for 100*s*).[172] In debt cases, however, according to the answers given in 1327 in response to an enquiry by Oxford about the city's customs, all unsuccessful defendants were liable to have their goods

[168] CLRO, HR CP40, m. 5 (*atte Waye* v. *Wadenhos*, 1315).

[169] CLRO, HR CP40, mm. 5 (*atte Waye* v. *Wadenhos*, 1315), 23 (*Forsham* v. *Thame*, account, 1315), HR CP43, m. 4v (*Jannoie* v. *Brunlesqe*, debt, 1318); there are no awards of costs in such cases recorded in the Sheriffs' Court roll for 1320, nor in the records of similar cases from the late fourteenth century (e.g., above, fn. 166).

[170] CLRO, HR CP147, m. 5v (*Hanwell* v. *Bakton*).

[171] Riley, *Munimenta Gildhallae*, I, pp. 184–5. [172] *CalPMR 1323–64*, p. 145.

and chattels and half their lands adjudged to their creditors in satisfaction of the debt.[173] The arrangements designed to compensate a plaintiff where the defendant failed to offer to repay the debt immediately do not seem to have applied in the Mayor's Court until the fifteenth century. A case from 1437 is the first recorded example of the award of damages which was specifically said to be partly for delay in payment of a debt in a case determined according to law and custom in this court. This suggests that the statement made in 1327 that '[n]o damages are given to persons recovering debts in the Chamber of the Guildhall or the Husting' remained true until changes in the conduct and workload of the Mayor's Court, culminating sometime (perhaps shortly) before 1440, made a nonsense of this distinction between the penalties awarded there and in the Sheriffs' Court.[174] That possibility is reinforced by the fact that on no other occasion did the court say what the damages were for, suggesting that the practice of awarding damages in debt in this court was a novelty which required explanation. This is also the first case in which the award of costs is mentioned. Costs were again awarded in two debt cases from 1444, and the award of costs in debt and trespass cases seems to have been routine practice thereafter.[175]

Finally, in most personal actions (not just debt, as 'Liber Albus' implies in relation to the Mayor's Court) there were set levels of amercement. These varied according to the court, in that, although both the Mayor's and the Sheriffs' Court imposed amercements of 4*d* and 1*s*, depending on whether the sums in dispute were small or large, in the Sheriffs' Court the higher amount was charged if the action involved a sum in excess of 40*s*,

[173] *CalPMR 1323–64*, p. 23; *ibid.*, pp. 138–9, 142; see also *CalPMR 1364–81*, p. 229, for the same procedure where a recognizance had been entered into.

[174] *CalPMR 1437–57*, p. 2; alternatively, the earliest recorded example is from 1444: *ibid.*, p. 62, *CalPMR 1323–64*, p. 23; for later examples in the Mayor's Court, see *CalPMR 1437–57*, pp. 150, 156, *CalPMR 1458–82*, pp. 1, 2, 15, 64, 144. The court did not award damages unless the defendant appeared in court and denied the debt, but did award costs in such cases: *CalPMR 1437–57*, pp. 64, 73, 122, 123.

[175] *CalPMR 1437–57*, pp. 62, 64; *ibid.*, pp. 73, 75, 102, 122, 123, 150 (debt), 13, 117–18 (trespass); *CalPMR 1458–82*, pp. 1, 2, 15, 64, 144 (debt), 23–4, 48, 82, 105 (trespass).

whereas in the Mayor's Court, it was imposed if the disputed sum was half that, 20*s* or more.[176]

'IN CONSCIENCE' AND MERCHANT LAW CASES

Cases adjudged according to conscience were initiated by a petition ('a certain bill') in the Inner Chamber. It seems likely, judging by the variety of handwriting, wording and the general literary quality of the surviving fourteenth- and fifteenth-century petitions, that petitioners could and did write them themselves or get amateurs to do so for them. In some, perhaps many, cases, the complaint may well have been made orally, particularly in the fourteenth century.

For most if not all of our period there was no such thing in cases determined according to conscience or merchant law as 'process', that is, set procedures by which the court itself was bound. How any summons was transmitted to those complained against in these cases is unclear (the record simply says that the '[defendant] appeared before us the said mayor and alderman' or similar).[177] They may have been summoned in the usual way by the mayor's sergeants at mace, or it may have been left to the petitioner to deliver the summons. In this type of case, where there was no possibility of a judgment in default and it was therefore never likely to be in the plaintiff's interest to fail to deliver a summons, the latter arrangement might well have been as good as any.

In cases determined according to conscience or merchant law, too, the mayor and aldermen could not force individuals to submit to their decisions when sitting informally. In order to avoid lengthy secondary actions, the best they could do was to get disputants to bind themselves with penal bonds to 'abide' (undertake to accept) their judgment, just as in arbitrations they would be asked to bind themselves to accept the arbitrators' decision.[178] As one might expect, there is no sign of any formal procedure beyond

[176] Riley, *Munimenta Gildhallae*, pp. 220, 390. With respect to the Mayor's Court, the two levels and sums involved were set, possibly for the first time (although fines were certainly being levied long before that), in 1365, when fines and any other profits made from pleas heard before the mayor and aldermen were granted to the sheriffs.

[177] *CalPMR 1458–82*, p. 26.

[178] *CalPMR 1381–1412*, pp. 287–8; *ibid.*, pp. 285–6; for examples of binding-over to abide judgments: CLRO, Jor. 7. fo. 149v, Jor. 6, photo. 542.

this point. In a situation in which the 'defendant' was not bound to accept the court's authority, let alone appear or reappear, essoins were redundant.

This was not true, however, of all the cases which were described by the city authorities as being 'brought' or 'heard' according to merchant law. Where these were determined informally, the general principle that parties involved in merchant law cases could refuse to accept the court's authority or decision applied.[179] However, if the case appeared to be determinable at common law despite involving questions of mercantile practices, it was begun in the same way as cases heard according to law and custom, with an original bill of debt, detinue, and so on.[180] What happened subsequently depended on the nature of the pleadings. So long as the case was still being heard in open court, process was, as far as one can tell, identical to process in any other personal action. Only for so long as the issues were being examined in the Inner Chamber did more informal methods apply; and if, as might happen, the main issue between the parties turned out to be one which could indeed be determined according to law and custom, that is what happened. In these cases, normal enforcement measures applied. As the mayor and aldermen explained to the chancellor in 1469, in the event of a bill being brought according to merchant law by merchant strangers or others against a freeman of the city, it was city custom that, just as in common-law actions, a defendant who failed or refused to find sufficient security to 'await the plea' was imprisoned.[181]

In 'conscience' cases, the mayor and aldermen clearly normally tried to reach a conclusion that would be acceptable to the disputants. In a dispute over the use and maintenance of a privy in 1466, for example, the decision was that one side should remove a

[179] *CalPMR 1381–1412*, pp. 285–6, 287–8.

[180] *CalPMR 1437–57*, pp. 101, 102, 105–6 (where the defendant by his sealed bill undertook payment to the plaintiff or the bearer of the bill); see also, e.g., *ibid.*, p. 8, *CalPMR 1458–82*, pp. 2, 30, 40–1, 68, 139, 140–1. Conversely, for a case which should have been determinable by the ordinary course of the law but could not be, see TNA (PRO), Chancery *Corpus Cum Causa* Writ Files C244/123, item 33, where the problem was that the court which should have dealt with the dispute was at Antwerp, and the defendants had allegedly been careful, ever since payment fell due, to ensure that neither they nor their goods came within that court's jurisdiction.

[181] TNA (PRO), Chancery Writ Files *Corpus cum Causa*, C244/108, item 170.

pipe belonging to the other which they had blocked and that the other should replace it; that the first parties, being poorer and with a smaller household, should pay 1*d* towards the cost of cleaning, the second, 'at our instaunce and Request by wey of charitee', 3*d*, and that both should thenceforth have use of the privy.[182] They would however impose damages in actions of most if not all types heard and determined according to merchant law, although it does not appear that costs were awarded, presumably because it was, in theory at least, unnecessary to incur any in such cases.[183]

As to the physical presentation of pleadings, the full range of written pleadings were in use in Inner Chamber cases by the 1470s at the latest. There is an extremely lengthy record of a case from 1471, *Herell* v. *Lambard /Basingthwaite*, which has clearly been stitched together from what the clerk describes as the 'tenour of the ... bill. Answere. Replicacion. With all other thinges dependying upon the same' (it is as if he had absent-mindedly copied down his instructions).[184] Actual examples of these documents, or copies of them at least, still survive, attached to Chancery writs of *certiorari* of the 1470s.[185] And while there is no evidence to demonstrate that written pleadings were in use in the Inner Chamber before that date, it would be surprising if they were introduced there much later than they were in the Outer Chamber. Given the restrictions on the employment of legal representatives, the main attraction of written depositions for petitioners would be that they provided a means by which their lawyers could present the alleged facts and any relevant points of mercantile practice to the mayor and aldermen. By the sixteenth century, when common lawyers were increasingly penetrating Chancery, it was probably less true than it might previously have been to say that one's priest, or even one's mother, was as capable as any lawyer of determining the probabilities of success in cases adjudicated according to conscience in the Inner Chamber.

182 *CalPMR 1458–82*, pp. 36–7.

183 *CalPMR 1381–1412*, pp. 166 (covenant, 1389), 285–6 (detinue, 1407), 253 (debt, 1398); for restrictions on the employment of legal representatives in the Inner Chamber, see p. 272.

184 *CalPMR 1458–82*, pp. 57–64, esp. 57–62, with the record of the proceedings beginning 'Wherupon the xiii day of septembre'.

185 TNA (PRO), Chancery Writ Files *Corpus cum Causa*, C244/119, item 70, C244/123, item 33.

There, too, rules were beginning to be laid down, starting with the 1475 restriction on the circumstances in which the mayor and aldermen could summon cases before them for informal determination. Rules (or 'certainty') give something for lawyers to chew on, and their absence tends to deprive them of sustenance. Even in cases determined in conscience, therefore, some disputants were very probably seeking legal advice, and having their complaints and responses drawn up by lawyers, by the later fifteenth century.

6

JUDGES, JURORS AND LITIGANTS

INTRODUCTION

This chapter examines developments in relation to the laymen who played their parts, in and out of court, in the administration of the law by the city of London. The reason for examining these developments is that the character of tribunals inevitably owes a fair amount to the character of its presiding judges, and the nature and quality of the judgments will be affected both by the judges and by anyone else who is involved in arriving at those judgments. If city judges differed in their backgrounds, attitudes and practices from the Westminster judges, and indeed also from those in other inferior courts, the city courts themselves are likely to have differed from other courts. Jurors, too, were judges of a sort in some instances: judges of the fact. Given the prominent place accorded to the jury in the history of the common law, the composition of city juries during the Middle Ages warrants detailed examination. And, as we have seen, the jury as a method of trial also occupied a fairly prominent position in the city courts. Litigants can also affect the character and workings of a court. Their influence is not always as obvious as that of judges and juries. In our period, however, when both courts and laws were developing, often at local level, litigants almost certainly affected that development. Their demands for new interpretations of the law and for new legal remedies to meet their changing needs, the types of advice and representation they preferred, their responsiveness (or otherwise) to legal procedures, their attempts to corrupt and to pervert the course of justice and their petitions against malpractice and misuse of procedures, all had an impact on the administration of the law.

JUDGES

Judges can, in Professor Maitland's words, be 'presiding magistrates' and (or) 'judges of the law'; and someone or something has to be the 'judges of the fact'.[1] Some confusion has arisen in the past over who the judges of the city courts really were, in any of these senses. A rather separate issue is the question of who 'kept' the court (managed the proceedings) between 1300 and 1550. Court managers, such as present-day court clerks, are not necessarily judges of any kind.

What we do know is that three of the city's law officers, the recorder and the two undersheriffs, eventually assumed the presiding and law-giving judgeships of the London courts; it has been suggested that this happened as early as the fourteenth century. The first time the recorder's duties were described, however, in 1304, only court-keeping was included. The same was true of the undersheriffs, whose duties were not enumerated until, probably, the latter end of the century. Court-keeping is admittedly a relatively small step from presidency, and the recorder was from the beginning sitting on the bench which the mayor and aldermen eventually vacated, leaving him to preside alone over their courts. Whether that step had been taken by 1550, however, much less by the fourteenth century, is doubtful.

Presidency of a court, with or without court-keeping, may or may not also involve judging the law or the fact. Presidents may, for instance, give judgments on points of law, but leave the question of judging the fact – the guilt or innocence or the better right – to others. This had been the position in the central common-law courts since the beginning of our period. Or they may rely on others for advice about points of law, but judge the facts for themselves, as modern magistrates do. The evidence from English local courts other than London's indicates that, before 1300 in most courts, and well into the seventeenth century in a few, it was usually persons other than the president who decided points of law or custom (men known as the suitors of court); and the facts were sometimes not judged by any human being at all, but were left to God.

[1] Pollock, Maitland, *History of the English Law*, I, p. 548.

So, what type of men were the judges in the city courts during our period?

As far as judges of the law are concerned, one thing we can say is that there is no evidence at all of suitors of court in any of the city's courts after 1300. Indeed, in 1321 the justices in eyre were invited to condemn the citizens of London because 'they have held the king's courts by one sheriff, without suitors or aldermen'.[2] Given the comparatively late emergence as formal entities of both this court and the Mayor's Court, at a period when the suitor of court had been ousted, or was busily ousting himself, in favour of the juror, it would have been difficult to impose new obligations of this sort on Londoners. Possibly certain city properties had once owed suit of court to the Husting. Dr Thomas thought he detected evidence of suitors in the late thirteenth-century Husting rolls. Since, however, it appears that some of these men required to be specially summoned by the alderman's servant (possibly another way of describing the ward beadle), it may be that these sessions were, or included, special assemblies convened to deal with governmental matters, rather than legal cases.[3] If so, the obligation to do suit of court in the Husting had probably been abandoned by the early 1270s at the latest. It may even be that there had never been such an obligation, and that the aldermen had been the judges of the law for as long as the Husting had existed.[4] In 1277 an ordinance which altered the procedure to be followed in certain writ-initiated cases was said to have been granted and established 'by all the aldermen present to render judgment this day'.[5] Certainly the discussions which they are recorded as holding on difficult points of law and custom in the late thirteenth and early fourteenth centuries suggest that this was their role at that time; and the comments of the justices in eyre in 1321 likewise imply that they were expected to act in this capacity.[6] But it seems clear that, if they ever had fulfilled this function in the Sheriffs' Court, they were no longer doing so by 1321.

2 Cam, *Eyre 1321*, I, p. liii, *ibid.*, II, p. 255.

3 *CalPMR 1323–64*, p. viii (the Husting references, where they can be identified, are to the issue of ordinances by the 'whole commonalty').

4 Bateson, 'London Municipal Collection of the Reign of King John', pp. 481, 487–8, 493.

5 CLRO, HR PL6, m. 2.

6 CLRO, HR CP23, m. 25(a)v (referring to a discussion held in the Pleas of Land), CP25, m. 21v, CP47, m. 20, HR PL44, m. 19v, PL46, m. 13; see HR PL24, m.

Judging by the lack of references in the Husting rolls to their discussions after 1324, it may well be that by this date they were no longer regarded, even in the Husting, as judges of the law. If so, it could be that the establishment of the common serjeanty, probably in 1319, meant that the court was no longer relying primarily on the legal knowledge of the aldermen but was increasingly seeking advice from a specialist in the common law.[7] By 1330, and possibly even earlier in the Sheriffs' Court and Mayor's Court, therefore, it may well have been a city law officer who was the real judge of the common law, with the common clerk providing advice on city custom.

What, then, of the presiding judges and judges of the facts?

As the headings of the city's court rolls not uncommonly state before whom a session of that particular court was held, it ought theoretically to be easy to discover the composition of the bench. And, in theory, it is. Judging by these headings, in 1300 the mayor and sheriffs presided over the Husting, the mayor over the Mayor's Court, and each sheriff over his side of the Sheriffs' Court. In practice, the aldermen appear to have formed part of the quorum of the Husting by this date, although they may not formally have been its presiding judges. By the 1330s, though not before, pleas in the Mayor's Court were sometimes said to have been held before the aldermen as well as the mayor.[8] Although the situation remained rather muddled for some while thereafter, in hindsight at least, it looks as though the aldermen should be included among the judges of the Mayor's Court from the 1330s on. So theory and practice did not always coincide, even in 1300. And, not only were there sometimes more judges than the heading acknowledged, but sometimes there may have been fewer. In the opinion of the editor of the city's surviving rolls of the possessory assizes, '[t]he heading of the roll cannot be accepted as a sure indication of the presence of the officials named therein', as there are a few occasions on which it appears that named office-holders

5v for reference to a 'roll [or rotulet] of discussions'; a surviving example is HR CP23, mm. 25(a–d).

[7] For the common serjeant's role, see the next chapter.

[8] *CalPMR 1323–64*, pp. 46, 95; compare these headings with those in *CalEMCR*, where the one mention of aldermen, other than as *locumtenentes*, is in relation to a session 'for the keeping of the King's Peace': *CalEMCR*, p. 155.

were in fact absent.[9] Moreover, just as there was no requirement for the king to be present for cases to be heard *coram rege* at Westminster, so the presence of the mayor, aldermen and sheriffs eventually came to be a fiction.

According to P. E. Jones, editor of the later plea and memoranda rolls, 'the Lord Mayor and Aldermen have continued in theory to be Judges of the Mayor's Court, but in practice the Recorder has exercised this function ever since the fourteenth century'. Likewise, the Sheriffs' Court in due course 'came to be presided over by suitably qualified Undersheriffs'.[10] By the later eighteenth century, the Husting was still being 'held before the *Lord Mayor*, *Aldermen*, and *Sheriffs*, when any point of law is to be argued, or matter of fact to be tried, the *Recorder* sits with them, to assist them therein, & to pronounce the judgements of the Court'.[11] In the Mayor's Court, however, although 'the *Mayor* and *Aldermen* [are] considered as judges ... the *Recorder* is the acting or officiating judge' and 'each [Sheriffs'] Court has its own Judge, appointed to his office by the Court of Aldermen ... [who] must be an utter barrister'.[12] Could it be, then, as Mr Jones thought, that the recorder was presiding over the Mayor's Court (and each under-sheriff over one side of the Sheriffs' Court, perhaps) even in the 1300s?

It certainly seems likely, from the way the Husting rolls are organised if nothing else, that routine business in the Husting was transacted separately from the pleadings, perhaps even on separate days when the court was still busy enough to justify two sessions a week. It is clear, too, that all sorts of routine activities were undertaken 'outside court' in the Mayor's Court, presided over by whoever was to hand. And it is undoubtedly true that the early recorders presided over the Mayor's Court as aldermen and deputies to an absent mayor, continued throughout our period to sit on the bench at the mayor's right hand, and sometimes held minor sessions alone. From the first emergence of the office,

9 Chew, *London Possessory Assizes*, p. xvii, fn. 1; in the first of the two instances referred to (item 11, pp. 3–4), the assize was respited because of the deputy coroner's absence; in the other (item 139, pp. 51–2), it was held in the absence of one of the sheriffs. But in fact the rule as stated in 1338 was that 'saunz un des viscounts et coroner ne poet le play estre tenuz': Chew, *London Possessory Assizes*, p. xvi.

10 Jones, 'City Courts of Law', p. 302.

11 Emerson, *Concise Treatise*, p. 7.

12 *Ibid.*, pp. 33, 88–9.

recorders were sitting as the mayor's deputy, as Recorder John de Wengrave did in 1304, the year of his election.[13] In 1372, we hear of the mayor and recorder 'sitting as a tribunal' to receive the petition of a Florentine merchant and to hear the testimony of witnesses on his behalf.[14] By the sixteenth century, when the Husting clerks routinely recorded who received the appointments of attorneys, the recorder was more likely than the mayor or an alderman to be named.[15] In a Common Council petition of 1502, reference was even made to the recorder, common clerk, or 'any other persone lerned sittyng in Juggement'.[16]

All this sounds impressive, and may well be what led Mr Jones to believe that the mayor and sheriffs had ceased to preside over their courts as early as the fourteenth century. But what the Common Council wanted in 1502 was for the officers concerned to be granted authority to award an automatic non-suit after a term if the plaintiffs failed to proceed against defendants held in custody. These sessions at which routine process was handled were not on a par with full sessions of the respective courts. There was nothing remarkable or significant about a senior city officer holding minor sessions of court. To the extent that these officers took procedural decisions, they were indeed judges, and were referred to as such; but this does not demonstrate that they presided over, and were judges of, the Mayor's Court and Sheriffs' Court in full session.

As far as the Mayor's Court is concerned, the role of the recorder was stated clearly in the late fourteenth century. As a petitioner remarked in a case brought in 1389 and appealed the following year, 'judgment lies with the mayor and aldermen in all pleas brought before them, and the recorder has no authority except to pronounce judgment'.[17] The record of this case demonstrates both that the mayor and aldermen were supposed to be present to hear actions brought in their courts and that, even in this instance, when they failed to give judgment (state what the outcome of the case was and what the awards and fines should be), they clearly were present. There is no reason to suppose that what was true in 1389 was not true a hundred or indeed a hundred and

[13] *CalECMR*, p. 164. [14] *CalPMR 1364–81*, p. 138.
[15] And see, e.g., CLRO, HR PL159, m. 3, for the recorder receiving attorney appointments in the 1430s.
[16] CLRO, Jor. 10, fo. 246v. [17] *CalLBH*, p. 395.

fifty years later. Although eventually only the recorder was left sitting on the bench of the Mayor's Court, that stage had probably not been reached even by the middle of the sixteenth century. In 1514, for example, Alderman Haddon was authorised to sit as the mayor's deputy together with his fellows 'to keep [the Mayor's C]ourt'.[18] In 1539 Alderman Bowes reported that he and others had been nominated to hold the Court of Requests.[19] These provisions echoed like arrangements for the Husting, where, there is no doubt, the mayor and sheriffs still presided.[20]

At first sight, the evidence relating to the Sheriffs' Court seems to suggest that even the main sessions were not genuinely presided over by the sheriff whose name headed the court roll. In 1291, Roger de Portlaunde, sheriff's clerk, accused another man of insulting him 'in the full court of [the sheriff], which the said Roger was holding in the name of his master'. As 'undersheriff' was not at that date the title invariably given to the sheriff's chief clerk, Portlaunde could well have been an early undersheriff; and it certainly sounds as though he was presiding over the Sheriffs' Court when the incident occurred.[21] In the early fifteenth century a former undersheriff endorsed a record with a note which seems to say that an assize of 1427 had been 'tried before me Johnn Fortescu somtyme undesherve of London' (the words which might be 'tried before' are particularly indistinct).[22] In a similar vein, in 1536 the undersheriffs were forbidden to give judgment in any matter depending before them on the same day that a verdict was rendered.[23] A year previously, Undersheriff Onley had been described as 'kepyng the Court apperteynyng to the Counter in Bredstrete'.[24] Then there is Thomas More's description of the various ways in which he dealt with 'public cases' in the 1510s; as he said, 'at times I, as judge, determine them'.[25] It is possible that he was referring to his work as undersheriff. Finally, a rare report of a Sheriffs' Court case from the 1540s, made or preserved by the future undersheriff Randolph Cholmondley, says that it 'fuit

[18] CLRO, Rep. 2, fo. 203. [19] CLRO, Rep. 10, fo. 137.
[20] CLRO, Rep. 9, fo. 138; CLRO, HB3, fo. 27.
[21] CLRO, MS LBA, fo. xcvi, printed in Riley, *Memorials*, pp. 27–8.
[22] Chew, *London Possessory Assizes*, p. 105 (CLRO, Rolls of Mort d'Ancestor, Roll EE, bottom of m. 15v).
[23] CLRO, Rep. 9, fo. 152. [24] CLRO, Jor. 13, fo. 44v.
[25] Rogers, *Correspondence of Sir Thomas More*, p. 78.

argue devaunt Crafford, donques southvisconte la'.[26] But again, it does not follow that the undersheriffs were judges of their courts at this period, save in the limited sense that they presided over and made judgments about process during the preliminary stages (for example, by refusing to admit an improperly written bill).[27] The city's common clerk, too, was a judge in this sense by the sixteenth century: in 1544, the Waxchandlers paid 3*s* to William Blackwell, 'the judge in the maiors Courte for the Bayle', Blackwell being the common clerk, and formerly a Mayor's Court clerk.[28]

That the undersheriffs did often hold the counter courts by the sixteenth century, and perhaps earlier, there is no doubt. It is certainly possible that, as soon as a separate counter court developed, it was presided over by the undersheriffs, unless the sheriff himself chose otherwise. In 1520, for example, the Court of Aldermen decided to allow the undersheriffs to take turns keeping their courts on Tuesdays and Thursdays, apparently with one undersheriff holding both counter courts for one week, his colleague, the next. (This was an extension of a concession granted in 1509, which had allowed them to sit for one another whenever one was absent 'for reasonable cause'.)[29] But even this practice may not have been regarded as quite proper or desirable. Certainly when, in 1532, a sheriff decided to challenge his deputy's right to hold the counter court, the mayor and aldermen supported him.[30] Nor does it follow that, when undersheriffs or others spoke of courts being held before them, the sheriffs were absent. The undersheriffs' oaths, from their first appearance in, probably, the late fourteenth century, referred to cases being heard before them. There is little reason to doubt that the sheriffs could be present at this period, however. In 1376, a sheriff complained that he was insulted while 'holding his court at Guildhall'.[31] Even Fortescue's comment about a case being 'tried before me', if that is indeed what he wrote, could well mean no more than that he had been present as chief clerk of the court. Sheriffs' Court records of the early 1420s, which are almost contemporary with Fortescue's period of office, refer on several occasions to actions taken by the

[26] Baker, *Reports ... of King Henry VIII, Vol. II*, p. 450; for the date, see *idem*, *Reports ... of King Henry VIII, Vol. I*, p. xlii.
[27] CLRO, Jor. 8, fo. 93. [28] Dummelow, *Wax Chandlers of London*, p. 160.
[29] CLRO, Rep. 5, fo. 82, CLRO, Jor. 11, fo. 91. [30] CLRO Rep. 8, fo. 277.
[31] *CalPMR 1364–81*, p. 225.

sheriff: it is, for example, the sheriff who is said in one case to have questioned the defendant and who gave the final judgment.[32] Even though there is some evidence that in the late 1380s and 1390s, when the city's jurisdiction was being subjected to challenge by and interference from the king's uncle, John of Gaunt, the mayor and aldermen were inclined to lose their nerve and abandon legally doubtful issues to their law officers for resolution, it seems clear that they were considered by contemporaries to have been acting improperly.[33] It was a specific ground for an appeal of error when in 1395 a case was removed 'from the court held before the sheriff to the court held before Mayor Fressh ... and then committed by the mayor for determination jointly before Thomas Colred and John Weston, undersheriffs'.[34] The undersheriffs' oaths from 'Liber Albus' and of 1488 enjoined them to give good counsel to the mayor and other judges of the city, which rather implies that the undersheriffs were not then regarded as judges themselves.[35] As late as 1536, the problem created by Undersheriff Onley's preoccupation with his work at the Court of Augmentations was not that it left the Sheriffs' Court short of a president but that 'diverse weighty cawses' were pending because the Court was 'not fully furnysshed of counsayll'.[36] And although Randolph Cholmondley's report from the 1540s, mentioned above, could have recorded arguments made in court, it seems more likely that it was a discussion between lawyers during an adjournment, of the sort occasionally held in the fifteenth century for the benefit of the city's courts in the presence of its law officers in the Exchequer Chamber and elsewhere. So, although it is not possible to demonstrate that the undersheriffs of our period never held the full Sheriffs' Court in the absence of the sheriffs, there is equally no definite evidence that they ever did so. It looks as though the city continued to regard the presence of the presiding judges, as given in the session heading, as necessary, and any absences resulted either in an adjournment or in a formal substitution. Indeed, the only reasons for thinking that the session headings were fictions seem to be that they eventually became so

[32] CLRO, HR CP146, m. 2v; HR CP147, m. 5v.
[33] *CalPMR 1381–1412*, p. 229, and see also 156–7, 158–60, *CalLBH*, pp. 395–6.
[34] CLRO, HR CP120, m. 4.
[35] Riley, *Munimenta Gildhallae*, I, p. 317, CLRO, Jor. 9, 220v.
[36] CLRO, Rep. 9, fos. 195, 197.

in London and that undersheriffs sometimes presided over shrieval courts elsewhere in our period.[37] But the circumstances which led to the undersheriffs assuming the presidency of rural courts – the numbers of relatively small courts to be visited on the sheriff's tourn, the distances involved and difficulties of travel, not to mention the heavy burden of general administration on the rural sheriff's staff and the rather different class of man employed as a rural sheriff – did not exist in London.

The situation may have remained unchanged for some years after 1550. In the Elizabethan 'Book of Oaths', the original heading of the undersheriff's oath was simply 'The Oath of the Undersheriffs of London'. At some later stage, this was amended to 'The Oath of the *Judges of the Sheriffs' Court, or* Undersheriffs of London'.[38] Although it is likely that the undersheriffs' role had expanded considerably by the end of the century, that change had either not occurred or was not yet formally acknowledged when the original heading was written.[39]

The one city law officer who was definitely not a presiding judge, nor even a court-keeper, until the early sixteenth century was the common serjeant at law; and, even then, he merely presided over the Court of Orphans, just as the city's chamberlain, an office-holder who was not, until the sixteenth century at least, legally trained, presided over the Chamberlain's Court.[40] When the situation did finally change, in the nineteenth century, and the common serjeant, too, became a presiding judge, it was because the recorder was overworked and the common serjeant underemployed.[41]

So the presiding judges of the full sessions of the city courts for most, and quite possibly all, of our period were the mayor, sheriffs and, in practice if not initially in theory, the aldermen. Such men were of course the elite of the city magistracy (though not necessarily of the London-based merchant class as a whole; not every successful merchant sought civic office). The judges of the Mayor's Court, the mayor and aldermen, were the elite of the

[37] Morris, *Medieval English Sheriff*, p. 189.

[38] CLRO, Book of Oaths, fo. 8v. [39] [Stow] *Survey of London*, p. 92.

[40] Carlton, 'Administration of London's Court of Orphans'; for the early Chamberlain's Court, see *CalEMCR*, pp. 46–8 (1298/9) and CLRO, HR CP35, m. 13v (1309/10).

[41] Masters, 'The Common Serjeant', p. 381.

elite. They were, even by city standards, wealthy men: in 1469 it was decided that no-one would be obliged to serve as an alderman if he would swear that his goods, chattels and hopeful debts were worth less than £1,000 a year, a decision which probably simply formalised earlier informal assumptions about what constituted 'sufficiency' for high office.[42] In contrast, even in the sixteenth century the effective minimum wealth level for a common councilman, on the next rung down of the civic ladder, was probably less than a twentieth of this.[43]

But what of the sheriffs? Given the way that Common Clerk Carpenter described them (in relation to the Husting, moreover) as being, not judges, but merely 'the executors of the judgments and orders of the mayor', one might assume that the status of the sheriff was by this period considerably lower than that of the alderman.[44] In fact, however, it was uncommon for a sheriff not to become an alderman, and a substantial minority by the fifteenth century were already aldermen when elected to the shrievalty.[45] Even the one sheriff in five who never became an alderman does not appear to have belonged to a different social group: early death and misconduct or misfortune are more likely explanations for the failure of a minority of sheriffs to advance further in the city hierarchy. Thus, of the nine sheriffs, in the period 1461–83, who did not become aldermen, Thomas Muschamp evidently left the city sometime before 1468 rather than face prosecution in the Mayor's Court for abusing his apprentice; Henry Brice died in office; Simon Smith, elected the following year, was accused of maltreating a prisoner, though eventually cleared; and Robert Byfield had earlier on several occasions been imprisoned for contempt and was described as 'beyng some deal rude for lacke of conynge'.[46] In two years (1471/2 and 1478/9), neither sheriff became an alderman; both were years of political tension

42 CLRO, Jor. 7, fo. 198.

43 Based on an oral account of the work of M. R. Benbow and colleagues, summarised in Benbow, 'Notes to the Index of London Citizens', 2 vols. (copy at the Institute of Historical Research, University of London).

44 Riley, *Munimenta Gildhallae*, I, p. 42.

45 Of those serving, 1461–83, 41% were already aldermen, and a further 28% were elected alderman during their shrievalty.

46 CLRO, Jor. 7, fo. 181; *ibid.*, fos. 181, 187, 187v, 191, 191v; *ibid.*, fos. 23, 105v; Ellis, *Fabyan's New Chronicles*, p. 666.

and their conduct at a difficult time may have damaged their prospects.[47]

So the judges in all the city courts were of very similar status, part of a small minority of leading citizens who were wealthy enough and willing to take on the highest civic offices. As was mentioned in Chapter 1, at the beginning of our period a fair number still belonged to city dynasties; by the end of it, the majority had begun life, and had almost certainly made their first fortunes, elsewhere. In addition, since aldermen not infrequently served a ward other than the one in which they lived, whereas common councilmen normally if not always lived in the ward they served, they almost certainly seemed more detached both physically and socially than the common councilmen from their fellow Londoners. A further mark of their distinctiveness was the increasingly common royal practice, during our period, of knighting leading Londoners: over a third of aldermen serving during the reign of Edward IV (1461–83) were knighted by him, for instance. On the other hand, they were certainly much more familiar figures to Londoners than their modern counterparts. Even aldermen were expected to spend a substantial part of the year living in the city: prolonged absence could lead to an alderman being required to resign.[48] Moreover, they tended by the fifteenth century to govern not only the city, but also the city's trade companies: nearly 60 per cent of later fifteenth-century aldermen were at some stage masters or high wardens of their company. Although by this stage they did not necessarily follow their professed trade, their activities as employers and wholesalers are likely to have brought them into contact with quite a range and number of non-freemen, too.[49] And however elevated their status may have been, Londoners do not appear to have been particularly intimidated by them or their courts: in late 1364, for example, a woman called an alderman a 'knackered old yokel', and less than a month later a second woman accused the mayor of taking bribes, a man accused him of denying him justice, and three other men were imprisoned for using bad language in court.[50]

[47] TNA (PRO), KB Plea Rolls, KB27/854, m. 18 *et seq.*, KB27/858, mm. 2v *et seq.* (*Talbot* v. *Shelley and[or] Aleyn*).
[48] Tucker, 'London's Government and Politics', pp. 54–6, 58–63.
[49] Tucker, 'Government and Politics', pp. 105–21, 124–33 and App. 2C.
[50] *CalPMR* 1364–81, pp. 15, 17.

The 'hands-on' nature of medieval urban government meant that a great many cats had the opportunity to look at their local kings: and they not only stared, but they hissed at them, too.

THE JURORS

Nowadays we rather take it for granted that all but the most civic-minded or under-employed individuals will attempt to avoid jury service. But it may be unwise to make the same assumption about attitudes towards jury service in medieval London's courts. Most modern jurors probably do not themselves anticipate having to rely on the public-spiritedness of their fellow-citizens. The chances of a juror today litigating or defending himself before a jury in his turn are not great. But one of the noticeable features of London's Husting is that a large proportion of its jurors, as of its administrators and judges, litigated in that court. Even in the other two courts, where jurors do not figure as prominently as litigants, their chances of doing so were nevertheless much higher than they would be today, partly because jury trial was available in a far wider range of private actions than it is nowadays. This is important when one considers questions such as the relatively high incidence of jury defaults in some courts and at some periods. To illustrate this, in 1316 a couple of Gilbert Pynnote's neighbours in or close to Langbourn Ward had their Husting cases impeded partly by his failure to turn up for jury-service. In 1320, it was the turn of Pynnote's widow Agnes to rely on the public-spiritedness of her neighbours when it came to be her turn to litigate.[51] There are many other examples in which a man who had been summoned to serve on a jury in litigation involving someone living nearby would subsequently have reason to hope that this person would appear when summoned in his turn. Knowing this, one wonders why jurors in city courts defaulted so often, and why they did so increasingly (though not as frequently as they did when summoned by the central courts). The answer seems to be that, when successive epidemics had reduced the population but not the number of actions brought in the Sheriffs' and Mayor's Courts, and particularly after all city juries became subject to quite stringent wealth qualifications in the 1490s, jurors

[51] CLRO, HR CP41, m. 7, HR CP45, m. 2.

simply felt that they were summoned too often: it was after all the burden imposed by jury service which was used to justify the establishment of the Court of Requests in 1518.[52]

Formal qualifications for jury service

A criticism levelled at city juries in Parliament in 1495 was that jurors were 'persones of litill substaunce discrecion and reputacion'.[53] This seems surprising. London contained a great concentration of wealth and its pool of citizens was large: if, as was suggested in Chapter 1, about 6 per cent of London's residents were freemen in the first half of the fourteenth century and about 11 or 12 per cent by 1550, it would probably have consisted of some 5,000 men at the beginning of our period, rising to about 10,000 by the end. However, by no means all these men were qualified to serve on a jury. To be liable for service before the justices of King's Bench, a man had not merely to be a freeholder in the ward in which the case had arisen and not to be 'of the affinity' of either litigant, but had also to hold property which, according to an act passed in 1414, had to be worth at least £2 a year (some discretion was allowed in actions involving assets worth forty marks (£26 13*s* 4*d*) or less, when the judges could decide whether a juror's yearly income was adequate).[54] If a similar level of property qualification was applied from then onwards to jurors in the city, the ward beadles would have had as much difficulty in finding enough suitably qualified freeholders for their jury lists in the smaller and poorer wards as the sheriffs had in supplying jurors for the central courts.[55] In Lime Street Ward in 1582, for example, fifty-eight Englishmen or -women were assessed for a subsidy. Of these, only thirty-six were considered to be worth more than £3 in either goods or in annual rents and fees; and all but four were assessed on goods, as being the more valuable of their resources. Subsidy assessments considerably undervalued wealth, particularly in relation to goods, and the later Tudor assessments were almost certainly more unreliable than the earlier ones; but there had also been both

[52] CLRO, LBN, fo. 70v. [53] *Statutes of the Realm, Vol. II, 1377–1503/4*, p. 584.
[54] Chrimes, *Fortescue, De Laudibus Legum Anglie*, p. 59.
[55] TNA (PRO), KB27/801, m. 11 (1461), KB27/805, m. 25 (1462).

considerable inflation in the 1540s and a considerable increase in London's population by the 1580s.[56]

Until 1495, it seems probable that the city did not always take notice of the 1414 act: either that, or it frequently took advantage of the discretion the act allowed. There is an example from 1421 of a litigant challenging a Mayor's Court jury on the grounds that the jurors were not qualified under the act, but it seems to be the only recorded instance before 1495 when this happened and the circumstances (involving a very large debt and a half-alien jury) were unusual.[57] In 1495, however, it was enacted that everyone serving on a city jury should have assets worth at least forty marks (£26 13*s* 4*d*), rising to 100 marks (£66 13*s* 4*d*), if the sum or property in dispute was itself worth forty marks or more.[58] The requirement of the 1495 act was probably lower than that of 1414, if one ignores the discretion allowed in disputes over low-value assets, assuming that real property yielded an annual income in rent equivalent to perhaps a twentieth of its value. The problem was that it applied to juries in all the city's courts. Requiring such a qualification of every juror in every case must have created great difficulties, at a time when the jury was an increasingly common method of determination and there was no lower limit to the value of the asset which could be subject to a jury trial. It was over twenty years before the city took effective steps to tackle these problems. If, after 1495, it ceased to be true that city juries sometimes contained 'persones of litill substaunce', it was probably the case that, until the establishment of the Court of Requests in 1518, jurors were individually overworked and probably more than usually uncooperative.

Another question which it is worth asking in this context, particularly in relation to fourteenth-century city jurors who seem still to have been expected to act as informants to the court, is whether they really were property-holders in the neighbourhood in which the offence occurred or the cause of the action arose. When a royal writ of *venire facias* was sent to one of the London sheriffs, ordering him to empanel a jury in the course of an action

[56] Lang, *Two Tudor Subsidy Assessment Rolls*, pp. lxx, lii–liii.

[57] *CalPMR* 1413–37, p. 92; in the 1470s, the sheriffs' and mayor's sergeants were merely ordered to ensure that they summoned the 'richer and more substantial men of the neighbourhood' for jury-service: CLRO, Jor. 8, fo. 167.

[58] *Statutes of the Realm, Vol. II*, p. 584.

brought in the central courts, it was the 'worthy and lawful' men of the *parish* and of its nearest neighbours whom he was ordered to summon.[59] Entries in the plea and memoranda rolls regularly refer to cases being put to 'the jury of the said parish(es)'.[60] Coroner's inquest juries, however, were invariably said to be 'the worthy and lawful men of [the ward in which the person had died] and of the three other nearest wards'.[61] This was stated to be in accordance with the custom of the city; and the evidence of the Husting and assize rolls suggests that there, at least, jurors were in fact placed on a ward panel, not a parish one.[62] The examples just given from the plea and memoranda rolls raise doubts about these 'parish juries', too. John Mason, for example, appeared in cases relating to the parishes of Allhallows Bread Street, St Olave by the Tower, and St Dunstan in the East.[63] The two latter parishes were certainly neighbouring, but Allhallows Bread Street was separated from them by some dozen parishes. So it may be unwise to take it for granted that the 'juries of the parish' were any such thing.

How true is it, then, that jurors were men of the wards concerned? At the lowest level of jury, the wardmote inquest, it seems certain that they were: in the fifteenth-century Portsoken inquest presentments, the same names reappear quite regularly, and a fair proportion of jurors served in other ward offices.[64] But when one turns to the jurors who served in the Sheriffs' and Mayor's Courts and on central court juries, the evidence initially suggests, at best, a modest relationship between any one juror's ward of residence and the location of any particular offence he might be called upon to consider. True, that evidence covers over twenty years. Even taking only those who appeared at relatively close intervals, however, the evidence is contradictory. Thomas York, who served

59 For example, TNA (PRO), KB Indictments, KB9/319, m. 2, TNA (PRO), KB Plea Rolls, KB27/805, m. 25.

60 For example, *CalPMR 1458–82*, pp. 23, 53, 82, 95.

61 For example, TNA (PRO), KB Indictments, KB9/311, m. 102, KB9/312, m. 19.

62 Chew, *Possessory Assizes*, items 276–9, 281.

63 *CalPMR 1458–82*, pp. 82, 94, 144.

64 CLRO, Portsoken Wardmote Presentments 1466/7–1483; for inquest jurors holding other offices, see, for example, Richard Sisworth (juror, 1468/9–1473/4; scavenger, 1476/7) or William Segrim (juror, 1473/4, 1480/1–1483, raker, 1475/6–1477/8): *ibid.*, fos. 5–7, 9–12 (Sisworth), 7–14, 2 (Segrim).

on Sheriffs' and Mayor's Court juries in January and April 1473, dealt only with cases from Aldersgate Ward.[65] Over longer periods of time, too, some men were repeatedly associated with one ward. William Aleyn, for instance, is to be found in July 1468 on the panel of two petty juries summoned for Tower Ward during a session of *oyer et terminer* and in 1475 and 1479 on two Mayor's Court juries, again for Tower Ward.[66] Likewise, Henry Field served on Mayor's Court juries dealing only with cases arising in Tower Ward at quite widely separated intervals (1470 and 1479).[67] However, if Field was the member of the Fletchers Company of that name, as seems quite likely, he was a common councilman who represented Bridge Street Ward, and very probably lived there in the 1450s or 1460s. Moreover, he died in 1486 as a parishioner of St Margaret Moses, Bread Street Ward.[68] Although only Billingsgate separates Bridge Street from Tower, and it is quite possible that Field lived in one of the three parishes which overlap the boundaries of Bridge Street and Billingsgate Wards, Bread Street Ward is separated from Tower by a minimum of three wards. Presumably he moved house sometime after 1479. Even more difficult to explain is the fact that William Aleyn, as well as serving on juries for Tower Ward, also seems to have served on juries considering cases arising in Bread Street Ward (1461, 1468), Cordwainer Ward (1470), and Langbourn Ward (1475, 1482).[69] Although Langbourn shares a boundary with Tower Ward, and Cordwainer with Bread Street, between Langbourn/Tower and Cordwainer/Bread Street lies Walbrook Ward. Likewise, in 1470, 1474 and 1475 Thomas Rock served on Mayor's Court juries dealing with cases arising in Cordwainer, Aldersgate and Tower wards; John Vicary, also in the 1470s, dealt with cases arising in Cordwainer, Aldersgate and Langbourn wards.[70] In only one case (Langbourn and Tower) could these wards be considered to be 'neighbouring'; indeed, Aldersgate Ward

[65] CLRO, Jor. 8, fo. 220, *CalPMR 1458–82*, p. 80.

[66] TNA (PRO), KB Indictments, KB9/319, mm. 9, 5, *CalPMR 1458–82*, pp. 104, 144.

[67] *CalPMR 1458–82*, pp. 60, 144.

[68] Fitch, *Index to Commissary Court of London Testamentary Records*, I, p. 70.

[69] *CalPMR 1458–82*, p. 23, TNA (PRO), KB Indictments, KB9/319, m. 22, *CalPMR 1458–82*, pp. 64, 104, TNA (PRO), KB9/360, m. 67.

[70] *CalPMR 1458–82*, pp. 64, 82, 95 (Rock), *CalPMR 1458–82*, pp. 64, 82, 104 (Vicary).

lies in the far north-west of the city, Tower Ward in the far south-east. All this may help to explain why it was found necessary in the early sixteenth century to warn the mayor's and sheriffs' sergeants not to summon jurors from anywhere except the appointed wards.[71]

The reason for these anomalies might lie in the way juries were employed. In major criminal trials it seems to have been normal practice by the later fifteenth century for the prosecution to draw up the accusation for the presenting jury to consider, rather than to leave the jurors to devise the bill themselves. Sometimes the same bill would be submitted to several juries, if the first failed to endorse it as the prosecution wished.[72] In 1468, although one of three original juries of presentment empanelled during sessions of *oyer et terminer* dealt mainly with offences committed in Aldersgate Ward, the other two original juries handled indictments covering offences committed in five different wards.[73] Presenting jurors in central court criminal cases, at least, could thus be required to return a verdict on bills covering offences committed both in their own neighbourhoods and elsewhere. There is however nothing to suggest that the London Mayor's and Sheriffs' Courts followed the same practice of asking several juries, even those presenting offences and nuisances, to consider a bill. It could be, of course, that city panels were made up in order to provide coverage for all the cases due to be heard by the court that day. Alternatively, it might be that if men summoned to serve on another jury failed to turn up, other juries were required to deal with their business. However, the fact is that the Mayor's Court records, like the central court records relating to private litigation, regularly state that jurors had to be distrained for non-appearance, supplemented with additional jurors, and resummoned. It seems odd that the court should go through this process, if it was acceptable to use one jury on another's case.[74] It seems much more likely that the practice of King's Bench and commissions when dealing with certain (political?) crimes was anomalous, and

71 CLRO, Jor. 11, fo. 340.

72 Virgoe, 'Some Ancient Indictments', pp. 262, 264–5.

73 TNA (PRO), KB9/319, mm. 24, 25, 39; *ibid.*, mm. 31–5, 42–4, 26–30, 36–7, 40–1; and see Holland, 'Cook's Case', pp. 25–8.

74 For example, *CalPMR 1458–82*, pp. 41, 53, 64 (with extra jurors), 82 (with extra jurors).

that the anomaly was confined even then to presentment juries, and did not apply to trial juries.

That jurors tried cases arising in different wards does not prove that they were not originally empanelled for the ward in which they held property. Certainly in the Husting, where the number of cases which reached the jury stage was never great, the evidence indicates strongly that jurors were genuinely of the ward concerned: the majority of those who appeared repeatedly did so for the same ward. More detailed examination of the backgrounds of the Husting jurors of 1372/3 reinforces this impression.[75] Just under 40 per cent of these jurors can be associated with a ward at some stage between the early 1360s and 1400. Of these, 85 per cent had a significant link with the ward they served as jurors and 15 per cent had a similar link with another ward.[76] The figure of 85 per cent is high enough to suggest that the exceptions had simply moved house before or after they appeared on the Husting jury panel.

It is likely that much of the variation in the wards represented by city jurors arose because the practice which applied in coroner's cases was indeed the custom of the city and applied in all three main city courts: each jury panel (though of course not necessarily each jury) was composed equally of men drawn from parishes which lay within the ward concerned and the three closest to it. This was clearly the case in the possessory assizes at the end of the sixteenth century, and it is probably only the recording habits of clerks which hides it from us at earlier periods.[77] As all city wards were bounded by at least three others – Cripplegate, despite being in part a suburban ward, bordered on no fewer than seven other wards – and parishes rarely lay in a single ward, the opportunities for service on a jury trying a case from another ward would have been considerable. Moreover, a good many jurors had common names. There were several contemporary William Aleyns, for example. The man who served as a juror for Bread Street and Cordwainer wards in the 1460s and early 1470s was probably the goldsmith who died in 1473 as a parishioner of St Matthew Friday Street, a parish which overlaps the wards of

[75] Based on jury-lists in CLRO, HR CP96.
[76] For a fuller discussion of the offices held by them, see below.
[77] Chew, *London Possessory Assizes*, items 276–9, 281.

Bread Street and Farringdon Within.[78] The William Aleyn who was empanelled for Langbourn and Tower wards between 1468 and 1482 was clearly another man. Jurors empanelled in the city courts were therefore probably not of the particular parish but almost certainly were of the particular ward concerned and its neighbours: of the vicinity, in other words.

The personal status and activity levels of jurors in city courts

Two main groups have been used to obtain information about city jurors as individuals and to see whether anything significant about them changed over time. The first consists entirely of men summoned to serve on Husting juries during the period when the court was still fairly busy (to be precise, 1315/6 to 1381/2). The second consists of all city jurors recorded in the city's surviving court records and King's Bench plea rolls (KB27/801 to KB27/885) between 1461 and 1483. This group numbers just over 1,100 individuals. Within the first group, which numbers at least 2,400 individuals, jurors listed in the Husting of Common Pleas roll for 1372/3 have been examined in more detail, to try to find out more about their status. These men were selected for closer scrutiny both because large numbers are listed (86) and because civic political upheavals of the mid-1370s and 1380s resulted in the names of an unusually large number of common councilmen being recorded, enabling the identification of more men from this level of city government.

The advantage of using the Husting jury-lists is that they begin fairly early. Until 1315, the clerks normally noted merely that a jury of such-and-such vicinity appeared by John Brown and his fellows. Thereafter, however, they took to recording the names of all defaulters (which suggests that, at a time when the Husting's workload was approaching its peak, defaulting was coming to be regarded as a problem); and, sometimes, they recorded the names of all those summoned. Even though variable practice has affected the completeness of the record, the evidence does not reveal any significant skew, apart from in the 1330s. The distribution of city wards represented is, for example, broadly what one might

[78] Fitch, *Index to Commissary Court of London Testamentary Records*, I, p. 4 (Cordwainer Ward borders Bread Street Ward to the east).

expect: tiny wards like Lime Street, or large but underpopulated suburban ones, like Portsoken, and wards to the east of the city are relatively under-represented (between 1 and 2.5 per cent of references); those in the fashionable west-central district, like Cheap and Bread Street, or in the western suburbs, like the two Farringdons, are over-represented (between 5 and 8 per cent of references). Nevertheless, the range is small: no part of the city or the suburbs under its jurisdiction was so poor as to contain no property worth litigating over.

Over half of the 2,400 or so names of Husting jurors appear just once, over a fifth just twice; but almost 10 per cent were noted at least five times. This group is clearly unrepresentative in that it contains more men who repeatedly defaulted than the others, but it is not necessarily unrepresentative of jurors generally in other respects. There is no obvious reason, for instance, why those who defaulted should have been eligible for jury service over a different period of time from those who appeared when summoned.

Undoubtedly, some of these names are those of different men. For example, it is clear that there were three John [de] Cressynghams who served as jurors between 1320 and 1370.[79] But although it is necessary to be wary of conflating or double-counting individuals, the evidence allows us to answer a couple of basic questions about Husting jurors. It shows that jurors could remain on their ward's panel for very many years. Of those who were summoned five times or more, over half appear to have served for between eleven and twenty years, and almost a third for over twenty-one years. More significantly, those who appeared repeatedly tended to do so for several years in succession. They were, as one might expect if the wealth qualifications for service as a Husting juror were comparatively onerous, men of some standing in the city. Of the 86 Husting jurors of 1372/3, two were future aldermen and 21 were future common councilmen. Other offices held by this group were as masters or wardens of companies (nine men), or as surveyors of butchers in the city markets of St Nicholas Shambles and East Cheap (six men). In all, 37 of the 86 held some kind of relatively important city appointment.

[79] CLRO, HR PL44, m. 5, HR CP55, m. 4v, *CalHW&D*, I, p. 434 (John de Cressyngham I); HR CP68, m. 14v, HR PL86 m. 8v, *CalHW&D*, II, p. 85 (John [de] Cressyngham II); HR CP93, m. 24v (John Cressyngham III).

Bearing in mind that the aldermanry was 24 men strong at the time (the Portsoken aldermanry was held *ex officio* by the prior of Christchurch) and that the Common Council then had a normal membership of between 60 and just under 100 men, the Husting jurors of the 1370s were evidently a socially superior group.[80]

This was not typical of all city jurors. Very few of the Portsoken wardmote inquest jurors, one hundred years later, penetrated even the lowest rungs of the governmental ladder. Indeed, very few of them served on any other city jury. At the most, eight of the 71 identifiable individuals did so.[81] It might be, of course, that Portsoken was unusual in this respect. Not only did it figure infrequently in Husting litigation, but it made the lowest contribution, after Lime Street Ward, to the various taxes and loans of the period; as we have seen, wealth and a liability to perform civic public service went together. On the other hand, in 1449 five Portsoken residents gave substantial sums towards the money being raised for the relief of Rouen. Portsoken was not unusual in only having about half-a-dozen contributors, nor in having a top-rate contribution of £1; only four men in the whole city exceeded this sum.[82] It seems on balance likely that what was true of Portsoken was true of other wards: men who served as wardmote inquest jurors only very rarely served on other city juries. When they did so, it was because they had progressed socially.

The majority (over three-quarters) of jurors in the second, fifteenth-century, group served exclusively either in the Mayor's Court or before the sheriffs. Of these, over two-thirds served on Sheriffs' Court or coroner's inquest juries only, and less than 10 per cent on Mayor's Court juries only. One might perhaps expect that those who served before the sheriffs would be of a lower

[80] See Table 6 in Thrupp, *Merchant Class of Medieval London*, p. 79. Figures of over 100 are probably in fact 'congregations' or afforced councils rather than normal common councils, but, as common councils were often afforced with the more senior ward or company office-holders, these additions were still men of some importance.

[81] John Arding (Arden?), John Bull, John Gardiner, Robert (John?) Knight, John Michell, Robert Nore, John Saunder[s] and Stephen Smith: CLRO, Portsoken Wardmote Presentments, 1466/7–1483; *CalPMR 1458–82*, pp. 66, 41, 104, 124; TNA (PRO), KB Indictments, KB9/301, m. 82, KB9/303, m. 43, KB9/311, m. 192, KB9/319, m. 47, KB9/339, m. 16, KB9/350, m. 74.

[82] CLRO, Jor. 5, fo. 21.

social status than men who were empanelled in the Mayor's Court, given that the Sheriffs' Court was the inferior court. At first sight, this appears to be true. Less than a fifth of those who appeared only in Sheriffs' Court or coroner's cases are known to have been common councilmen. Not one became an alderman. By contrast, half of those who appeared on both Sheriffs' Court or coroner's juries and in the superior courts were common councilmen at some stage; in addition, over 7 per cent became aldermen. On the other hand, men who only appeared in the Mayor's Court had an even worse record of civic advancement. Less than a twentieth became common councilmen; none became an alderman. Even of those Mayor's Court jurors who also served in the Husting or on central court juries, little more than a third became common councilmen, and, again, none became an alderman.

When summoned by the Court of King's Bench, however, it was usual for the jury panels to contain several future aldermen and a few serving common councilmen. About a third of names on the panels and juries for the politically sensitive 1468 sessions of *oyer et terminer* are of known common councilmen. Indeed, not merely serving aldermen, but the mayor himself, who presided over the sessions, are listed. (Needless to say, none of these august persons was pricked as appearing to answer the summons.) These jurors were important citizens, equivalent to the 'twenty-four knights or other worthy and lawful men', to whom the Westminster records make reference elsewhere. Juries in the city courts were of more mixed social composition, however. Even though Mayor's Court juries were not normally full of city governors, a single panel of 1470 contained no fewer than eleven men, or just under a third of those empanelled, who had served or were currently serving as common councilmen. This was similar to the proportion to be found in important King's Bench cases.[83] So it is probably misleading to talk about the social composition of juries in this city court or that, at least above the level of the wardmote inquest. There was clearly a certain level of wealth and status below which no man could serve on any city jury, even before 1495. That apart, however, the status of the jurors in private lawsuits varied according to the importance, not of the court,

[83] TNA (PRO), KB Indictments, KB9/333, m. 28; *CalPMR 1458–82*, pp. 64–5.

but of the case: of the asset being disputed or of the litigants themselves.

LITIGANTS

We cannot know for sure what influence the majority of individual litigants had on the administration of the law by London. What we can do, however, is get some sense of litigants as a group: what their social status was, whether litigants of differing social status used different courts, whether there was an imbalance between the sexes, and, if so, whether it differed between courts, and so on. That may, on the assumption that litigants of different social standing, wealth or sex had somewhat different priorities, help us identify the ways in which they might have influenced the conduct of the city's courts.

As far as the sex balance is concerned, there is a point that needs to be borne in mind. It relates to the opportunity available to married women in London, should they so choose, to trade as *femes soles* (as though they were single) and therefore to sue and be sued without involving their husbands. The likely effect of the latter provision would be to make women generally somewhat more visible as litigants in local courts like London's than in the central common-law courts, where husbands and wives were usually treated as one person, the husband. *Feme sole* status may have made women more visible in the records, because they appeared as individuals, but did not necessarily mean that they were more active commercially. Under English common law married women could trade, and therefore sue and be sued, together with their husbands or under their husbands' names; and some of this trading may in fact have been carried on by the woman alone.

The Husting

Legal actions brought in the Husting were often important cases, because they involved rights in land and, sometimes, important people – the early 1300s found both the dowager countess of Cornwall and the earl of Hereford among the demandants there.[84]

[84] CLRO, HR CP27/5, HR PL24/13.

Because of the nature of the assets in dispute, one would not expect to find many poor people litigating in the Husting, even in pleas of naam. It is true that small parcels of land or modest rents were sometimes involved (a piece of ground ten feet by five feet, for example, or a rent of 2*s* a year).[85] That seems to have been atypical, however. More common were demandants seeking to recover substantial houses and large numbers of shops. In 1368, for example, William Walderne, draper of London, was litigating over two messuages with 38 or 39 shops: possibly two large town houses, each with a range of shops along the street front.[86]

At first sight, Walderne himself seems atypical in that the majority of demandants in the Husting were not, if we may judge from those provided with a designation, freemen of the city. The great majority of identified demandants, nearly 75 per cent, were heads of religious houses, clergy or otherwise associated with the church (including chaplains and, in one case, churchwardens) or masters of institutions such as hospitals. Such men and women are much more readily identifiable than laymen, however: the clerks commonly identified heads of institutions, including the wardens of London Bridge, because this was relevant in the context of litigation, but did not need to note, for example, that litigants were aldermen. Taking all demandants, those with some sort of an ecclesiastical connection probably constituted 15 per cent of the total at most. The men and women who brought actions in the Husting may not always have been identified as freemen and freewomen, or even as Londoners, but it is probable that the majority of them were – like the Asshewys, the Ba[u/n/t]quelles, the Basinges, the Bokerels and the Boxes who are to be found among the demandants in the late thirteenth- and early fourteenth-century Pleas of Land rolls, to go no further down the alphabet.[87]

As to the sex of litigants, the great majority were men. That said, women were frequently demandants in actions of dower, naturally enough, but they also appeared quite regularly as one of the demandants in other types of action (rather less commonly as

[85] CLRO, HR CP38, m. 13; HR PL87, m. 27.

[86] CLRO, HR PL91, m. 20.

[87] See, e.g., the list of aldermen in 1291, *CalLBC*, pp. 1–3 (Basinge, Batquelle, Box (*bis*), Asshewy) and the explanation of 'Bokerellesbiry' (Bucklersbury) in *CalLBB*, p. 197, fn. 1.

tenants): about one in seven first or sole demandants in the Husting of Pleas of Land was a woman.

The Mayor's Court

As there is no doubt that the Mayor's Court was not only superior to but also more prestigious than the Sheriffs' Court, one would expect it to attract wealthier litigants and to involve litigation over more valuable assets. To some extent, that is true. When Henry VI sought to recover the vast sum of £3,000 from an Italian merchant and a (German?) shipman, the case was heard in the Mayor's Court. Excluding this unusual case, in a file of bills from the late 1450s the smallest sum sued for in that court was 3*s*, the largest, £260. In 20 per cent of disputes the assets involved were worth under 20*s*, however, and 54 per cent involved sums of less than £5. Contrariwise, only 11 per cent involved assets worth £50 or more.[88] Of the plaintiffs named in the first 50 bills contained in the same file, excluding the king, almost half (22) were definitely city freemen, whereas only eight seem unlikely to have been, either because they were alien merchants or because they described themselves as esquires, on the one hand, or husbandmen, on the other, or were said to be from other parts of the country. In addition, 'Thomas Bryan, gentleman' and 'William Norburgh, sergeant' should be included among the Londoners: Bryan, because he may have been a senior Sheriffs' Court attorney at the time, and Norburgh, because he was a Mayor's Court sergeant.[89]

None of the plaintiffs in these 50 bills were women. A widow did however figure as the defendant in one instance, and two others who had been trading as *femes soles* when the debts were incurred appeared as the only or second defendants in other cases. A wife who was summoned as the second defendant in fact answered by herself and, having denied she owed the sum demanded, waged her law as a freewoman of the city.[90]

88 Based on CLRO, Mayor's Court File of Original Bills MC1/3A, esp. item 15.
89 Chapter 8, Appendix 7.2 (Bryan); CLRO, Recognizance Rolls 20, m. 4 (Norburgh).
90 CLRO, Mayor's Court File of Original Bills MC1/3A, items 29, 3 (Agnes Smith, who had been trading as a butcher), 12 (Mrs Margery Barley, who had been trading as a tallowchandler).

The overall impression gained from the details given in the later files of Mayor's Court bills is that this was a court, above all, for city freemen, and particularly for wealthy and prominent freemen. One file, which contains bills brought between 1440 and 1456, has nine involving serving aldermen and a further 21 involving future aldermen out of some 370 items, not all of which were bills.[91] Around 10 per cent of bills at this period therefore involved men in or about to join the highest level of the city's governing class. In addition, a good many foreign merchants, together with a few merchants from other parts of England, used the court to sue both one another and denizens.[92]

These bills, however, all appear to have been used to initiate cases on the ordinary or common-law side of the Mayor's Court. Plaints and petitions may well have been the preferred initiation methods of poorer litigants, and in the 1440s and 1450s evidence relating to them is scant.[93] Possibly, therefore, both sides of the Mayor's Court were more frequented by men and women of modest standing and means than the surviving evidence suggests. Even so, what was true of the Court of Requests in its earlier days was true of the 'Inner Chamber' side of the Mayor's Court. It was not the poverty of the petitioners, but the fact that their problems could not for some reason be resolved at common law, which dictated whether they brought a bill in the Chamber or a petition in the Inner Chamber. In the second half of the fourteenth century, and quite possibly a hundred years later, apprentices and their parents complaining about the alleged failure of masters and mistresses to carry out the terms of an apprenticeship predominated among petitioners. These parents may not have been wealthy, but they will have been able to afford to pay to apprentice their child. In the rare instances where the parents' occupation is described, they are of middling status (carpenter, chapman, saddler, and so on).[94]

91 CLRO, Mayor's Court File of Original Bills MC1/3, items 5, 20, 42, 73, 162, 312, 314, 328, 334 (aldermen), 9, 64, 100, 110, 127, 142, 152, 177, 178, 193, 211, 215, 218, 219, 238, 299, 313, 322, 327, 335, 338 (future aldermen).

92 E.g., CLRO, Mayor's Court File of Original Bills MC1/3A, items 1, 14, 61; *ibid.*, item 33.

93 Bills marked 'supplication' are rare by this stage, apprentices' petitions apart. There are no definite petitions in *CalPMR 1458–81*, and only four (all brought by apprentices) in *CalPMR 1437–57*, pp. 50, 65, 114 (twice).

94 CLRO, Mayor's Court File of Original Bills, MC1/2A, items 62–72, esp. items 62, 66, 67; MC1/3, items 171, 290, 295, 339.

The Sheriffs' Court

There is a contrast between the names and designators of Sheriffs' Court litigants recorded in the Husting rolls and in the one surviving part of a Sheriff's Court roll which underlines the need for caution when attempting to use records of appeals (in the modern sense) in order to assess the social and financial status of parties to cases in the city's courts. Whereas plaintiffs and defendants in Sheriffs' Court cases listed in the Husting rolls tended to belong to leading city families or to be foreign or denizen merchants, the majority of Sheriffs' Court litigants had rather more homely names and many of these were probably of much more modest status: Henry Herdeman, Roger and Amicia Trugge, and Henry Cook of Westminster, for instance.[95] On the other hand, lists of plaintiffs and defendants who appeared at or were summoned to a court held on 1 July 1320 provide the occupations of fifteen individuals across quite a broad social range: a stockfishmonger, a tableter [tablet or gaming-board maker, herald?], two goldsmiths, a 'copour' [cooper, coper?], two clerks, two skinners, a baker, a butcher, a porter, a nurse, a sawyer and a merchant. Of the 94 litigants 12 were women (just under 13 per cent), divided equally between plaintiffs and defendants; two were acting as their late husbands' executrices, and three were suing or being sued together with their husbands.[96]

The comparative commonness in this court of cases alleging trespasses involving genuine physical violence brought relatively more poor men and women into it: whether or not poor people were more violent than their wealthier contemporaries, they were almost certainly more likely to be sued or prosecuted for violent behaviour. For those of limited means, the Sheriffs' Court was, during our period, evidently the cheapest and probably the easiest way of formally going to law in the city. In 1320, Thomas Orpedeman sued a client for 1*s* 8*d* owed to him for acting as an essoiner on several occasions, and William le Despenser sought to

[95] CLRO, Sheriffs' Court Roll (1320), mm. 3v, 7, 7v.

[96] CLRO, Sheriffs' Court Roll (1320), mm. 1, 1v. Occupations are only included here if given separately from the surname, though it is possible that at this date the surname indicated occupation wherever no additional designator was provided ('William le Taverner' as opposed to 'William le Taverner, chaucer').

recover the comparatively modest sum of 12*d*.[97] That said, it was not a poor man's court: in 1321 the plaintiff in a trespass case, Bartholomew Muscard, spicer, briefly recovered the enormous sum of £1,000 in damages from the defendant, Benedict Reyner of Florence, saddler.[98] The social status of litigants no doubt varied as widely as the value of the assets over which they litigated.

Among litigants, therefore, there is a noticeable relationship between two of the city's courts and their own wealth and status. Litigants in the Husting, like Husting jurors, included significant numbers of men and women from the higher social and economic groups, both within and outside the ranks of the city's freemen. The Mayor's Court, too, attracted more than its fair share of such people, and on its common-law side seems normally only to have dealt with poorer individuals if they broke city ordinances. Relatively poor men and women may nevertheless have used the services of the mayor and aldermen to resolve their disputes informally more often than the surviving records show, perhaps particularly when they were with wealthy or important citizens. For most litigants and accused persons, however, it was the Sheriffs' Court where they sued, were sued, or were prosecuted.

[97] CLRO, Sheriffs' Court Roll (1320), m. 13v. In 1320, 12*d* equated to six days' to a week's wages for a London labourer: Dyer, *Standards of Living in the Later Middle Ages*, pp. 215, 220.

[98] CLRO, HR CP53, mm. 22–22v.

7

THE CITY'S LAW OFFICERS

INTRODUCTION

This chapter examines developments in the city's law offices. Whether or not any of the city's law officers presided over the city courts during our period, their characteristics, too, will have had an impact on the character of the courts in which they worked. At the beginning of our period, in 1300, there were probably no law officers: meaning, men employed by the city specifically for their legal expertise. By the end, in 1550, there were four (and not only had several common clerks trained as common lawyers, but one had recently quitted office on his creation as a serjeant at law). They were the recordership, the common serjeanty, and the two undershrievalties of London.

London was well ahead of other English cities and towns in establishing law offices which were distinct from its clerkships. Since no other borough was a county before 1373, when Bristol was granted that privilege, and therefore only London had its own sheriff before that date, naturally no other borough had under-sheriffs before 1373 either.[1] More surprising is that recorderships were still very rare in 1400; and there appear to have been no other common serjeanties in our period. The first mention of a recorder in the records of Bristol, which was the leading provincial city at the beginning of our period, occurs in 1344, although the office may have been introduced in the 1330s. The first known recorder of the next wealthiest and, probably, largest, provincial city in the late fourteenth century, York, was Thomas Thornhill (1388?–1408); an ordinance of 1385 decreed that the office should be filled by a man 'knowing the law and of good repute' and possibly established the office for the first time. Other cities

[1] Veale, *Great Red Book of Bristol: Text, Part III*, p. 14.

among the 'top twelve' provincial cities of the time do not seem to have had recorders in the fourteenth century. Winchester and Norwich did not have recorders *eo nomine* until the early fifteenth century. The medium-sized towns were even slower to establish the office. Gloucester, for example, did without until 1534.[2] As to common serjeanties, Bristol had an officer known as the 'common attorney' by 1449, when he was ordered to process before the mayor on certain feastdays, 'after the rewle of the Citee of London'. Little seems to be known about this officer, who was still being fee'd by the city in 1627/8. He might have discharged some of the functions of the London common serjeant (for example, acting as public prosecutor), but that is far from certain.[3] Two of the questions addressed in this chapter are, therefore, Why were the recordership and the common serjeanty established when they were, and how, if at all, did their functions change?

Other questions examined here relate to the professionalisation of the city's law offices. The introduction of law offices with specified functions which could overlap with, but were clearly distinct from, the general run of city clerkships and other mainly administrative offices was part of a process of differentiation and specialisation which was well under way in London by the end of the thirteenth century. Almost from the moment of their introduction, these offices appear to have been held by 'professionals', that is, men who specialised in work of this type and were not simply, for example, freemen who undertook the offices as part of their involvement in city government. That is not to say that all the holders of the city law offices were necessarily specialist lawyers at any given point thereafter, or that, even if they were specialist lawyers, they were lawyers of similar status throughout our period. One aim of this chapter is therefore to try to demonstrate the extent to which the city's law officers were or became legally

[2] Bickley, *Little Red Book of Bristol,* I, pp. 24, 15; Basile and others, *Lex Mercatoria*, pp. 116–18; Pugh, *Victoria County History of the City of York*, p. 74; Furley, *City Government of Winchester,* pp. 49–50; Hudson, Tingey, *Records of the City of Norwich*, I, p. 104; Elrington, *Victoria County History of the City of Gloucester*, p. 55.

[3] Veale, *Great Red Book of Bristol: Text, Part I*, p. 121; Livock, *City Chamberlains' Accounts*, p. 102. Edward Dowtinge was elected 'to the office of common attorney and undersheriff of the city of Bristol' in 1571: Stanford, *Ordinances of Bristol*, p. 46.

professionalised between the early fourteenth and the mid-sixteenth centuries and the reasons for these developments.

It is not the easiest of issues to address, not least because legal professionalism was identified or proved in different ways at different times: for example, simply by occupying certain law offices or by repeatedly being employed as a legal adviser or representative in the fourteenth century, by membership of an inn of court in the fifteenth century, by successful completion of a specific course of legal study in the sixteenth. To some, every man who ever attended a legal inn, held a session of a manor court, acted as a legal representative or regularly offered advice on the law was a lawyer. Others would restrict the status to those who worked almost exclusively as legal advisers and representatives, and even then would exclude scriveners and others whose functions were as much clerical as legal. Here, as far as possible the approach will be to use the designators of lawyerliness employed by contemporaries (not least, describing someone a 'countor/narrator/pleader' or 'attorney in X court') and to regard as lawyers those men whose training and career patterns corresponded to the training and career patterns of other undoubted lawyers of the period.

DEVELOPMENT OF THE CITY'S LAW OFFICES

The recordership

According to A. B. Beaven, who compiled a list of London aldermen from the thirteenth century to the early twentieth century, the first holder of the recordership was Geoffrey de Nortone. Nortone, who was elected an alderman in 1297, is supposed to have held the office between 1298 and his death in 1303 or 1304. Beaven gave no source for his belief; he was, at the time of writing his notes on Nortone, unable to find the relevant reference.[4] The probability is, however, that he was thinking of an entry in Letterbook B which notes that in November 1298 the mayor and aldermen 'granted to Geoffrey de "Norte", their

[4] Beaven, *Aldermen of London*, I, p. 378, followed by e.g. Thrupp, *Merchant Class of Medieval London*, p. 358, Chew, Kellaway, *London Assize of Nuisance*, 'Index', *sub* 'Norton'.

co-alderman, the sum of £10 and the fee of deeds and wills for making records in the Husting from Easter [1298] until the Easter following'.[5]

In support of Beaven's early date for the establishment of the recordship are a few specific references to a recorder before 1304, the date at which the first man definitely to hold the office was sworn in. In February 1302, for example, it was decreed that the sheriffs were to provide clerks to enrol the pleas of the Husting at their own expense. These enrolments were to be read out before the mayor, recorder and four aldermen on the following day, to confirm that they were correctly entered.[6] If Nortone was not the recorder in 1302, who was?

That question may however be misconceived. There is another entry of almost the same date (1303, although the words may be older than the entry), which refers to the claim by the grandson of the sometime castellain of the city to be entitled, among other things rather derogatory to the city's honour and liberties, to deliver 'touz les jugemenz ... parmy sa bouche, solonc le record des Recordours de la Gihale'.[7] This is interesting, both because it provides an unexpected ancestor for the recorder in his role of the record personified, and because it may well explain why the city felt it necessary, shortly afterwards, to set up its own recorder. It also rather suggests that the word 'recorder' was being used even at this date simply to describe those responsible for ensuring that records were kept. This would be perfectly in accord with the task given to Nortone in 1298. The need for a 'recorder', in the sense of someone with a particular responsibility for and knowledge of the records, may already have been apparent some years before he was appointed. In 1286/7, when a litigant claimed that an action had been brought previously, an officer described as the clerk of the commonalty, Hugh de Waltham, was consulted about the written record and his recollection seems to have prevailed, even though no alderman 'could be found to record or remember it'.[8] It may therefore be that the word 'recorder' did not become exclusively associated with a particular and important office until after 1300. If so, it might explain why the city's counsel claimed in the

[5] *CalLBB*, pp. 218–19.

[6] Riley, *Munimenta Gildhallae*, II, i, p. 88 (for the date); *ibid.*, I, pp. 402–3 (for the main text).

[7] Riley, *Munimenta Gildhallae*, II, i, pp. 149–51.

[8] CLRO, HR PL22, m. 18.

1321 eyre that Londoners had been accustomed since time immemorial to claim their franchises and free customs (before the royal justices in eyre) by the mouth of their recorder.[9] Given that the last London eyre had been in 1276, either the city was wrong, or someone who was known as a recorder was active long before Geoffrey de Nortone was appointed to supervise the city's legal records. M. Weinbaum, editor of the rolls of the 1276 eyre, suggested that the alderman who was most knowledgeable about city custom had in the early days been assigned the task of ensuring that records were kept.[10]

Whether or not this is so, the first recorder to have his admission noted as such in the surviving city records was John de Wengrave. Wengrave was already an alderman (just: he had been elected the previous year) when he was sworn in as recorder in January 1304. He succeeded Nortone in the function of overseeing the proper and lawful enrolment of Husting pleas, and, again like Nortone, was paid £10 a year and received a fee (specified as 1*s* 8*d*) for 'every deed, writing and testament enrolled in the aforesaid Husting'. In 1310, however, his fee was raised by an additional £5.[11] This higher level of remuneration reflects the very marked difference between the scale of his activities and Nortone's, if indeed Nortone can be considered as his predecessor in anything more than a partial sense.

By the first quarter of the fifteenth century, the recorder was clearly established as London's foremost law officer. In 'Liber Albus', the chapter describing his office begins: 'he will be and has customarily been one of the most learned and most able apprentices at law in the whole realm' – in other words, a man already rising towards the heights of the legal profession. His duties were to sit at the mayor's right hand, recording and pronouncing (proclaiming) judgments, and to 'record orally' the process of courts presided over by the mayor and aldermen whenever cases were heard on error before the central court justices at St Martin le Grand. It was also customary by this stage that the recorder would act as the mayor and aldermen's mouthpiece before the

[9] Chew, *Eyre 1321*, p. 15; see also Clanchy, *From Memory to Written Record*, p. 77.

[10] Weinbaum, *Eyre 1276*, p. xxviii.

[11] *CalLBC*, pp. 132–3; *CalEMCR*, p. 13; *CalLBD*, p. 313.

king and council, and indeed in any court, including the high court of Parliament, in any matter relating to the city.[12]

This account of the recorder and his office is however almost certainly misleading in its emphasis. It comes from a section of the custumal which appears to have been composed personally by the then common clerk, John Carpenter, shortly before the work was completed in 1419. Carpenter was clearly keen to emphasise the knowledge and brilliant eloquence of this great city officer. More importantly, perhaps, his focus on the recorder's pre-eminence as a common lawyer unbalances the picture and reflects the pre-occupations of his time. It is unsafe to assume that the duties and responsibilities of the recorder were the same in the earliest days of this office as they were in the fifteenth century.

He was probably not initially regarded primarily as a law officer. He appears to have been employed above all as a record- and court-keeper, being responsible for ensuring that the city's courts were duly and efficiently administered, its court records properly kept, its judges well-advised on its laws and custom, and that the court's staff did not make mistakes which might render the city vulnerable to external intervention in its judicial activities (for example, that royal writs were correctly dealt with).[13] As we have seen, what is known of the origins of the office suggests that it was literally the requirement for a 'recorder', a record-keeper, which generated it. This appears to have been the case in Winchester, where there was a clerk who had responsibility for the records by the fourteenth century. His duties came to embrace the provision of legal advice and eventually, in the early fifteenth century, his office was divided between an underclerk and the first man known to have been described as the recorder.[14]

Nevertheless, the notion that the recorder personified the record was from the outset, perhaps, rather old-fashioned. Certainly in later years the personal appearance of the recorder before the royal justices was accompanied by a degree of ritual explanation and ceremony, suggesting a self-consciously anachronistic process. Even in the early fourteenth century, what was really needed, because of the ways that royal justices were thinking and

[12] Riley, *Munimenta Gildhallae*, I, pp. 42–3.
[13] *Les Reports de les Cases ... , The Seconde part of Henry the Sixt ...* , fo. 4, pl. 12.
[14] Furley, *City Government of Winchester*, pp. 49–50.

behaving, was someone who ensured that pleas were correctly enrolled and that due process was observed so that the city's jurisdiction would not be challenged.[15]

In practice, the city also needed someone to run its courts. In 1304, the recorder's duties were said to be to 'well and truly render all judgments in Husting after the Mayor and Aldermen have come from consultation, and have arrived at an agreement, and also all other judgments touching the commonalty of London'; to 'do justice as well to poor as to the rich', which probably means to see that the court was administered without fear or favour; to ensure that all pleas in the Husting were enrolled promptly, accurately and in an orderly manner; and to 'be prepared to expedite the business of the city' whenever required, on due warning. This early oath is in fact similar, allowing for the greater precision and elaboration of the later oaths, to the one administered at the end of the century to the sheriffs' secondaries and clerks of the paper. The 1304 oath is, in short, the oath of an officer who is chiefly an administrator, but not just an administrator: he is also the embodiment of the court, its memory and its mouth. Another version of the recorder's oath survives from the last quarter of the fourteenth century; this version was 'Englished', almost unchanged, about a hundred years later. It, too, is primarily concerned with the need to protect the rights, customs and profits of the city, and with the just and efficient administration of its courts. The recorder was certainly required to give good advice to the mayor and aldermen, but it was not specifically legal advice and it was neither given solely in the city's law courts nor confined to legal and legislative matters. Loyalty to and activity and alertness on behalf of the city was what was demanded.[16]

The common serjeanty

The role of the common serjeant was quite different and distinct from that of the other city law officers, in that this officer seems

[15] Martin, *Husting Rolls of Deeds and Wills*, p. 8; Chew, Weinbaum, *Eyre 1244*, pp. xx–xxi and 102–4.

[16] *CalLBC*, pp. 132–3; *CalLBD*, pp. 4–6; Kellaway, 'John Carpenter's Liber Albus', p. 75; Riley, *Munimenta Gildhallae*, I, pp. 308–9 (referring to the 'Roi Richard [II, 1377–99]'); *CalLBD*, p. 33 (substituting for King Richard, 'Kyng Edward [IV, 1461–83]', in a fifteenth century hand).

from the outset to have been regarded mainly as an advocate and specialist legal adviser, possibly with an emphasis on expertise in the common law rather than city custom. As with the recordership, there is some doubt about the date when the office was first established. Much confusion has been caused by the fact that the same title, *communis serviens*, was for many years used without distinction for the city's law officer and for the city officer known later as the 'common sergeant crier' (1343), 'common crier' (1370), and 'common sergeant at arms/mace' (early fifteenth century on).[17] It remains difficult to determine when the common serjeanty at law was estabished. Certainly the first note of the admission of an undoubted common serjeant is not evidence that the office was first established at that point. Equally, it is doubtful whether the first known common serjeant was the first man to carry out at least some of the functions which were in the future to be closely associated with the common serjeanty: acting as the city's prosecutor and looking after the interests of city orphans.

There are a number of contenders to be considered as the first common serjeant. One is Ralph Pecok, a city clerk of whom it has been said, 'the first attorney to appear for the commonalty[, he] was common serjeant in all but name'.[18] He did indeed prosecute for the commonalty on a number of occasions, although he does not seem to have had any special responsibility for orphans. It is possible, therefore, that he was being employed as the common serjeant in everything but name from the mid 1290s on.[19] In fact, however, if Pecok was common serjeant in all but name – or even in name, but unrecorded as such – one of his colleagues was prosecuting on the commonalty's behalf during his period of office.[20] Moreover, for very many years men who acted as

[17] *CalLBF*, p. 87, *CalLBG*, p. 265, *CalLBI*, p. 189. For the confusion, see Cohen, *A History of the Bar and Attornatus to 1450*, pp. 251–3 (Thomas de Kent and Thomas Juvenal were common sergeants at arms, not common serjeants at law); *CalLBD*, pp. 196–7, fn. 2; Williams, *Medieval London*, p. 95, again, mistakenly including Juvenal and his successor, 'the lawyer' Kent; for the correction, see Masters, 'The Common Serjeant', p. 379.

[18] Chew, Kellaway, *London Assize of Nuisance*, p. xxix.

[19] *CalLBC*, pp. 14, 11 (in this instance, when the city was in the king's hand, Pecok prosecuted for the king), *CalEMCR*, pp. 80, 113; Chew, Kellaway, *London Assize of Nuisance*, p. 15, where he is described as the commonalty's attorney; *CalLBA*, p. 78, *CalLBC*, p. 107.

[20] *CalEMCR*, p. 46 (1299, John de la Chaumbre, then 'clerk of the city', twice prosecuted on the commonalty's behalf).

attorneys in the city's courts, and who may or may not have held other city offices, occasionally prosecuted for the city while common serjeants are known to have been in office. As late as the 1390s an attorney, Gilbert [de] Meldebourne, was acting for the commonalty in a Husting case. Prosecuting on behalf of the city may have been one of the common serjeant's main functions, but it was not exclusive to him, at least until the fifteenth century.[21]

A second contender is Robert de Kelleseye, who claimed to have been 'common serjeant' in 1312. At about this date, Kelleseye had been granted a fee of 100*s* (£5) instead of the 40*s* (£2) allowed him for unspecified services in 1310 or thereabouts.[22] Given that Kelleseye was very closely associated with the first recorder, later mayor, John de Wengrave, it is possible that the common serjeanty emerged in the 1310s, and that it was initially conceived as an adjunct to the recordership. If so, it may not have fully separated out from the other office until after Kelleseye's dismissal – hence, perhaps, the failure of the city records to mention Kelleseye's appointment (and his son's belief that it was in fact the recordership that Kelleseye had held).[23] On the other hand, Kelleseye's reference to being common serjeant was in response to the allegation that he had been implicated in attempts in 1312 to enable a murderer to evade justice. He protested that he had merely accepted a cask of wine from the man in return for helping him, and requested 'judgment whether he should be molested about it, *especially since he was not at that time holding any office in the said city*' [my emphasis].[24] What Kelleseye may therefore have meant was that he was a serjeant licensed to practise in the city courts – which he undoubtedly was, having been admitted to that office in 1305 – and had simply been retained privately to act for the accused man.

The third contender is John de Waldeshef. Before he received his fee and the freedom of the city in March 1319, he had represented the city in various Westminster courts; he was subsequently the city's member for Parliament and one of a deputation sent to see the king in 1321.[25] Although Waldeshef was described in 1322 as 'sworn serjeant of the city', this probably meant either that he was the city's counsel at Westminster, or,

[21] *CalLBC*, pp. 34–5; *CalPMR 1323–64*, pp. 205–6; *CalPMR 1364–81*, p. 174; CLRO, HR PL113, m. 3v.

[22] *CalLBD*, p. 31. [23] *CalHW&D*, II, p. 177.

[24] Chew, *Eyre 1321*, pp. 50–1. [25] *CalLBE*, pp. 20, 103, 104, 139.

more likely, that he, like Kelleseye, had been licensed to practise as an advocate in the city courts.[26] There is no other evidence to suggest that he was the common serjeant.

The first common serjeant, in the later sense of the city's own advocate and legal adviser, was almost certainly Gregory de Nortone, son of Geoffrey, who was appointed common serjeant and countor of the city shortly after Waldeshef received his appointment in March 1319, with what became the standard fee of 100*s*.[27] Even then, the office may have been regarded as an experiment, or perhaps Nortone, as the son of an alderman, received special treatment, because the next certain appointment of a common serjeant was not until three years after Nortone junior became recorder in 1327.[28] From then onwards, however, appointments to the common serjeanty appear to have become regular and routine.

What prompted the creation of this office is nowhere stated. One reason for its establishment may have been to provide the city with a law officer of its own who could advise it and act for it at Westminster and elsewhere before the royal justices. Even before 1300, the city was paying annual retainers to men who worked in the Westminster courts to provide it with legal advice and, probably, to act there as advocates on its behalf.[29] However, it looks as though the city had ceased to appoint standing counsel by the late 1320s. At least, it is very difficult to see how the annual expenditure on fees between 1328 and 1337 could be stretched to cover the number and types of retainers that were being paid to Westminster-based counsel and attorneys in the 1310s.[30] Providing advice and perhaps acting as the city's advocate at

[26] *CalLBE*, pp. 31–2. Waldeshef appeared on a couple of occasions in 1318 as an attorney in Chancery: *CalCR 1318–23*, pp. 47, 106.

[27] *CalLBE*, p. 20. [28] CLRO, HR PL49, m. 9; HR CP54, m. 6v.

[29] In 1311, three men were retained 'to serve ... the commonalty before the justices of the lord the king': *CalLBD*, p. 251.

[30] In the 1311/2 list of annual fees, city officers cost the Chamber over £45 a year; attorneys acting for the city in other courts cost it a further £6 16*s* 8*d*; and counsel acting for the city cost it £10 13*s* 4*d*: CLRO, LBE, fos. 201v–2, 229v–30, 243v–4. Summary city Chamber accounts covering all but six months between October 1328 and May 1337 show that the cost of the city bureaucracy had risen, and cannot have come to much less than the £57 a year which was then its maximum total expenditure on annual fees: LBF, fos. 2v, 9v–10; *CalLBE*, pp. 20 (common serjeant's fee of £5 paid for first time, 1319), 242 (recorder's fee increased by £5, 1329).

Westminster may therefore have been one of the common serjeant's functions.

Against the proposition that this was a consideration at the time that the office was established is the fact that, almost contemporaneously with the appearance of the first man definitely to have held the common serjeanty, the city appointed (if very briefly) as its recorder someone who was an experienced Westminster-based serjeant, Geoffrey de Hertpole.[31] As he was appointed to succeed Wengrave, who had been dismissed in disgrace, and was moreover appointed in the year preceding the last full eyre undergone by the city, that is however not the strongest of objections. More convincing, perhaps, is the fact that none of its early common serjeants appears ever to have practised at Westminster. Nortone and his immediate successors were not well-equipped either to advise the city when it litigated elsewhere or to represent it.

It seems much more likely that the main aim initially was to provide the city with a public prosecutor who acted in its own courts, this being the one function which for many years clearly distinguished the common serjeant from the recorder. There is no evidence that any of the men appointed in the late thirteenth and early fourteenth centuries to represent the city's interests in the Westminster courts also acted as the commonalty's prosecutor in cases which were brought in the city itself against those who breached its laws. So there was scope for the creation of such an office. A related aspect of the common serjeant's role was his responsibility for the protection of city orphans (the minor heirs of dead freemen) and their inheritances, which were a valuable source of capital for citizens who needed to fund new enterprises or expand existing ones. Although the city's chamberlain was responsible for controlling the assets themselves, it was the common serjeant who advised the city about, and who most commonly prosecuted on behalf of the orphans during, any litigation resulting from the debtors' failure either to pay for the orphans' maintenance or to repay the principal when the heirs achieved their majority.[32]

[31] *CalLBE*, pp. 11–12.
[32] Carlton, 'Administration of London's Court of Orphans', pp. 22, 24–31, 32.

It is also possible that initially it was the common serjeant, and not the recorder, who was expected to provide legal advice to the bench in the city courts. The very fact that the man usually regarded as the first common serjeant was described as the common serjeant and countor suggests that this officer was not simply seen as the city's advocate, but also had a more general advisory role. His oath, as preserved in 'Liber Albus', says that he is to defend the city's laws, customs and liberties and give good and loyal 'counseille' in everything relating to the city's profit and welfare, as well as protecting and maintaining the rights of city orphans.[33] This version of the oath appears to be roughly contemporaneous with the recorder's oath of Richard II's reign, although it does not appear among the many fourteenth-century oaths recorded in 'Letterbook D'. It was translated into English without significant change, probably in the second half of the fifteenth century. In practice, the medieval and early modern common serjeant was by turns city attorney and advocate, adviser to the city on the intricacies of the common law and mouthpiece for the city's Common Council.[34]

Having said that there is no evidence to show that common serjeants in our period ever acted as the city's advocate in open court at Westminster, it is certainly likely that, at least until the later fifteenth century, the recorder was usually accompanied by the common serjeant when he headed a deputation to the king or royal council or appeared before the Westminster justices to deliver the city's record orally. Nor were common serjeants confined, when acting externally, to supporting the recorder. In 1454 Common Serjeant Ursewyk accompanied his predecessor to see the justices of the Common Bench to complain about the alleged abuse of writs of privilege by officers of that court. Their orders were to consult with the justices and 'to show them what damages and inconveniences would result from such writs'.[35]

When accompanying the recorder, the common serjeant may merely have been present to advise and support the other, but it could also be that any legal argument resulting from the recorder's rehearsal of the record was in fact conducted by him. Unfortunately, the records are generally uninformative about his role.

[33] Riley, *Munimenta Gildhallae*, I, p. 310; *CalLBD*, pp. 196–7.
[34] *CalLBH*, p. 15, *CalLBI*, p. 85. [35] *CalPMR 1437–57*, p. 136.

In 1453, for example, in the course of a prosecution launched against bakers who failed to use the authorised weights for corn and flour, one of the sheriffs appeared in Chancery accompanied by the recorder, the common serjeant and both undersheriffs. The case was then transferred to the Exchequer Chamber and heard before the two chief justices, three justices, and the master of the rolls (of whom, three were former city law officers). Although the civic record mentions 'counsel for both parties', no further details are given. What precise role the common serjeant had when he appeared in Chancery, and whether he spoke for the city in the Exchequer Chamber, is therefore unclear.[36] It could be, however, that he was the man who attended specifically 'to prosecute for the city's affairs'. A reason for suspecting that this was so is that one glimpse we have of informal discussions between the city law officers and other lawyers shows the common serjeant taking a full part in the debate, with the recorder doing little other than to raise or press particular points. This seems to be what was happening in the discussion in 1492 of an issue raised in the Mayor's Court, in which the participants were Recorder FitzWilliam, who is reported as merely putting forward one proposition, Thomas Frowyk, who was either the current or the recently departed common serjeant, his successor, Thomas Marowe, and two other men: 'More', quite possibly John More, who was then the bridge house counsel, and [Edward?] 'Grantham'.[37] The common serjeant also took a full part in the discussion of a Sheriffs' Court case from the 1540s reported by the future undersheriff, Randolph Cholmondley.[38] Any contribution made by the undersheriff himself went unrecorded, perhaps because, as apparently was the case with the recorder in other instances, the discussion was being held 'before him' in the sense that it was being argued out in his presence and for his benefit, in order to resolve some tricky point of law.

The undershrievalties

The two city sheriffs were in fact the sheriffs of London and Middlesex: they shared the two roles. This was not true of their

[36] *CalLBK*, pp. 359–60, CLRO, Jor. 5, fos. 128v, 137, 138v.
[37] Thorne/Baker, *Readings and Moots*, II, pp. 259–60.
[38] Baker, *Reports … of King Henry VIII, vol. II*, p. 453.

undersheriffs, however. From the very start of our period there was a sheriff's clerk known specifically (from time to time, at least) as 'the undersheriff of Middlesex'. This is how Roger Appelby, elsewhere referred to simply as 'Sheriff *N*'s clerk', was described in 1298.[39] William de Londonstone, Appelby's contemporary, was also on one occasion described as the 'undersheriff', and he was probably the first known undersheriff of London, although Roger de Portlaunde, mentioned as holding his sheriff's court in 1291, is also a contender.[40] The Middlesex undershrievalty in due course became completely separated from its London counterpart, and was for much of the fifteenth century usually held in annual rotation by the clerks of King's Bench, into which the London sheriffs made their Middlesex returns.

It looks as though there was still only one London undersheriff in 1300, and possibly for quite some time after that. When in 1309 the sheriffs' clerks were listed, only the senior sheriff had clerks described as 'first' and 'second'.[41] It seems likely that his first clerk was, or was the equivalent of, the London undersheriff. Likewise, regulations (undated, but probably pre-1324) refer to the '*clericus capitalis unius vicecomitis* of London', probably meaning 'chief clerk of one of the sheriffs'.[42] Part of the difficulty in determining when the second London undersheriff emerged lies in the fact that, in the early days, the word itself was rarely used. Londonstone was on most occasions, like Appelby, simply called 'Sheriff *N*'s clerk'. In the 1309 list John de la Chaumbre, the former city clerk (or clerk of the Chamber – whence, no doubt, his name) was simply described as 'primus'.[43] At this date, it is probable that the first and second clerks' vernacular titles would have been closer to the 'prothonotary' and 'secondary' of the fifteenth century and beyond. A 'chief clerk acting as undersheriff' is however mentioned in ordinances of 1356, and from this date onwards 'undersheriff' appears to have been the standard title.[44]

[39] *CalEMCR*, p. 23, *CalLBC*, p. 179.
[40] *CalEMCR*, pp. 236–7 (1301); Riley, *Memorials*, pp. 27–8.
[41] *CalLBC*, p. 181. [42] Riley, *Munimenta Gildhallae*, II, i, p. 98.
[43] *CalEMCR*, p. 106. There is however apparently a reference to a London undersheriff in the early twelfth century: Macray, *Chronicon Abbatiae Ramsiensis*, I, p. 249.
[44] *CalLBG*, p. 72.

By the 1330s, nevertheless, there may already have been two London sheriffs' 'chief clerks'. Roger de Depham and John de Hardyngham are listed directly after their sheriffs in a witness-list of 1332 and are said to have received two writs on their masters' behalves from the chamberlain a few years later, so might both have been dealing with city business on their respective masters' behalves.[45] If so, things remained rather fluid for a while. There was a period of experimentation in the middle of the fourteenth century, possibly associated with the physical separation of the Middlesex undershrievalty from the sheriffs' staffs. In 1356 the city ordered the sheriffs to hold their counters in common, so there could be only one undersheriff. Two years later, this particular section of the ordinance was reversed.[46] It may well have been this decision, and the reasons behind it, which led to the emergence of a fully duplicated organisation, with each sheriff having his own undersheriff, secondary and clerk of the papers.

The version of the oath of the undersheriffs and their clerks recorded in 'Liber Albus', and probably of late fourteenth-century origin, required that they were incorruptible and unbiased in their dealings with 'all who plead before [them]'. They were only to summon for jury-service men who were of good character and close to neither party; they were to record the pleadings accurately and to take reasonable fees for enrolments; they were not to delay judgments unnecessarily, nor to fine people more than was due; they were to show all (royal) writs relating to the city's liberties to the mayor and city counsel; they were to report to the chamberlain any violent acts involving the spilling of blood, and to raise and to pay to the Exchequer all that was due from the shrievalty, not taking anything for themselves; and they were to supervise the sheriffs' sergeants, who had certain rights of carriage within the city. Above all, obedience to the city's governors, loyalty to the city itself, and the provision of sound honest counsel were what was expected.[47]

In practice, the late medieval undersheriff supervised the running and administration of his sheriff's court and counter: in 1475, for example, the undersheriffs were ordered not to admit

[45] *CalLBE*, pp. 286, 300. [46] *CalLBG*, p. 72; CLRO, HR PL80, m. 11.
[47] Riley, *Munimenta Gildhallae*, I, pp. 317–18.

any bill unless it had been written and signed by a duly appointed writer of court bills.[48] The name of one of the first undersheriffs to be recorded as such, John de Morton, is known to us because in 1380 he was accused of soliciting a bribe to 'render judgment and enter it', whereupon Morton allegedly had not only endorsed an obligation with a note that it had been paid, but had also falsely told the plaintiff that judgment had been enrolled, with the result that the defendant was released from prison.[49] As has already been mentioned, by the sixteenth century, if not earlier, sheriffs tended to leave the undersheriffs to preside over the court held 'in the hall of the counter', at which routine process was undertaken. This was however evidently not a particularly onerous duty. In the 1510s, Undersheriff Thomas More was said by his friend Erasmus to be acting 'as a judge in civil causes ... (but only on Thursdays until lunchtime)'.[50]

In the 1340s and 1350s, the Husting rolls refer occasionally to the fact that Sheriff *N*'s clerk had testified on his behalf. At first sight, it looks as though these men might have been undersheriffs, with, for example, John Lucas taking over from Stephen de Waltham in 1343, Henry de Padyngtone taking over from John Lucas in 1350, and all three men's tenure being overlapped by that of John de Morton. Unfortunately, Lucas was still active, though not in this particular role, after Padyngtone had 'taken over' from him.[51] So it may be unsafe to assume that testifying on a sheriff's behalf was at this stage an activity confined to undersheriffs. It became so, however. From the 1350s onwards, the possessory assize rolls quite often mention that the record was brought in by an undersheriff.[52] This suggests that 'recording' whatever had occurred in the Sheriffs' Court, whether orally or in writing, was by the second half of the fourteenth century considered to be one of the undersheriffs' special functions. It is also possible that this was part of a recent formalisation of their roles and duties. In 1423, it was stated as settled custom that an undersheriff who had left office could not return as of record

[48] CLRO, Jor. 8, fo. 93. [49] *CalPMR 1364–81*, pp. 266–7.

[50] Suger, *Roper's Life of St Thomas More*, p. 9.

[51] CLRO, HR PL64, m. 6v, HR CP67, m. 12v; HR PL77, m. 3; HR CP82, m. 9; but HR PL78, m. 11v.

[52] Chew, *London Possessory Assizes*, pp. 46, 100 fn. 1, 105, 111, 114 fn. 2, *et seq.*

anything done before him, which of course implies that a serving undersheriff did have this authority.[53]

PROFESSIONALISATION OF THE CITY'S LAW OFFICES

The recordership

Legal professionalism can be judged both positively (by what a man was) and negatively (by what he was not). Recorders, from the moment that the office definitely existed, were aldermen. This might suggest that they were not professionals, that is, specialists in this type of work. The early recorders were, however, not aldermen for any significant period before they became the recorder. They were invariably elected to the aldermanic bench at much the same time as they were admitted to the recordership. With the possible exception, therefore, of John de Wengrave, who went on to be mayor, recorders very probably were professionals from the outset.[54]

Why the city felt the need to admit its recorders as aldermen is nowhere explained. As aldermen were not formally part of the bench of the Husting or Mayor's Court in the early 1300s, it is unlikely that they had to be made aldermen in order to justify their position on the benches of those two courts. It may have been intended to bind them more closely to the city's interests than would otherwise have been the case. The aldermen may also have felt that the recorder needed to be clearly both on a level with, and one of, them. Or it may simply have been a continuation of former practice: advisers on city law and custom had generally been aldermen in the past. Either way, practice and attitudes changed in the last quarter of the fourteenth century. William Cheyne (1376–89) was not elected alderman at the time he was appointed recorder, and this established a new pattern.[55]

The reason for this might be that the recorder's standing as a member of the bench was by now taken for granted. What the

[53] CLRO, Jor. 2, fo. 10v.

[54] For details of the city's recorders, see Appendix 7.1.

[55] An entry in Letterbook H which appears to include him in May 1377 among the aldermen is misleading; he was listed, as was by then customary for recorders, directly after the mayor, and his designation was omitted in error: *CalLBH*, p. 64.

evidence suggests, however, is that he was beginning to be seen by the aldermen not as a fellow, however specialist his knowledge, but as a lawyer employed by the city. By the early fifteenth century at the latest, the recorder did not, for instance, vote during mayoral elections. Instead, he acted as a supervising and returning officer.[56] A good example of the way he was viewed by this stage is provided in the record of a 1389 case, appealed the following year (*Walpole* v. *Botlesham*). The mayor, aldermen and sheriffs, being unable to decide what should be done in the case of a verdict which was clearly false, had, on the grounds that 'they were not expert in the law', left the matter in the hands of Recorder Cheyne. Cheyne was instructed to consult the common serjeant and William Cressewyk, who was probably one of the under-sheriffs at the time.[57] Although this was an unusual and indeed improper decision, made when the city's jurisdiction and authority was under pressure from the king's uncle, John of Gaunt, it is one of a number of factors which suggest that the city's governors were beginning to distinguish between the various elements of their judicial responsibilities and to regard some (such as city custom and the merchant law) as being more comfortably within their understanding and knowledge than others.

These developments were the culmination of quite a lengthy process. The city had certainly employed recorders who were clearly professional lawyers in the fourteenth century: notably Geoffrey de Hertpole and Hugh de Sadelynstanes.[58] Cheyne, too, would have a good claim to be considered a professional lawyer, if Recorder Cheyne is to be identified with the future chief justice of King's Bench. However, the identification is improbable, since it would require Cheyne to have had an active career of well over sixty years; although it is just possible that the reason that Cheyne was not admitted to the aldermanry on election was that he was an able but youthful 'rising star'. But whether or not Recorder Cheyne and the chief justice were the same man, it is certain that, by the end of the fourteenth century, London recorders were indeed professional lawyers. None of Cheyne's successors seem to have emerged, as Roger de Depham had done in the late 1330s,

[56] Riley, *Munimenta Gildhallae*, I, p. 21.
[57] *CalLBH*, pp. 395–6, *CalPMR 1381–1412*, pp. 158–60.
[58] For a biography of Hertpole, see Brand, *Earliest English Law Reports, II*, pp. lv–lvii.

from the city's bureaucracy. John Carpenter's comment that the recorder was 'one of the most learned and most able apprentices of the law in the whole of the kingdom' was a fair description of the recorders with whom he worked.

And yet the subsequent careers of the majority of the recorders of London before the sixteenth century are not quite what one would expect of the most learned and able apprentices at law in England. After 1400, it did become more common for them to be appointed to the benches of one of the Westminster courts. Of the recorders who served before 1440, five received appointments to the Westminster benches (six, if Chief Justice William Cheyne had been recorder), three to judgeships in King's Bench or the Common Bench.[59] At this period, judged by success at Westminster, recorders were undoubtedly progressing further than most undersheriffs or common serjeants. For the rest of the fifteenth century, however, they were less successful in this respect. Of seven recorders admitted to that office between 1440 and 1500, only three reached the Westminster benches, and two of the three did so as chief barons of the Exchequer, a position regarded as junior to the judgeships of the two main common-law courts.[60]

This is curious. It may be the case that some were reluctant to give up lucrative city offices (the fees granted by the city were certainly not their sole or even main source of income). John Bartone senior, for example, was admitted to the recordership in 1415, possibly shortly after refusing to accept creation as a serjeant.[61] Perhaps he had been discouraged by the experience of his immediate predecessor, Prestone, who had just been appointed a Common Bench justice, having had little or no time in which to concentrate on the extremely lucrative employment opportunities which were available to serjeants at law.[62] And bad luck evidently

[59] Robert de Swalclyve; Thomas de Lodelawe; [Cheyne?]; John Cokayne; John Prestone; John Fray: for details of the careers of these men, see Baker, *Order of Serjeants at Law*.

[60] Thomas Ursewyk, Humphrey Starkey, Thomas Billyng.

[61] The writ notifying him that he was to be created serjeant was issued on 11 July 1415: Baker, *Order of Serjeant at Law*, pp. 161, 33, 38 fn. 1. The date of his election to the recordership is not noted, but he was present as recorder at the shrieval elections on 21 September 1415: *CalLBI*, p. 143.

[62] Prestone was created serjeant at law in 1412 and a justice in 1415, but was serving as recorder until at least late November 1414, when he was noted last, in the place usually occupied by the recorder, in a commission of gaol delivery;

played a part: both Alexander Anne and his successor, Thomas Cokayne, died within a couple of years of being appointed recorder. Anne had actually been selected for a serjeanty at law when he died and Cokayne is probably the 'Cokain apprentice' who appeared in an assize in 1428, so he, too, died at about the time when he might reasonably have hoped for further advancement.[63]

It could also be that Carpenter was over-egging the pudding a little. It was not necessarily in the city's interests to select the very highest fliers among the rising legal eagles of the day. Those who received appointments to the Westminster courts tended to have foreshortened careers as city officers. As the city's journal rather plaintively put it, John Fray's appointment as a baron of the Exchequer in 1426, after a mere four years in office, left it 'destitute of a recorder'.[64] Stability was almost certainly one of the things that the Court of Aldermen aimed to achieve by its choice of recorders. Reducing the rapidity with which recorders succeeded one another during the early years of professionalisation, particularly in the 1390s, may well have required a degree of compromise in terms of quality or ambition.

Nevertheless, the shift towards a more professional recorder at the end of the fourteenth century inevitably caused the city some problems. Thereafter it was impossible to avoid electing some future serjeants and central court justices to the recordership, because the level of demand was bound to be unpredictable and the city was no doubt reluctant to employ lawyers who were second-rate or too junior. As a result, the city found itself competing for the recorder's attention. Thomas Billyng expressly cited the demanding workload at Westminster and the fact that he was receiving commissions to sit all over the country when he asked to be allowed to relinquish the recordership in 1454, a year after he was created serjeant at law.[65] At this period, the city

probably in fact until his appointment to the bench: Baker, *Order of Serjeant at Law*, p. 232; *CalLBI*, p. 131.

[63] Baker, *Readers and Readings*, pp. 19 (Anne), 144 (Cokayne); Thorne, Baker, *Readings and Moots*, I, xx, p. lix (Cokayne); CLRO, Jor. 3, fos. 173, 173v. I am most grateful to Jessica Freeman for correcting a misunderstanding which led to Anne's selection as serjeant at law being attributed to 'Alexander Anne senior' rather than to the recorder of London.

[64] CLRO, Jor. 2, 85v.

[65] CLRO, Jor. 5, fo. 196.

fathers took the view that, if a man's duties as a recorder conflicted with his desire to act privately or his royal duties, he must resign the recordership. In 1438 the Court of Aldermen explicitly forbade recorders to take fees from anyone or any body other than the city itself, 'in accordance with the ancient statutes [of the late fourteenth century] contained in "Liber Albus"'.[66] The first recorder to be created serjeant while serving was John Cokayne, who was called to assume the degree about three years after he had been appointed recorder. The introduction of the rule may well have been prompted by this novel situation: it looks as though Cokayne resigned almost immediately.[67] But the fact that it was clearly not enforced in Prestone's case, that it was felt necessary to confirm the ban forty years later, and that Billyng did not resign immediately upon being created serjeant, just five years after the ban had been confirmed, tells its own story: the pressure to relax it was almost impossible to resist. When Humphrey Starkey was elected recorder in 1471, over a decade before he was created serjeant, he was permitted not only to retain all his existing (private) clients but also to acquire new ones.[68]

This concession raises some ethical questions. Was Starkey being permitted to advise or even represent private clients in the London courts? Or was he limited to working for and advising clients who litigated elsewhere?[69] There is no doubt that Starkey's predecessors as well as his successors counselled certain types of litigants in the city courts: many city companies recorded payments to them for advice. But city companies were a special case. They played a part in the city's system of law, their ordinances, once approved, functioning as a kind of subset of the city's own, and enforced by the companies on the city's behalf. In 1468/9, for instance, the Cutlers gave the recorder a share of 15*s*, 'for to examine our [in]corporation by the act of the Parliament', and a gift worth 1*s* and 10*s*, 'to be of our counsel in certain matters sued to the Mayor', just as they gave 5*s* to the common clerk 'for his counsel in the same matter'. These payments, which were not at

66 CLRO, Jor. 3, fo. 173, Riley, *Munimenta Gildhallae*, I, pp. 308–9.
67 Baker, *Order of Serjeants at Law*, p. 505; *CalLBH*, p. 417; Chew, Kellaway, *London Assize of Nuisance*, item 641.
68 CLRO, Jor. 8, fo. 9.
69 E.g. Ives, *Legal Profession in Pre-Reformation England*, p. 297; Stevenson, *Records of the Borough of Nottingham, Vol. 2*, pp. 396–8.

any standard rate, are neither regular fees nor mere bribes.[70] It seems unlikely, however, that ordinary private clients were permitted to employ the services of the recorder in the city courts. To begin with, one would expect the practice, if allowed at all, to be regulated, for example, by forbidding the recorder to represent foreign litigants against citizens, or anyone against the city itself; which did not happen. Moreover, in 1455 a man was ordered to appear before the mayor and aldermen to account for his 'scandalous words', having said 'that the Recordor [Thomas Ursewyk] was chief of counseill with his adversary Simon Dawdeley'.[71] Whether or not the accusation was true, it seems clear that, at this date at least, the recorder was not supposed to be retained by private clients litigating in the city courts.

Ethical considerations aside, the Court of Aldermen's readiness to allow Recorder Starkey to continue in private practice was a bad omen, if control was the city's aim. Starkey's successors were visibly becoming detached from the city. In 1521 Recorder Shelley managed to persuade a manifestly reluctant Court of Aldermen to allow him to remain in office after he had been created serjeant, assuring the court of his continued diligence and attendance.[72] Evidently he was not diligent or attentive enough, because it was agreed on the election of his successor, John Baker, an undersheriff, that he must resign if created serjeant. The court took the view that a recorder who was also a serjeant could not 'well & duely occupye & excercise the matters & busynes of this citie & also his own clyants matters'. It did, however, fully appreciate the nature of its dilemma. In discussing its decision, reference was made to John Carpenter's comments, as recorded in the late fifteenth-century custumal, 'Liber Dunthorne', about the legal experience and standing of the recorder.[73]

By now, the court was fighting a losing battle. Two years later, it again changed its mind, agreeing that Recorder Baker could remain in office if created serjeant – which he was not.[74] It had no choice in the matter when it came to the election of Baker's successor in 1535: Sir Roger Cholmondley had to be exempted from the 'ancient law' forbidding recorders to be serjeants because he

70 GH Library, Cutlers' Accounts, Microfilm 7146/16/2.

71 CLRO, Jor. 5, fo. 254. 72 CLRO, Rep. 5, fo. 19.

73 Rep. 7, fo. 148 (with reference to CLRO, Liber Dunthorne, fo. 459).

74 CLRO, Rep. 8, fo. 36v.

already was one. He was also elected on the king's recommendation, the first example of successful royal interference in the elections of city recorders.[75] And Cholmondley's successor, Common Serjeant Robert Broke, was not only admitted to the freedom free of charge on election in 1545, but was granted £10 towards the costs of 'proceeding to the degree of serjeant at law' seven years later.[76]

Similarly, in 1438 the city had not only forbidden its recorder to accept fees from any other; it had also demanded that he attend the city courts on a daily basis.[77] In 1464, Recorder Ursewyk had had to seek permission (in Common Council, moreover, though no doubt the question had already been settled in the Court of Aldermen) to go to his home county for up to six weeks over the summer. Come Michaelmas, he was to be back in London, where he belonged.[78] Recorder Shelley, in 1522, also sought permission to absent himself for a couple of weeks in the summer.[79] In July 1563, however, the city had to write to the then recorder, requiring his presence at Guildhall; he does not appear to have had to seek permission to absent himself.[80] It may therefore be that the lack of noted permissions to be absent in the later sixteenth-century records reflects, not the continual presence of the recorders in the city, but the fact that it was by now taken for granted that they would be absent for at least part of the summer.

The city's inability to command the recorder's attention and presence whenever it wanted to was symptomatic of a significant shift in the balance of power between the parties, resulting both from the fact that the recordership had become simply one available step on a wider professional ladder and from changes in the structure and functions of the legal profession as a whole. By the middle of the fifteenth century, in contrast to the situation a century earlier, the published law reports contain a considerable number of references to men who at some time held a city recordership. And whereas in the second half of the fifteenth century the city could probably normally rely on its former city law officers, as serjeants and justices of the central courts, to defend its interests, by the sixteenth century the loyalty of these

[75] CLRO, Rep. 9, fos. 112v *et seq.* [76] CLRO, Rep. 11, fos. 223, 223v, 535v.
[77] CLRO, Jor. 3, fo. 173. [78] CLRO, Jor. 7, fo. 72.
[79] CLRO, Jor. 10, fo. 120v. [80] CLRO, Jor. 18, fo. 120v.

men could not even be counted upon when they were still in the city's service. In the early years of the century, Recorder Robert Sheffelde was accused of abusing his position as one of the city's members for Parliament in order to promote a bill attacking the city's company courts because they 'grew to the prejudice of the learned men of the city'.[81] Towards its end, the former recorder, William Fletewode, delivered himself of a treatise condemning the powers of the city's court of Bridewell in which he described local custom (in contrast to the [common] law) as being something defended merely 'through simplicity or ignorance'.[82] It was very much the work of a man who identified with his profession: and not just as a lawyer, but as a lawyer of the Common Bench.

The common serjeanty

One of the curious features of the fourteenth-century London common serjeanty at law is that none of the holders of the office, with the possible exception of Thomas Moryce (1356–1360/3?), who was created serjeant in 1362, were in fact serjeants at law while they were in office.[83] Indeed, apart from Moryce, none of the common serjeants before John Tremayne seem to have been particularly distinguished members of their profession. Yet it does seem clear that the city was employing these men for their advocacy skills and legal expertise, and, from the mid-fourteenth century on, at least, for not much else. It is almost certainly significant that Roger de Depham, who was probably an undersheriff or sheriff's chief clerk before he was elected common clerk and then recorder, was never the common serjeant.[84] The fact that, certainly after the first few decades of the fourteenth century, common serjeants were not automatically admitted to the freedom of the city *ex officio* on appointment, if not already freemen, suggests that they were regarded in a rather different light from the rest of the city officers (Common Serjeant Broke, it will be recollected, had to be admitted to the freedom on being elected recorder in 1545).[85]

[81] Clode, *Early History of the Guild of the Merchant Taylors*, I, p. 40 (1504).
[82] GH Library, MS 9384, 'Observations on Statutes & Customs', fos. 1–9v.
[83] See Appendix 7.2. [84] *CalLBC*, p. 181; *CalLBE*, pp. 286, 300, 5.
[85] CLRO, Rep. 11, fos. 223, 223v.

The appointment of Tremayne, who went on to be recorder and was created serjeant at law in 1401, heralded the beginning of a change. Until the 1450s, the summit of the common serjeant's achievement tended to be the city recordership.[86] Thereafter, however, common serjeants quite frequently progressed to the highest reaches of the legal profession. Between 1455 and 1545, not one went on to become the recorder. Instead, from the early 1440s until the early 1500s, former common serjeants were more likely than not to be created serjeant at law, in a proportion of three to two.[87] And if they were created serjeant at law, they had a similar chance of becoming a justice in the Common Bench or King's Bench or (in one case) a chief baron of the Exchequer.[88] Bearing in mind what was said earlier about the greater prestige of the judgeships of the King's and Common Benches compared to the Exchequer, it seems likely that contemporaries would have regarded these later fifteenth-century common sergeants as having had more successful careers in the common law than city recorders at the same date.

John Grene's admission as common serjeant in 1495 signalled another major shift. Thereafter, common serjeants not infrequently went on to one of the undershrievalties, and possibly to the recordership at a later stage. Only one, Robert Broke, pursued the once familiar route to the central court benches via a serjeanty at law. The men who held the common serjeanty were – if they were active lawyers at all - either relatively junior, or sinecurists, or both. Indeed, the last common serjeant of our period, John Mersshe, appears to have devoted his final few years in office to his duties as governor of the Merchant Adventurers.[89]

The probability that common serjeants were the first 'professional lawyers' to colonise a city office on a permanent basis may explain why, despite the fact that the status of the common serjeanty was undoubtedly lower than that of the recordership, fifteenth-century common serjeants were more likely to end up as

[86] Of the eight men serving between 1420 and 1455, Fray, Anne, Robert Danvers and Thomas Ursewyk became recorder.

[87] Of fourteen men, nine, Danvers, Moyle, Thomas Billyng, Nedeham, Guy Fairfax, Thomas Bryan, John Haugh/Hawes, Thomas Frowyk and Thomas Marowe, were all serjeants at law.

[88] Danvers, Moyle, Billyng, Fairfax, Haugh, Frowyk.

[89] Masters, 'The Common Serjeant', p. 386.

serjeants at law or on the Westminster benches. Contrariwise, common serjeants may have suffered the same fate as the serjeants at law when a relaxation of procedures in the sixteenth century led to greater competition in areas over which they had previously enjoyed a monopoly.

It certainly looks as though the common serjeant's role as the city's principal legal adviser was coming under challenge at quite an early date. By the end of the fourteenth century, he had lost to the recorder any role he might once have had as an adviser to the mayor and aldermen, and had come to be regarded specifically as the Common Council's counsel.[90] By the 1500s the Court of Aldermen reckoned that the 'common counsellors retained by the city' included, not merely the common serjeant, but also the chamberlain, the common clerk and one of the undersheriffs.[91] The practice of appointing former common serjeants as city counsel did not survive much beyond the late 1460s. Indeed, the simultaneous appointments in October 1480 of Serjeants William Husee and John Vavasour and of King's Attorney William Huddesfeld as city counsel look very much like a clean sweep, and might reflect a positive change of approach.[92] It might also reflect a change of priorities among the the city's governors, who, as the Court of Aldermen put it in 1542, were hoping that their appointee would not only 'dylygentlye & redelye' offer his advice in the city's affairs but would 'be alwayes towards theym in the same'.[93]

That final comment probably reveals a large part of the reason why former common serjeants both began and ceased to be appointed as city counsel. It would appear that, after about 1500, the common serjeants as a group were no longer of the right calibre – or, perhaps rather, no longer ambitious for advancement in the central courts – and, in consequence, they would not in the longer term be able to influence events at Westminster in the city's favour. At that point, the Court of Aldermen did not hesitate to look elsewhere for its counsellors and for influential persons whose 'good & lovyng mynde' would in future smooth relations with the central courts.[94]

[90] *CalPMR 1437–57*, p. 136. [91] CLRO, Rep. 1, fo. 150.
[92] CLRO, Jor. 8, fo. 234.
[93] CLRO, Rep. 10, fo. 294 (said of [Robert] Townesende).
[94] CLRO, Rep. 9, fo. 186v.

Moreover, even in the 1450s and 1460s the common serjeant's role as the principle city prosecutor and legal representative was being challenged by others.[95] By the early sixteenth century, Common Serjeant Grene and his successors were taking pot luck with a large number of alternative sources of legal advice and representation. A decade later, the bridge masters were more likely to employ the future bridge counsel and undersheriff John Pakyngton than Grene, who seems not to have attended court on their behalf at all.[96] In 1520, it was the undersheriffs, not the common serjeant, who had to be excused regular attendance at the city's courts because they were so busy about the city's affairs at Westminster.[97]

In addition, when the city's judges adjourned cases to advise themselves on particularly difficult points of law, they seem no longer to have been satisfied to do what they had done in *Walpole* v. *Botlesham*, and simply tell the recorder to consult with the common serjeant, with or without an undersheriff's assistance.[98] Instead, the recorder would seek external advice. Sometimes, apparently, he would go alone, as seems to have happened in a case of the early 1460s discussed in the Exchequer Chamber.[99] At other times, as happened in the (probable) Mayor's Court case from 1492, the common serjeant would discuss the matter with a group of mainly or entirely 'city' common lawyers in the recorder's presence, perhaps at one of the inns; and then, if no clear answer emerged, both men would go on to consult with the Westminster justices. Both in this case and in another instance from the same year, the recorder and common serjeant were not entirely happy that the matter had been resolved, and sought the advice of the justices: to be precise, in the second instance they sought the advice of three justices who were also of the city counsel, Thomas Bryan CJCP, Guy Fairfax JKB, and John Vavasour JCP (no details about the justices are given in the first instance).[100]

95 CLRO, MS Bridge House Rental [and Accounts] 1460–84, translation, pp. 81, 83, 270, 454, 693, 546, 598.
96 CLRO, MS Bridge House Accounts, 1484–1509, fos. 281v, 297, 84v, 123–3v.
97 CLRO, Rep. 5, fo. 82. 98 *CalLBH*, p. 395.
99 Hemmant, *Select Cases in the Exchequer Chamber, Vol. I*, p. 181.
100 Thorne, Baker, *Readings and Moots*, II, pp. 259–60, 258.

Admittedly, such consultations were not new in the 1490s. Throughout our period, the city legal records note regular adjournments for consultations, some of which will have been with outside experts – indeed, in 1390 the city replied to a writ ordering it to proceed with an assize that 'the matter is so difficult and doubtful in law that both various justices of the lord king and various serjeants and apprentices at law differ in their opinions about it'.[101] Nevertheless, these earlier external consultations do not seem to have been either normal or regularised, in the sense of involving specific individuals or office-holders. The exhaustive consultation which allegedly took place in late 1389 or early 1390 may itself have been prompted by nervousness induced by the knowledge that the unsuccessful plaintiff in *Walpole* v. *Botlesham* had petitioned John of Gaunt's council and had received a favourable response. It was certainly unusual for city returns to writs to refer specifically to the sources from which advice had been sought. As was mentioned earlier, this was a period when the city became embroiled in several aggressive challenges to the decisions of its courts: a case which ran from the late 1380s to the early 1390s cost the bridge masters over £25 in a single year, 1390/1.[102] Apart from this period, in no year between 1381 and 1550 did total bridge house legal expenses, less standing fees, exceed £20.

By the 1490s, with a wealth of alternative sources of professional expertise formally available to the city, and perhaps an increasing tendency to make use of it for fear of being challenged, it would not be surprising if the particular contribution of the common serjeant no longer seemed so valuable and the office, in consequence, not quite so important. Professionalisation of the city's other legal offices and changes to the wider legal profession may even have threatened the common serjeant, like the Westminster common serjeants, with eventual extinction. Unlike the Westminster common serjeants, however, the city's common serjeant adapted and survived.

[101] CLRO, Rep. 1, fo. 150; CLRO, HR CP114, m. 13v; and see, e.g., Mayor Oulegrave's uninformative response to a similar complaint about delays in 1468: TNA (PRO), KB Plea Rolls KB27/827, m. 104.

[102] CLRO, MS Bridge Masters' Annual Account Rolls, 1381–9 (trans), pp. 257, 266, 275; CLRO, MS Bridge Masters' Annual Account Rolls, 1390–1405 (trans.), pp. 30, 74, 93.

The undershrievalties

The undershrievalties may have had a slow and comparatively obscure start, but the sheriffs' chief clerk or clerks were always potentially men of considerable influence, worth cultivating. So long as the sheriffs could and did bring their own clerks with them at the beginning of their shrieval year, that influence would have had its limitations. The evidence for sheriffs' clerks in general, however, suggests that even in the early fourteenth century they often served under successive sheriffs. John de Hardingham, who was sworn in as the senior sheriff's third clerk in 1309, was still in office, probably as a chief clerk or undersheriff, in 1336; he ended up as a junior member of the city's magistracy, as a master of London Bridge.[103]

In practice, therefore, sheriffs' chief clerks or undersheriffs were probably serving under successive sheriffs from an early date.[104] The history of the office, once it emerges into daylight, suggests that its prestige and the element of legal professionalism involved were not insignificant even by 1400 and that both rose further during the first half of the fifteenth century. Fourteenth-century and some early fifteenth-century undersheriffs either did not engage in formal legal training or did not progress far enough with any they undertook to be described as apprentices at law.[105] Most undersheriffs from Alexander Anne onwards, however, appear to have been in at least the early stages of advanced legal training by the time they were admitted to the office.[106] Thomas Burgoyne obtained exemption from creation as a serjeant at law a mere ten years after being admitted to an undershrievalty, and those of his successors who became serjeants at law continued the downwards trend: in other words, later undersheriffs were more senior lawyers on appointment. Undersheriffs were also becoming more likely to end up on one of the Westminster benches.

[103] *CalLBC*, p. 181; *CalLBE*, p. 300; Chew, Kellaway, *London Assize of Nuisance*, item 416.

[104] See Appendix 7.3.

[105] The only fourteenth-century undersheriff who might possibly have become a serjeant at law was John Weston (*fl.* 1394–99, created serjeant in 1425?).

[106] Of the nineteen undersheriffs known to have served between 1400 and 1500, six (John Fortescue, John Markham, Billyng, Fairfax, Haugh and Marowe) became serjeants at law and three (John Bartone senior, Burgoyne and Edmund Dudley) sought exemption.

Between 1420 and 1450, no fewer than three chief justices of King's Bench were former undersheriffs of London (Fortescue, Markham, Billyng; though Billyng had been recorder meanwhile), and two were appointed to Exchequer baronies. It is as though the criminal side of the sheriffs' work led to London undersheriffs being regarded as particularly well-suited to work in King's Bench, just as recorders, at about the same period, seem to be have regarded as particularly suited to the Exchequer bench. Although their immediate successors were not so illustrious, John Haugh or Hawes was appointed a justice of the Common Bench and might well have gone further, had death not cut short his career three years later.

The increasing legal professionalism which is evident in the fifteenth century was a later echo of the changes that occurred in the common serjeanty. In due course, the two offices came to form part of a civic legal career. Of the few undersheriffs known before 1441, one, John Fray, definitely went on to become common serjeant. John Wilton's career seems to have been unusual, in that he served as an undersheriff in the 1430s, was nominated as common serjeant in 1437 and apparently served in that office until 1439, before returning to an undershrievalty, at least intermittently, for a further decade. His fellow for this second term, Thomas Billyng, was also common serjeant before election to an undershrievalty; and this was the case with two other mid-century undersheriffs, Guy Fairfax and John Rigby.

It is conceivable that the early fifteenth-century city fathers deliberately set about enhancing the attractions of the undershrievalty. Although a 1441 decision that the undersheriffs should not be subject to annual re-election was annulled in 1450, in practice the undersheriffs admitted between 1441 and 1485 were, unless they wished otherwise, routinely re-elected and served for many years.[107] A reason for doubting that this was the reason why the mayor and aldermen decided to take control of the admission of London undersheriffs, however, is that the almost immediate effect was in fact quite different. Assuming that the short tenures of former common serjeants Billyng, Fairfax and Rigby were no more than an aberration, temporary expedients, perhaps, what the city's control produced was stability at some cost to prestige. The

[107] CLRO, Jor. 3, fo. 88v, Jor. 5, fo. 47v.

men who spent very many years as undersheriff did not then go on to greater things. Indeed, as has already been mentioned, Thomas Burgoyne followed the example of the former recorder, John Bartone, and obtained an exemption from being created serjeant.[108] Evidently the attractions of the undershrievalty, once security of tenure was effectively ensured, outweighed those even of the highly-remunerative Westminster serjeanties.

As far as the relationship between the offices of undersheriff and common serjeant are concerned, it looks as though the relative rise in the legal status of the undershrievalty was halted at about mid-century, and that thereafter, until the 1490s, it was generally regarded within the city as being of similar status to, or of rather lower status than, the common serjeanty. By the early sixteenth century, however, there is no doubt that the undershrievalty was more prestigious than the common serjeanty: it was the office routinely acquired by or promised to common serjeants as their next step in the city hierarchy of law offices. Under pressure from would-be undersheriffs, the city's governors were quite unable to hold the two offices in balance.[109]

There was of course a price to be paid for this. Whereas the later fifteenth-century undersheriffs stayed in office for many years together, their sixteenth-century successors came and went at dizzying speed. They also proved to be less firmly attached to the city even when in office. Like the recorder, the undersheriff was expected to be available constantly. In 1511, however, a precedent was set when Undersheriff Nevyle was allowed to go to his home area for three weeks over the summer and to discharge his office by deputy.[110] The precedent was shortly followed by Thomas More, who was allowed to appoint a deputy when he was sent on embassy to Flanders.[111] Although there are no further references to absences or deputies, this may merely be because they had come to be taken for granted. Indeed, the situation may have been formalised by the creation of a new office. One possible reason why in the 1510s Erasmus failed to mention Thomas More's activities in relation to the main Sheriffs' Court is that by this date another officer, the prothonotary, could well have been in

[108] Baker, *Order of Serjeants at Law*, pp. 38, fn. 2, 163, 516, 113, fn. 8.
[109] Masters, 'The Common Serjeant', especially p. 381.
[110] CLRO, Rep. 2, fo. 115. [111] CLRO, Rep. 3, fo. 22.

charge of the court held before the sheriff himself. Undersheriff More evidently had a busy private practice, and his colleague, Thomas Nevyle, and all three of their immediate successors were included in a list, probably of 1518, of the 'pleyders or prentyses of the kynges courts [at Westminster] supposed to be present at this terme'.[112] Changes in the type of men who held undershrievalties might well have led to the emergence of the prothonotaryship. That office did not exist in 1486 but had been established by 1513.[113] Thomas Rysshton's appointment in the latter year is the first noticed, and there is no mention of a predecessor; but the second recorded appointment, of Richard Staverton to the other prothonotaryship in August 1519, was in place of John Baker, who must therefore have been admitted to the office at some earlier date, possibly before Rysshton was appointed.[114] So perhaps the prothonotaries were running the main Sheriffs' Court when Erasmus described Undersheriff More's duties. Whether that was so or not, it was almost certainly they who came to discharge the clerical functions of the earlier undersheriffs, leaving the undersheriffs of the 1510s or 1520s onwards to occupy offices which seem to have been little more than sinecures, held in the main by Westminster-based lawyers and senior clerks.

[112] CLRO, Rep. 5, fo. 82, TNA (PRO), Chancery Warrants, C82/474 m. 36.
[113] *CalLBL*, p. 236. [114] CLRO, Rep. 2, fo. 165v, Rep. 4, fo. 18v.

8

LEGAL REPRESENTATION IN THE CITY

INTRODUCTION

In 1300, there were three main types of function undertaken by legal representatives in court: advocacy, personal substitution, and excusing absence. An advocate spoke for his client in the client or attorney's presence and his pleadings could be 'disavowed' or repudiated, whereas the attorney substituted for his client, his words and actions being as binding as the client's own, and an essoiner excused the absences of both the litigant and his attorney.

The one place in the city in which legal representatives were definitely not permitted to appear, certainly by the later fourteenth century, was the Inner Chamber; and the only types of cases in which they were definitely never permitted to act formally for their clients were those heard and determined according to merchant law or conscience.[1] It is likely enough that legal representatives had never appeared in such cases, and that it was the increase and formalisation of the activities of the Mayor's Court which made it necessary to clarify the situation, rather than any change in practice. The explanation given for the restriction in 1390, that the mayor and aldermen wished 'to examine [the parties in such cases] ... and put questions to them [on oath] and to use other means of eliciting the truth ... without any counsel or any other form of plea', probably does accurately reflect their motivation.[2] Where there were no points of law or custom to be considered and decided, they may well have genuinely felt that legal counsel was superfluous; and attorneys (who were not mentioned, but who must surely also have been barred) would merely have constituted a barrier between them and the parties.

[1] *CalLBI*, p. 80. [2] *CalPMR 1381–1412*, pp. 171–2.

The protection afforded even in the Husting to litigants who were ignorant of the law and 'how to speak' might suggest that there was little need to spend money on legal counsel and advocates. So the first of the questions to be examined in this chapter is whether litigants in the city's courts did in fact often employ advocates, and, when they did employ them, whether they were obliged to retain only licensed lawyers or whether they could pick and choose as they pleased.

Attorneys, on the other hand, had their practical uses even when they had no more knowledge of the law than the litigant himself had. But being allowed to appoint an attorney instead of having to appear in person at every stage of an action was not a privilege that early medieval courts felt bound to grant litigants. While there is no doubt that attorneys were employed in the city courts throughout our period, what is not certain is that those who appeared as attorneys were, or were necessarily, anything more than 'friends'. Litigants whose mothers and sisters acted as their attorneys and guardians were probably not, even on an optimistic view of the opportunities open to women in the late thirteenth and early fourteenth centuries, employing them primarily because of their knowledge of the courts' procedures or their legal expertise.[3] This was no doubt also true of the majority of husbands, brothers, sons and fathers who acted as attorneys.[4] Most of them were probably simply personal substitutes. The second question to be considered here, therefore, is whether any constraints were imposed by the city on the employment of attorneys, and on the type of people so employed.

In addition to advocates and attorneys, there are two further types of legal representative to be considered. The first is the essoiner; and there is another, much less distinct, group, known as 'counsel'. Because essoiners and attorneys were both types of personal substitute, they are discussed together. So are advocates and counsel, even though, functionally, they could be quite different. The word 'counsel' did not have the same association

[3] CLRO, HR PL25, m. 8 (Mathilda Bat), HR PL28, m. 5 (Alice, daughter of Richard de Newerke); see also Brand, *Origins of the English Legal Profession*, p. 73.

[4] CLRO, HR PL9, mm. 4, 5 [*bis*], 5v (Roger de Aulton, Hugh de Cestre, Thomes le Perer, Nicholas le Barber), 9 (Thomas Brakele) and 9v (John de Wood), HR PL24, 10 (Thomas Bat).

with advocacy in the early Middle Ages as it does nowadays. Indeed, there seem to be no identifiable examples in the city's records before 1350 of the word being used of men who were definitely acting as advocates rather than advisers. The reason for discussing counsel together with advocates nevertheless is that the line between oral advocacy in court and the preparation of pleadings out of court was probably more blurred in the city's courts than it was in the central common-law courts. Paper pleadings seem to have appeared in the city's courts relatively early on, perhaps in the 1380s or shortly afterwards. [5] This means that for most of our period the quality of counsel, particularly the advice given when preparing the case and during any intermissions, was at least as important as the quality of advocacy in determining the standards of legal assistance available to litigants and defendants in the city's courts. Moreover, in the Common Bench it appears that, until about 1500 at least, the counsel who advised litigants and the advocates who were involved in all but the routine stages of the pleadings tended to be the same men. That may not be so in the city, since paper pleadings need not have been drawn up by whoever appeared for the litigant in court. Indeed, it is possible that 'pleader' was not a synonym for the earlier 'countor', 'narrator' or 'serjeant', but, in the city and by 1400 at least, was used of a man whose role straddled the existing functional boundaries, much as that of a modern 'solicitor-advocate' does. When considering the types of people who acted as representatives in the city's courts, therefore, we need to look specifically at the men who acted as counsel, who may have 'spoken' to the court on paper, and not just at the men who acted as advocates.

CONTROL

Advocates and counsel

Even in the thirteenth century the city undoubtedly did permit litigants to employ advocates, variously described in the records as 'causidici', 'serjeants', 'countors' (or 'serjeant-countors') and 'narratores', in its main courts. Indeed, they may in some cases

[5] See Chapter 4.

have been obliged to do so. Until 1260 all real and mixed actions appear to have been classed as 'pleas of land'. The assertion made in a London chronicle that in 1259 Henry III granted 'for the improvement of the city a new statute ... namely, that in future it would not be necessary to have an advocate in any plea brought in the city, neither in the Husting nor in other city courts, except in pleas of the Crown and pleas of land, with the exception of pleas of naam', therefore rather suggests that, until then, the parties had been required to employ advocates in all writ-initiated actions, at least for the formal business of making the count and of pleading the plea.[6] Just possibly, it was the 1259 statute which encouraged the city a year later to move some (later, all) mixed actions to the Husting of Common Pleas, thus converting them, by a sleight of hand, from 'pleas of land' to 'common pleas', in an attempt to limit further the actions in which advocates had to be employed.

Before the 1280s at least it does not look as though the city normally tried to control who could act as an advocate.[7] The only earlier restrictions on who did what in terms of legal representation appear to have been on attempts to undertake two or more incompatible functions in a single case: essoining a client while being retained as his advocate, for example.[8] In 1244 the royal justices in eyre decreed that aldermen were not to be permitted to render judgment in any case in which they had been consulted by one of the parties or had 'supported one of them in a plea in court', and that no advocate was to act as an assessor (meaning, probably, a judge of or adviser on the law) in any case in which he had represented a client.[9] The first recorded formal admission of men as advocates occurred in 1280, when five men were admitted and sworn in as countors, thereby, presumably, acquiring a monopoly on the automatic right of audience. In regulations associated with, but possibly of a slightly later date than, these admissions they were said to have been made because men 'who did not know how to speak properly' in court were offering their services as [serjeant-]countors, attorneys and essoiners.[10] In the early sixteenth century, too, admissions to 'common pleaderships'

[6] Stapleton, *De Antiquis Legibus Liber*, p. 70. [7] *Ibid*, p. 42. [8] *Ibid*, p. 170.
[9] Weinbaum, *Eyre 1244*, pp. 96, 97–8.
[10] CLRO, LBA, fos. 108v–9, printed, with some omissions and variations of spelling, in Riley, *Munimenta Gildhallae*, II, i, pp. 280–2.

were regularly recorded in the city's journals and repertories.[11] By 1550, therefore, it looks as though these offices were well-established. The attempt to admit groups of men all at one time may have been abandoned, if indeed that was what was happening in the 1280s, and the number of offices had reduced by one.[12] Otherwise, little had apparently changed.

Sixteenth-century common pleaders were clearly being licensed to work predominantly in the Sheriffs' Court: hence a note, marginated 'Clerks and Counsayllers of this city' in the same hand as that of the main entry, which records the summoning of the sheriffs' clerks and 'all other clerks attorneyes & pleders of the Shreves Courts of this City' to appear at the next Mayor's Court day.[13] They were, however, certainly permitted to speak for clients in the Husting, and probably in the Mayor's Court, too.[14]

There is however no evidence at all that men were being admitted as pleaders and (or) sworn to obey the city's regulations governing legal representatives before the Court of Aldermen at any time after 1305 and before 1518. Nor does it appear that they were being sworn in before the sheriffs instead. No common pleader was recorded among the sheriffs' staffs, including common attorneys, who took their annual oaths with their new masters in 1416, 1420 and 1424.[15] No common pleader's oath was recorded in the letterbooks, even in the fifteenth century when the oaths of the lowliest members of the sheriffs' staffs, the sergeants' valets, found a place there.[16] When the first known common pleader of the sixteenth century, Roger Cholmondley, was admitted to office in 1518, the attorneys' oath had to be amended for the purpose; he was 'sworn in as one of the common pleaders [*placitatorum* deleted, *Narratorum* substituted] of this city according to an attorney's oath, Except that the word "attorney" [was replaced] throughout by "in the office of one of the *placitatorum*"'.[17] The pattern of admissions from then onwards confirms what this suggests, namely, that this was a new

[11] For details of all the men admitted as common pleaders, 1518–50, see Appendix 8.1.
[12] Tucker, 'First Steps towards an English Legal Profession'.
[13] CLRO, Rep. 10, fo. 190.
[14] CLRO, HB2, fo. 171v; Emerson, *Concise Treatise*, p. 10.
[15] CLRO, Jor. 1, fos. 2, 69, Jor. 2, fo. 28v.
[16] *CalLBD*, pp. 1–13, especially 7.
[17] CLRO, Rep. 3, fo. 207.

introduction, or, rather, a reintroduction. For just over a decade, there were only the two common pleaderships, with the numbers being increased to three in 1526, and to four from 1542 onwards.[18]

Yet there is no doubt that men were working in London as advocates and as counsel, both in and out of court, during the fourteenth and fifteenth centuries. Regulations associated with the ordinance of *circa* 1280 referred to 'such counsel as [the litigant] should wish to employ for his business, whether ... a foreign, or a citizen [*prive*]', who, unlike the advocates (and attorneys and essoiners) 'qi generalment hauntent noz Courtz, et entre nous demoerent continuelment', were not subject to control.[19] Likewise, articles governing the Sheriffs' Court in 1356 referred to 'pleaders of the city', who were in 1356 contrasted with unspecified 'gentz de lei qe veillent pleder en court des viscountes'.[20] The same regulations commanded 'qe touts les attournes du dite cite qe usent loffice dattourne en la Guyhall & autres communes pledours qe sont residents deins mesme la cite soient chescuns an estreitement charges & sermentes devaunt le Mair & Andermans ... de bien & louelment faire leur office' and that 'men of law ... who were free of the city' should likewise be sworn to obey the regulations. In other words, there were men who acted as countors or pleaders in the city courts, both regularly and occasionally, who were supposed to be sworn to obey the city's regulations, yet for whom no evidence of oaths or oath-taking survives between 1305 and 1518.

These references, opaque though they are, suggest that the city recognised two main types of advocate: 'men of law' who might or might not be freemen and who, if they were not, could not be obliged to swear to obey the regulations; and 'common pleaders', who might or might not also act as 'common attorneys', who certainly could and should take their oath. Given that 'common' could be used both of someone who held a city office and of someone who simply offered his services to the public at large, and that 'office' could also mean 'function' or 'duty', this does not advance our understanding much.[21] It is possible, nevertheless,

[18] CLRO, Rep. 3, fo. 213, Rep. 1, fo. 34; CLRO, Rep. 8, fo. 43, Rep. 7, fo. 87v, 223; Rep. 10, fo. 269v.

[19] Riley, *Munimenta Gildhallae*, II, i, p. 281.

[20] CLRO, LBG, fos. 54–54v, LBH, fo. 286v.

[21] E.g., a 'common scrivener' of London (1399/1400): Hudson, Tingey, *Records of Norwich*, p. 53.

that some of these pre-1518 advocates held other city offices, enjoying the privilege of offering their services as legal representatives *ex officio*. That was the situation in a number of other courts. The most regular attorney noted in the Winchester city court roll for 1425/6, for example, was Sergeant John Ocle, followed by the underclerk, Richard Erle or Erell, and Sergeants Thomas Porter, Thomas Stokes, and William Mersshe.[22] Judging by contemporary ordinances, the same type of men could and did act as pleaders and counsel.[23] On the other hand, given the proximity of the city courts to Westminster and the restrictions on the type of advocacy that anyone who was not a serjeant could undertake there, it is quite likely that some apprentices at law would have been keen to act as advocates and counsel in the lower courts while gaining the experience necessary to prepare them for admission to practise in the higher ones. While the ordinance of *circa* 1280 was never intended to exclude such men, it is not clear whether, at the time, they would have been allowed to address the court. In 1356, however, it was specifically stated that litigants in the Sheriffs' Court were to be permitted the assistance of 'gentz de lai' who could act as advocates if the lawyers were competent and were prepared to plead in English. This final caveat does rather suggest that some of the men of law concerned might normally have worked at Westminster, since it was not until 1362 that an attempt was made to ensure that pleadings there were in English.[24]

The only way of discovering whether any of the pre-1518 common pleaders did indeed hold other city offices, and whether the independent advocates did normally work at Westminster, is to find out more about the men themselves: beginning, of course, with their names. Since many of the litigants in the city courts were city organisations, the best source for this type of information should be their financial accounts, where they survive. Although they are not as helpful as they might be (the accountants

[22] HRO, Winchester City Court Roll W/D1/56; Bird, *Black Book of Winchester*, p. 40; Winchester City Court Roll W/D1/106, fo. 11 (1416/7), [c] (no date, *c* 1416–25); Britnell, 'Colchester Courts and Records', p. 137; Bateson, *Borough Customs*, I, pp. 15, 16 (Worcester, Lancaster).

[23] Bird, *Black Book of Winchester*, pp. 40 (1402), 18 (1412); or Veale, *Great Red Book of Bristol, Text Part I*, pp. 122 (1449), 254 (1453/4).

[24] CLRO, LBF, fo. 54, CLRO, LBG, fo. 54v (article 15: 'de la citee' omitted in error in *CalLBG*, p. 74).

or their clerks seem to have believed that one 'man of counsel' was much the same as any other), the men of law and counsel they employed usually seem to have appeared at Westminster. The only exception in the nine sets of company accounts examined for this study seems to have occurred in an action between the Tailors and the parson of [St Matthew?] Friday Street in 1423/4, which cost the company well over £4.[25] This case evidently began life in the city courts, as Common Clerk Carpenter and his clerk were paid to enter a plea and replication; two of Carpenter's clerks were also later paid for a further replication; and several payments, totalling 16*s* 8*d*, were made to John Fortescue, who was probably undersheriff at the time. Woven around and between these entries are payments to 'Fulthorp seriaunt' [Thomas Fulthorpe], to [John] 'Hody of Temple', to 'Goodrode sergeant' (presumably William Godered), and to men who either were, or were probably, attorneys.[26] The accounts do not say what the payments to the other men of law were for; whatever it was, they were paid no more than the 'attorney's rate' of 1*s* 8*d*.[27] Some payments undoubtedly or almost certainly related to litigation at Westminster (Godered was paid 'for a plea at Westminster', and there were previous payments for a writ of trespass and 'a new writ'). Nevertheless, it looks as though Fulthorpe was engaged before litigation was begun at Westminster, and it is possible that these payments – up to eight of them, if one assumes that he was being paid at the 'advocate's rate' of 3*s* 4*d* a time – included his fees for court appearances or attendances. If so, the Tailors, a company which spent lavishly on advancing its civic ambitions in the fifteenth century, had employed a senior member of the legal profession as its advocate and/or counsel in, probably, the Mayor's Court.

All that said, this is the only occasion, as far as the Tailors' records of the fifteenth century show, when there is any reason to

[25] GH Library, Merchant Taylors' Accounts, I, fo. 146. The company accounts were those of the Carpenters, the Cutlers, the Drapers, the Founders, the Grocers, the Ironmongers, the Tailors/Merchant Taylors, the Skinners, and the Vintners, with additional information from the records of the Mercers and the Waxchandlers.

[26] Neither Fulthorpe nor Godered was created serjeant until 1425, in fact (accounts were often written up some time after the financial year concerned): Baker, *Order of Serjeants at Law*, pp. 161, 162.

[27] Hody got 1*s* 8*d*, Fulthorpe and the unnamed others, 2*s* 5*d* between them.

suppose that the company might have paid lawyers of this standing to advise and represent it in a city court. Moreover, it is possible that its payment to Fortescue covered counsel and appearances in court – perhaps representing up to five individual payments of 3*s* 4*d* – rather than the undersheriff's fees. Even in the second half of the century, the Tailors almost always sought advice and, possibly, representation from the likes of Thomas Rigby (undersheriff, 1460–?1484) and Thomas More (clerk, 1420, common attorney, *floruit* 1446–63), who were both paid 'for counsel here in defence against the prior of Christchurch' in the late 1450s.[28] Similarly, payments made by the Grocers' Company to named senior common lawyers in the first half of the century appear – insofar as it is possible to tell anything about them – to have related to actions brought at Westminster or bills presented to Parliament.[29] When payments are recorded to named counsel in relation to matters which might have involved litigation in the city courts, the Grocers, like the Tailors, tended to employ current or future law officers: men like Thomas Burgoyne, who was very probably undersheriff at the time (*floruit* 1432–?1470; he seems to have died in office). Burgoyne was employed again in 1461/2, when, like the future recorder, Humphrey Starkey, the following year, he provided advice about a large bequest to the company.[30] Others so employed were 'Watnow man of law' (John Watno, who had succeeded Burgoyne as undersheriff by 1470), who advised the Grocers on three occasions in the 1460s and 1470s, and 'Rikby [Rigby] man of law', who provided counsel on two occasions in 1466.[31]

The surviving churchwardens' accounts tell a similar tale. Judging by its records, one of the more litigious of the London parishes in the fifteenth century was St Peter, West Cheap. Between 1448 and 1450 the churchwardens spent over £4 on three cases which were without doubt heard at Guildhall, since they involved payments to 'a man of law at the Guildhall' in the first instance, to 'Bryan [almost certainly the future common serjeant, Thomas Bryan] at the Guildhall' and to 'an attorney in the

[28] GH Library, Merchant Taylors' Accounts, II, 1445–70, fo. 137.
[29] GH Library, Grocers' Ordinances, 1345–1463, pp. 241, 297, 347.
[30] GH Library, Grocers Wardens' Account Book, 1461–71, fos. 19v, 40, 128v.
[31] *Ibid.*, fos. 19v, 40, 128v (*bis*, plus 2 payments to the recorder for counsel), 200, 221.

Mayor's Court' in the second, and (twice) to an undersheriff 'on the first day of our plea' and on another occasion, in the third.[32]

The churchwardens' expenditure on these three cases, like that of the Tailors a quarter of a century before, was both unusual and extravagant by city standards. In 1466 or 1467, the churchwardens of St Botolph, Aldersgate, spent 5*s* 6*d* on consulting 'Mr Bryan [and others] of a matter touching the church', which could well have been in connection with a case brought – if it was brought anywhere – in one of the city courts.[33] When they brought a bill in the Exchequer Court a couple of years later, they spent over 18*s*, including modest sums on breakfasts for the barons of the Exchequer and their counsel, Nicholas Stathum, and others.[34] These are the only references to the employment of men as counsel in the accounts, which cover the years 1466–72 and 1479–83. None of the other churchwardens' accounts of the period refer to payments for men of law or counsel to appear in the city courts, or even definitely for providing advice in cases heard there.[35]

The Bridge House accounts of the late fourteenth century are also insufficiently explicit for it to be possible to say for sure who was being paid to do what, where. Although they mention payments to named individuals for 'prosecuting pleas' and also to 'various men of law of the London Guildhall' and the like, they never do so in conjunction. So it is quite likely, but not certain, that the occasional named individuals (William Nafferton and John Seymour) were acting elsewhere, probably at Westminster (an attorney named John Seymour was active in the Common Bench in the final decades of the fourteenth century).[36] In a case from the mid 1420s, however, 13*s* 4*d* was paid for four 'legistae'

[32] GH Library, Churchwardens' Accounts, St Peter, West Cheap, 1435–1601, fos. 217–27, esp. fos. 220–4.

[33] GH Library, Churchwardens' Accounts, St Botolph, Aldersgate, 1466–7, fo. [1].

[34] GH Library, Churchwardens' Accounts, St Botolph, Aldersgate, 1468–72, fo. 3.

[35] Litigation, or possible litigation, is mentioned in GH Library, Churchwardens' Accounts, St Stephen, Wallbrook, 1474–1538, fos. 1–24, esp. fo. 5v; GH Library, Churchwardens' Accounts, All Hallows, London Wall, 1455–1535, fos. 1–19v; GH Library, Churchwardens' Accounts, St Michael, Cornhill, 1455[-] 1608, fos. 1–24v, esp. fo. 8; GH Library, Churchwardens' Accounts, St Martin Orgar, 1471 [*recte*]- 1469–1615, fo. 6v.

[36] CLRO, MS Bridge Masters' Annual Account Rolls, 1381–9 (trans.), p. 266; *ibid.*, p. 192; MS Bridge Masters' Annual Account Rolls, 1390–1405 (trans.), p. 26; *ibid.*, p. 30; Thornley, *Year Books, 1387–1388*, pp. 239, 247, 271, 275, TNA (PRO) CP Plea Roll, CP40/555, attorney rolls.

brought in by Common Serjeant Anne and retained as counsel 'tam in consilio quam in placito' in a possessory assize brought against the Bridge House.[37] The role played by Anne makes it seem certain that these were independent lawyers, probably in fact apprentices at law. It also suggests that the bridge masters needed some assistance in securing the services of men like this. The next and final time before 1550 when we have what looks like evidence of anyone acting as the Bridge House's advocate in the city courts is in the late 1490s, when 'Nicholas Pagman' was paid 3*s* 'for defending the suit of the parson of St Sepulchre's' in a dispute over tithes.[38] This was Nicholas Pakenham, who, though legally trained, was the city's common clerk.

For reasons discussed earlier, it is unlikely that the recorder represented or was permitted to advise litigants in the city's courts, certainly before the later fifteenth century. It is, however, just possible that the licence that Recorder Starkey received on admission to the office in 1471 to retain his existing clients and to acquire new ones might have extended to representation in the city courts.[39] If so, it seems probable that his successors enjoyed the same privilege. On the other hand, city ordinances of 1393 clearly assumed that the fourteenth-century undersheriffs sometimes represented and advised litigants; and, as we have seen, they did not stop doing so even after 1393.[40] It was, however, the common serjeant who seems to have been the law officer to represent litigants (and not just city organisations) most often. His duties, providing he was not representing someone whose claims were prejudicial to the interests of the city or its freemen, were not incompatible with such activities. There are a relatively large number of references to common serjeants acting as advocates and counsel. John Weston was common serjeant in both 1410 and 1416 when he appeared as an advocate, as was Ralph Strode when he was sued over advice given to a litigant in 1382.[41] As we have just seen, in the mid 1420s Common Serjeant Anne assisted the bridge masters in an assize brought against the Bridge House. His involvement in a number of Exchequer chamber discussions in

[37] CLRO, MS Bridge House Weekly Payments, III: 1421–30, fos. 128, 131, 135v.
[38] CLRO, MS Bridge House Accounts 1484–1509, fo. 197.
[39] CLRO, Jor. 5, fo. 254.
[40] CLRO, LBH, fo. 286, printed in Riley, *Munimenta Gildhallae*, I, p. 519.
[41] *CalLBI*, p. 85, *CalPMR 1413–37*, p. 43, *CalPMR 1381–1412*, p. 16.

the 1430s may in part be explained by his private activities rather than by his city office: he certainly seems to have been acting for a private client in a case discussed in the Michaelmas term 1435, very shortly indeed after he had been admitted to the recordership.[42] A similar explanation may lie behind the presence of Common Serjeant Robert Molyneux in a Star Chamber discussion of the 1473 case of the 'carrier who broke bulk'.[43] It was probably also Molyneux ('master Molenars') whom Richard Cely consulted in 1482 about some lands which might have been subject to an escheat, although there is nothing to suggest that he also acted as Cely's advocate.[44] The John Grene gentleman who 'assigned the errors orally' in a case brought in the Husting in 1519 may have been the then common serjeant.[45] Finally, although the common serjeant's contribution to the arguments in a 1544 Sheriffs' Court case reported by Randolph Cholmondley may have been made because Undersheriff Crayford had been ordered to consult with him on a point of law, his momentary lapse into the third person plural is typical of the way that advocates referred to their clients and might indicate, if it is not an error, that he was present as the defendant's legal representative rather than as one of the city counsel.[46]

The surviving evidence indicates that the great majority of payments by civic bodies to independent lawyers, where litigation in the city courts was envisaged, were for consultations; and even then they were not commonly employed. It confirms the impression given by the city's own court and administrative records: before 1518, the usual choice, and probably preferred option, of city organisations was to engage one of the city's law officers. What is probably a good example of the different ways in which lawyers were employed by city organisations and Londoners – in this case, by the city itself on behalf of a city orphan (minor heir of a freeman) – is the action brought by Thomas Pynchon in 1392 against his father's executors in the

[42] Hemmant, *Select Cases in the Exchequer Chamber*, I, pp. 52, 64, 67 (his predecessor as recorder was still in office in October 1435, so it is probable that he undertook the case while he was common serjeant).

[43] Hemmant, *Select Cases in the Exchequer Chamber*, II, p. 31.

[44] Hanham, *Cely Letters*, letter 147 (p. 134). [45] CLRO, HB2, fo. 179.

[46] Baker, *Reports … of King Henry VIII, Vol. II*, p 453.

Mayor's Court six weeks after the father's death.[47] The case was prosecuted on young Thomas's behalf by the common serjeant, the executors (who included the two undersheriffs) being represented by their attorney. To protect the city against charges of failing to safeguard the youngster's interests, the final agreement, after eight months of adjournments, was witnessed by an Exchequer clerk and six 'friends' of the orphan: no fewer than four serjeants at law, and Thomas Skelton and Walter Skrene, described as Thomas's counsel.[48] While there is every reason to believe that Skelton and Skrene, at the very least, were actively involved in the negotiations leading up to the agreement, there is nothing to show that they represented Thomas or even were present in court during the earlier proceedings.

City organisations were more privileged than other litigants in enjoying the services of the common serjeant. In 1425, that officer was forbidden to 'be of counsel with foreigns against freemen or with freemen against freemen in any pleas or actions'; he could however be retained in other circumstances, that is, in cases between foreigns or brought by freemen against foreigns.[49] This prohibition probably represented a clarification or restriction of earlier practice, not a relaxation of an earlier total ban on accepting private legal work. When the former common serjeant, Ralph Strode, was retained as the city's counsel for seven years in 1386, he was ordered 'not to plead against any freeman of the City during that term', except in cases affecting the city, its trade companies or its orphans or himself.[50] Restrictions of this type were clearly not novelties in the 1420s. It was, however, not until the later sixteenth century that common serjeants were entirely forbidden to take fees from private clients, probably because by then the common pleaders were struggling to maintain their position.[51]

The evidence relating to private litigants is scant, but, such as it is, it suggests that the litigants who were most likely to employ independent advocates were important non-citizens. In a case which was probably brought in the Mayor's Court in 1369, [*Thomas*] *Sapillow* v. [*John*] *Jois and Another*, in which the

[47] *CalPMR 1381–1412*, pp. 201–3; *CalLBG*, p. 250.
[48] *CalPMR 1381–1412*, p. 202. [49] CLRO, Jor. 2, fo. 39v.
[50] *CalLBH*, p. 288. [51] CLRO, MS Book of Oaths, I, fo. 8.

defendants were represented by 'Parshay', [52] there seems to be nothing to connect any of the litigants, or Percy, with the city.[53] It is also possible that foreigners were even more inclined than Englishmen generally to employ independent advocates. There are several references to advocates and counsel in Sheriffs' Court cases brought on error by Italian defendants in the Husting.[54] These cases may be misleading, however, in giving the impression that it was the Italians above all who expected to get expert assistance in court: the other substantial group of foreigners which enjoyed similar levels of wealth was the Hanse, a company of northern European merchants, whose privileges in London included holding their own court. Consequently, cases involving them appear only rarely in the city's records. No doubt, too, had England not been at war with France for much of our period, Frenchmen would have appeared more often in the records; and they might well have employed relatively expensive legal counsel. Unusually, a consolidated list of costs was submitted to the mayor and aldermen for approval by Reyner Lomner, a Cambrai lawn merchant, in the 1470s. Lomner had been engaged in prolonged litigation (the best part of £4 was paid to a kind of private detective who 'lay in wait for [the defendant] by the space of a year and half') in the Mayor's Court, Chancery, the Common Bench and King's Bench. An unnamed man, or possibly men, described as 'my counsel in the said bill before my lord the mayor' or 'my counsel before my lord the mayor', received 8*s* 4*d* on one occasion, 6*s* 8*d* on two occasions, and 3*s* 4*d* on another occasion.[55] Whether this man was or these men were acting as advocates, accompanying Lomner into court as advisers, or being consulted outside the court, there is, however, no way of telling.

Private litigants (and city organisations, too) also sometimes employed holders of middle-ranking city offices as advocates and counsel. The 1393 ordinance not only forbade the undersheriffs, but also the secondaries and the clerks of the papers, to act as counsel in their courts. The very fact that the city felt the need to prevent them from undertaking this work rather suggests that

[52] Probably Henry Percy; see p. 302.

[53] *Les Reports del Cases en Ley ... 40 and 50 ... Edward le Tierce*, 43 Edward III, p. 32, pl. 33.

[54] For one of them, see p. 228.

[55] CLRO, Rep. 8, fos. 81–1v.

they had been doing just that.[56] Indeed, the disciplining of Prothonotary Thomas Rysshton in 1524 for 'occupying [his office] by deputy and acting as a common pleader' indicates that some sheriffs' clerks may have continued to act as advocates into the early sixteenth century, until the establishment of the pleaderships finally rendered this intolerable.[57]

It is clear from the 1356 regulations that the category of 'resident' common pleader included men who also offered their services as attorneys. Certainly in the fifteenth century, by which time there was undoubtedly such a thing as a city-controlled 'office of common attorney', attorneys acted as pleaders on occasion. In June 1421 an Italian defendant in the Sheriffs' Court complained that he did not have sufficient counsel to enable him to respond to the plaintiff, and asked the court to assign to him men learned in the law; he had been represented thus far, including during the oral pleadings, by William Louther, a common attorney.[58] A Chancery petition of 1504–8 raises the possibility that former as well as serving common attorneys could act as pleaders. The petitioner described the difficulties he was facing in an action of trespass brought by Robert Pynkney in London, where Pynkney allegedly was 'gretly acqueynted for asmych as he is on of the pleders there'.[59] Pynkney had resigned his common attorneyship in the summer of 1500.[60] But perhaps the petitioner, who was not a Londoner, was simply behind the times – and rather unlucky: by the time he submitted his petition, Pynkney was working as a pleader in Chancery, and had had several years in which to become 'gretly acqueynted' in that court, too.[61]

The ordinance of *circa* 1280 had forbidden men who undertook one type of legal representation to undertake another, at least in a single case. Nevertheless, it is clear that, when attorneys represented litigants during our period, they, like William Louther in 1421, could indeed plead; they did not just request adjournments

[56] CLRO, MS LBH, fo. 86, printed in Riley, *Munimenta Gildhallae*, I, p. 519.
[57] CLRO, Rep. 4, fos. 194, 195–5v. [58] CLRO, Jor. 1. fo. 69.
[59] TNA (PRO), Early Chancery Proceedings, C1/88, item 90. TNA (PRO), PCC, PROB11/16/1 (fos. 4–4v).
[60] CLRO, Rep. 1, fo. 71.
[61] TNA (PRO), Early Chancery Proceedings, C1/244, item 83 ('Pynkney' in top lefthand corner; the petition refers to Aleyn's mayoralty, 1500/1).

and other similar routine matters. In 1345, Christian de Bury, who had allegedly been retained as an attorney, was sued by his clients for failing to 'plead an action of debt' when it came before the jury.[62] In 1426, in another Mayor's Court case, both litigants 'pleaded by their attorneys', and their pleas were recorded.[63] In 1510, the defendants in a Husting case 'again pleaded by their attorney orally at the bar' and were then given a day to produce a written version of the plea.[64] Indeed, even after 1518, common pleaders continued for a time to act as attorneys and attorneys continued to plead.[65] Whatever the case may have been in the Common Bench, where the serjeants at law enjoyed a monopoly of pleading, apparently even as against the most senior apprentices at law, in London there was until the sixteenth century no equivalent group which monopolised pleading, apart possibly from the first few years of the fourteenth century. At least until 1518, the city appears to have taken the view that an attorney, who was his client's personal substitute, could do whatever his client could do in person; and there seems to be no doubt that, even in the Common Bench, a litigant in person could plead.[66] It presumably follows that those attorneys who pleaded in their client's absence could not be disavowed in the way that an advocate, who appeared in company with his client or the client's attorney, could be.[67] Perhaps this safeguard was superfluous in the city's courts, given that most pleas could be amended freely, with no apparent time limitation, up to the point when the verdict was to be taken or judgment rendered.

Most of the advocates and counsel mentioned so far can with fair confidence be assigned to one of two main categories: they were either entirely independent advocates or were holders of city offices (including, by the fifteenth century, common attorneyships) who acted from time to time as pleaders. Some, however, are harder to categorise. Thomas Bryan, employed as a 'man of law' by the churchwardens of St Peter, West Cheap, between 1448

[62] *CalPMR 1323–64*, p. 218. [63] *CalPMR 1413–37*, p. 198.
[64] CLRO, HB2, fo. 39v; see also fo. 190v. [65] CLRO, HB2, fo. 189.
[66] Hemmant, *Select Cases in the Exchequer Chamber*, II, p. 190.
[67] The only example of a 'disavowal' (of sorts) noted in the city records during our period is a case from 1378, when the defendant's counsel was held to have pleaded, in her presence, in such a way as to exclude the plaintiff from his action; whereupon the court examined the defendant, a widow, who 'confessed that she did not acknowledge the facts set forth by her counsel', who in turn admitted not having been instructed by her: *CalPMR 1364–81*, p. 247.

and 1450, is an example: he was a future city law officer. If, as seems likely, the 'Brikes' employed at the same time as Bryan is Roger Byrkes, he too was a future undersheriff. Why they should have been so employed before being elected to office is unclear. It is likely, nevertheless, that they did in fact belong to one of the two main categories. On the one hand, they may in fact have been independent lawyers. The future serjeant at law, William Wangford, whom the churchwardens also retained in these cases, was one of the city counsel appointed in 1455 to advise the mayor and aldermen in an important case involving a breach of sanctuary. Roger Byrkes was sufficiently closely associated with him (four years later, he would appoint Wangford his executor) to suggest that it might have been Wangford's influence that allowed him access to the city courts – possibly, indeed, as Wangford's pupil.[68] Then again, Wangford himself might have come to the governors' attention because he was, like most if not all of the law officers serving in the 1450s, a member of Gray's Inn. Perhaps a serving city law officer, or one of the former law officers among those appointed as city counsel at the same time, recommended him.

Two other men who may have been independent advocates can be identified. When the Italian defendant in the 1421 case mentioned above complained about the standard of counsel available to him, the court duly appointed Thomas Basset and Robert fitzRobert. This was done with little delay, apparently, for, even after having had 'maturo tempore interloquendi', the two men were able to continue with the defendant's response that day; so they were probably already in court, the defendant having, perhaps, requested their presence in the expectation of being allowed to employ them.[69] There is a good case to be made for regarding men like Basset, Bryan and Byrkes as independent lawyers who, despite having no prior association with the city's administration, tried their luck in its courts and, perhaps because they happened to make useful contacts through their legal inns or in other aspects of their professional lives, were successful. Even fitzRobert, who did have close personal connections with the city, may well not

[68] *CalLBK*, pp. 370–1, CLRO, Jor. 5, fo. 266; TNA (PRO), PCC, PROB11/4/18 (fo. 138).

[69] CLRO, HR CP146, m. 3.

have held any city office; in 1428 he was described as a 'man of law' by his company, the Grocers.[70]

It is also possible, on the other hand, that all four men had associations with the city which its surviving records do not reveal. Certainly it is unlikely that the mayor and aldermen needed any introduction to Wangford, assuming him to have been the city orphan of that name, the son of a London draper, for whom provision had been made in 1426.[71] We have seen that undersheriffs and future undersheriffs, some of whom were almost certainly more junior clerks, acted as attorneys and pleaders in the period before the common attorneyships were securely established as city offices. So perhaps Bryan and Byrkes were sheriffs' clerks. Equally, however, a number of those who acted as pleaders in the city courts before 1518 were common attorneys; and it is only after 1450 that we know the names of the majority of these men. Like the common pleaders a century later, fifteenth-century city attorneys appear to have enjoyed something approaching a monopoly of practice in their own courts (see below). Foreign attorneys could evidently only appear if they did so in conjunction with an attorney who held office in the court. And there is no suggestion that Bryan and Byrkes, who also acted as attorneys for the churchwardens, only appeared as attorneys at Guildhall in conjunction with others. So perhaps they were common attorneys.

The same may even be true of Basset and fitzRobert. It certainly seems very likely that Basset was in some sense licensed to plead in the Sheriffs' Court, and quite possibly in the city courts generally. Two months before he appeared in the case just mentioned, an entry in the first of the surviving journals recorded that he was 'admitted to the same status in which he was on the day he was deprived &c from the exercise [of it] &c'.[72] Fortunately for us, whatever it was that caused Basset to be deprived of whatever status it was that he had had before, the problem persisted. In February 1424 another journal entry recorded that at a meeting of the Common Council there was presented a 'petition of the commonalty about Thomas Basset &c that he may not be heard in court &c until he has corrected his life'.[73] These journal entries,

[70] GH Library, Grocers' Memorandum Book, fo. 176. [71] CLRO, Jor. 2, fo. 68.

[72] CLRO, Jor. 1, fo. 90 (journal entries to Basset taken from Professor C. M. Barron's card index at CLRO).

[73] CLRO, Jor. 2, fo. 14.

combined with the description of him in the Sheriffs' Court records as 'learned in the law', suggest that Basset was not only regarded as a specialist, but that some form of misconduct (not necessarily in court, of course) had led to a proposal to suspend his right to appear in the city's courts. In the absence of any evidence that men were being licensed specifically to act as common pleaders, the obvious possibility is that he enjoyed the right to be heard in court as a result of being a common attorney.[74] We do have lists of those sworn into office as common attorneys in 1416, 1421 and 1424, from which his name, and fitzRobert's, are absent; but they vary in number, containing six, nine and eleven names respectively. One of the common attorneys who was definitely active by 1416, William Strensall (or Transall), is not included until 1424.[75] The lists are therefore incomplete; they are probably the names of those who were sworn on a particular day, not of all common attorneys active at that time.

Attorneys, and essoiners to circa *1350*

None of the surviving city ordinances comments on the right of city freemen to appoint attorneys or essoiners. It looks as though London 'citizens', which probably then meant residents, were by the early thirteenth century able to appoint both attorneys and essoiners whenever they chose. The rights of non-citizens may not have been so extensive, however. There is nothing to suggest that they could not employ essoiners as freely as citizens, but foreign tenants in real and mixed actions may have had to wait until 1221 to be granted the right to appoint attorneys. Even then, it was specifically denied to foreign demandants on the grounds that, if they were allowed to do so, they would find it easier to pester London citizens with lawsuits than if they had to appear in person.[76] In March 1267, however, Henry III's final charter to the city extended to foreigns, both as tenants and demandants, the right to appoint attorneys in real and mixed actions.[77] Even

74 See below, fn. 134 for Basset's connections in the city.

75 CLRO, Jor. 1, fos. 2, 69, Jor. 2, fo. 28v; CLRO, HR CP140, m. 5, HR PL145, m. 10.

76 Riley, *Munimenta Gildhallae*, I, p. 63; Chew, Weinbaum, *Eyre 1244*, pp. 95, 97–8.

77 Riley, *Munimenta Gildhallae*, I, p. 138; Stapleton, *De Antiquis Legibus Liber*, p. 104.

though evidence from the city assize records in the fourteenth century suggests that some form of restriction might have been maintained in these cases, the article appears to have been enforced in the Husting.[78] Foreign demandants certainly did occasionally appoint attorneys in the Husting in the late thirteenth and early fourteenth century.[79] By 1300, therefore, both demandants and tenants, whether citizens or foreigns, could appoint an attorney in real and mixed actions heard in the city's courts. The only proviso was that it had to be done either in open court or before at least one alderman (or the mayor or recorder).[80]

Whether the early thirteenth-century restriction imposed by the city on the appointment of attorneys by foreigns in real and mixed actions applied to personal ones, too, is uncertain. The 1221 provision stated specifically that foreign tenants' right to appoint attorneys related to real actions, but the denial of the right to demandants merely spoke of 'any foreign who wishes to implead any citizen'. So it is conceivable, if unlikely, that the restriction extended to foreign plaintiffs in personal actions, too. What is certain is that by the early fourteenth century foreign plaintiffs were appointing attorneys to represent them in personal actions in all three city courts: men like Adam de Forsham, merchant, who in 1315 appointed an attorney in his action of account in the Husting against Robert de Thame of London, merchant, who, he alleged, had been his receiver in the city.[81] By the fifteenth century aliens could also demand the services of an

[78] Chew, *London Possessory Assizes*, p. xx, fn. 1, where most of the relatively few plaintiffs who appointed attorneys may only have been allowed to do so because of special circumstances (e.g. because they were abroad, minors, in holy orders): item 14 and p. 6, items 27, 47, 48, 61, 94, 103 and pp. 32, 110, 125. Not until about 1400 do plaintiffs, foreigns as well as city freemen, appear to have routinely appointed attorneys in the possessory assizes: Chew, *London Possessory Assizes*, items 195, 196, 197, 199, 200, 202, *et seq.*

[79] CLRO, HR PL23, mm. 9 (John Baudewyn of 'Wolfeswike', demandant, appointed John de Ware), 10 (Emma, widow of Ralph le Mareschal of Standon, demandant, appointed John de Cornhull).

[80] Riley, *Munimenta Gildhallae*, I, p. 222.

[81] CLRO, HR CP40, m. 23, CLRO, Sheriffs' Court Roll (1320), mm. 11v (le White 'Esterlyng', plaintiff, appointed Reginald Wolleward), 13 (le Bakere of Pottenheth, plaintiff, appointed Thomas de Bury), and possibly also *CalEMCR*, p. 132 (le Brun, executor of Bree of Dublin, plaintiff, appointed three city attorneys to act for him); *CalEMCR*, pp. 146 (Geoffrey Hubertyn of Lucca, plaintiff, appointed Nicholas Teste) and, probably, 122 (John de Croily, plaintiff, appointed Jakemin de Sessoln).

interpreter: this occurred in the Sheriffs' Court in 1421, and it may well be that such assistance was by that date available in all the city's courts and in all types of action.[82]

In addition, the city recognised that some English litigants could not speak for themselves. Under-age demandants, or tenants in actions in which demandants were not obliged to await the tenant's majority before suing them, could be permitted a 'guardian', an experienced attorney or advocate who would conduct the case for them; and city orphans could automatically rely on the city's common serjeant at law or some other city clerk or attorney to act in this capacity for them.[83] From the record, it sounds as though the court decided who the guardian should be, but that may not be correct, or not always so; there is certainly a case of a minor 'removing' his guardian (by royal writ) and replacing him with someone else, and another is said to have asked that a certain attorney should act for him.[84]

So it is clear that by 1300 litigants could, regardless of their status, employ attorneys and other personal substitutes in appropriate circumstances in all types of actions heard in the main city courts; and by the next century they could expect to get other forms of practical assistance as well. The Husting records show that it was quite usual, throughout our period, for litigants to appoint an attorney in that court: in the Husting of Pleas of Land roll for 1301/2 (PL24), there were more attorney appointments (38, treating joint appointments as one) than there were new writs brought (27). (This does not of course mean that attorneys were employed in every case, much less that all litigants employed them; each case involved at least two litigants, some many more.) In the decade 1431/2–1440/1, 19 attorneys were appointed and 19 new writs were brought.[85] The Sheriffs' Court part-roll for 1320, too, shows that attorneys were quite commonly appointed in that court. On 1 July, 30 appointments were noted.[86] On average, a little over 30 cases appeared on the roll for the first time at each

[82] CLRO, HR CP146, m. 3; see also HR CP53, mm. 21v, 22 (1334).
[83] CLRO, HR PL26, m. 7v. For two aldermen being appointed to represent minors, even though their father was the co-tenant, see HR PL23, m. 2v (*Durham* v. *la Rose*).
[84] CLRO, HR PL41, 27v, 31; HR PL43, m. 5v.
[85] Based on CLRO, HR PL156–162.
[86] CLRO, Sheriffs' Court Roll (1320), mm. 1–2v; joint appointments are again treated as one.

common court. Again, there is a rough parity between the number of actions brought and attorneys appointed. At first sight, the Mayor's Court appears to be an exception. Of 374 original bills on a file which covers the 1440s and 1450s, fewer than 50 (13 per cent) note attorney appointments or activities.[87] Bearing in mind that these files include bills relating to actions abandoned at such an early stage that they would probably not have made it onto the sheriff's roll, however, the difference may not be as great as it appears. The company, churchwardens' and Bridge House accounts also confirm that attorneys were quite commonly employed: indeed, by 1381 the bridge masters were retaining an attorney to act for them at Guildhall (one of the two most active later fourteenth-century city attorneys, Gilbert [de] Meldebourne) for an annual fee.[88] With the possible exception of the Mayor's Court, therefore, nothing suggests that litigants of one type, litigating in one court or over one type of asset, were more likely to employ attorneys than other litigants in other situations.

Whether any positive attempt was made before about 1400 to control who could act as attorneys and essoiners is impossible to say. The city may not have admitted even attorneys formally at any stage before the fifteenth century, although it is possible that a group of six men who took their oath in 1289, having been 'elected' by the countors, were attorneys, and it would certainly appear to have been the intention to record the names of those who took an oath to obey the regulations in 1305 (two headings, 'Attorneys Sworn' and 'Essoiners Sworn', appear beneath the entry recording the swearing-in of five advocates, but the spaces were never filled).[89] As for essoiners, it seems probable that they were never expected to do more than take the oath: there is certainly no surviving evidence of any selection or licensing procedure. In the longer term, the question became academic. Essoiners disappeared as a distinct type of legal representative, with names of common essoiners becoming fictionalised, in the 1350s.[90]

[87] CLRO, Mayor's Court File of Original Bills, MC1/3.
[88] CLRO, MS Bridge Masters' Annual Account Rolls 1381–9 (trans.), p. 29.
[89] CLRO, MS LBC, fo. 87v.
[90] Essoiners with rhyming or locative names, or combinations of both, appear in the Husting rolls from the mid-1350s on: e.g. Posse, Bosse, Bosswode, Posselonde, Possemouth, Possedore, Mossebrok, Bourne, Ponde, Bromegate, Huntegate: CLRO, HR PL77 (1355/6). Few if any of these were real men.

If attorneys were indeed admitted in 1289, that was the first and last recorded instance of a group admission during our period. Indeed, the only recorded example of the granting by the Court of Aldermen of a licence to practise at large as an attorney before the 1450s occurred in October 1389, when the former sergeant and keeper of Newgate Gaol, David Berteville, was admitted.[91] In 1393, however, it was decreed that none of the sheriffs' clerks should act as an attorney for any litigant in their court. This article no doubt explains why, when the sheriffs' staffs took their annual oath in 1416, the list of oath-takers included a group of men who were described as common attorneys and who were clearly differentiated from the clerks.[92] A similar list of the names of clerks and sergeants who were sworn in together with the newly elected sheriffs had been entered in Letterbook C in 1309; there were, however, no attorneys included in this early list.[93] (The 1416 oath-taking was not part of an admission ceremony, but merely an event which was supposed to occur annually, after the sheriffs' election: three of the attorneys had appeared in that capacity before 1416.)[94] Then, in the 1450s, the Court of Aldermen began to admit men as common (or city) attorneys. In 1460, evidently encountering some resistance, the mayor and aldermen had to insist that no-one who had not been formally admitted and sworn before them as an 'attorney of the city' should be allowed to appear as an attorney in the Sheriffs' Court.[95] By this they seem to have meant that common attorneys, even if they were freemen of the city, could not simply be sworn in annually before the sheriffs. This may have been the practice previously: although Richard Lovell and Thomas Chaumbre were admitted and sworn as attorneys before the mayor and aldermen in 1453 and 1455 respectively, three other attorneys of the period, John Crokker, admitted to the freedom in 1451, and Hugh Warter and Robert Chapman, both admitted to the freedom in 1454, do not appear to have been.[96] Likewise, although, according to his petition of 1427,

[91] *CalPMR 1364–81*, p. 104, *CalLBH*, pp. 185, 344.

[92] *CalLBH*, p. 344; CLRO, Jor. 1, fo. 1v. [93] *CalLBC*, p. 181.

[94] Chew, *London Possessory Assizes*, items 140, 142–3, 157, 159, 168–9, 184, 186, 191 (Robert Louthe). For the other two men, Louther and Strensall, see pp. 286, 290.

[95] CLRO, Jor. 6, fo. 262v.

[96] *CalLBK*, pp. 350, 369; CLRO, Recognizance Roll 20, 1v, Recognizance Roll 23, m. 3v.

Ralph Stoke, the former renter of the Bridge House, had been admitted to the freedom 'in the office of attorneys' in March 1413, this seems not to have been done before the mayor and aldermen.[97] We can be sure, therefore, that all the fifteenth-century common attorneys were somehow being formally admitted to office and thereby obtaining a licence to practise at large in the Sheriffs' Court. At this period, it also seems certain that they were being admitted to a 'city' rather than merely to a 'public' office. That is certainly the inference that can be drawn from the enrolment of an 'oath of the attorneys' in the letterbooks in about 1400.[98] And in due course, what may have begun as an attempt to ensure that common attorneys were approved by the Court of Aldermen transmuted into selection by the mayor and aldermen.

If we want to know whether, and if so how, attorneys and essoiners were being controlled before about 1400, however, we need to find out who the many men were whose names appear in the city's court records.[99] Personal information about such men is extremely scant before the sixteenth century, and particularly so before 1350. Of essoiners, therefore, it is impossible to say anything much, other than that there is some evidence to suggest that there may have been an association between certain essoiners and attorneys. William and Walter Gladwyne (essoiners) and Richard Gladwyne (attorney), for instance, were working together in the Husting in the 1310s. Although William disappeared from the records after a couple of years, Walter went on to act as an attorney, his first recorded appearance in that capacity occurring a few years after Richard's death.[100] What was shared by some of these attorneys and essoiners, such as the members of the great fourteenth-century Horewode 'dynasty', was perhaps merely a toponym; they may not have been related. Thomas and Christian de Bury were father and son, however, and it seems likely that they and Solomon and Reginald de Bury, the Gladwynes, and

[97] *CalLBK*, p. 61. [98] *CalLBD*, pp. 6–7.

[99] For attorneys who appeared more than once in the city's courts between *c.* 1300 and 1550 (almost all before 1400), but are not known to have been either common attorneys or mayor's court clerks, see Appendix 8.2.

[100] CLRO, HR PL31 mm. 6v, 1, HR PL33 mm. 4v, 1v, HR PL36, m. 13v, *CalHW&D*, I, pp. 229–30.

perhaps also attorney(s) Adam Orpedeman (I and II?) and essoiner Thomas Orpedeman, were likewise relatives.[101]

There is something more that can be said of the men who acted as attorneys. Of 108 who appeared in the Husting between 1300 and 1399, 27 definitely or almost certainly held city offices. John de Waltham, for instance, was a clerk; although he may have been regarded chiefly as an advocate by 1309, he had been appearing as an attorney since the late 1290s.[102] John Cook (who appeared as an attorney over almost a quarter century) was also a clerk; so were Richard de Crofton, Nigel de Lutterworth (although it is not certain that he was a city clerk), John de Guldeford, William de Horewode, Philip Rykhall, Henry Perot, the common clerk, John Byrom and Richard Osbarn, clerk of the city's Chamber.[103] Henry de Suttone, William de Hockele and Nicholas Symcoke were deputy coroners and probably therefore city clerks, since the two offices were quite closely associated.[104] Six others were, or very probably were, sergeants (John de la Barre, William de Greyngham, Richard de Olneye, John Chamberleyn, John Broun and John Watlyngton).[105] More unusually, John de Horewode I was bailiff of Queenhithe in 1327.[106]

To say that twenty-five per cent of fourteenth-century attorneys were holders of city offices may not seem too impressive. Such a proportion would be compatible with a situation in which there was no systematic control at all: one in which some attorneys and essoiners were holders of court offices, others were regular practitioners who may have specialised in legal representation in the city courts despite not holding any court office, and others

[101] CLRO, HR CP62, m. 6, HR PL43, m. 16, HR PL33, m. 9; HR PL22, m. 17v, HR PL36, mm. 22, HR PL37, mm. 1 *et seq.*

[102] CLRO, HR PL21, *CalLBC*, p. 172.

[103] CLRO, HR CP37, m. 3; *CalEMCR*, pp. 107, 210, Chew, Kellaway, *London Assize of Nuisance*, item 70; HR CP56, m. 8, HR PL61, m. 7; HR PL64, m. 20; CLRO, HR W&D89, m. 4; TNA (PRO), PCC, PROB11/1/9 (fos. 68v–9); *CalLBH*, p. 8, TNA (PRO), PCC, PROB11/1/9 (fos. 68v–9); CLRO, Jor. 3, fo. 25, CLRO, MS Bridge House Weekly Payments vol. 3, 1421–30, fos. 12, 151, MS Bridge House Weekly Payments vol. 4, 1430–45, fo. 72v; CLRO, HR W&D129, m.9.

[104] Chew, *London Possessory Assizes*, pp. 20–68; *CalCorR*, pp. 272–3, 274–5; Chew, *London Possessory Assizes*, pp. 52–130, also item 142.

[105] CLRO, HR PL26, m. 9v; *CalLBF*, p. 124, *CalLBH*, p. 15; HR CP77, m. 6; *CalLBG*, pp. 249, 288; CLRO, Mayor's Court File of Original Bills MC1/1, item 136; *CalLBG*, p. 202.

[106] CLRO, HR CP51, m. 6.

again appeared occasionally, may or may not have been specialists, and were entirely independent of the city. It is however worth bearing in mind that this study has identified only eighteen sheriffs' clerks, and no underclerks, who served between 1300 and 1373. Later evidence suggests, first, that clerks and underclerks were more likely than other office-holders to act as attorneys, and, secondly, that it tended not to be the clerks responsible for record-keeping (about whom we know most, because their names were sometimes noted when they brought the records into the Husting or Mayor's Court) who offered their services as legal representatives. So we may well know least about the city office-holders who were most active as attorneys, particularly in the first half-century of our period. Moreover, the twenty-five per cent of 'office-holders' among the fourteenth-century Husting attorneys excludes men who very probably did hold a city office but who cannot be associated with a particular one. Gilbert [de] Meldebourne was such a man. He, together with Richard Forster, appears to have been the most active attorney in the city courts between the mid 1360s and the early 1390s, when he died.[107] One of his last recorded appearances was as the commonalty's attorney, Forster representing the mayor.[108] He acted as mainpernor with a known city officer (Common Serjeant Ralph Strode), and in 1384 was chosen to deputise for an alderman while the latter was away from the city.[109] While none of this proves that he held a city office, it is quite likely that both he and Forster did.[110]

That the one isolated example of an admission to the 'office of attorney' before 1393 involved a man who occupied a city office, but one which was, at best, on the fringes of the city's courts and their staffs, is almost certainly significant. It suggests that it was then unusual to admit men specifically in the 'office of attorney'; and that was probably because, although *ad hoc* appointments of friends, family and independent lawyers continued to be permitted, at least so long as another attorney was appointed jointly with the foreign one, the attorneys – and probably also the

[107] CLRO, HR PL88, m. 14v; *CalHW&D*, II, pp. 289–90.

[108] CLRO, HR PL113, m. 7.

[109] CLRO, Mayor's Court File of Original Bills, MC1/1, item 165; *CalLBG*, p. 247.

[110] Forster acted as a viewer and a summoner in a Husting case, tasks which tended to be performed by office-holders: CLRO, HR CP113, mm. 4–4v.

essoiners – who appeared regularly either held city offices themselves, or were the 'servants' of office-holders. A fair number of them, particularly before 1350, very probably were younger relatives working for office-holders.

The situation in all the city courts during the fourteenth century may well have been very similar to the one that obtained in the Mayor's Court for most of our period. There, at least by the second half of the fifteenth century, the clerks enjoyed an effective monopoly of the right to practise as a regular attorney in their court.[111] It is possible that something approaching a monopoly for court officers, if not clerks, existed earlier, given that five of the six attorney appointments noted in the early fifteenth-century *querelae levatae* were of Mayor's Court Clerks John Carpenter and William Kyngeston and Mayor's Sergeant John Byrkrygg, the sixth being of Simon Cook, about whom nothing else seems to be recorded.[112] Moreover, as early as 1302 a defendant argued that the attorney admitted for the plaintiff in the Sheriffs' Court 'should not be admitted for the defence here [in the Mayor's Court]' (though this may have meant that he should not be admitted on the strength of his Sheriffs' Court admission alone).[113] Either way, such a monopoly existed in later years. In a Mayor's Court file of the 1440s and early 1450s, nearly sixty per cent of the recorded appointments and activities of attorneys involved Mayor's Court Clerk Thomas Lambourne, and, of the other six who acted alone, the only one who might not have been a Mayor's Court clerk was 'RH' (Robert Hylsay?), of whom nothing more seems to be known.[114] The only limitation on the clerks' activities, introduced in 1454, was that the clerk responsible for the court records and his underclerk(s) were forbidden to act as attorneys; and in the sixteenth century it was the fourth, or most junior, clerk who specialised in this type of work.[115] By 1500 (and

111 For attorneys active in the Mayor's Court, see Appendix 8.3.

112 CLRO, Sheriffs' Court Rolls, Sheriff Wotton, 1406/7, items 2, 4; Sheriff Brook, 1406/7, items 4, 6; Sheriff Halton, 1407/8, items 4, 7.

113 *CalEMCR*, pp. 130–3.

114 CLRO, Mayor's Court File of Original Bills, MC1/3; CLRO, Jor. 5, fo. 219; *CalPMR 1437–57*, p. 40. Thomas Segrym and Giles Nase, who were not clerks, were jointly appointed together with Lambourne: Mayor's Court File of Original Bills, MC1/3, item 242.

115 CLRO, Jor. 5, fo. 166.

therefore possibly until 1500) the offices were in the gift of the common clerk, although it may be that the normal route was for candidates to procure an underclerkship, so that *de facto* control lay with the incumbents themselves. That was certainly so in the case of Common Clerk John Carpenter, who succeeded his former master, John Marchaunt, in that office in 1417; and Marchaunt himself, who received a legacy from the former common clerk, Henry Perot, may well have been Perot's sometime underclerk.[116] On a number of occasions after 1500, however, the Court of Aldermen admitted men to Mayor's Court clerkships, noting the common clerk's right merely in order to disregard it.[117] This made it theoretically more likely that 'outsiders' would be admitted, but there are in fact few recorded instances of this occurring before the end of our period.[118]

In the Sheriffs' Court, any monopoly on working regularly as an attorney that the sheriffs' clerks and sergeants and their underlings might have enjoyed did not last beyond the end of the fourteenth century. On the other hand, the 1393 ordinance was evidently not fully effective in separating out clerks from attorneys, certainly in the short term, since later clerks did apparently sometimes evade the prohibition. A [sheriff's?] clerk, William Aston, for example, is probably the man who acted as an attorney in a number of Husting cases between 1400 and 1406; and he is probably also to be identified with the future undersheriff of that name.[119] (Indeed, serving undersheriffs evidently acted as attorneys before 1393, and may possibly have done so afterwards: William de Iford represented a litigant in an assize of freshforce, of all things, in 1355, while he was an undersheriff; William Cresswyk, who was jointly appointed as an attorney in 1374, might also have been an undersheriff at the time; and the same was true of the John Weston who was appointed attorney in a Husting case brought in 1401.)[120] The decision by the Court of

116 *CalLBI*, p. 179; TNA (PRO), PCC, PROB11/1/9 (fos. 68v–9).

117 CLRO, Rep. 1, Rep. 5, fo. 267v, Rep. 7, fo. 78v, Rep. 8, fo. 17.

118 CLRO, Rep. 10, fo. 165; most such requests were made by serving or former city officers: Rep. 4, fos. 109v, 161, Rep. 5, fo. 267v, Rep. 10, fos. 253v, 254, Rep. 11, fo. 69.

119 CLRO, Bridge House Weekly Payments, 1st series, vol. 2, p. 72, CLRO, HR CP125, m. 6, HR CP 130, mm. 1, 2v, HR PL130, m. 3.

120 CLRO, HR CP79, m. 28; CLRO, Mayor's Court File of Original Bills, MC1/1, item 147; CLRO, HR CP126, m. 4.

Aldermen in the 1450s to control admissions to common attorneyships does however seem in the longer run to have had the effect of eliminating Sheriffs' Court clerk-attorneys altogether; or, at least, clerks who wished to act as attorneys had formally to transfer.[121] For example, Richard Lovell, admitted as an attorney in 1453, may well be the man of the same name who was discharged (temporarily, probably) from his sheriff's clerkship in 1444; the Richard Cote admitted as a Sheriffs' Court attorney in 1460 may be the sheriff's clerk (probably, the secondary) sworn into office in 1439; Richard Grene, admitted in 1462, may well be the scrivener of that name, and, more doubtfully, was possibly employed as a clerk or writer of court bills in the Sheriffs' Court beforehand; and in 1535, Thomas Went was on his admission as a common attorney described as having been 'of longe tyme exercised in the Shryeffs Cortes' (in what capacity is unfortunately not stated).[122]

PROFESSIONALISATION

Advocates and counsel

The thirteen years during which the city was being governed directly on the king's behalf (1285–98) were probably anomalous, in that the advocates who were newly appointed by the warden and his advisers in 1289 may have been of roughly similar status and expertise to the serjeants who worked in the eyres and the Common Bench.[123] This contrasts with the five men admitted in 1280, three of whom seem to have been drawn from the so-called 'populist party' among the city's governing families (it is almost as though an attempt was being made to mend fences after the defeat

[121] For common attorneys, see Appendix 8.4.

[122] *CalLBK*, p. 350, CLRO, Jor. 4, fo. 82; CLRO, Jor. 6, photo. 422, Jor. 3, fo. 25; *CalLBL*, p. 19, GH Library, Commissary Court of London Register 6, fos. 260v-261; CLRO, Jor. 9, fo. 142.

[123] One, William de Mareys, was shortly to become a Common Bench serjeant: Brand, *Origins of the English Legal Profession*, pp. 80 and 193 (fn. 45); Baker, *Order of Serjeants at Law*, p. 525. Although Mareys held property in the city by 1291, it does not look as though the connection predated 1285 or lasted beyond 1298: *CalHW&D*, I, p. 102, CLRO, HR CP19, m. 4, HR CP20, m. 3v, HR CP16, m. 9, HR CP22, m. 8, HR PL21, m. 12v.

of this group).[124] In contrast again, none of the five men who took the oath to obey the city's regulations governing the conduct of countors in 1305 appears either to have worked in the eyres or central courts or to have been drawn from the city's leading families, even though one of them, Robert de Kelleseye, was later to become an alderman.[125] There is however much more evidence of activity by this third group, and three of them at least appear to have been working in the city's courts for some years before they took their oath.[126]

We know so little about anyone else who might have appeared as an advocate or counsel in the city's courts in the fourteenth century that it is impossible to draw any general conclusions about the level of expertise of these men. Whether even those who took their oath as countors in 1305, in some cases after several years of activity in the city's courts, can safely be regarded as specialist advocates is doubtful. This is also true of the one fourteenth-century common serjeant known to have acted as counsel for private clients in the city. Indeed, it is doubtful whether he would have been regarded by contemporaries as a lawyer of any kind, if Common Serjeant Ralph Strode is to be identified with the fellow of Merton College, Oxford, of that name.[127] Other than that possibility, nothing seems to be

[124] One of them, Walter Hervy, was almost certainly the former mayor, alderman and sheriff, disgraced in 1274, and another, Roger Hervy, was presumably a relative: Williams, *Medieval London*, pp. 167, 235–46; Stapleton, *De Antiquis Legibus Liber*, pp. 168–70. For his activity as a legal representative, see CLRO, HR CP2, m. 6, and CLRO, HR PL3, m. 4, TNA (PRO), Special Collections: Ancient Petitions, SC8/280 item 13992 and *CalPR 1272–81*, p. 407 (I am most grateful to Dr Paul Brand for the last two references). Another, John Duraunt, who was described as a countor in the records of the 1276 London eyre, was evidently also of some social standing in the city: Weinbaum, *London Eyre, 1276*, items 669, 715, TNA (PRO), Chancery Ecclesiastical Miscellanea, C270/22, m. 5. For the two others, Richard de Wylton and Walter Wolleward, see CLRO, HR CP3, m. 5, HR CP19, m. 3, *CalEMCR*, p. 191.

[125] Kelleseye seems to have held some sort of city office previously, as no charge was made for the enrolment of an acknowledgement of a debt to him in 1301, a privilege normally accorded to aldermen and officers: *CalLBB*, p. 110; *ibid.*, pp. 230, 249, 133–4.

[126] For the activities of Kelleseye and his colleagues, Robert de Suttone and Reginald de Oundle, see *CalLBB*, p. 119, *CalLBC*, pp. 185–7, 82, 101; CLRO, HR CP19, m. 4v, *CalLBA*, p. 192, *CalLBB*, p. 133, *CalLBC*, pp. 130–1; *CalLBB*, p. 81. The others, William de Graftone and Richard de Honewyk, are only known to have appeared afterwards: *CalEMCR*, pp. 253–4, 264, *CalLBD*, p. 296, CLRO, HR W&D39, item 91, printed in *CalHW&D*, I, p. 216.

[127] Emden, *Biographical Register of the University of Oxford*, III (1359, 1360).

known of his training and career before he was elected common serjeant in 1373. On the other hand, the 'Parshay' who seems to have acted for the defendants in a Mayor's Court case in 1369 may have been Henry Percy, who was created serjeant at law in 1371.[128] But the appearance of such an experienced lawyer in the city courts seems to have been highly unusual.

By the 1420s, however, things were changing. John Weston, the undersheriff and common serjeant who acted as an advocate on occasion, might have been the man who was created serjeant at law in 1425.[129] The doubt arises because two London freemen called John Weston, either of whom could have been the city law officer, made their wills in 1420, one in February, the other in October. The second died almost immediately; the other lived for another seven years.[130] Both were probably members of Lincoln's Inn, since a Weston senior and a Weston junior had been admitted sometime before 1420.[131] If so, the first testator must have been Weston junior, since he was alive in 1421. Despite the fact that Weston had been replaced as common serjeant sometime between the summers of 1416 and 1421, and therefore could well have died in 1420, Weston junior's choice of second executor (Richard Teweslee, who was a sheriff's clerk) suggests that it might have been he who was the former undersheriff.[132] If Weston junior was our man, there is no doubt that he did very well professionally. If Weston senior was the undersheriff and common serjeant, however, all that one can say is that he probably enjoyed some standing as a 'man of law', over and above the status conferred by his city offices. Even at his first recorded appearance as an advocate in 1410, he was probably already quite an experienced lawyer; he had evidently been representing clients as an attorney at least since the early 1400s.

Whether or not Weston is to be identified with the serjeant at law, by the 1420s city law officers were certainly beginning to

[128] *Le Livre des Assises*, pp. 265–6, 43 Ed. III, pls. 2, 3, 4; HRO, [Winchester] Mayor's Account Rolls, W/E1/6, mm. 4, 7v (but note reference to *William* Persay on 4v); Baker, *Order of Serjeants at Law*, p. 530.

[129] Baker, *Order of Serjeants at Law*, pp. 162, 543.

[130] TNA (PRO), PCC, PROB11/2B/50 (fos. 171v–2v), PROB11/13/8 (fos. 59–9v).

[131] *Lincoln's Inn Admission Register*, pp. 3, 4.

[132] CLRO, Jor. 1, fos. 1v, 39v (1416).

acquire the level of legal expertise necessary for such advancement. Alexander Anne and John Fortescue both served as undersheriffs in the 1420s and received the call to assume the degree of serjeant in 1438. Fortescue probably did not read at his inn of court for the first time until the autumn of 1425, and Anne is likely to have had his first reading at much the same time.[133] So both men, though well-launched on their legal training, were relatively junior in the 1420s. But by the 1440s, undersheriffs who appeared as advocates occasionally included men like Undersheriff Thomas Burgoyne, who received an exemption from the 1443 call.[134]

Of the law officers who were active as advocates and counsel in the second half of the fifteenth century, Thomas Rigby and John Watno were both probably considered quite senior apprentices at law in the 1460s and 1470s, although they seem not to have advanced further.[135] Perhaps Watno's social circle helps to explain why. He noted in his will that he had borrowed a book from a former common attorney, James Bradman; and his closest friends appear to have been the secondary of the Bread Street counter where he worked, Giles Claybrooke, and his former colleague as undersheriff, Roger Byrkes, whose executor he had been.[136] In this respect, he and Watno differed from their contemporary, Common Serjeant John Baldwyne, whose will gives no hint that he was serving as a city law officer when he made it.[137] Common Serjeant Robert Molyneux, too, was probably of similar professional standing to Rigby and Watno when he was first recorded in the yearbooks as acting as an advocate, five years after he read at his inn for the second time.[138] Like Watno, he was never a serjeant at law, although he lived for some time - eleven years - after his second reading. And if the John Grene who appeared as an advocate in a

133 Thorne, Baker, *Readings and Moots*, I, p. ix; Baker, *Order of Serjeants at Law*, p. 512.

134 Baker, *Order of Serjeant at Law*, pp. 38, fn. 2 & 163.

135 Thorne, Baker, *Readings and Moots*, I, pp. xxv, xli (Rigby); *ibid.*, pp. xxiv, xxxi (Watno).

136 TNA (PRO), PCC, PROB11/8/6 (fos. 50–1). Byrkes had also left a legacy to Claybrooke's wife.

137 TNA (PRO), PCC, PROB11/5/27 (fo. 226). Burgoyne also made a point of noting that he was one of the undersheriffs of London in his will: PCC, PROB11/6/1 (fos. 4v–6v).

138 Thorne, Baker, *Readings and Moots*, I, p. xxxiii.

Hustings case in 1519 was indeed the common serjeant, his legal career, judging by what is known of it, seems to have been relatively undistinguished.[139]

Not all the named counsel who were consulted by (and could possibly have appeared for) litigants in the city's courts in the fifteenth century were city officers, of course. Serjeants John Vavasour and Thomas Fulthorpe, and to a lesser extent William Wangford (created serjeant in 1453), were certainly senior common lawyers in the 1480s, 1420s and late 1440s respectively. In a rather different category were Thomas Basset and Robert fitzRobert, who, as we have seen, may also have been independent lawyers. 'Men of law' they may have been, but the evidence suggests that they were not particularly prominent ones. They seem to have belonged in the large grey area which then existed between the more experienced attorneys and the serjeants at law. FitzRobert [junior] was the son of a London grocer, and is often mentioned in contemporary city records, but he had much wider interests; in 1420 he received a one-year appointment as the earl of Ormond's attorney (he remained associated with the earl and countess until his death in 1436), and he was later appointed to a number of commissions of the peace and the like in Middlesex and Surrey.[140] There are a number of Thomas Bassets recorded at this period. Our man was, like fitzRobert, an active 'man of business' with plenty of legal connections, inside the city and out; in May 1434, for example, he was one of those required to take an oath in London not to maintain peacebreakers.[141]

In addition, there are the men who acted as advocates who were either common attorneys or city clerks. The evidence in the case of the common attorneys suggests that membership of a legal inn of court might have become more common among them in the course of the fifteenth century. Not much seems to be known about the legal training or career outside the city of Common Attorney Thomas More, apart from the possibility that he was the

[139] *Ibid.*, II, p. lxviii.

[140] *CalPR 1416–22*, p. 261, *CalPR 1422–9*, pp. 546, 566, *CalPR 1429–36*, pp. 303, 353, 620, 625; *CalHW&D*, II, pp. 506–7.

[141] *CalPR 1429–36*, p. 401; TNA (PRO), Chancery *Habeas Corpus Cum Causa* Writ File C250/14, item 11, TNA (PRO), Early Chancery Proceedings, C1/11, item 518; *CalCR 1422–9*, pp. 152, 184, 335, *CalCR 1429–35*, pp. 162, 222, *CalFR 1422–30*, p. 114.

man admitted to Lincoln's Inn in 1435 and that he was one of many city office-holders involved as feoffees in a grant of Gray's Inn in 1456 (and so might perhaps have moved on to Gray's Inn later in his career).[142] On the other hand, like Christian de Bury (*floruit* 1334–45) in 1345, he was an experienced and active attorney in the city's courts.[143] And if Thomas Bryan and Roger Byrkes were common attorneys, that was also true of them by the time they first appeared as advocates and counsel. Bryan had reached an almost identical stage in his legal career in 1450 as Fortescue had in 1424 (the same may have been true of Byrkes, but the evidence is lacking; he may have been relatively young when he died in 1459).[144] It is probably also true of Robert Pynkney, depending upon when he came to be regarded as a pleader; he is likely to have read at his inn for the first time in 1500.[145] Moreover, had he not died eight years later, he might possibly have gone on to enjoy a level of professional advancement not too far short of that achieved by his colleague, near-contemporary, and (perhaps) fellow Middle Templar, Common Attorney Richard Lyster, assuming him to be the man who figured in the 1518 list of apprentices of the central courts and ended his career as chief justice of King's Bench.[146]

A rather different case is that of Thomas Rysshton, whose activities as an advocate in the years before he was finally admitted as a common pleader are known to us only because he was disciplined for them. Within two years of being appointed one of the Sheriffs' Court prothonotaries, he had been admitted to Lincoln's Inn.[147] He seems nevertheless to have been in two minds about

142 *Lincoln's Inn Admission Register*, p. 7, Williams, *Early Holborn*, I, p. 653. More's executor was the common attorney James Bradman: TNA (PRO), PCC, PROB11/5/11 (fo. 85v).

143 His father, Thomas senior, with whom he acted jointly in the early years, was also an active attorney (*fl.* 1315–39): CLRO, HR PL56, m. 5, HR CP69 m. 8v; HR CP62, m. 6.

144 Bryan probably read at his inn of court for the first time in Autumn 1450: Thorne, Baker, *Readings and Moots*, I, p. xxxii. Having been described and paid as an attorney up to January 1450, he was paid at the 'pleader's rate' from February onwards: GH Library, Churchwardens' Accounts, St Peter, West Cheap, 1435–1601, fos. 222v, 223; ibid., fos. 223 (*bis*), 224. Likewise, 'Brikes' was paid as an attorney until February 1450, but as a pleader from March onwards: *ibid.*, fo. 223.

145 Thorne, Baker, *Readings and Moots*, I, p. xv.

146 Baker, *Order of Serjeants at Law*, p. 169.

147 *Lincoln's Inn Admissions Register*, p. 25.

which of the now-diverging career paths, primarily clerical or primarily legal, he wished to follow. It was only after the mayor and aldermen had disciplined him on several occasions for undertaking advocacy work that he finally accepted their invitation to apply for a common pleadership: and within six years he had stepped back onto the clerical ladder, being admitted as common clerk in 1533.[148] That was, however, also the year in which he read for the first time at his inn of court. A further six years later, he was created serjeant at law, and was, evidently somewhat controversially, granted the reversion of a city under-shrievalty in return for his continuing support, although he does not seem to have been admitted before his death three years later.[149] He remained resident in London and his will suggests that his relationship with the sheriffs' staff continued to be close.[150]

At the other end of the professional scale, it is also clear that the men who continued to be employed by individual Londoners as counsel were not necessarily lawyers of any kind, not even part-time ones. In 1482/3, the Drapers paid 20s for a 'repast made to Robt Olney [a member of the company] to herr' Ashbone & to other lernyd men of his counceill'. 'Harry Ashbone' was Henry Assheborne, secondary of the Bread Street counter (*floruit* 1466/7–1486), a scrivener by trade, who did not have any other training or education in the law, as far as can be ascertained.[151]

All the common pleaders admitted after 1518 were members of inns of court.[152] There is nevertheless a noticeable difference between the career patterns of those appointed in the first fourteen years after the office was formally established and of those appointed afterwards. Of the first six men appointed, two were created serjeants at law, one eventually becoming chief justice of King's Bench, and two obtained Exchequer baronies. Of the

148 CLRO, Rep. 4, fos. 195–5v, Rep. 6, fos. 114v, 116, 223; CLRO, Jor. 13, fo. 371v.

149 Baker, *Readers and Readings*, p. 120; CLRO, Rep. 10, fo. 108v (see also fo. 111).

150 His wealth was assessed at £1,000 in 1541: Lang, *London Subsidy Assessment Rolls*, p. 57. His daughter married a common attorney, John Osborne, and Rysshton left bequests to two other common attorneys: TNA (PRO), PCC, PROB11/29/F24 (fo. 184).

151 GH Library, Merchant Taylors' Accounts, II, fo. 296, *CalLBL*, p. 236; Steer, *Scriveners' Company Paper*, pp. 110–11.

152 See Appendix 8.1.

fourteen others who served before 1551, one, Thomas Atkyns, went on to become a city law officer, but the rest seem to have died in office, and relatively little is known of their professional careers or training.[153]

Attorneys, and essoiners before circa *1350*

In the late thirteenth and early fourteenth centuries, the attorneys and essoiners were becoming smaller and more individually active groups. Several dozen attorneys were noted in a number of the Husting of Pleas of Land rolls for the 1270s and 1280s, for example, with a dozen or fewer being common by the 1330s.[154] This was also true of the Sheriffs' Court: there were probably no more attorneys working regularly in the Sheriffs' Court in the 1320s (twelve being noted in the part-roll for 1320) than there were a hundred years later (eleven are recorded as having taken the attorneys' oath in 1424).[155] The drop is even more dramatic in the case of essoiners: down from sixty-five in the first surviving Pleas of Land roll, for 1273/4, to less than a dozen, normally, by the 1300s. Moreover, most attorneys active in the early 1300s had worked their way up from being an essoiner, and there was a tendency for individuals to stop acting as essoiners once they started to receive appointments as attorneys. Examples of men who began as essoiners before moving on to become attorneys include William Westwode (essoiner, 1306–12, attorney 1313–32), Walter Gladwyne (essoiner, 1308–15, attorney, 1315–42) and William Momby (essoiner, 1313–16, attorney, 1316–47).[156]

By the fifteenth century, nevertheless, the fact that the Sheriffs' Court was confined to dealing with litigation according to law and custom and its clerks were no longer supposed to act as legal representatives, combined with the probability that its workload had risen since 1320, is likely to have meant that the common attorneys were even more specialised, both as attorneys and as

[153] Richard Gooding was promised a law office, but died before a vacancy occurred: CLRO, Rep. 11, fos. 321v, 474v.

[154] CLRO, HR PL1, PL5, PL6, PL8–10, PL13–15.

[155] Up to twelve may well have been normal in the fifteenth century, but in 1545 the limit was eight: CLRO, Jor. 15, fo. 171v, CLRO, Rep. 10, fos. 6, 8.

[156] Westwode: CLRO, HR CP32, HR PL34, HR CP37, m. 12, HR PL51, m. 5; Gladwyne: HR PL31, HR PL36, HR PL36, m. 13v, HR CP66, m. 16v; Momby: HR PL35, HR PL37, HR PL37, m. 18v, HR PL69, m. 18.

practitioners of the common law, than men like Westwode, Gladwyne and Momby had been. Over the course of the century, it looks as though this resulted in a closer alignment between their training and, eventually, career patterns and those of attorneys based at Westminster. John Mordon, one of those sworn in as common attorneys in the 1410s and 1420s, may be the man who was in 1431 granted a retainer by the prior of Charterhouse, in return for 'his counsel and labour in his faculty ... in all causes and matters'.[157] With three possible exceptions, none of the common attorneys active before 1440 appear to have belonged to an inn of court. From the later 1440s onwards, however, it becomes increasingly common to find the names of men who might have been common attorneys among those admitted to, or associated with, inns of court. This is certainly in part a trick of the evidence: we know much less about membership of the inns of court before 1450 than afterwards. But that may not be the whole explanation. Of thirteen common attorneys listed as having been sworn in in 1416, 1420 and 1424 or active between 1400 and 1430, two, William Louther and [William?] Kellow, might be the men admitted to Lincoln's Inn sometime before 1420 and in 1444 respectively.[158] Of the same number of common attorneys admitted or active between 1430 and 1460, however, William Blyton, Thomas More, John Jeny, John Crokker, James Bradman, Hugh Warter, and (possibly) Richard Lovell, may all have been members of Lincoln's Inn or Gray's Inn.[159] If the majority of these identifications are correct, it looks as though the common attorneys active from the 1430s onwards either joined an inn of court earlier or were more senior men on appointment than their predecessors. Of the nine common attorneys known to have been active in the late 1470s and early 1480s, none apparently joined Lincoln's Inn, but three, J[ohn] Chamberleyn, R[ichard, probably] Elyot and [?] Burrell, may have been members of Inner

157 Williams, *Early Holborn*, II, item 1811.

158 *Lincoln's Inn Admission Register*, p. 2. (Louther); CLRO, Jor. 2, fo. 28v, *Lincoln's Inn Admission Register*, p. 10 (Kellow). In addition, John Heth, who received an appointment as an attorney in 1400, might possibly be the 'Heth' admitted to Lincoln's Inn sometime before 1420: CLRO, HR CP125, m. 6, *Lincoln's Inn Admission Register*, p. 2.

159 For Jeny, see Thorne, Baker, *Readings and Moots*, I, p. xii, TNA (PRO), PCC, PROB11/6/7 (fos. 52v–53v), CLRO, MS Bridge House Rental (Accounts) 1460–84 (trans.), pp. 234, 511.

Temple, Middle Temple and Gray's Inn respectively.[160] This suggests that some common attorneys were by this date joining the more 'senior' inns of court, presumably with their sights set on higher things. By way of comparison, about a third of the attorneys practising in the central common-law courts in 1480 have been identified as members of legal inns, a proportion which, given how few membership records survive for this period, is said to be 'quite consistent with them all having been members'.[161]

If this also applied to the late fifteenth-century common attorneys, it may have been a reflection or result of the fact that quite a few of them were by this date working in the central courts. (In contrast, there seems to have been virtually no overlap between Common Bench attorneys and attorneys who appeared in the city courts in the previous century.)[162] Chamberleyn was a Chancery clerk, and Elyot, since he was admitted at the request of the Master of the Rolls, probably was, and may have been the man who was active as an attorney in King's Bench in the 1470s; J[ohn] Joys or Joce (promised the next common attorneyship in 1467) was probably the man who was described as an attorney of the Common Bench in 1463.[163] The process of alignment reached its zenith around 1500, when the London Sheriffs' Court numbered among its attorneys such legal luminaries – if the identifications are correct – as Richard Lyster, the future chief justice of King's Bench, and Elyot himself, attorney-general to Henry VII's queen.[164] Similarly, as we have seen, Robert Pynkney was evidently working in the Court of Chancery and perhaps elsewhere at Westminster as well as in the city's courts, apparently, by the early 1500s, having just resigned from a common attorneyship and, probably, read at his inn of court for the first time. It is true that Elyot, Pynkney and Lyster were the only ones among the

160 Thorne, Baker, *Readings and Moots*, I, pp. cxxiv, xv, xxxvi.

161 Baker, 'English Legal Profession', p. 87.

162 Only Thomas Melreth, active in the Sheriffs' Court between *c.* 1382 and 1399, seems to have appeared in the Common Bench: Thornley, Plunknett, *Year Books of Richard II: 1387–88*, p. 286; CLRO, HR PL104, m. 11v, HR CP122, m. 11v, HR CP125, m. 3 (Sheriffs' Court cases); conversely, none of the attorneys listed in the yearbooks, nor of the 'London' attorneys in the Common Bench attorney roll for Michaelmas 1399, seems to have appeared in the city courts: TNA (PRO), CP Plea Roll, CP40/555 (the roll is however badly damaged).

163 CLRO, Jor. 8, fos. 205, 146v; TNA (PRO), KB Plea Roll KB27/809, m. 20.

164 Baker, *Order of Serjeants at Law*, p. 169; Ives, *Common Lawyers*, p. 60.

common attorneys of our period to progress to a more exalted career at Westminster.[165] William Martyn, however, another late fifteenth-century common attorney, went on to read at his inn seventeen years after his admission and was subsequently granted the second common pleadership.[166]

Despite the coincidence of rising professional achievement and the assertion by the mayor and aldermen of their right to control the common attorneyships, it was probably not their involvement which caused standards to improve. Certainly they were unable to prevent them declining again. A decree made in 1537, requiring that common attorneys should in future be approved by the city counsel, was probably never given effect.[167] No doubt as a consequence, eight years later the Court of Aldermen was again lamenting the 'lack of good knowledge and learning' among contemporary incumbents compared to the 'sad discreet and well learned men' of yesteryear, and determining both to reduce the numbers and increase the competence of these office-holders.[168] Although the mayor and aldermen blamed the problem on the fact that admissions had been 'at the special labour instance and suit' of various great men, relatively few admissions were of this type, and those that were, were not necessarily of men who lacked learning. Some of these attorneys were evidently well-educated, like George Mountford, admitted in 1465, sometime fellow of Gonville College, Cambridge, Richard Staverton (a scrivener and Sir Thomas More's brother-in-law), granted the next vacancy at Cardinal Morton's request in 1498, who was a member of Lincoln's Inn, and John Adams of Inner Temple, admitted at the instance of Undersheriff Pakyngton in 1526.[169] But the Court of Aldermen, despite its periodic concern about the standards of the attorneys in the Sheriffs' Court, failed to resist the temptation to make use of these offices as a way of currying favour or paying off debts: as happened in 1527, when the son of a deceased draper was

[165] TNA (PRO), Chancery Warrants 10 Henry VIII, C82, 474, item 36.
[166] CLRO, Rep. 1, fo. 34; Baker, *Readers and Readings*, p. 31.
[167] CLRO, Rep. 10, fo. 8. [168] CLRO, Jor. 15, fo. 171v.
[169] *CalLBL*, p. 61, Fitch, *Index to the Testamentary Records in the Commissary Court of London*, I, p. 130; CLRO, Rep. 1, fo. 41, *Lincoln's Inn Admission Register*, p. 27 (the city prothonotary of the same name was Staverton's son: *Lincoln's Inn Admission Register*, p. 39; GH Library, Commissary Court of London, Reg. 10, fo. 315); Rep. 7, fo. 88.

admitted 'in recompense for his father's great expenses in city offices'.[170]

In fairness to the sixteenth-century Court of Aldermen, however, the workload and therefore profits to be made out of the city courts may have been dropping sharply by the 1530s. It might well have been difficult to attract the more able and ambitious lawyers, just as it had been easy to do so, when the courts were still busy. In addition, with the establishment of the common pleaderships in 1518, the city was under a duty to protect the profits and interests of those office-holders. For these reasons among others, common attorneyships ceased to be a normal avenue to professional advancement both in the city and outside. Whereas, of the seven men admitted sometime between 1482 and 1501, five are known to have been members of an inn of court, no more than ten of the thirty-six men whose admissions were recorded between 1502 and 1550 were members of these inns, with one or two more being members of an inn of Chancery. Given that more information is available about memberships at this period, it is likely that this represents a real reduction since the late fifteenth century in the proportion of common attorneys who became members of inns of court.

Of course, not all the attorneys at work in the city's courts were common attorneys. The modest level of litigation in the Mayor's Court compared to the Sheriffs' Court even in the fifteenth century, and the fact that the Mayor's Court clerks maintained their near-monopoly of work as attorneys to the end of our period, means that one might expect the common attorneys to have been much more proficient and more familiar with common-law procedures than those who normally only represented clients in the Mayor's Court and the Husting. In fact, the evidence suggests a rather different situation, at least at first sight. On the one hand, of twenty-three fifteenth-century attorneys who appeared in the Mayor's Court, as many as nine may have been members of a legal inn. John Stafford, John Crowton, Robert Langford, Roger Spycer *alias* Tonge, Thomas Kyrton, Robert Cartleage and, much more doubtfully, William Hamond, may with very varying degrees of confidence be identified with men who were admitted

[170] CLRO, Rep. 5, fos. 128–8v.

to Lincoln's Inn.[171] In addition, it is possible that Robert Blount and John Lambourne were members of Gray's Inn, and William Fox might well have been a member of an inn of Chancery, Clifford's Inn.[172] On the other hand, there is no evidence that any of them, apart from Stafford, who may be the man who read at his inn in 1428 and 1434, advanced their legal education much beyond the level available in the inns of Chancery.[173] At least one of the early fifteenth-century Mayor's Court attorneys appears to have got his basic training as an apprentice in the Scriveners' company.[174] The probability is that most of those who were members of inns of court were either admitted *ex officio*, as Robert Cartleage was and Thomas Kyrton may have been, or sought admission for social rather than educational purposes. Where anything more is known of their careers, they tended to progress to more senior clerical positions in the city.

Even in the sixteenth century, when more information is available, not much seems to have changed. Belonging to an inn of Chancery, perhaps either having begun as a scrivener's apprentice or being admitted *ex officio* to an inn of court afterwards, but with no evidence of more advanced education, is the best that most Mayor's Court attorneys achieved by way of a career as a lawyer; and half appear not even to have bothered with this. William Goldyng seems to have been unusual in being, not only a scrivener and a member of Thavies Inn, but also admitted to Inner Temple in 1516, three years before he died.[175] Roger Coys was probably unique, in the event of him being the 'Mr Coys' mentioned in the Lincoln's Inn records in 1518 as an university

171 *Lincoln's Inn Admissions Register*, pp. 4, 7, 2, 24 (Thomas Kyrton, 'specially admitted' in 1487, by which time, if it is the same person, he was probably retired), 14 (Cartleage, admitted in 1458 as clerk of Mayor's Court, so almost certainly an honorary admission), 12 (Hamond, admitted 1454, so probably another man).

172 A Robert Blount was sued by Gray's Inn for unpaid dues in 1486, and Lambourne was one of feoffees of Gray's Inn in 1456: Sir John Baker (private communication), Williams, *Early Holborn*, item 653. Fox may be the man who was sued for unpaid dues by Clifford's Inn in 1508: Sir John Baker (private communication).

173 Thorne, Baker, *Readings and Moots*, I, p. xii.

174 William Kyngeston (active as an attorney, 1402–8), was probably apprenticed to [his father?] Nicholas Kyngeston sometime before 1404: Steer, *Scriveners' Company Paper*, p. 21.

175 Steer, *Scriveners' Company Paper*, p. 215, Sir John Baker (private communication).

man.[176] Less unusual was the fact that he had worked for Common Pleader Atkyns before being admitted as a Mayor's Court clerk; probably at least five other sixteenth-century Mayor's Court attorneys owed their admissions as clerks in this court to their time in the service of city clerks or law officers.[177] The typical Mayor's Court attorney continued throughout our period to be primarily a clerk, learning the skills of an attorney on the job. One or two, like William Marshall and, possibly, John Palmer, may have gone on to work in the central courts.[178] But if we assume that Marshall is not to be identified with the man listed in 1518 among the pleaders working in the central courts, none of them seem to have aspired to greater things, as far as their legal work was concerned.

176 Baildon, *Records of Lincoln's Inn*, p. xiii.

177 CLRO, Rep. 10, fo. 253v, TNA (PRO), PCC, PROB11/35/3 (fos. 20–20v).

178 Marshall, who resigned his Mayor's Court clerkship in 1519, may have been working as an attorney in the Common Bench by 1520; he was certainly employed as a clerk by Richard Broke, CB(Ex), the former undersheriff and recorder, until 1526, before returning to city employment as deputy to Secondary Giles Claybrooke. There were a number of contemporary John Palmers, two being members of Thavies Inn, one of Lincoln's Inn, and one being a filacer of King's Bench; and a John Palmer was in the service of Thomas Bryan CJCP (the former common serjeant) in 1495: Sir John Baker (private communication), CLRO, Rep. 7, fo. 239v, Baker, *Order of Serjeants at Law*, p. 500.

9

THE EFFECTIVENESS OF THE ADMINISTRATION OF THE LAW BY THE CITY

INTRODUCTION

Since the nature and variety of legal remedies offered by the city's courts, and the process employed for each of them, have already been described, it is the implications of these remedies and processes for litigants, and consequently how attractive the city is likely to have been as a place in which to litigate, which are of interest here. Likewise, as far as the city's own priorities are concerned, its effectiveness in protecting its jurisdiction and citizens against adverse intervention by national authorities has also been described and discussed, as has been its ability to influence those authorities. It is however also clear from the letters which survive in the early plea and memoranda rolls, in particular, that the city's governors engaged in a considerable amount of correspondence with important individuals and with other towns and local authorities, both on the city's behalf and, where necessary, on behalf of its citizens.[1] Unfortunately, in later years this type of correspondence seems normally to have been recorded and held elsewhere, and much has probably been lost.[2] The probability is, nevertheless, that within England changes in the relationship between local and central courts and the greater willingness of the larger local courts to entertain suits brought by outsiders meant that the need for such *ad hoc* interventions had reduced by the end of the fourteenth century. For so long as they continued, the ability of the wronged parties to obtain either royal letters authorising reprisals against third parties from the localities concerned or, from the city itself, a withernaam against them,

[1] *CalPMR 1323–64*, pp. 3, 4, 6, 10, 70. [2] *Ibid.*, p. 277.

secured some measure of cooperation, at least when these letters were addressed to authorities.[3]

The limitations of the evidence also mean that we cannot know for sure what impact the city authorities generally and the Sheriffs' Court and the Mayor's Court in particular had on crime and public disorder in our period. The problem is compounded by the fact that attitudes towards criminality and anti-social behaviour have changed so much. On the one hand, while some modern offences did not then exist at all, a good many activities which medieval man regarded as offences would be not be viewed in that light today. On the other hand, it is probable that some of the minor offences and nuisances which nowadays would go to the Magistrates' or Juvenile Courts would in the Middle Ages and early modern period have been handled informally by the aldermen or city officers (and so would often go unrecorded).[4] Indeed, allegations relating to serious crimes, including alleged treason, conspiracy to murder and riot, and rape, were sometimes dealt with informally, and on occasion the city authorities appear to have kept these matters under their own control.[5] The powers exercised by the aldermen in the Court of Bridewell in the later sixteenth century, which so outraged the sometime recorder of London, Serjeant Fletewode, were almost certainly inherited from their predecessors and formerly employed either independently within their wards or collectively, in the Inner Chamber.[6]

We are on slightly firmer ground when it comes to asking how successful the city courts were in resolving inter-personal disputes formally. At least, we can get some answers to such straightforward questions as 'What proportion of plaintiffs (or demandants) won their cases?', 'Did you have to be rich in order to litigate?' and 'Was it very time-consuming?'. Having asked these straightforward questions of the evidence, we also need to consider how accessible the city's courts really were and whether there is any evidence of the subversion or perversion of justice in them.

[3] *Ibid.*, pp. 76–7.

[4] E.g., TNA(PRO), Early Chancery Proceedings, C1/32, items 34, 53, 56, 79, *et seq.*

[5] TNA(PRO), Early Chancery Proceedings, C1/32, item 48, CLRO, Jor. 7, fo. 25v, CLRO HR CP34, m. 16v (*Refham* v. *Br[aye?]*), HR CP80, m. 4v (*le Patenostrer* v. *Wascon*).

[6] GH Library, MS 9384, esp. fos. 6–6v.

EFFICIENCY AND EFFECTIVENESS

The maintenance of law and order

The city was active at a number of different levels in its attempts to enforce law and order. On the basis of the evidence discussed in Chapter 4, it looks as though serious and violent crimes were not nearly as common as one might expect given that, although the carrying of swords and other weapons within the city was normally forbidden, knives as personal tools were ubiquitous. Although both the proportion and the number of private cases of trespass brought in the Sheriffs' Court had probably risen considerably by the second half of the fifteenth century, to perhaps 1,200–1,500 a year if the estimates of totals and percentages are correct, the increase was very probably in non-violent trespasses, rather than in assaults on the person.

If so, demographic, social, economic and political factors largely beyond the city's control might account for the improvement. On the other hand, by the later fifteenth century London appears to have found ways of containing factionalism and violence among its governors and administrators. The city's administration was also much more tightly controlled by the fifteenth century than it had been even a hundred years before, with clear roles for freemen at all levels of government. It is certainly possible that one historian's vision of a seventeenth-century London kept orderly – despite the political upheavals of the period – by the mundane busyness of lowly officials, which itself echoed the scarcely less mundane busyness of the city's governors, is close to the reality for most of our period, too.[7] How much the city's administration of the law itself contributed to this, however, is best judged by considering how successfully it met the standards others might reasonably expect of it.

Informal dispute resolution

As we have seen, informal dispute resolution, both in court and out, was a feature of the administration of the law in the city in relation to private litigation. Adjudications in conscience and

[7] Pearl, 'Change and Stability'.

arbitrations delivered by or organised under the auspices of the mayor and aldermen, however, probably never constituted more than a tiny proportion of their workload. Whether their intervention in such cases was successful or not clearly depended on whether both parties were equally willing to accept their authority and, no doubt, on the heat generated by the dispute. Nevertheless, arbitrations supervised by the Court of Aldermen probably did perform a useful service in difficult times, and there is no reason to suppose that the Mayor's Court, as a court of conscience and, later, equity, lost popularity over the course of time. In the seventeenth century it not only still existed, but was apparently both cheaper and faster than Chancery.[8]

In arbitrations, it was common practice to require the arbitrators, and the umpires if appointed, to return their findings promptly, usually within a month of the original agreement or first adjudication date.[9] Where there undoubtedly was potential for delay and uncertainty was when disputes were brought in conscience in the Inner Chamber. Given that the law and custom as it worked in the city was comparatively flexible, informal adjudications were likely on occasion to be particularly difficult, involving cases in which the truth or right was hard to discern. That was the burden of Mayor Oulegreve's argument in 1468, when he had to defend himself against a charge of delaying such a case unreasonably.[10] In the circumstances, it is surprising that there were not more complaints about delays that occurred when the mayor 'took cases into his hands' in order to determine them in accordance with conscience.

A potential limitation on the effectiveness of the informal side of the court has already been mentioned: the fact that, in theory, the mayor and aldermen could not force individuals to submit to their decisions when sitting *in camera*. That there do not in the event appear to have been great problems is probably owing to the ability of the court to bring considerable pressure to bear on anyone who wished to live and work in the city, and particularly on freemen.[11] Moreover, the petitioners in some of these cases were defendants in actions brought in the Sheriffs' Court or on

[8] CLRO, Misc. MSS 4/37, 'Remarks submitted to authority for reform', p. 4.
[9] E.g. CLRO, Jor. 6, photo. 475.
[10] TNA (PRO), KB Plea Rolls, KB27/827, m. 104.
[11] E.g. CLRO, Jor. 7, fos. 164, 164v, *CalPMR 1458–82*, p. 31.

the common-law side of the Mayor's Court. In such cases, plaintiffs at common law who wished to see an end to their cases had little choice but to cooperate. The experience of Richard and Beatrix Page in 1468, who found their Sheriffs' Court trespass case delayed after it had been removed into the Inner Chamber for examination in conscience, reveals how difficult it was to evade such examination: even King's Bench hesitated to interfere, beyond requiring the city to offer some sort of an explanation of the delay.[12]

The Husting

Process in the Husting was very often slow, even by the standards of the central common-law courts: a case rarely terminated in less than a year, if it was contested all the way. Actions begun by writs of right were particularly protracted, because there was a finality about the outcome which did not apply to the other writ-initiated actions, such as dower. And in practice process in the Husting of Common Pleas was also slow. In cases of dower, mesne and of customs and services, the in-built procedural delay created by the allowance of essoins effectively held the action up for at least six sessions, if, on the one hand, the tenant chose to take advantage of it, and, on the other, nothing went wrong. Had each side of the court sat once a fortnight apart from the main holiday periods, a demandant could have hoped to see his opponent in court, ready to plead, within three months. For much of our period, sessions on each side of the court were in fact held at approximately six-weekly intervals. This meant a delay of, not three, but about nine months. It was by no means the worst that a demandant could face. Clearly it did not account for the fact that some cases could take several years to get anywhere at all: a right action brought in 1449, for example, was not finally determined until the early 1450s.[13] And plaintiffs who brought writs alleging error in the Sheriffs' Court were liable to find themselves repeatedly delayed by the fact that 'the sheriffs did nothing', as the records say.[14] This fundamental flaw in the process for a writ of error could, of

[12] TNA (PRO), KB Plea Rolls, KB27/827, m. 104.

[13] CLRO, HB1, fos. 7, 11, 12, 16 (*Quartermayns* v. *Stafford*).

[14] E.g., *Hope* v. *Sewale*, CLRO, HR CP162, mm. 1, 2, 3, 4, 5, 5v, 6 (1438/9), HR CP163, mm. 1, 2 (1439/40), at which point the demandants seem to have given up.

course, help to explain why, in the fifteenth century, aggrieved litigants increasingly chose to turn to the informal sides of courts like the Mayor's Court or Chancery for a remedy instead.

It would be unfair to judge the efficiency of the Husting on the basis of these extremely protracted cases if they were exceptional; but in fact they were not exceptional. The average time taken to reach a judgment in the first ten determined actions begun by writ of right after 1 January 1300 was just under three years, ranging from just under one year to just under four. The average time to determination improved somewhat during the course of next hundred years, judging by similar checks done in the 1350s and 1400s: then, it was around two years. At the same time, however, the range got much wider: extending from between eight months and in excess of seven years in the earlier period to between five months and more than ten years in the later. In the Common Pleas, the average time to determination in the 1300s was about thirty months, but this had fallen sharply by the 1350s: down to just under eight months. Moreover, whereas the ranges increased in the Pleas of Land during the fourteenth century, in the Common Pleas, where they had been very wide in the 1300s (twelve months to six years), they shrank sharply in the 1350s (two months to two years).

Even once the parties had been brought to plead, a determination could be many months off, because of the difficulty of securing the attendance of enough jurors. In *Hyde* v. *Illingworth & Others*, for instance, although attorneys were admitted for both parties at the Husting of Pleas of Land following the first summons of the tenants in July 1443, and the matter pleaded to issue then, too few of the jurors appeared for a verdict to be taken. Thereafter, the sheriffs on three occasions claimed to have received the order to distrain jurors too late to act. It was not until February 1444 that judgment was secured for the demandant. This was despite the large number of jurors summoned: thirty jurors were initially empanelled, and in November 1443 extra names were added to the panel in an attempt to produce the twelve jurors needed.[15] Even worse, the jurors in *Lawes* v. *Sudbury*, an action for dower which was well under way by April 1459, did not

[15] CLRO, HR PL163, mm. 3v, 4, 4v, HR PL164, mm. 1, 1v; HR PL163, m. 4, HR PL164, m. 1v.

return their verdict until March 1463.[16] An early-fourteenth-century provision that judgments in the city's courts should not be deferred after verdict for more than three sessions could not overcome the problem of delays which occurred because the jurors defaulted.[17] Nor could it help when the evidence was not of a kind which could sensibly be put to a local jury. One case, *Roos* v. *Kyng*, lasted for at least seven years, and involved a Chancery petition by Kyng against the prior of Wymondley for (allegedly falsely) certifying that the demandant, Roos, was not a monk. Faced by evidence of uncertain value, as here, the court simply adjourned *ad infinitum* until either the truth eventually emerged or the parties gave up or reached an accommodation.[18]

There was, however, one significant exception to this general tendency towards dilatoriness: and all these exceptional cases appear from the 1450s onwards, were begun by writ of right and were entered separately in formal plea rolls dedicated to them. In almost all cases, the actions recorded on these rolls were over in a single session, and ended up with the tenant defaulting, so that the demandant recovered the property. These cases were of course collusive recoveries. While they were useful and, relatively speaking, popular, they are not evidence of more efficient processing of contested actions by the Husting.

The slow pace of legal actions in the Husting might have been less significant had the outcome usually been favourable to the demandant. On the whole, as far as one can tell, it was not. The proportion of determined writ-initiated cases was quite low by city standards throughout our period (averaging less than 18 per cent, 1272–1448). Indeed, the 1308/9 Pleas of Land roll (PL31) records the presentation of fifty writs of right but a mere two determinations. Perhaps more importantly – since low rates of determination are also a feature of modern civil courts and are not necessarily a sign of inefficiency[19] – the demandant was unsuccessful in both determined cases: although the tenant was

[16] CLRO, HB1, fos. 40v, 48v.

[17] Riley, *Munimenta Gildhallae*, I, p. 143 (the 'three-session' rule also obtained in rural county courts: Palmer, *County Courts of Medieval England*, p. 62).

[18] CLRO, HR PL162, mm. 1 *et seq.*, HR CP164, mm. 1–3v (misfiled) and TNA (PRO), Early Chancery Proceedings, C1/45, item 42, C1/17, item 177.

[19] In 1961, 16–17% of 438 plaints in the Norwich Guildhall Court, and in 1962, 6–7% of 673 plaints, came to trial: *Atkin's Encyclopaedia of Court Forms in Civil Proceedings*, XXIX (1964), p. 72, fn. b.

dismissed *sine die* in one case because he had a royal writ of protection. The most common developments recorded on this roll, process apart, were adjournments because the jury failed to appear when summoned; the death of one of the litigants; and, unsurprisingly in view of this, the granting of a licence to the demandant to withdraw from his or her action. The year 1308/9 does not appear to have been unusual. Checks of determined cases begun in the 1300s and 1350s show that demandants either failed to prosecute or were defeated by a faulty writ, someone's death, an allegation which removed the case from the city's courts (such as bastardy), or a minority or writ of protection in some 60 per cent of actions at both periods. Demandants' chances of winning in court in fact decreased somewhat over time: they were successful on average in 30 per cent of decided cases in the 1300s, 24 per cent in the 1350s. Process which was grindingly slow and, it would seem, frustratingly inconclusive, was nothing new when *Jarndyce* v. *Jarndyce* was first launched on its hopeless course.

Confronted with relatively low chances of success and with the probable inconvenience of protracted process, genuine would-be litigants and their advisers would no doubt be eager to explore any alternative avenue. In the early years of our period, however, it looks as though the alternatives were limited. Many of the failed Husting actions were simply begun again. At times, this happened sufficiently promptly to create the impression that demandants were running two actions concurrently, or even starting the case afresh, having lost. However, although the reason for abandoning an action (or the fact that it had been abandoned) seems not always to have been recorded, it does not appear to be the case that litigants were ever permitted to bring a second writ before the first action had been abandoned. None of the determined actions on the Pleas of Land side (there are insufficient details given in the initial Common Pleas entries to make such a check) can be shown to have involved two current cases. Often, the reasons for the abandonment of the earlier writ are obvious even when the record is silent: a widow replaces her husband as the first tenant, the details of the disputed property change, and so on.[20]

[20] CLRO, HR PL26, m. 4, HR PL27, m. 5 (tenant John de Herfeud succeeded by his widow Margery); HR PL24, m. 13, HR PL27, m. 1 (land stated to be 165 ft by 25 ft, amended to 150 ft by 24 ft).

In the case of the action of mesne, it is possible that the lack of success for demandants was as real as it was apparent, with a mere two identified, if successful, outcomes for sixty writs; and perhaps it was for precisely this reason that the action ceased to be brought in the Husting after 1342 (although other factors, such as the development of alternative remedies or the effective disappearance of the mesne landlord, are at least as likely explanations; and the tendency to bring pleas of naam concurrently with actions of mesne may well have contributed to the latter's apparent ineffectiveness). In any event, other mixed actions were not so 'unsuccessful'. Of eighty writs *ex gravi querela* brought to enforce the execution of testaments between the beginning of 1348 and the end of 1359, twenty-four had an identifiable conclusion, with the demandants enjoying success in ten of these cases. This compares favourably with the results a plaintiff might expect today, bearing in mind that a proportion of cases will presumably have been without merit, and that some non-prosecutions may well have involved alternative settlements: mere notification of the purchase of a writ is likely to have persuaded some tenants to cooperate, and not all demandants may have troubled to ask for permission to concord. As in the central common-law courts, it does not seem to be the case that demandants who sought licence to withdraw from their action for some reason were penalised. Only in the case of naam was there a rule which prevented the demandant bringing any further actions after he had failed to prosecute on three occasions. To that extent, therefore, the lack of success of Husting demandants is exaggerated. Providing they did not go too far (and they could withdraw at any stage before a jury's verdict was actually rendered), they could try, try and try again.[21]

The Mayor's Court

According to the author of a seventeenth-century tract, at that date 'the determination of causes in the city courts [was] of far greater speed · · · than in others'.[22] Certainly process on the common-law side of the Mayor's Court was normally quite swift,

[21] Riley, *Munimenta Gildhallae*, I, p. 188.
[22] CLRO, Misc. MSS 4/37, 'Remarks submitted to authority for reform', p. 3.

and it was an object with the mayor and aldermen to keep it so. In 1463, the Court of Aldermen decreed that anyone who brought a plaint in the Mayor's Court and failed to prosecute it within three months would be fined. This was not merely aimed at speeding up procedures. As the record of the ordinance states, the process could be abused by a plaintiff intent on outmanoeuvring an opponent by pursuing the action when the latter's guard was down.[23]

The combination of customary procedures which had absorbed merchant law ones and a court which was prepared to sit on any day of the week made the Mayor's Court potentially exceptionally speedy. In a *querela levata* originally levied in the Sheriffs' Court on 28 July 1416, the parties appeared at Guildhall the following day. There the plaintiff requested to have the case removed into the Mayor's Court. The litigants duly appeared again on 30 July, this time before the mayor and aldermen; a jury was summoned for the next day, and, when the defendant defaulted, found against him on the spot.[24] This was admittedly an unusual case, in that the plaintiff was a former mayor who had been slandered by a non-citizen, and the defendant's default might simply have been a recognition that he was at a marked disadvantage for reasons which had little to do with the merits of his case (although, in fairness to the court, it did not permit the plaintiff to supplement his original charge with one of attempted intimidation). Even in ordinary *querelae levatae*, however, progress was usually quick. A case from 1415 was levied in the Sheriffs' Court on 14 February, removed into the Mayor's Court on 5 March, and the jury assessed the plaintiff's damages on 21 March.[25] Actions originating in the Mayor's Court, even when defendants took full advantage of opportunities allowed them to delay, were also swiftly dealt with. In a case brought on 8 June 1414, the defendants failed to respond to the summons on three occasions, then, having appeared on 22 June, requested an adjournment to allow them to take advice. The case was finally heard on 8 July.[26] Even actions which were plagued with procedural problems were dealt with comparatively speedily. Jury defaults on two occasions,

[23] CLRO, Jor. 7, fo. 42v, also CLRO, MS 'Liber Dunthorne', fo. 428, CalLBL, pp. 38–9.

[24] *CalPMR 1413–37*, pp. 43–4. [25] *Ibid.*, pp. 30–1. [26] *Ibid.*, pp. 6–7.

repeated challenges to the jury by the parties, and the court's eventual agreement that half should be aliens, resulted in an action which had been brought on 25 February 1421 being delayed until 10 April. Even so, judgment for the plaintiff was given less than seven weeks (forty-four days, to be precise) after the action was begun.[27]

At first sight, the rate of determination in personal pleas in the Mayor's Court, although it appears to have been better than that in the Husting, was modest nevertheless. Less than a third of the bills from a file of the later 1450s (MC1/3A) record process of any kind; less than a tenth record a judgment. Indeed, only in twenty-six cases on the file is it certain that the court was actively involved in a hearing (that is, one party opted for trial by jury, waged his or her law, or the defendant acknowledged the debt). As with the other city courts, however, the initial entry might have served the same function then as does the summons issued by a modern small claims court today, being enough to persuade a good many debtors to settle their account immediately. It is also worth bearing in mind that some of the Mayor's Court bills which seem to have been abandoned almost immediately might well not have been entered onto the formal roll, had the court been maintaining one at that date. This alone could explain the apparently higher rate of determinations in the Sheriffs' Court.[28] There seems to be no way of knowing how many non-suits represented an informal settlement in the plaintiff's favour and how many, a recognition by the plaintiff that his case was hopeless or without merit. Moreover, it looks, from the details entered on the surviving bills, as though a quarter of cases (65 out of 264) may in fact have resulted in a judgment, despite the absence of a note to that effect in a number of cases.[29] This seems to have been similar to, possibly slightly better than, the outcomes in civil pleas today or on the civil side of King's Bench at much the same period. According to Dr Blatcher, in Michaelmas term 1488 only 27 entries, excluding two non-suits, recorded a judgment.[30] Using the same assumptions as were employed earlier in relation to the workloads of the central courts (that about 4,000 personal pleas a year were

[27] *Ibid.*, pp. 91–3. [28] See p. 326.

[29] If simple defendant defaults are included, the total of probably determined cases rises to 85.

[30] Blatcher, *Court of King's Bench*, p. 59.

brought in the two main central common-law courts in 1490, and that King's Bench was entertaining some 12 per cent of the civil litigation), it looks as though the court could have expected to be dealing with perhaps 120 cases that term. Thus the ratio of conclusions to cases was apparently a little less than one to four in King's Bench in Michaelmas 1488. What is more, in the Mayor's Court in the late 1450s plaintiffs seem to have obtained a judgment in their favour in the great majority of cases which resulted in one.[31] Usually this happened after the defendant defaulted and either the plaintiff or his attorney swore that the money was indeed owed to him.[32]

The Sheriffs' Court

The Sheriffs' Court also offered a relatively quick procedure to litigants, although the fact that common courts were at most held twice a week imposed some restriction on speed compared to the arrangements made for foreigns and in the Mayor's Court. Delays evidently could and did occur, and very occasionally resulted in complaints.[33] Nevertheless, process was normally swift, with interim determinations commonly achieved within fourteen days. It seems to have been extremely unusual for a case to take longer than six months. It took just sixteen days to prosecute an alleged assault in 1315; a more complicated action, again involving an assault, was delayed by the need to establish whether the assault had taken place before or after a concord between the parties.[34] It lasted from 19 March to 2 July 1310. An action entered in the sheriff's counter on Monday 11 March 1398 had reached the stage of pleading by the following Friday.[35] In one case from 1302, it took a month to progress from pleading to a jury; in another case from the same year, pleading took place on 5 April, judgment was rendered on 12 May, and a jury assessed damages on 19 June.[36] Moreover, as most of our detailed information about Sheriffs'

[31] In 58 (78) cases, judgment was probably for the plaintiff; in a further two, a judgment was for him in respect of part of the sum owed.

[32] In 52 of the 58 (78) cases which plaintiffs probably won.

[33] TNA (PRO), Early Chancery Proceedings, C1/49, item 27, TNA (PRO), KB Plea Rolls, KB27/828, m. 11, Early Chancery Proceedings, C1/46, item 266.

[34] CLRO, HR CP40, m. 5, HR CP36, m. 4.

[35] *CalPMR 1381–1412*, pp. 251–2. [36] *CalEMCR*, pp. 134–5, 133–4.

Court cases comes from records produced on allegations of error, they could well have been more vigorously contested and hence slower than average.

The many actions in which a debtor's goods were arrested in the defendant's absence by the procedure of foreign attachment reached an interim determination very quickly indeed.[37] Speed seems, moreover, to have characterised those actions which in effect alleged disseisins, but were brought on plaints of trespass and contempt against the statutes prohibiting forcible entries. Although less than a month from start to finish would be highly unusual, perhaps impossible, more than six months was probably uncommon. In the first of the 'forcible entry' trespasses for which the record survives, *Barton* v. *Barantyn*, the action was levied on 15 December 1424 and the jury found found for the plaintiff, in part, a week later; and even though the verdict was not entirely straightforward and the case was adjourned while the court sought advice, judgment was finally given on 7 February 1425.[38] In *The Earl of Essex & Others* v. *Marsh*, the defendant was summoned for 15 July 1461 and the verdict was returned, after jury defaults and respites, on 18 September.[39]

Cases in the Court for Foreigns naturally tended to be swifter. One of the most protracted recorded cases was *Rothinge* v. *Staunford* (1311), which turned on the question of whether a bailee who had no means of knowing the contents of a sealed purse and who claimed to have been robbed of it was liable for the large sum of money it had contained. This occupied the court through no fewer than twenty-five adjournments, with the defendant being eventually adjudged undefended on 14 March 1312, the case having begun on 17 November of the previous year.[40]

As with other courts, only a minority of recorded actions resulted in a trial or determination: under fifty per cent of those recorded in the roll of 1320, for instance, seem to have done so. In addition, if, as seems to be the case, bill-initiated actions were not enrolled until process had begun, there will have been other cases which were abandoned without ever making it onto the record.

[37] E.g. TNA (PRO), KB Plea Rolls, KB27/806, m. 76 (*Hill* v. *Peke*, plaintiff recovered within a fortnight).
[38] *CalPMR 1413–37*, pp. 191–3. [39] *CalPMR 1458–82*, pp. 23–4, 81–2.
[40] CLRO, HR CP36, m. 18.

Because of the different nature of the surviving records, it is impossible to tell whether outcomes in the Sheriffs' Court in 1320 were more or less favourable to the plaintiff than they were in the Mayor's Court nearly a century and a half later. All one can say is that if the 165 cases being processed in the summer of 1320 for which an outcome is known were representative of Sheriffs' Court cases generally at this period, then outcomes were more favourable there than in the later Mayor's Court: 53 resulted in a judgment for the plaintiff; in a further 23 cases, there was an agreement between the parties. On this basis, although plaintiffs were slightly more likely to withdraw from their action (in 40 per cent of cases) or lose (about 14 per cent) than reach an agreement or win, the Sheriffs' Court would by any standards – including today's – have to be judged effective in terms of delivering the verdict the plaintiff wanted or was prepared to accept.

ACCESSIBILITY

The mayor and aldermen themselves had no doubt that the city offered access to justice to rich and poor alike. In 1417, when Henry Pountfreit (probably a former sheriff) sought to justify forcibly ejecting a man from a house on the grounds that it was his own, they ordered the reinstatement of the ousted tenant, saying that 'forcible entries of this kind [are] an injustice to the public, since the portals of the law [are] wide open to all who [need] it'.[41] Just how wide open those doors were, and whether they gave equally free access to everyone, is however another matter.

The Husting

In the seventeenth century, it was claimed that costs in personal actions in the city courts were 'of much less charge' than in other courts, although, as there is little evidence of the costs of engaging in litigation in the London Court of Husting, it is unclear whether this was as true of that court as of the Mayor's Court or Sheriffs' Court.[42] In the eighteenth century, however, it was said to be

[41] *CalPMR 1413–37*, p. 58.
[42] CLRO, Misc. MSS 4/37, 'Remarks submitted to authority for reform', p. 3.

much cheaper to use the Husting for a common recovery than it was to use the central Court of the Common Pleas (the Common Bench), the cost of this predictable action in the Husting being £4 7*s* in about 1700.[43] Almost 20*s* of this sum went to the common vouchee and city pleader, and as it is by no means certain that it was necessary to employ either a vouchee or a pleader in the second half of the fifteenth century, the cost might well have been proportionately lower at that date. Evidence of the costs incurred by the bridge masters in suits over city properties and rents belonging to the Bridge House suggests that cases brought in the Husting in our period did usually end up being cheaper than those brought in the central common-law courts. Suing to recover a quitrent in the Husting cost the Bridge House 13*s* 4*d* in 1381, and in most years at this period the annual retainer of 13*s* 4*d* which the masters were then paying to their attorney, Gilbert [de] Meldebourne, was all they spent on litigation.[44] In contrast, a similar case from about the same period which required the services of a Common Bench attorney, among others, and was therefore almost certainly sued in that court, cost £1 12*s* 6*d*.[45]

By city standards, nevertheless, the Husting was an expensive court. Indeed, any advantage it offered over the central courts probably had more to do with the payment of fewer fees to clerks and lawyers (for example, because litigants in the Husting less frequently employed advocates in addition to attorneys) than with the relative cheapness of the fees themselves. As in the central courts, charges for routine matters were modest, typically 4*d* a time for an entry recording process, and attorneys and pleaders, if retained, were paid the standard medieval fee of 1*s* 8*d* and 3*s* 4*d* respectively for an appearance. The often protracted nature of contested cases, however, meant that many such payments must have been made, at perhaps 8*d* or 2*s* a time for the record entry plus the essoiner's or attorney's fee, before the action was eventually abandoned, compromised or determined.[46] Moreover, less

43 Emerson, *Concise Treatise*, p. 16, Bohun, *Privilegia Londini*, p. 176.

44 CLRO, Bridge Masters' Annual Account Rolls, 1381–9 (trans.), p. 26.

45 CLRO, Bridge Masters' Annual Account Rolls, 1390–1405 (trans.), p. 26 (the attorney was John Seymour).

46 For essoiners' fees, see the 'salary' of 20*d* claimed by the plaintiff in *Orpedeman* v. *le Tapicer*, 'for various essoins [five?] cast in various courts', CLRO, Sheriffs' Court Roll (1320), m. 13v.

routine or more time-consuming activities could be costly.[47] Costs could on occasion equal those incurred in some of the most expensive cases in the Common Bench. In 1457/8, what appears to have been a relatively quickly resolved and straightforward case resulted in the Tailors' Company paying £1 for the prior of Christchurch's costs.[48] Consolidated costs for a case brought in 1514/5 'at Guildhall', quite possibly in the Husting, amounted to £3 12*s* 4*d*.[49] And in the politically charged atmosphere of the late 1380s and early 1390s, the bridge masters spent the enormous sum of £45 12*s* 9*d* on defending their rights in four properties against John Lyndesseye.[50] What was said of the Sheriffs' Court in the early eighteenth century seems to have been true of the Husting in our period: 'by reason of Devices of Continuance ... the charge of a Tryal there comes to much more'.[51]

Part of the demandants' calculations in deciding whether to bring a case must have depended on the balance between risk (quite high, apparently), cost (high by city standards) and potential benefits (the value of the disputed asset). As the value of properties litigated over in the Husting is rarely if ever given and it is not possible to assess value from the standardised descriptions given, the nearest we can get to judging how much the disputed rights were worth is from those cases in which demandants were attempting to recover rents alone. The first fifty such cases taken alphabetically (by the name of the first tenant) from those brought in the Husting of Pleas of Land between 1272 and 1448 produced an average of £2 17*s* 2½*d* per case, with a range of 2*s* (but several such claims were brought by a single demandant; the lowest individual claim was for 4*s* rent) to £20.[52] If it is correct to assume that land and property of any quality could command a price

[47] In 1512/3, the bridge masters paid 5*s* 8*d* to the Mayor's Court clerk, Peter [Saxton], simply for 'entering and writing' three pieces of evidence relating to a single case: CLRO, Bridge House rental (and accounts) 1509–25, fo. 83v.

[48] GH Library, Merchant Taylors' Accounts vol. II, fo. 137.

[49] GH Library, Skinners' Company, Receipts and Payments vol. I (unfoliated), 6–7 Hen. VIII.

[50] CLRO, HR PL110, m. 1, CLRO, Bridge Masters' Annual Account Rolls, 1381–9 (trans.), pp. 257, 275, CLRO, Bridge Masters' Annual Account Rolls, 1390–1405 (trans.), pp. 30, 74, 93.

[51] Bohun, *Privilegia Londini*, p. 192.

[52] See also CLRO, HR PL84, mm. 3, 20, 27 (*Carlill* v. *Baudewyn*, 1362), HR PL9, m. 6 (*FitzJohn* v. *Prior of 'Ockeburn'*, 1281), HR PL24, m. 5 (*FitzPeter* v. *Alegate*, 1302; Alegate being the city's chief clerk).

equivalent to twenty years' rent during the Middle Ages, then the £20 rent that Ralph fitzPeter and Ralph de Alegate were litigating over in the early 1300s related to a property worth some £400. On the other hand, elsewhere in the records one occasionally encounters claims for tiny sums, such as the 2¼*d* of rent claimed by Agnes la Yongge from Nicholas Derman in 1309.[53] This was, it is true, one of three claims made by the demandant in this session of the Pleas of Land; but as the total still amounted only to 3½*d*, one wonders why it was worth pursuing.

A possibility is that the city had some arrangement for assisting poor litigants. In the late fifteenth century Hereford, for example, required its bailiff and steward to help widowed and orphaned plaintiffs, both in court and outside.[54] Despite the quite frequent ordinances regulating the conduct of the city's courts and those who worked in them, however, there is no trace of any formal provision of this sort in London. The nearest to it is the admission of guardians to act for minors; and even here it is not certain that they gave their services free. It could be that individual aldermen assisted on an *ad hoc* basis, or perhaps the bench did so. Again, however, there is no evidence of aldermen 'standing with' litigants after 1300 (and even before then they tended to 'stand with' wealthy litigants). It may well therefore be that poor people were encouraged to place their disputes in the hands of the mayor and aldermen for resolution in conscience instead of going to law. As we have seen, some of the surviving petitions relate to matters which should have been capable of resolution at common law. If that was the sum total of the support provided to the poor, one would be bound to conclude that the Husting itself was not accessible to those of modest means. As there can have been very few poor Londoners who needed to litigate over rights in and arising from real property (even over rents, given that most of the rents disputed in the Husting were owing from whole or substantial parts of tenements), however, this may not in practice have mattered much.

It may therefore also not have mattered much that the Husting sat in the comparatively awe-inspiring vastness of the great hall of Guildhall, that its procedures were probably more formal than

53 CLRO, HR PL32, m. 1. For the relationship between the prices paid for land and its value in annual rent, at least in the later Middle Ages, see McFarlane, *Nobility of Later Medieval England*, p. 57.

54 Bateson, *Borough Customs*, II, p. 16.

those of the other city courts, and that it may even have been necessary in the earlier part of our period to employ advocates once the case came to the stage of pleadings. Nor may it have made much difference to a wealthier (and, therefore, perhaps, somewhat more legally experienced and sophisticated) class of demandant that, except when they were seeking to recover a distress, they were obliged to negotiate the Chancery bureaucracy before they could begin their case.

It is possible that Anglo-Norman French continued in use in the Husting, at least for the formal business of counting on the writ and for the technical language of the law, well beyond the point in time by which it had ceased to be understood by most Englishmen. Even this would not necessarily have created problems for a comparatively well-educated or worldly-wise type of litigant, if that was what many Husting litigants were. There is unfortunately not much evidence relating to the language actually spoken in the Husting.[55] That English was by the 1360s the first language of most litigants, even in this court, is, however, indicated by the increasing use of that language for personal descriptions given in the vernacular (for example, 'ceynturer' in 1323, 'chaucer' in 1337, 'le sisme, chivaler' in 1357; but 'grosser' (Middle English, though derived from the French *grossier*) in 1358, 'goldesmyth' in 1360, 'fisshemonger' in 1362).[56] On the other hand, not only were knights still describing themselves in French but city clerks appear still to have been thinking in French at this period, judging by the faint note at the bottom of a Husting roll for 1359/60, which reads 'Mauld mere Robt piere Thomas le Dynisour'.[57] So perhaps the court persisted in conducting at least part of its business in that language for some while longer.

The Mayor's Court

Even in the nineteenth century, the total cost of process to the plaintiff in a Mayor's Court case, where the value of the sum in

[55] CLRO, HR CP107, m. 1v.

[56] CLRO, HR CP48, m. 15, HR CP60, m. 9v; HR CP82, m. 14, HR PL82, m. 2, HR PL84, m. 16; but 'Adam Rous le Leche' also occurs in 1362, and another 'chivaler' in 1360: *ibid.*, m. 6, HR CP83, m. 6; the earliest examples of English are from 1359: see also HR PL80, m. 13.

[57] CLRO, HR CP83, m. 20v.

dispute was £19, was apparently only £1 1*s* 6*d* (5 to 6 per cent of the sum); and what would in our period have been a typical case, ending with a judgment by default, cost a further £1 9*s* for the attorney's fees (giving a total cost of just over 13 per cent).[58] It is said that in the early 1700s a Mayor's Court case could be brought to trial for £1 10*s* (about a third of the cost of a common recovery in the Husting at that date).[59] By contrast, although there is no means of telling what would have been the costs in a typical case from our period, at first sight the Mayor's Court looks then to have been fairly expensive. In the early 1490s, the Skinners' Company paid 1*s* to a Mayor's Court clerk to enter a plea in that court, and six years later spent £3 6*s* 8*d* suing various alien skinners, probably also in the Mayor's Court.[60] In the 1470s, a single case cost the Cambrai merchant Reyner Lomner £1 11*s* in all, of which £1 5*s* went on attorneys and counsel (this sum almost certainly included payments by the attorneys for routine process).[61] In a case between the [church]wardens of St John Zachary and the Waxchandlers' Company in 1543/4, the Waxchandlers spent the large sum of £7 13*s*.[62] This was however a complex case, which involved a counter-action of trespass brought by the churchwardens in the Sheriffs' Court, which was removed into the Mayor's Court.[63] Likewise, Lomner's case seems to have been exceptionally protracted and the defendant, unusually elusive. Moreover, Lomner, being a foreigner in a country which was just about to go to war with his own, might have felt the need for considerable legal support. By contrast, suing one Thomas Dalan in the Mayor's Court for not providing torches in accordance with the will of one of the company's benefactors cost the Skinners a relatively modest 13*s* 4*d* in 1513/4.[64] In the majority of cases, judging by those for which an outcome is known, the plaintiff's

[58] Brandon, 'Observations on County Courts', pp. 15, 20.

[59] Bohun, *Privilegia Londini*, p. 188.

[60] GH Library, Skinners' Company, Receipts and Payments 1491–1510, vol. I (unfoliated), 7–8 Hen. VII and 13–14 Hen. VII.

[61] CLRO, Jor. 8, fo. 81.

[62] Dummelow, *Wax Chandlers of London*, pp. 159–61.

[63] The 'querelaint [*querela levata*] for removinge out of the Sherifes Court' alone cost 1*s* 4*d*: Dummelow, *Wax Chandlers of London*, p. 160.

[64] GH Library, Skinners' Company, Receipts and Payments vol. I (unfoliated), 5–6 Hen. VIII.

costs will probably have amounted to less than 15*s* on unavoidable expenses.[65]

Given that over 50 per cent of claims in the 1450s appear to have been for £5 or less, however, even 15*s* (at least 15 per cent) sounds like a slightly discouraging price to have to pay.[66] But that assumes that it was normally plaintiffs who paid. A significant advantage possessed in the nineteenth century by the Mayor's Court, like other borough courts, was that it awarded actual costs, even for actions brought over small amounts, unlike contemporary county courts.[67] That may well have been true of the Mayor's Court in our period, in cases in which costs were available. The long list of costs incurred by Lomner in the Mayor's Court, Chancery, the Common Bench and King's Bench was granted in full by the mayor and aldermen.[68] Moreover, it looks as though plaintiffs could choose whether or not to incur extra expense by employing writers of bills, attorneys, and even, if they were city freemen, sergeants at arms to arrest defendants and their goods.[69] 'Self-help' at this period was clearly not prohibited or even, as far as one can tell, discouraged.[70]

Finally, although the Court of Requests was not established until the early sixteenth century, its appearance merely formalised an existing situation. By the end of the fourteenth century at the latest, plaintiffs with small claims who for some reason did not wish (or perhaps could not afford) to sue in the Sheriffs' Court could present a petition and expect to have their dispute dealt with in the Inner Chamber. By so doing, they obliged their opponents to do without legal representation and a jury, and were themselves able to spend relatively little without fear of being 'outgunned' by a wealthier defendant. It looks, therefore, as though the Mayor's Court as a whole was accessible to plaintiffs from quite a wide social range, although the type of dispute resolution offered to the poor (and also, therefore, to those with whom they were in dispute) differed from and was limited compared to that available to wealthier individuals.

65 For the likely costs, see, e.g., GH Library, Cutlers' Accounts, sections 12/2, 13/1.
66 See Chapter 8. 67 Brandon, 'Observations on County Courts', pp. 6–11.
68 CLRO, Jor. 8, fo. 81. 69 Riley, *Munimenta Gildhallae*, I, p. 220.
70 Lomner spent £4 partly on 'a man that lay in wayte for [the defendant] by the space of a yeere and a half': CLRO, Jor. 8, fo. 81.

The Mayor's Court may also have been comparatively accessible in the sense that litigants were not unduly intimidated by the experience. The almost domestic scale of the Outer Chamber, and the intimacy of the Inner Chamber, may have been seen as an advantage, as (to some) was the restriction on the employment of counsel in the Inner Chamber. A possible barrier was the language that was employed by the court. There seems to be nothing to indicate what language was actually spoken there until the second half of the fifteenth century, when some oral testimonies and interrogations in English are recorded in the plea and memoranda rolls and journals.[71] It could therefore be that the court, because of its prestige and monopoly of cases determined according to merchant law, continued to conduct its affairs in French well into the fifteenth century. Written testimonies in English begin to be recorded from the early 1400s on, however, with the earliest recorded wardmote presentments in English being from 1422 (mixed in with those written in French).[72] So it seems more likely that the spoken language of the Mayor's Court had ceased to be French by the early fifteenth century, whereas that language continued to be used for written depositions, awards, petitions and the like well into the 1420s.

The Sheriffs' Court

The Sheriffs' Court was, during our period at least, almost certainly the cheapest of the city courts. In the 1650s, a plaintiff might apparently expect to spend just over £1 7*s* on a straightforward case that went to jury, with the jury summons and verdict contributing a third of the cost.[73] Certainly in the earlier part of our period, a case involving a jury trial would have been unusual and comparatively expensive. In 1448/9, the churchwardens of St Peter, West Cheap, seem to have spent about 11*s* on what was probably a Sheriffs' Court case.[74] In a case brought in the 1460s, which was either not prosecuted or was settled by agreement, but which nevertheless required the services of fifteen sergeants and

[71] E.g., *CalPMR 1437–57*, pp. 153–5 (1457).
[72] *CalPMR 1381–1412*, pp. 279–82 (1406), *CalPMR 1413–37*, pp. 125, 127–8, 136–9.
[73] CLRO, 'Practise of the Sheriffs' Court', p. 11.
[74] GH Library, Churchwardens' Accounts, St Peter West Cheap, fos. 221, 221v, 222, 222v (suing Robert Butler).

their yeomen to arrest nine horses and sequestrate a debtor's property, the Grocers' Company spent a total of 11*s* 4*d*, over half of it being paid to the arresting officers.[75] At what appears to have been the higher end of the scale, the Skinners' Company spent £1 17*s* in 1513/4 on defending an attachment made by them.[76] Even process seems to have been unusually inexpensive. In 1550 entering a plea only cost 2*d* in the Sheriffs' Court; although this might represent a reduction in costs since the previous century, since in 1459/60 the Grocers' Company paid 4*d* to 'put in a bill' to the Sheriffs' Court.[77] It is conceivable that, at a time when it was losing business and, possibly, other costs were rising because of an increasing tendency to employ legal representatives in an increasingly formal court, there had been an unrecorded decision to improve its competitiveness by reducing court fees. On the other hand, until the 1520s at least the court appears normally to have been inexpensive to use. The Bridge House accounts record many modest payments for Sheriffs' Court cases in the early fifteenth century, such as the 18*s* 6*d* paid to Sergeant John Tramell 'for his labour together with an amercement for prosecuting many various debtors of the Bridge in the Sheriffs' Court during the past year' or the £1 2*s* paid to 'various sheriffs' sergeants for summons and arrests of various debtors together with the costs of pleas this year'.[78] Two individual cases brought in 1415/6 cost the bridge masters 1*s* 10*d* and 1*s* 2*d* apiece, which may well have been all that they paid in addition to the annual retainer of £1 then being given to John Hethyngham, the Bridge House's 'attorney-general in all actions [real?] and personal' brought in London.[79] A hundred years later, by which time the Bridge House accounts are full of references to cases brought at Westminster or elsewhere outside the city's jurisdiction, payments remained low: such as the 4*s* 2*d* 'paid in the Mayor's Court and the Sheriffs' Court for various actions against debtors' in 1517/8.[80] Costs in the many

[75] GH Library, Grocers' Account Book 1461–71, fos. 70v-71.

[76] GH Library, Skinners' Company, Receipts and Payments, vol. 1 (unfoliated), 6–7 Hen. VIII.

[77] CLRO, Jor. 12/2, fo. 263, GH Library, Grocers Wardens' Account Book 1454–60 [*recte* 1461], fo. 121; GH Library, Grocers' Account Book 1461–71, fo. 71.

[78] CLRO, Bridge House Accounts: Weekly Payments 1412–21, II, pp. 156, 213.

[79] CLRO, Bridge House Accounts: Weekly Payments 1412–21, II, p. 268; Bridge House Accounts: Weekly Payments 1421–30, III, p. 17.

[80] CLRO, Bridge House Rental (and Accounts), vol. 5, fo. 105v.

cases which were not prosecuted were naturally particularly low (the churchwardens of St Martin Orgar were paying between 1*s* and 2*s* a time for such cases in about 1470).[81]

Whether the Sheriffs' Court would award full costs to a successful litigant at any stage during our period is unclear. In the 1650s, it was apparently only allowing the standard fee of 3*s* 4*d* for '[e]very Councell extraordinary, though the Plaintiff pay 10*s* or 20*s*' except 'on a good cause', when it might allow three or four standard fees.[82] This may however have been a restriction imposed in order to discourage the employment of foreign counsel rather than a reflection of a more general policy of limiting the awards of costs. If so, it may also have been a post-1550 development, since the encroachments of foreign counsel did not become a major source of irritation to those who held the city pleaderships until the later sixteenth century.[83]

There is nothing to suggest that the costs involved in Sheriffs' Court cases discouraged small claims (an essoiner's suit for 1*s* 8*d* has already been mentioned, although it is possible that he enjoyed the privilege afforded to court clerks and more senior officials of not having to pay court fines). Nor is there anything to suggest, even in the fifteenth century, that plaintiffs seeking to recover large sums preferred to do so in the Mayor's Court.[84]

In the first stages of an action, at least, the Sheriffs' Court may have seemed even less intimidating to law-abiding litigants than the common-law side of the Mayor's Court: assuming, that is, that the atmosphere of the medieval and early modern counters was similar to that of a modern police station and that the Mayor's Court clerks and other members of staff carried on their business in the Outer Chamber when the Mayor's Court itself was not in session. Conversely, the great hall of Guildhall might well have overawed litigants more than the relatively cosy Mayor's Court. In one respect, however, the Sheriffs' Court was, after 1356, probably more accessible to litigants than the other city courts, for in that year it was decreed that all pleadings there should be in

[81] GH Library, Churchwardens' Accounts, St Martin Orgar, [1469]–1615, fo. 6v.
[82] CLRO, 'Practise of the Sheriffs' Court', p. 13.
[83] CLRO, Jor. 17, fo. 212, Jor. 18, 280. See also CLRO, Torr, 'Sheriffs' (City of London) Court . . . ', pp. 8–9, for later practice.
[84] CLRO, Sheriffs' Court Roll (1320), m. 26, and CLRO, 'Sheriffs' Court Roll', Wotton, 1406/7, item 4.

English.[85] It is possible that most of the proceedings had in fact been conducted in English for some years before this, with only the pleadings, or perhaps only pleadings by foreign advocates, being in French, since in 1335 an Italian defendant complained that he was put at a disadvantage in the Sheriffs' Court because he was ignorant of the 'lingua istius patrie'.[86] At this date, however, French might have been the language meant. But that was clearly not the case by 1422, when another defendant in the Sheriffs' Court expressly objected that he was unable to speak English ('lingua anglicana') and did not understand it well enough to follow the court's proceedings.[87] Given the limited evidence, it is not possible to be certain that the 1356 decree was obeyed immediately. In the absence of any complaints about non-compliance, however, or of any repetition of the decree, it seems likely that it was.

LEGAL AND ETHICAL STANDARDS

Standards of legal administration

We have seen that many of the law officers who advised and managed the city's courts from the later fourteenth century to the early sixteenth went on to reach the highest levels of the legal profession, whereas that was not so true of their predecessors and immediate successors. What impact this development had on the administration of the law by the city, and whether the presence of able and ambitious common lawyers prompted some of the changes in the conduct of its courts, is, however, hard to say. For instance, the trend towards routinely appointing law officers from the 'Westminster mainstream' of the legal profession, which began in the final quarter of the fourteenth century, took place at much the same time as a sharp increase, relatively speaking, in the numbers of writs of error recorded in the plea and memoranda rolls. Whereas only two such writs were recorded in the fifty-nine years between 1323 and 1381, there were ten in the thirty-two years between 1381 and 1412. This was probably in part a

[85] CalLBG, p. 73. [86] CLRO, HR CP53, m. 21v.
[87] CLRO, HR CP146, mm. 3–3v.

result of the successful assertion by the mayor and aldermen in 1397 that alleged errors in their court were not subject to an appeal to the Husting, but had, like appeals of error in the Husting itself, to be heard before the royal justices sitting at St Martin le Grand.[88] It was evidently not just that, however. In the Husting, too, decennial totals of writs of error rose to over thirty in the two decades to either side of 1400. While these levels were not unprecedented (totals in the low thirties had also occurred in the 1310s and 1340s), the concentration of such cases and the maintenance of high levels for eight years or so was exceptional.

This development probably owed a good deal to the prevailing political situation; evidence of forceful challenges to the city's jurisdiction and of exceptionally high legal costs incurred by the Bridge House in the late fourteenth century has already been mentioned. But it is also possible that the period around 1400 was one during which political tensions allowed the city's maladministration of justice to be exposed. The decrease in the number of complaints of error by the middle of the fifteenth century, taken together with the recovery to the fourteenth-century average in the sixteenth, might perhaps suggest that the influence of the city's law officers in the interim had effected an improvement in standards.[89] But the increased activity of Chancery by the 1440s could well be sufficient to account for what is, after all, a difference in tiny numbers. As the examples of unsatisfactory decisions by the city's judges in the later fourteenth century are suggestive of a collective loss of nerve rather than incompetence, perhaps they deserve to be given the benefit of the doubt.

Other decisions taken by them in the later fourteenth century might well, however, have contributed to the increase in the numbers of complaints of error. The majority of such complaints recorded in the plea and memoranda rolls in the late 1390s and early 1400s related to *querelae levatae*. That the Court of Aldermen decided to declare the 'immemorial custom' concerning these

88 CalPMR 1381–1412, pp. 258–9; despite this, instances of writs of error relating to Mayor's Court cases brought in the Husting can be found: CLRO, HR CP45, m. 7 (1320, *Getlom* v. *de la Chambre*), HR CP49, m. 32 and HR PL47 [*recte* CP'49A'], m. 3 (both 1325, both *Pampesworth* v. *Causton*, but two different cases), HR CP75 (1351, *Schirborne* v. *Rede*).

89 Only 27 writs of error were recorded in CLRO, HB1, October 1448–November 1484, compared to 2 writs apiece in 1507 and 1550: HB2, fos. 4v–15, HB3, fos. 163–90, or just under 300, 1303/4–1439/40.

removals in 1397 and again in 1398, as well as the rules governing appeals from the Mayor's Court itself, in the context of complaints of error, suggests that some Sheriffs' Court litigants were either unhappy with recent developments, or regarded them as novelties which might well be successfully challenged either in King's Bench or Chancery.[90] So it may be that the very process of formalisation and definition which occurred in the later fourteenth and early fifteenth centuries, designed no doubt to improve the city's administration of the law, created short-term problems.

As far as it is possible to assess such matters from the surviving records, it looks as though it was relatively uncommon for the city's courts to make straightforward errors in law or record-keeping. Of eighteen allegations of error recorded in the Mayor's Court rolls between 1298 and 1305, for example, two were annulled, ten were affirmed, and the rest were either not prosecuted or the outcome was not recorded.[91] Where judgments in cases of alleged error in the Husting have been traced, the only ground which seems to have had much success was a complaint that the court, and not a jury, should have taxed the damages awarded.[92] This appears to have been an aspect of city custom about which there was some genuine doubt. Such as it is, therefore, the evidence neither suggests that the administration of the law and courts by the city was 'unprofessional' before about 1400, nor that the increasing tendency to employ high-flying common lawyers as law officers during the fifteenth century was of itself a factor which significantly altered standards of administration. The one change which probably did make quite a difference, in that the aldermen ceased to have the major role as judges of the law, was the creation of the law offices themselves; and that had happened long before.

Attempts to prevent misconduct by legal representatives

We have seen that the degree of 'professionalism' of legal representatives working the city's courts varied over time, and indeed

[90] *CalPMR 1381–1412*, pp. 242–3 (a removal on grounds of alleged 'maintenance', however), 250–1, 251–3, 267–70, 294, 203–4.

[91] *CalEMCR*, pp. 134–5 and 139, 140–1 and 181–4; *ibid.*, pp. 89–91, 98, 99–100, 110, 117–18, 121, 127–36, 202, 242, 261–2; *ibid.*, pp. 168–9 and 167, 15, 69–70, 144–5, 263.

[92] CLRO, HR CP53, mm. 21v–22, 22–22v (*Brunlesge* v. *Reyner*, *Muscard* v. *Reyner*), HR CP79, mm. 18–18v (*Herpesfeld* v. *Prior of St Bartholomew West Smithfield*).

between the courts. Another factor which would have affected the effectiveness of the administration of the law by the city through its courts was the standard of conduct by legal representatives that its governors maintained or failed to maintain. The only specific provisions for the disciplining of advocates before the 1280s were said to have been made in 1259, as part of Henry III's 'statute': this prescribed heavy but unspecified punishment for any advocate found guilty of undertaking a plea in return for part of the property in dispute (the offence known as champerty).[93] This did not mean that improper behaviour by men who were acting in some legal capacity in connection with cases brought in the city's courts went unpunished until the 1280s, merely that they could be punished on other grounds. In 1275, for instance, the former alderman Walter Hervy was accused of arranging for a man who was not authorised or duly appointed to present himself in the Husting as the attorney of one of the queen's ladies in waiting, and of lying about what had happened. For his falsehood, 'done to the great deception of the King's court and of the city, he who had been sworn and bound to be a Judge', Hervy was summoned to the next court to be told what his punishment would be. As he turned up with 'a huge multitude' of supporters, however, he may not in fact have received his (presumably) just deserts.[94]

In contrast with the earlier approach to misconduct in, or in relation to, the city's courts, the regulations associated with the ordinance of *circa* 1280 did not merely prohibit misconduct by legal representatives: they laid down specific penalties for specific forms of wrongdoing. Advocates were to plead 'saunz vileinie' and without criticising or slandering anyone or using foul language. They were forbidden to take money from both sides (and to abandon their client mid-suit). They were not to challenge the record or judgment save by the proper procedure in error, and they were not to go beyond the bar nor participate in the judgment in any way in any case in which they were involved. These faults were to be punished by temporary suspensions, ranging from suspension from acting in the plea in question to suspension for three Hustings or more. In addition, they were not to seek to undermine the city's jurisdiction nor to undertake a suit for a

[93] Stapleton, *De Antiquis Legibus Liber*, p. 42. [94] CLRO, HR CP2, mm. 6, 8.

share in the profits, the penalty in both cases being a permanent disbarment. The same penalties for the same offences applied to attorneys, with the additional penalty of imprisonment if, 'by their default or their negligence', they lost their clients' cases, a penalty which was said to be statutory. Why attorneys alone should have been liable to this extra penalty is unclear: chapter 29 of the Statute of Westminster II (1275), which was presumably what prompted it, imposed a lengthy term of imprisonment and permanent disbarment on serjeants as well as unspecified 'others' who were found guilty of serious misconduct.[95]

The disciplinary provisions associated with the ordinance may have reflected the concerns of the warden, who was then governing the city on the king's behalf, rather than of the city itself. If so, however, the mayor and aldermen appear to have absorbed the lesson. During our period there were three major revisions of the regulations governing legal representatives, in 1345, in 1356 and in 1393. On each occasion, they formed part of a group of articles which sought to regulate the administration of the law in the city. In 1345, the regulations specifically ordered attorneys to undertake not to act for anyone unless their appointment had been duly accepted and enrolled (which had long been a requirement), and, evidently for the first time, required them to keep proper notes of their clients' pleas.[96] Eleven years later, it was additionally provided that pleaders and attorneys take reasonable fees (no more than 3*s* 4*d* in any event), that they refrain from encouraging their clients to engage in unjust or vexatious litigation on pain of being suspended for a year, and that those who wanted to act as pleaders in the Sheriffs' Court should be free of the city as well as being sworn to carry out their office 'well and loyally'. As was mentioned earlier, pleaders were also required to plead in English.[97] In 1393, regulations governing the sheriffs' staffs, counters and city prisons ordered the attorneys of the city and other common pleaders (essoiners were no longer an issue) to take their oath before the mayor and aldermen. This ordinance also decreed that clerks should no longer act as counsel and attorneys in the

[95] Riley, *Munimenta Gildhallae*, II, i, pp. 281–2, *ibid.*, II, ii, 596–7; Brand, *Origins of the English Legal Profession*, p. 120.
[96] CLRO, LBF, fo. 105, printed in Riley, *Munimenta Gildhallae* I, p. 473.
[97] CLRO, LBG, fo. 54, printed in *CalLBG*, pp. 74–5.

Sheriffs' Court. Otherwise its provisions were similar to those of 1356, if differently ordered; the only addition was that 'those who wished to sue for the king or the city' were permitted, unlike other legal representatives, to stand within the bar of the court.[98]

If the original regulations and subsequent revisions worked as they should have done, one would expect the prescribed penalties to be applied in appropriate circumstances. Before 1356, suspension, disbarment and imprisonment (for attorneys) ought to have been the main sanctions; from 1356 onwards, temporary suspensions and, in serious cases, loss of the freedom appear to have been the only penalties envisaged.

Between 1280 and 1300, we have a single reported instance of the disciplining for misconduct of a man who was acting as an advocate. This was Robert de Suttone, who in March 1291 was suspended from practising because he had knowingly told a lie on a client's behalf. The mayor and aldermen, having received a writ ordering them to consider whether his action was contrary to the statute of 1275 which made it an offence for countors to put forward false exceptions with the intention of deceiving the court, took the view that it was.[99] The record does not say what penalty was imposed, but Suttone was clearly suspended for at least four months, for in July he was found guilty of the further offence of behaving contemptuously towards a clerk who attempted to prevent him from pleading in the Sheriffs' Court while under suspension. For this, he was imprisoned. Again, it is not made clear how long this was for (the record ends 'until, &c'), but Suttone was certainly not permanently disbarred.[100] Although his second punishment was not exactly what had been prescribed by the regulations, neither was his offence exactly what the regulations had proscribed. Allowing for the tendency of contemporary courts to exercise discretion in such matters, it looks as though, on the second occasion, the city was indeed attempting to enforce discipline much as had been envisaged in the regulations.

There are few if any references to the disciplining of men who acted as advocates – just one, perhaps – in over two centuries between 1300 and 1518. The one possible reference relates to the

[98] CLRO, LBH, fos. 286–7, printed in Riley, *Munimenta Gildhallae*, I, pp. 519–25.
[99] CLRO, HR CP19, m. 4v (*Scrip* v. *le Felipp*).
[100] CLRO, LBA, fo. xcvi, printed in Riley, *Memorials*, pp. 27–8.

temporary suspensions imposed on Thomas Basset, although it is far from certain that these resulted from misconduct while acting as an advocate.[101] The sixteenth-century common pleaders did however require disciplining. In June 1529, little more than a decade after the first of their number was admitted, they had to be reminded to conduct themselves properly in office.[102] One of them, Thomas Rysshton, despite a distinguished future career as city undersheriff and, later, a serjeant at law, proved to be an undisciplined common pleader. He may well have been the principal offender against whom the 1529 order was directed, for little more than a month after it was issued he was briefly 'sequestered' from office and forbidden to plead in any city court.[103] Similarly, William Hone, admitted as one of the common pleaders of the city in 1542, was discharged from office in January 1550 for behaving contemptuously towards the mayor and forbidden to plead in any of the city courts, although he was readmitted a month later when he apologised.[104] These two 'sequestrations' were probably, as the word implies, intended to enforce better behaviour rather than to be permanent disbarments. They were in effect, assuming the pleaders did not prove obstinate, temporary suspensions, and are what one would expect as a penalty for misdemeanours not amounting to serious misconduct, both before and after 1356.

The disciplining of attorneys follows a similar pattern. There is a single example in the early records, involving Terry de Enefeud, who was punished in 1298 for losing his client's writ and failing to appear to sue for him, thus losing him his case. He seems to have been imprisoned for six months, which would be in line with the penalty prescribed by the original regulations.[105] Between 1289 and the 1450s, there is no further evidence of the disciplining of attorneys for misconduct by the city authorities. From the 1450s, however, when formal admissions by the Court of Aldermen were instituted or reinstituted, attorneys were subject to disciplinary measures imposed by them. John Laurens was thrice discharged

[101] See pp. 289–90. [102] CLRO, Rep. 8, fo. 43. [103] CLRO, Rep. 8, fo. 51.
[104] CLRO, Rep. 12/1, fos. 187v, 200.
[105] CLRO, HR PL21, m. 8v (9 June 1298); Enefeud next appeared in court on 20 February 1299: HR PL22, m. 5. This case may well be what prompted the discussion on 9 June 1298 among the aldermen 'concerning the order [*ordo*] of countors, serjeants, attorneys and essoiners': HR CP23, m. 25a.

and twice readmitted as an attorney in a twenty-one year career which finally ended in 1481.[106] Thomas Acton junior, admitted 'in the office of attorney in the Sheriffs' Court' in 1463, was discharged four years later.[107] Sometimes, as in the case of John Mey, discharged and replaced in 1472 after a two-year career 'discharge' meant what it said, but often it was clearly no more than a suspension.[108] In 1536, John Melsham got away with a warning to be obedient towards the judges of the Court of Requests, but seven years later Thomas Went and John Huchecok were discharged for challenging a petty jury on the grounds of insufficiency. In their case, three days' suspension was considered sufficient punishment.[109] More exemplary punishment was awarded to Robert Maddy in 1548, when he was imprisoned overnight and suspended *pro tempore*. Maddy, admitted at the behest of the chancellor of the Court of Augmentations, Sir Richard Rich, in 1539, seems to have specialised in upsetting the president of the city's Court of Requests, Alderman Sir Martin Bowes.[110] These penalties are in line with the provisions of the 1356 and 1393 ordinances, although no reference was made to them.

That we have little or no evidence of the disciplining of advocates and attorneys between 1300 and 1517 is not of course evidence that men were never disciplined for misconduct when performing these functions at this period. If office-holders working as advocates and attorneys in the Sheriffs' Court were being disciplined by the city in the fourteenth and first half of the fifteenth centuries, it was presumably done by the sheriffs or, if they were employed as underclerks, by the more senior sheriffs' clerks. Even legal representatives involved in misconduct, in or out of court, serious enough to have attracted the attention of the mayor and aldermen and consequently to have been recorded in the journals will be hidden from us: Richard Lovell, the sheriff's clerk who was discharged for fornication in 1444, might possibly have been working as an attorney in his master's court before he was formally admitted to that office, in 1453.[111] We do have a few

[106] CLRO, Jor. 6, photo. 397, Jor. 7, fo. 135v, Jor. 8, fos. 12, 250v.
[107] *CalLBL*, p. 30, CLRO, Jor. 7, fo. 157. [108] CLRO, Jor. 8, fos. 2, 12.
[109] CLRO, Rep. 9, fo. 152, Rep. 10, fo. 352.
[110] CLRO, Rep. 12/1, fos. 14, 29v, Rep. 10, fo. 79; Rep. 10, fo. 137.
[111] CLRO, Jor. 4, fo. 82, *CalLBK*, p. 350.

examples of complaints made against more senior officers who were acting, or were alleged to have acted, as legal representatives, such as the complaint made against Recorder Ursewyk in 1455.[112] Otherwise, we have only one known instance when a lawyer was sued by his clients (Christian de Bury, the attorney, in 1345).

Limited though it is, this evidence does suggest that the disciplinary provisions of the original ordinance as subsequently amended were on the whole applied appropriately. Gross misconduct by legal representatives was apparently uncommon, and litigants seem rarely to have had reason to complain that any defaults had not been addressed by the city authorities. In later years, insubordination towards the city's courts, judges and officers appears to have been the main reason why legal representatives were disciplined; and, in these cases at least, the authorities were certainly not reluctant to act.

Attempts to prevent misconduct by judges and jurors

Bias, unreasonableness and corruption among, and interference with, juries were quite frequently alleged by Chancery petitioners in the fifteenth century, when such petitions become numerous.[113] It seems likely that some at least of these complaints were justified; but what of the allegation made in Parliament in 1495, that 'perjurye is muche and customably used [by juries] within the Citie of London' because of the low status and impoverishment of many city jurors?[114] As we saw in Chapter 6, identifiable fourteenth- and fifteenth-century jurors were generally men of some standing within the city, whether or not all of them met the strict financial qualifications for jury service. Had something changed by the end of the fifteenth century, or was the allegation a gross exaggeration?

One possibility is that the picture we have of city jurors is distorted because few cases involving disputes over low-value

[112] See p. 261.
[113] Of 20 surviving Chancery petitions relating to such complaints, *c.* 1465–*c.* 1485 (C1/31–C1/67), thirteen are in a single file which covers the civil war years of 1467–73: TNA (PRO), Early Chancery Proceedings, C1/64, item 302; C1/47, item 81; C1/32, item 439; C1/65, item 208; C1/64, items 603, 802, 883; C1/46, items 38, 40, 75, 103, 149, 164, 221, 237, 264, 411, 433, 438, 455.
[114] *Statutes of the Realm, Vol. II, 1377–1503/4*, p. 584.

assets were recorded in the plea and memoranda rolls or became subject to a complaint of error. That might well mean that we do not know the names of the sort of men who served as jurors in these cases; and, since discretion over juror qualifications was permitted when the value of assets was low, these jurors may well have been of lower status and less wealthy than those we do know about. They may even have been hired hands. By the middle of the fifteenth century, there are a good many references to men described as 'common jurors' or 'professional jurymen'. These were evidently men who made a living partly out of serving on juries, presumably attracted by the sums paid by litigants to jurors – both the modest standard payments of a few pence a head and, if petitioners to Parliament, Chancery and the city's governors are to be believed, the much larger sums offered as bribes. If many or indeed any of the jurors who served on city juries in our period made a living out of this activity, juror qualifications were probably, at least sometimes, entirely fictitious.

At first sight, it looks as though the possessory assizes, which were held in the city if not, strictly speaking, in a city court, were regarded as a particular haunt of the common juror. In 1323, an ordinance required the examination of juries in the possessory assizes; and Stow's comment about 'divers persons, being common Iurors, such as at Assises were forsworne for rewards, or favour of parties' who were punished in the later 1460s by being paraded on horseback to the pillory at Cornhill, made to stand there with paper hats on their heads and placards proclaiming their wrongdoing, and then paraded back to Newgate again, indicates that the perceived problem with assize juries continued into the fifteenth century; indeed, into the sixteenth.[115] As the editor of the city's surviving rolls of possessory assizes commented, they 'afford no clear evidence of the existence of professional jurors, but the frequent recurrence of certain names should not be overlooked'.[116]

The impression may be misleading, however. The rather different origins and characters of juries in the possessory assizes and in private litigation generally may well have meant that the conduct of the former continued to be a focus of special concern to

[115] [Stow], *Survey of London*, p. 208.
[116] Chew, *London Possessory Assizes*, p. xxvii and fn. 3.

the authorities throughout the Middle Ages.[117] And if there was a particular problem with common jurors on assizes, it was probably confined to them. Jurors summoned into city courts in other cases do not seem to have been common jurors. For example, two men called Robert Trott and Robert Anon (despite appearances, these are not fictitious names) were described as professional jurymen by a London petitioner to Chancery. Neither is recorded as having served on a city jury of the 1460s to 1480s, the period to which the petition belongs; Trott in fact lived in Southwark, which was not then within the city's jurisdiction.[118] Another fifteenth-century 'common juryman' mentioned by a London Chancery petitioner who does not appear on any surviving city jury panel of the period is William Derby, tailor.[119] In 1454, a future mayor listed among the qualities demanded of witnesses in city courts that they should not be 'common jurors, nor witnesses at St Paul's [before the Ordinary] nor regularly sworn elsewhere'. Given that the witnesses referred to here were apparently not operating in the city courts, it may well be that the common jurors also were not.[120]

Corruptible and subject to influence though a few individual jurors clearly were, lacking in 'substaunce discrecion and reputacion' though they may sometimes have been, therefore, and despite the fact that some of them were summoned repeatedly, it seems unlikely that the city juries consisted even partly of men who made a living out of appearing on them. The apparent absence of common jurors probably owes a good deal to the more persistent attempts by the city's governors to stamp out jury misbehaviour than vice, vagabondage or usury.[121]

Allegations of corruption or abuse of power on the part of city officials were rarer than allegations against juries, but by no means non-existent.[122] Judges, too, were occasionally accused of bias or

[117] Pollock, Maitland, *History of English Law*, II, pp. 541–2.

[118] TNA (PRO), Early Chancery Proceedings, C1/32, item 293,C1/66, item 413.

[119] TNA (PRO), Early Chancery Proceedings, C1/64, item 603; for the sixteenth-century Laurence John of London, 'a common juror of the city', see C1/384, item 56.

[120] *CalPMR 1437–57*, p. 150.

[121] E.g., CLRO, Jor. 7, fos. 111, 129–30, 139v–40, 148, 148v, Jor. 8, fos. 107–8.

[122] E.g. TNA (PRO), Early Chancery Proceedings C1/45, item 287, C1/32, item 346, C1/46, item 197 (alleged corruption); C1/46, items 39, 68 (alleged false arrest/imprisonment), and possibly 75 (incorrect venue named in bill, in order to obtain a partial jury). This was no novelty: a number of city clerks and others

misconduct. There are examples of this in the city records almost from the first. After his political eclipse, Walter Hervy, mayor in 1271/2–1272/3, was presented for what appears to have been misconduct in office by several ward inquest juries, in addition to the more serious charges relating to abuse of power levelled against him by Alderman Arnald fitzThedmar.[123] Former mayors John de Wengrave and John Pecche were both subject to similar allegations in the first and last quarters of the fourteenth century respectively.[124] In the next century, two successive mayors were accused of bias in their handling of a case.[125] For what it is worth, the surviving records and other sources do not normally show clear evidence of bias or impropriety in the handling of cases by the court. There are however some possible exceptions. Refusals to accept the jurisdiction or informal judgments of the mayor and aldermen occurred in a handful of fifteenth-century disputes in which leading citizens were in conflict with aldermen.[126] And in another dispute from the same period, *Herells* v. *Lambard / Basingthwaite*, one of the aldermen who delivered the court's judgment in favour of the plaintiffs, George Ireland, subsequently obtained the disputed properties from them.[127]

The readiness of Londoners to make generalised accusations of bias and corruption against their governors was mentioned in Chapter 6. Specific allegations, however, like those levelled against Wengrave and Pecche, were most likely to be made at times of political tension. It is even more difficult than in the case of complaints of error to tell whether they were justified, reflecting widespread misconduct among judges who were normally protected from accusation by their continuing political power, or largely unfair attacks on vulnerable men made by or on behalf of their political enemies. The possibility is that, before about 1430, London's governors and officials could normally expect to prevent

were accused of corruption in 1305: Pugh, *Calendar of London Trailbaston Trials*, item 104.

123 *CalLBA*, p. 178, fn. 3; Stapleton, *De Antiquis Legibus Liber*, pp. 168–70, and see also CLRO, HR PL1, m. 4, HR CP2, m. 8.

124 Cam, *Eyre 1321*, I, p. xviii; Williams, *Medieval London*, p. 103; *CalLBH*, pp. 38–40.

125 CLRO, Jor. 7, fos. 23, 25v.

126 CLRO, Jor. 6, fos. 561–3, 565; Jor. 7, fos. 202v, 203, 204v, 205.

127 *CalPMR 1458–82*, pp. 57–64, GH Library, Skinners' Company Records (section 5), pp. 88, 89, 90, CLRO, HR PL168, mm. 27–7v.

their misdeeds and prejudices being exposed, other than in times of conflict between the city and the central government. By the 1440s, however, the availability of Chancery as a routine recourse for those who claimed that they had been treated unjustly enables a view to be taken. At this stage, at least, ethical standards appear to have been reasonably high. It is probable that, as was apparently the case in the central courts, blatant corruption on the part of judges and court officers was under control if not entirely eliminated by the fifteenth century. The frequency with which such men litigated in their own courts nevertheless suggests that they benefited considerably, if on the whole lawfully, from their positions. It is therefore not surprising that their opponents were occasionally unwilling to entrust their disputes to the courts concerned.

10

INTERCHANGE AND EXCHANGE BETWEEN THE CITY AND THE COMMON LAW

INTRODUCTION

Chapter 1 described the ways in which royal decrees, parliamentary legislation and the decisions of the judges of the central courts had the potential to alter city custom, and the ways in which the city sought to defend its jurisdiction, privileges and practices. What it did not do was draw any conclusions about the overall state of play by the end of our period. Likewise, although it was argued in Chapter 2 that a number of London remedies and procedures antedated or preserved ones which were later adopted by the central common-law courts, nothing was said about the significance of this to the development of the English common law as a whole. The aim of this chapter is to remedy both deficiencies.

THE IMPACT OF THE ADMINISTRATION OF THE COMMON LAW ON CITY CUSTOM

There are a number of ways in which developments in the central courts and the national common law could have affected the city's courts and custom. Negatively, the supervisory role of the central courts could have been used to undermine the prestige of the city's courts and litigants' confidence in them. The privileges afforded to officers of the former could have been employed to divert 'London' cases into them. The closer alignment between remedies and procedures might simply have enabled the central courts to poach what could, and in earlier days would, have been city litigation. Conversely, just as parliamentary legislation could sometimes strengthen the city's administration of the law, so developments in the administration of the law centrally might have been beneficial to the city and its custom.

As regards the first possibility, it seems to have been rare by 1350 for the two main central courts to intervene directly in city cases, whether on an allegation of error, or by issuing a writ either of *habeas corpus*, ordering the production in King's Bench of a defendant imprisoned in the course of an action in the city courts, or *recordari*, requiring information about a case in the city's courts.[1] The most complete record available to us now is contained in the sheriff's register of writs for the year following Michaelmas 1458. Of some 220 judicial writs sent to this sheriff by the central courts (excluding those concerned solely with their own procedures, for example, ordering the process leading to outlawry), only two are writs of *habeas corpus*, and there appear to have been no writs of *recordari* or error at all sent to him that year.[2] On the other hand, the first half of the fifteenth century saw a significant extension of the activity levels of the Court of Chancery, particularly, though not exclusively, in relation to 'conscience' cases. The register contains only one Chancery writ [*habeas*] *corpus cum causa*, but this is misleading. The writ is either recorded in the wrong place or, much more likely, relates to a case heard according to the common law, and was therefore entered in the section of the register which held writs issued by the common-law courts or common-law 'sides' of courts (Chancery, in dealing with the original part of its legal business – litigation involving the activities of Chancery itself or its officials – proceeded according to common law, and this might well have been true later of cases which involved the supervision of other courts and officials).[3] The register once had a separate section devoted to Chancery writs of *corpus cum causa* (which may well have included writs of *certiorari*, just as the equivalent Chancery writ files did), which has been lost.[4] Even if there was no other evidence to show how important these Chancery writs were, the very fact that they merited a

[1] E.g., 9 writs are recorded in CalPMR 1413–37 (pp. 6, 14, 114, 218, 241, 262, 282, 292, 296).

[2] CLRO, MS 205C/15, Sheriffs' [*sic*] Register of Writs. This is probably a register of writs received by the counter of the junior sheriff, Richard Nedeham: *ibid.*, fos. 4v, 6, 9, 11, 12v, 16 *et seq.* (original foliation).

[3] Tucker, 'Early History of the Court of Chancery', pp. 802, 804–5.

[4] CLRO, MS 205C/15, Sheriffs' Register of Writs, fos. 32v, 37 (original foliation).

section of their own would be suggestive. The surviving Chancery *corpus cum causa* writ files for 1458/9 contain 55 of these writs and a further 9 writs of *certiorari* directed to the London authorities. Moreover, many more Chancery writs of *attachias* (probably all in fact writs of privilege) are recorded in the register than now survive in the Chancery files.[5] So there may well once have been many more writs of *corpus cum causa* and *certiorari*; in the next two decades, over 200 a year was not unknown. And even if in fact only 64 were issued in 1458/9, there were still very many more of them than there were writs of *habeas corpus* or *recordari* issued by the central common-law courts.

Although even two hundred such interventions a year by Chancery might not have had much effect on the workload of the city's courts, they had the potential to provide an effective means of supervising the administration of the law by the city. Despite the apparent success of the response made as late as 1441 to a writ of *certiorari* that 'all plaints and processes begun in the king's courts of the city must be determined there', unless they were brought on error before the justices at St Martin le Grand, it is clear that by the middle of the fifteenth century Chancery did normally manage to obtain from the city authorities, not only a written 'certification' of the record and process in individual cases, but also the transfer of the case itself, if that was demanded.[6] By this date, interventions by Chancery in city cases wholly dwarfed those of the two main central common-law courts.

So, although the common-law courts had not lost their power to summon cases before them, the impression that the Court of Chancery began to take over the task of supervising the activities of the city's courts and officials in the fifteenth century is probably accurate. The effect of the 1475 decision of the Court of Aldermen not to permit cases to be brought before them for determination in conscience unless they were either ones which had run their course at common law, or were incapable of resolution by that

[5] TNA (PRO), Chancery *Corpus cum Causa* Writ Files, C244/86, TNA (PRO), Chancery *Attachias Non Sunt Inventi* Writ Files, C251/16 (30–39 Henry VI); also TNA (PRO), Chancery *Subpena* Writ Files, C253/35, C254/36 (both 34–37 Henry VI).

[6] *CalLBK*, p. 257; a similar protest had been made, again apparently successfully, in 1355: *CalPMR 1323–64*, p. 247. For compliance with these writs, however, see *CalPMR 1323–64*, pp. 51, 99, 104, 106, 112–13 *et seq.*, *CalPMR 1381–1412*, pp. 242, 275, *CalPMR 1412–53*, pp. 10, 150.

means, has already been discussed in Chapter 1. It was taken at a time when university-trained civil lawyers are said to have been replacing clerks trained in Chancery itself, and shortly after the chancellorship of Robert Stillington, Bishop of Bath and Wells (1467–73), himself a civil lawyer.[7] If Chancery Clerk Piers Pekham's contemptuous comments in 1469 to Alderman Tate, and indeed his attitude towards the entire Court of Aldermen, is any guide to the opinions of his fellows, the 1475 decision might well have been provoked by challenges from a Chancery which by then saw itself, not as a court of conscience which was able to provide remedies where the common-law courts could not, but as *sui generis* in terms both of its superiority and of its freedom to act, compared to all other courts.[8] That is likely to have made for more effective supervision than had formerly been the case. Chancellors seem to have retained into the later fifteenth century what might be described as a casual or even cavalier attitude towards the application of particular laws in particular cases and particular forums.[9] Tactics such as those employed in earlier attempts to make difficult or even to defeat supervision by the central common-law courts would not have worked well against a court that demanded all the paperwork and sought to establish the truth by questioning the parties under oath.

The sizeable number of surviving Chancery writs of *attachias* in the sheriff's register of writs raises the question of what happened when the city's privileges clashed with those of the central courts. Although its governors fought some attempts by officials in the Westminster courts to arrest litigation in the city courts by exercising their privilege of suing and being sued in their own courts, success depended on the city being able to show, first, that the officials were also city freemen and therefore that their own court's privileges conflicted with the city's; and, secondly, that the litigation had been under way in London when the official had claimed his privilege of court.[10] Even that point seems to have

[7] Pronay, 'The Chancellor, the Chancery, and the Council', p. 91; Tucker, 'Early History of the Court of Chancery', p. 793.

[8] CLRO, Jor. 7, fo. 204v.

[9] Tucker, 'Early History of the Court of Chancery', pp. 810–11; *idem*, 'London's Courts and the Westminster Courts', pp. 133–7.

[10] On the grounds that, 'amongst like priviledged men, most speede carries it away': Blatcher, *King's Bench*, p. 112.

been in some doubt before 1469, when Chancery Clerk Pekham, who was also a city freeman, failed in his attempt to oblige a plaintiff in the city courts to sue him in Chancery. That the outcome of the case was recorded, not just in the relevant letter-book, but also, at length, in the near-contemporary city custumal, 'Liber Dunthorne', bears witness both to the city's triumph and to its uncertainty beforehand that it would be successful.[11] In instances where there was no conflict of privileges, the city was obliged to respond to writs ordering it to cease hearing the case concerned.

At first sight, it looks as though writs of privilege were a minor niggle compared to writs of *corpus cum causa* and *certiorari*. Regardless of which court sent them, only about ten per cent of entries in the sheriff's register relating to writs of privilege mention litigation pending in the city courts. There is nevertheless the possibility that the large number of Chancery writs of privilege which are recorded in the register, compared to those for King's Bench, the Common Bench and the Exchequer, is evidence of a problem (there are almost twice as many such writs on behalf of Chancery officials as there are for officials of all the other three courts combined). As was suggested in Chapter 2, it seems likely that one motive for recording gifts of goods and chattels in the rolls of Chancery (as of the Mayor's Court) was to enable private individuals who had no other connection with the court to take advantage of its equitable jurisdiction, should problems arise. There is, however, another possible reason for involving officers of those courts in transactions generally. It looks as though, for much of the fifteenth century, if one of the plaintiffs or defendants could claim privilege of court in relation to a particular dispute, his fellows would be protected likewise, on the grounds that they ought not to be sued separately. The question of whether this was permissible was apparently not squarely addressed until 1484; and although it was then decided that it was not allowed in the case of co-defendants, the issue was still creating uncertainty (in a London case) eight years later.[12] Until 1469, therefore, in those cases in which the Chancery official or servant was also a city

[11] CLRO, Jor. 7, fos. 202v, 203, 204v, 205, transcribed into *CalLBL*, pp. 89–90 and MS 'Liber Dunthorne', p. 409. For the outcome in a case involving a Chancery official who was not a freeman, see *CalPMR 1412–37*, pp. 264–5.

[12] Thorne, Baker, *Readings and Moots*, II, pp. 259–60.

freeman, and until 1484, in cases in which he was not, privilege of Chancery may sometimes both have protected those not personally entitled to it and have resulted in the bringing into or removal to Chancery of cases which would otherwise have belonged in the city courts. Judging by the surviving writs, however, it was rare for Chancery officers to sue out writs of privilege with others: of forty writs of *attachias* on a file covering the 1450s, all but one claiming privilege of Chancery, only one joined a Chancery clerk with another plaintiff: although, admittedly, that was also the only 'London' case.[13]

On the other hand, the fifteenth and sixteenth centuries saw the emergence of a number of uses or abuses of bill procedure in the central common-law courts which could have affected the workload of the city's courts adversely. There appears to have been a serious slump in the activity levels of the Common Bench and King's Bench, between about 1440 and about 1550 in the case of the former, and about 1460 and 1540 in the case of the latter.[14] It has been suggested that this encouraged the clerks and the justices of those courts to look more favourably than they would otherwise have done on changes which might make their courts attractive to litigants. The collusive recovery is one example of a legal device which could have increased the profits of, if not the amount of genuine litigation entertained by, the Common Bench, as it did in the Husting. Another, associated with the 'bill of Middlesex', originated in King's Bench. In its developed form, the device was a rather complex variant of bill procedure associated with the general jurisdiction that King's Bench had over crimes and offences committed in Middlesex, the county in which it sat. It enabled ordinary would-be litigants to get defendants (or to get themselves, it would appear[15]) into the court's custody by alleging, quite falsely, that they had committed a trespass in the county. When the sheriff of Middlesex returned that he was unable to find the defendant, the plaintiff would purchase a writ of *latitat* addressed to the sheriff of the county in which the defendant was said now to 'lurk' (his real place of residence). If this was successful in securing the defendant, he could be sued using a 'bill of custody' by anyone who cared to do so. The reason why even

[13] TNA (PRO), Chancery *Attachias Non Sunt Inventi* Writ Files, C251/16.
[14] Blatcher, *King's Bench*, p. 21. [15] See p. 359.

the original plaintiff (he who had employed the bill of Middlesex) might choose this three-stage process was that King's Bench jurisdiction did not normally cover non-trespassory personal actions. If someone was at least notionally a prisoner of King's Bench, however, the fact that litigation was pending in that court prevented would-be plaintiffs from bringing actions elsewhere. Rather than leave plaintiffs in non-trespassory actions without remedy for the duration, they were permitted to bring their cases in King's Bench. A characteristic of actions initiated by bills of custody, therefore, was not only that the defendant in custody could be sued by others but that he could be sued in any form of action.

M. Blatcher suggested that the fully developed procedure was a major contributor to the recovery of King's Bench business by the middle of the sixteenth century. It opened the doors of the court to a multitude of ordinary litigants who wished to bring personal actions and who could not otherwise have walked through them.[16] And litigating in King's Bench was attractive compared both to litigating in the Common Bench and in local courts. This was because, on the one hand, the Common Bench continued to insist that plaintiffs should sue by writ, with its comparatively lengthy and hence expensive mesne process and vulnerability to upset on technical grounds, even against prisoners of the court in custody; and, on the other, local courts lacked the national reach possessed by the central courts.[17]

Given that the activity levels of the Mayor's Court and the Sheriffs' Court appear to have reduced substantially in the 1530s and 1540s respectively, one is bound to wonder whether the development of the bill of Middlesex procedure had some adverse impact on their workload. The chronology looks to be wrong, however: the workload of King's Bench itself seems to have reached a sixteenth-century low in the 1530s. Not until the following decade, judging by the profits of the court, is there any visible improvement.[18] On the other hand, the profits received by the court up to the 1460s were rising at a time when those of the Common Bench had already started to decline substantially, reaching a peak in the 1450s, when they were about twice what

[16] Blatcher, King's Bench, pp. 112–20.

[17] *CalPMR 1437–57*, p. 136; Blatcher, *King's Bench*, p. 140.

[18] *Ibid.*, p. 21.

they had been in ninety years previously. This may at least partly be explained by an explosion in the amount of business begun by other types of bill, insofar as the number of bills can be gauged from the contents of the King's Bench plea rolls. S. Jenks, counting only custodial bills, found that the totals rose dramatically between 1422/3 and 1456/7. In 1422/3, there were fewer than twenty. By the mid 1450s, on average over 100 custodial bills were being recorded each year.[19]

Dr Jenks' analysis of bills of custody suggests that the increase in their numbers in the second quarter of the fifteenth century deserves to be studied both as a precondition of the development of the bill of Middlesex device and as an independent phenomenon.[20] A possibility is that the first stage in the development of the device, the growth in the use of custodial bills to bring actions in King's Bench which would not otherwise have been heard there, involved the active participation of the court's staff. Perhaps members of the court's staff made fictitious allegations by bill of privilege in order to get their associates' debtors into the custody of King's Bench. Allegations of collusion between plaintiffs, and between clerk-attorneys and their clients, was certainly not unknown at this period.[21] So, had bills of privilege been as commonly issued in King's Bench at this date as they were in Chancery, one might have suspected some form of collusion or other chicanery. As it is, the number of these bills seems to have remained low throughout the fifteenth century, and the proportion that can be associated with bills of custody is also low.[22] Nothing at present suggests that collusion between plaintiffs by bills of privilege and of custody in King's Bench was commonplace. One can perhaps therefore clear the officers of King's Bench of systematically misusing or abusing the privilege of their court.

[19] Jenks, 'Bills of Custody', p. 203.

[20] As late as the mid-1520s Dr Blatcher noted a mere 11 custodial bills in the plea roll for one term, with no more than 28 in any one term: Blatcher, *King's Bench*, p. 123.

[21] *Ibid.*, pp 119–20, TNA (PRO), Early Chancery Proceedings, C1/64, item 339, C1/46, item 197.

[22] A decennial check of files between Michaelmas 1400 and 1500 (or the nearest useable Michaelmas file) produced only one containing more than 10 bills of privilege (16 for 1463): TNA (PRO), KB *Panella* files, KB146/7/3/3. For an example of associated bills, see this file for *Kebell* v. *Neweman alias Smyth*, which resulted in 4 actions against the same defendant.

It does however remain possible that more bills of custody were being brought because more potential plaintiffs were somehow being informed of the names of defendants in the custody of King's Bench. At the same time, it may be that somewhat more individuals were being brought into custody by one means or another. Some fifteenth-century bills of Middlesex do look a little suspicious: one wonders, for example, about the bill brought in 1461 against Thomas Hill, grocer, alleging that he had robbed the plaintiffs of various goods in Middlesex. Hill is almost certainly the future London sheriff and alderman of that name; and it seems most unlikely that he supported himself in earlier years by robbery.[23] That William Blakeman brought a bill alleging trespass against Roger Poynte of Surrey and then, upon his arrest by the sheriffs of Middlesex, sued him for debt by bill of custody is also suggestive of some form of manipulation of the system.[24] In any case where a bill of Middlesex was abandoned in favour of a non-trespassory action pursued by bill of custody, rather than both actions being pursued, it is possible that the allegation in the original bill was fictitious. After 1448, it might well have been. That year it was decided that anyone 'in custody' would be assumed to be held lawfully, even though the process leading to his arrest had in fact been unlawful. Four years later, it was decided that a bill would also be accepted even when there was nothing on the record to show what had led to the detention.[25] This meant that a defendant could be brought into custody by an allegation of trespass which, providing it was initiated by some type of bill and subsequently abandoned, would not be investigated by the court. The decision may well both have enabled and encouraged plaintiffs to bring bills of Middlesex which contained fictitious allegations.[26] If so, one critical step in the development of the later bill of Middlesex device had been taken by 1452. Dr Jenks suggested that, by the end of the century, the fictitious allegation which brought the defendant 'into custody' was such a formality that plaintiffs simply presented their bill of custody to the court when the defendant appeared.[27]

[23] TNA (PRO), KB Plea Rolls, KB27/801, m. 4.

[24] TNA (PRO), KB *Panella* files, KB146/6/30/1; see also *Chatys* v. *Rolf*, on the same file.

[25] Jenks, 'Bills of Custody', pp. 212–13, 220, fn. 63. [26] *Ibid.*, pp. 211–12.

[27] In TNA (PRO), KB *Panella* Files, KB146/10/6/3, excluding bills associated with jury summons/returns and with determined cases (where it is unlikely that

These developments may well have been ones of which 'London' litigants, in particular, took advantage. They could benefit 'London' plaintiffs and defendants alike. For example, in the early 1480s a man indicted of a trespass in Middlesex claimed his privilege as a prisoner of King's Bench in order to obtain the removal of two actions of debt being heard in the city courts. It was alleged that he had himself arranged to be indicted 'by covin and collusion' because he wanted to wage his law and would not be able to do so in London, since, according to the custom of the city, his opponent had two witnesses prepared to swear to the contract between them.[28] A similar ploy was apparently used by Baptiste Gentili five years later when he was arrested in London for debt on a verbal undertaking to settle the account between them ('on a *solvere concessit*') brought by John Pynde, a London draper. He got himself indicted for trespass in Middlesex, was brought into King's Bench on a *habeas corpus*, and promptly admitted the offence when the jury was finally persuaded to appear, nearly a year later. By this time Pynde had presumably been non-suited in London (being unable either to prosecute his suit in the city courts while it was pending in King's Bench or to sue in King's Bench on a *solvere concessit*).[29] In Michaelmas term 1491, the majority of custodial bills in the King's Bench files were 'London' bills. Moreover, because of their wide commercial networks, even 'non-London' bills might in fact involve two London freemen as plaintiff and defendant.[30] And not only did Londoners loom large among litigants by bill of custody by the end of the fifteenth century, but 'London' bills seem by this stage mainly to have been used to bring actions of debt. The proportion was about six to one in Michaelmas 1491, whereas 'non-London' bills in the same file were predominantly, in a ratio of about two-and-a-half to one, brought in actions of trespass. So it is possible that Londoners in particular took advantage of the situation in King's Bench in order to bring non-trespassory personal actions by bill there. Because the

fictions were employed), less than 12% were bills of Middlesex; most of the rest were custodial bills, whereas, even in the 1460s, there were sometimes more unassociated bills of Middlesex than bills of custody: KB146/7/3/3.

[28] BL, MS Hargrave 105, fo. 83. [29] *Ibid.*, fo. 100; see p. 65.

[30] Blatcher, *King's Bench*, p. 120, and see TNA (PRO), KB *Panella* Files, KB146/10/6/3, especially *Davell* v. *Gunton*, a 'Surrey' bill brought by a London grocer against a London dyer.

defendants were at least notionally prisoners of King's Bench and therefore covered by its privilege, the city could not object. There is certainly some evidence to suggest that the activities of King's Bench and (or) the conduct of the Middlesex undersheriffs were causing the city's governors anxiety by the 1460s, a concern that continued into the sixteenth century.[31]

Before concluding that this anxiety was occasioned by the use of bill procedure to divert city cases into King's Bench, however, it should be said that Dr Jenks's work is not yet complete. It may be that her continuing researches will reveal that relatively few of the bills which led to some form of litigation in King's Bench involved disputes which could and should otherwise have been brought in the city's courts. A significant proportion of the bills filed by the chief clerk did not, as far as can be ascertained, result in any process (or resulted in nothing beyond the issue of a writ of *latitat* or, at most, the granting of an adjournment). Dr Jenks found that in two terms, Michaelmas 1443 and 1457, half or more of the cases in the custodial bills in the chief clerk's files could not be traced in the plea rolls. She suggested that litigants were producing custodial bills to the court, which the chief clerk was then filing, in the expectation or hope that the defendant would be brought into custody sometime in the future.[32] An alternative explanation is that the defendant did appear, which is why the bill was handed over to the chief clerk instead of being kept by the plaintiff or his attorney, but the action against him was abandoned immediately. (In King's Bench, process on bills was not normally enrolled in the plea rolls until after the defendant's appearance had been secured, and sometimes not even then.) In a minority of instances, the annotations to the bill show that the defendant had not only appeared, but had admitted the plaintiff's claim, although, again, nothing is entered on the plea roll.[33] In the majority of the 'disappearing' cases, however, either the parties came to an agreement, or something else happened which left no mark even on the bills but which may nevertheless have served the plaintiff's purpose. If so, the intention was clearly not necessarily or invariably to give ordinary plaintiffs access to King's Bench in order to

[31] Tucker, 'Relationships between London's Courts and Westminster Courts', pp. 128–9, CLRO, Jor. 8, fo. 72v, CLRO, Jor. 10, fo. 296v.

[32] Jenks, 'Bills of Custody', pp. 200–1. [33] *Ibid.*, p. 200.

litigate there. An obvious possibility is that these plaintiffs were taking advantage of the central courts' one great attraction over other courts: their national reach. The aim in the case of bills of custody may simply have been to get a defendant into a position – into court or under arrest or mainprise – where he could be put under pressure to come to an agreement without further litigation. This was just what was achieved by a seventeenth-century device: fictitious allegations of trespass were used as a way of arranging to have writs ordering the arrest of debtors sent to the sheriff in their county of residence, and the parties' attorneys would then attempt to come to an accommodation which would avoid any genuine litigation. According to Prothonotary Moyle, the court's records showed that this had produced a seventy-five per cent reduction in the amount of litigation generated by the four counties in which the device was first popularised.[34]

There is also the possibility that, in some of these 'disappearing' cases, once the defendant had appeared in King's Bench to answer the bill, the suit or suits would be abandoned and the defendant – no longer protected as a litigant in or prisoner of King's Bench – would be arrested as he left and carted off to face a genuine action in a court of the plaintiff's choice. A number of plaintiffs might well have found that course of action an attractive alternative to litigation in King's Bench in cases where the defendant appeared but refused to concede or compromise. It may even be that some actions were abandoned as soon as the defendant had been arrested in his home county or elsewhere.[35] Dr Jenks remarked on the 'massive increase' – admittedly from a low base – of writs of *latitat* recorded in the plea rolls, where nothing further is heard of the case concerned and no custodial bill appears to have been brought.[36] If so, far from taking work away from the city's courts, this growth in the use of bill procedure in King's Bench could have increased it by enabling the arrest of a defendant who was otherwise beyond the city's reach.

34 Brooks, *Pettifoggers and Vipers*, pp. 127–8.

35 For an example of a trespass action which was brought in the Common Bench in about 1410 but was then abandoned once the defendant had been arrested in his home town of Stockbridge, the intention being to take him to Winchester where the parties could settle all the outstanding disputes between them, see HRO, Winchester Court *Recorda*, W/D1/112, item '41' (*recte*, 42).

36 Jenks, 'Bills of Custody', p. 215.

So perhaps the developments in King's Bench were, from the city's perspective, like the curate's egg: excellent, in parts.

Likewise, it is probable that only a minority of city cases – possibly only a very small percentage – were diverted away from its courts by a Chancery writ of *corpus cum causa*, *certiorari* or privilege. Although the activities of Chancery almost certainly did affect the city's administration of the law, particularly from the 1470s on, it does not look as though it was simply poaching city cases: by 1500, only about sixty petitions a year (about six per cent of surviving petitions), and by 1550 fewer than two per thousand, judging by the surviving petitions, concerned cases brought in the city's courts or actions taken by the city authorities.[37] Even in the later fifteenth century, the evidence suggests that Chancery may in practice often have done no more than enable bail to be arranged for a defendant who could not obtain it in London.[38] For all we know (unfortunately the surviving Chancery documents rarely state the outcome), a good many of the few remaining cases may normally have been remitted to the city court concerned.

Taken overall, the impact of developments in the common law and its administration on the city's custom and courts during our period was, like the impact of royal decrees, parliamentary legislation and judicial decision-making, mixed and, probably, broadly neutral. Alignment and assimilation only went so far. Important differences remained, which is why Baptiste Gentili felt moved, as late as the 1480s, to go to such lengths to avoid being sued in the city's courts.

THE IMPACT OF CITY CUSTOM ON THE DEVELOPMENT OF THE COMMON LAW

The final question to be considered is this: did the existence of London custom, or the way that the law was administered by

[37] Based on calendars of TNA (PRO), Early Chancery Proceedings, C1/236–48 in *List of Early Chancery Proceedings, 1500–1515* and C1/1188–1267, C1/1269, C1/1316–17, C1/1271–85 in *List of Early Chancery Proceedings, 1544–1553.*

[38] Of the 55 'London' writs *corpus cum causa* in the Chancery writ files for 1458/9, all but 4 have memoranda of the bail arrangements attached, and of the remaining 4, 3 have clearly become detached from other documents, now missing: TNA (PRO), Chancery *Corpus cum Causa* Writ Files, C244/86, /87; see also Tucker, 'Early History of the Court of Chancery', pp. 800–5.

London, affect the common law and its administration during our period, and, if so, how?

The answer to that is 'Yes'. It certainly affected the 'whole common law', that is, the laws and customs of England. The early practice of granting the customs of London to other boroughs was mentioned in the Introduction. While it is impossible to be sure that all of these grants resulted in significant changes to any customs these places had had before, in some cases they clearly did. The example of Oxford, which wrote on several occasions to ask the London governors for advice in the 1320s, a century after being granted the customs of London, is well-known; the way that Bristol obtained a description of London's courts, perhaps in the late 1330s, not much less so.[39] During our period, several other cities drew on London's example when establishing their own Sheriffs' Courts. York, on being granted county status in 1396, obtained a copy of the portion of 'Liber Albus' relating to the conduct of the London Sheriffs' Court and copied it verbatim into its own custumal; and Lincoln acted similarly after it, too, became a county in 1409.[40] Since York and Lincoln were the only other urban counties which were permitted to do as London did, and hold regular courts of pleas presided over by the sheriffs in the intervals (in their case) between the monthly county courts, it is very likely indeed that their actions were prompted by the intention to copy London practice in respect of their new courts.[41]

At a local level, therefore, London was undoubtedly influential. It is also clear that the mere existence of the city's courts and custom had some effect on the administration and even the principles of the law at Westminster. When men got themselves indicted in King's Bench as Baptiste Gentili did or, like Piers Pekham, sought to exercise the privilege of Chancery in order to

[39] Riley, *Munimenta Gildhallae*, II, ii, pp. 671–3, *CalPMR 1323–64*, pp. 7–8, 23–4, 52. The extracts obtained by Bristol now only survive in a late fifteenth-century book, but as they were '*wretin oute of a boke that was Maister Henry Daarcy … in Kinge Edward the thirds daies*', they may once have been among the material collected by Bristol's first recorder, Colford, who may well have been serving when Darcy was mayor of London, in the late 1330s: *CalEMCR*, pp. xxv–xxvii, Toulmin Smith, *Ricart's Kalendar*, p. 93, Bickley, *Little Red Book of Bristol*, I, pp. xxxi–xxxii.

[40] Stell, *Sheriffs' Court Books of York*, pp. 49–68, esp. 452 on; Hill, *Medieval Lincoln*, pp. 270, 293, referring to Bateson, *Borough Customs*, I, p. xiv.

[41] Baker, *Spelman's Reports*, II, pp. 282, 318.

avoid being sued in the city, their actions affected both the courts concerned. Not only did they find ways of manipulating central court procedures and privileges in order to remove cases from one court to another, but their actions sometimes resulted in clarifications and even extensions of the common law, as the chancery clerks and judges worked out how to respond to these novel situations.

There are a number of other examples of the way that the existence of the city and its custom might have influenced the law and customs of the central courts in this passive manner. It is, for example, possible that a few of the remedies which were made available nationally by royal decree and legislation before 1300 were adaptations of local custom. As was mentioned in Chapter 2, the twelfth-century national possessory assizes could well have been a refinement of existing remedies offered by a number of local jurisdictions. Some of the men closest to Henry II must have known of any such remedy then available in London: Thomas Becket was not merely a Londoner but also, apparently, a former London sheriff's clerk.[42] The eyres, too, might well have offered a means of increasing awareness of these remedies among royal advisers. In the 1321 eyre the recorder claimed that the city's custom permitting landlords to recover the property concerned if the rents or services were in arrears, not merely to sue for the outstanding sum, and the tenant to get the property back by paying double the arrears, predated the statute which created the writ of *cessavit* (meaning either the Statute of Gloucester, 1278, or the Statute of Westminster II, 1285).[43] Although one of the justices dismissed the relationship between *cessavit* and city usage, it is certainly the case that London's courts had been offering a remedy of this nature, the action of gavelet, long before its method of doing so was formalised (or perhaps, rather, extended to include the city sokes) by the Statute of Gavelet, which was enacted a mere four years before the eyre.[44] 'Liber Albus' contains several descriptions of the procedure, one of which was provided to the justices in eyre as early as 1221.[45] It was not just

[42] Morris, *Medieval English Sheriff*, pp. 106, 268.
[43] Cam, *Eyre 1321*, I, p. 254; Plucknett, *Legislation of Edward I*, pp. 89–90.
[44] CLRO, HR CP4, m. 2.
[45] Riley, *Munimenta Gildhallae*, I, pp. 62–3 (1221), 468–9 (the Statute of Gavelet, which, from 'Si autem servitia sua eis denegaverint . . . ' to the end, closely follows the city's response in the 1221 eyre).

fourteenth-century Londoners who suspected that the form of remedy provided by the Statute of Gloucester owed something to pre-existing English custom.[46] Whether London custom was uniquely influential at this period is, however, more doubtful.

When it comes to the important 'new' remedies which appeared in the central courts in the second half of the fourteenth century, in particular the action known in the central courts as assumpsit, however, there are a number of instances in which it is probable that it was specifically London custom which was involved. The concentration of physicians and surgeons in London during the Middle Ages, for example, is likely to have meant that cases against doctors were much more commonly brought there than in other local courts, which is no doubt why Professor Palmer found no pre-1348 examples anywhere else.[47] So, if local custom provided the model for these particular 'new' remedies, it was probably London custom rather than borough or local custom generally.[48]

It is likely enough, as Professor Palmer suggested, that it was the royal council that initiated the process which led to their provision.[49] Perhaps the critical moment was in 1349, when the king, too enmeshed in warfare to be able to deal with the multitude of problems which the war itself, together with the first onset of the Black Death, had helped to generate, invited those who were unable to resolve their disputes by course of the common law to take their problems to the chancellor. This invitation has been seen as creating the conditions in which a court of conscience could develop in Chancery.[50] It could equally well have produced a readiness in Chancery to provide common-law writs to cover a wider set of circumstances than had previously been permitted.[51] But it is clearly not the case that Chancery clerks and royal justices between them would have had to develop new remedies from scratch, even if they did have to work out 'an appropriate conceptualisation' for these remedies 'as well as appropriate

[46] Plucknett, *Legislation of Edward I*, p. 90.
[47] Rawcliffe, 'Medicine and Medical Practice in Later Medieval London', p. 13.
[48] Baker, *Introduction to English Legal History*, p. 407, fn. 28.
[49] Palmer, *English Law in the Age of the Black Death*, pp. 187, 340–2.
[50] Baildon, *Select Cases in Chancery*, pp. xvii–xviii. The proclamation survives as a letter in the close rolls, addressed to the sheriffs of London.
[51] Palmer, *English Law in the Age of the Black Death*, pp. 296–8.

allocations of situations among the various writs' (to fit them into the existing forms of action and system of writs, in other words).[52] In the first place, most if not all the Chancery clerks and justices of the central courts had some personal familiarity with city custom by virtue of the proximity of Chancery and Westminster to London. Even if a few had not, there were ways in which they would have been made familiar with it. Litigants are likely to have played some part, both in the adoption of 'new' remedies by the central courts, and in shaping the particular form they took. As was mentioned in the Introduction to this study, an ever-greater proportion of litigants in the central courts after the middle of the fourteenth century were involved in cases in which the cause of the action arose in the city. Those litigants did not need to be London-based themselves in order to be familiar with city custom. The city's Sheriffs' Court for Foreigns was open to all comers, providing only that there was some connection between the dispute and the city. London seems never to have attempted to insist, as other cities and towns did in the early fourteenth century, that only those strangers who were merchants could sue one another in its courts.[53] Although it is impossible to prove the link, it is perfectly possible that the example of the city, in insisting in 1356 that English be spoken during pleadings in the Sheriffs' Court, inspired the 1362 parliamentary statute establishing a like requirement in the central and other local common-law courts.[54] The parliamentary petition of 1393 which attempted to prevent records clerks in the central courts acting as legal representatives, too, might have been prompted by the city's ordinance forbidding the employment of Sheriffs' Court clerks in those capacities.[55] Just as the particular use of the gift of goods and chattels to secure debts seems to have become popular in the city and then spread nationwide primarily through contacts between Londoners and others, so dealings between Londoners and non-Londoners will have increased awareness of city custom and practice among the

[52] *Ibid.*, pp. 142–3.
[53] HRO, Winchester City Court Rolls, W/D1/4, mm. 16v, 14 [*sic*] (1329/30).
[54] Ormrod, 'The Use of English', p. 752; *Statutes of the Realm: I*, pp. 375–6.
[55] *Rotuli Parliamentorum*, III, p. 306B; it was however unsuccessful, and for many years, indeed, several centuries afterwards central court clerks continued to act as attorneys: see, e.g., Hastings, *Court of Common Pleas*, p. 111; Baker, *Legal Profession and the Common Law*, p. 82; Brooks, *Pettyfoggers and Vipers*, p. 143.

latter; and they, too, might well have wanted similar remedies and procedures in the central courts, even if they had not encountered them at home. And this potential source of influence remained a factor throughout our period. Although the traditional workload of the central courts waxed and waned between 1450 and 1550, their jurisdiction, and hence the range of litigants and types of dispute they entertained, continued to expand. Likewise, the tendency to adopt the remedies available in the city's courts persisted to the end.[56]

In the fifteenth century, there was another possible channel of influence: the growing number of central court justices who were former city law officers. By this stage, the city was probably indirectly playing a more active part in influencing the central courts and the common law, if only because its governors seem to have taken a positive decision to employ high-flying common lawyers in its law offices and to secure influential 'friends' at Westminster. This could well have encouraged the reception by the central courts of practices employed in the city, just as the increasing presence of common lawyers at all levels of the city's courts made for a greater conformity there to current practice in the central courts. The discussion of written pleadings in Chapter 5, for example, suggests that they were probably in use in two of the city courts some time before they were introduced to the central courts. They were first mentioned in the yearbooks in the middle of the fifteenth century, at a time when up to half the justices sitting on the benches of the central common-law courts were former city law officers. Even in the Common Bench, where city law officers were not as prominent as they were in King's Bench and where only two became chief justice, it was unusual to have no former city law officers at all among the six or seven justices.[57] It is possible that the use of written depositions was encouraged, or at least tolerated, by these justices, who were accustomed to them.

It should be said that the use to which the central common-law courts put these papers appears to have been different from the way they were employed in the city courts. As far as can be

[56] Baker, *Oxford History of the Laws of England,* VI, p. 283; Tucker, 'London and "The Making of the Common Law"'.
[57] Thorne, Baker, *Readings and Moots,* II, pp. 357–74.

determined, in the city they served merely as *aide-mémoires* for the record clerks, and there is no sign before 1550 of their use by the court in session: nothing to suggest, for example, that draft papers were produced to the city courts and copies provided to the judges and the parties' legal representatives in advance of any oral pleadings or discussion of them.[58] Not only are the references in the city's records almost invariably to parties being 'given a day' to produce their pleadings in writing (clearly, in most cases, after having pleaded orally), but in one case the defendants were noted as having brought in their 'advocacio' written on parchment, which suggests a considerable degree of finality.[59] Throughout our period, the city had its own uses for remedies and practices which were familiar to, and, in the case of the collusive recovery in its 'common recovery' form, were evidently popularised, and almost certainly invented, in the central common-law courts. In the case of written pleadings, however, it looks as though the practice was first established in the city.

Their introduction may also be related to the increased levels, or at least to the recognition, of activity on the part of pleaders, lawyers of intermediate status, in the central courts.[60] The city's practice might even have given something of a boost to the process which led to the emergence of the two branches of the legal profession in its modern form. As a result of its success in preventing clerks from acting as legal representatives, the city was well ahead of the central courts, and almost certainly of other local courts, in establishing a specialist group of attorneys, who were not clerks or other holders of other city offices, and who had something approaching a monopoly of practice in its courts. It was also apparently the first to recognise, by creating an office and a monopoly of rights of audience in its courts for them, a specialist group of advocates who had more in common with the modern barrister than with the medieval serjeant at law. By the early sixteenth century, pleaders enjoyed good opportunities to practise in Chancery and in the other conciliar courts, but there seems to have been no formal system of admissions, no formal monopoly of rights of audience for those either admitted or permitted to plead

[58] Baker, *Oxford History of the Laws of England*, VI, p. 339.
[59] CLRO, HB1, fo. 40; CLRO, HB2, fos. 11v, 162, 179; HB1, fo. 198v.
[60] Baker, *Legal Profession and the Common Law*, pp. 88–92.

by reason of legal status (as readers, for example), and, probably, nothing like as much work available.[61]

The relationship between the staffs of the Sheriffs' Court and King's Bench, which was particularly close at the time, could well have contributed to developments in bill procedure in the latter court in the first half of the fifteenth century. Throughout our period, the same men served King's Bench as sheriffs of Middlesex as served the city as sheriffs of London; and by the fifteenth century if not earlier, King's Bench clerks were acting as undersheriffs of Middlesex. Indeed, King's Bench clerks may occasionally have served in the Sheriffs' Court itself. Sometime in the early 1460s a Chancery petitioner alleged that John Gibbon, goldsmith, who was attorney to another goldsmith, had brought a collusive action in the Sheriffs' Court; Gibbon may be the man of the same name who was undersheriff of Middlesex in 1461.[62] Common Attorney Richard Elyot (admitted sometime after February 1477) is almost certainly the man who was a King's Bench filacer at that date, having previously worked as an attorney there, and who served as undersheriff of Middlesex in 1480/1 or 1481/2.[63] Moreover, not only did three former city undersheriffs in succession sit as chief justice of King's Bench between 1442 and 1481 (John Fortescue, John Markham and Thomas Billyng), but until 1469 these chief justices normally had another former city law officer as one of their two junior colleagues.[64] Chief Justice Fortescue undoubtedly played a part in the expansion of bill procedure in King's Bench. In 1442, he himself brought a bill of privilege against one William Hodekyn of Somerset. Once Hodekyn was in custody, he could be sued by any third party using a bill of custody – and he was.[65] Much more significantly, it was Fortescue who took the 1448 and 1452 decisions which made it much less risky for plaintiffs to bring fictitious allegations of

61 Baker, *Oxford History of the Laws of England*, pp. 190, 197, Ives, *Common Lawyers*, p. 199.

62 PRO, Early Chancery Proceedings, C1/28, item 118; TNA (PRO), KB Ancient Indictments, KB9/295, item 10.

63 CLRO, Jor. 8, fo. 146v, and, for his work in the central courts: Ives, *Common Lawyers*, p. 60; TNA (PRO), KB Plea Rolls, KB27/865, mm. 110 onwards (he appears occasionally as an attorney from Trinity 1474 onwards); TNA (PRO), Chancery *Corpus cum Causa* Writ Files, C244/130, item 106.

64 Sainty, *Judges of England*, pp. 8–9.

65 Meekings/Baker, 'King's Bench Formulary', p. 91.

trespass which could be used to get defendants into the court's custody.

At what appears to have been a critical period for the reintroduction to and development in King's Bench of bill procedure as one available to ordinary litigants, therefore, the court was presided over by chief justices who had spent some years working in the Sheriffs' Court and served by men who knew its staff and its workings well.[66] Dr Blatcher suggested that the people who were most likely to have been responsible for the development of the bill of Middlesex device were the King's Bench clerks.[67] These men benefited directly from any increase in the court's workload, providing other fees were not unduly curtailed as a result: and in this case, they lost nothing, because any additional business attracted, however briefly, by the greater use of bills would not otherwise have been entertained by their court. And they also often acted as litigants' attorneys, possibly most often in the sort of abbreviated and perhaps fictionalised actions that the 'disappearing' or non-litigated cases may have represented. But if they did encourage a greater use of bill procedure in some way, the success of their efforts will have depended on the willingness of the justices to accommodate them. Given his background, it seems no more likely that Fortescue (or indeed his two successors) had a mind so far above office work that he failed to notice what was happening, as Dr Blatcher thought, than that the judges in the Husting failed to notice the use to which actions of right were being put from the 1450s onwards.[68] The former undersheriffs had experience of advising and managing a court in which informal methods of initiating actions were normal and where, even in the fifteenth century, the conduct of the case could be relaxed by the standards of the central common-law courts. This might well have led them to be more tolerant of a degree of laxity or informality in their court than their colleagues in the Common Bench then were.

[66] E.g. the sheriff's register of 1458/9 was 'signed off' by John Werall, a clerk of King's Bench, as well as on behalf of the secondary of the Counter: CLRO, MS 205C/15, Sheriff's Register of Writs, (original) fo. 63.

[67] Blatcher, *Court of King's Bench*, pp. 128–9 (the rather similar early seventeenth-century device was allegedly promoted by the Common Bench filacers in collusion with clients' attorneys: Brooks, *Pettyfoggers and Vipers of the Commonwealth*, pp. 127–8).

[68] Blatcher, *Court of King's Bench*, pp. 148–50.

It seems most unlikely, however, that the influence of former city law officers was as great in the final fifty years of our period as it had been in the fifteenth century. By this stage it was much less common for men to progress via a city law office to the benches of one of the two main central common-law courts. At a lower level, too, city lawyers appear to have been becoming separated once again from their equivalents at Westminster, at least temporarily. The reduction in litigation in both the Sheriffs' and the Mayor's Courts will have made them less lucrative to office-holders, and therefore less attractive. Where men did move from city offices to ones at Westminster, or vice versa, the city offices were clearly the poor relations, and the city was losing its grip even on its serving law officers and lawyers. The century or so following 1550 was, moreover, a politically fretful time, when Parliament and the common law were portrayed by some members for Parliament and lawyers (who were often the same men) as the greatest bastions of an Englishman's liberties. In these circumstances, the hostility generated by the supposedly arbitrary procedures of the conciliar courts tended to encompass other courts employing similar procedures. To the erstwhile London recorder, Serjeant William Fletewode, the origins of common law were the 'full and perfect Conclusions of reason', whereas those of custom were 'such things as through much often and long usage, through simplicity or ignorance, gain an entry and become hardened & then defended as firme & stable Lawes'.[69] These comments were made in the context of a fierce attack on the Court of Bridewell. The treatise duly found a place among a collection, dated to about 1640, of 'Observations on Statutes & Customs ... relating to the King, the Parliament, & the several Courts, &c'. It is not surprising that the city found it difficult to protect itself against direct attack and subversion between 1550 and 1650. In these circumstances, not only will the opportunities for cross-fertilisation have been reduced, but it seems likely that there would have been resistance to the very notion of the reception by the central courts of London ideas or practices.

Yet, unlike the conciliar courts which developed in the late fifteenth and sixteenth centuries, the city's courts survived the upheavals of the seventeenth century. By 1770, at a time when

[69] GH Library, 'Observations on Statutes', fos. 1–9v, esp. fo. 2.

other local courts were in the depths of a prolonged recession, the Sheriffs' Court was perhaps as busy as it had been at its peak during our period, with around 3,500 private lawsuits brought; and within a century, not only was its workload almost four times this, but the Mayor's Court was handling ten times as much private litigation as it had entertained three hundred years earlier.[70] Again unlike the equity or 'English bill' side of the courts of Chancery and the Exchequer, which did survive the seventeenth century, the city's courts did not shed their summary character. Some of its customs were eventually abandoned rather than (re-) adopted or adapted into the national common law, probably because things like wager of law only worked in relatively confined commercial and social circles. What London preserved for the future was arguably more important: attitudes to the law with which we are familiar today. Those attitudes covered a wide spectrum: from its resistance to manipulation of the technicalities of the law and to the employment of personal representatives and juries in less formal tribunals; through its treatment of real property as a form of personal property and its governors' preference for inexpensive, speedy and accessible justice; to its practical provisions for enforcing judgments and for handling disputes involving mutual indebtedness, negotiable IOUs, unwritten promises, alleged negligence and consequential harm. Whether or not its remedies and practices were all unique to it, London's custom and its administration of the law continued to make both direct and indirect contributions to the development of the English common law, long after the end of our period.[71]

[70] CLRO, [Poultry] Counter Registers A and B; Jones, 'City Courts of Law', p. 302; Brandon, 'Observations on County Courts', p. 12. For the situation elsewhere, see, for example, Champion, 'Litigation in the Boroughs', esp. pp. 207–13, 216–18.

[71] E.g., for the long-lived example and influence of London's Court of Requests, see Slatter, 'Norwich Court of Requests', pp. 97–8, Hanly, 'Decline of Civil Jury Trial', pp. 255, 267–9, 269–74.

APPENDICES TO CHAPTERS 7 AND 8

Appendix 7.1 – *Recorders of London, 1304–1550*

NAME	Recorder	Other City Offices	Inn	Serj-at-Law	Judge &c	Sources[1]
WENGRAVE John de	1304	Ald 1303, Mayor 1316				*CalLBC* p132
HERTPOLE Geoffrey de	1320	Ald 1320		'narrator', CB 1296		*CalLBE* p11
SWALCLYVE Robert de	1320	Ald 1319			BEx 1327	*CalLBE* p12, HR PL49 m9
NORTONE Gregory de	1327	CS 1319, Ald 1327				HR PL49 m9
DEPHAM Roger de	1338	?US 1332, CClk 1335, Ald 1338				HR PL60 m11v
SADELYNSTANES Hugh de	1359	Ald 1359		1344		*CalLBH* p 17
LODELAWE Thomas de	1361	Ald 1361			CBEx 1365	HR W&D II p57
HALDENE William	1365	Ald 1365				*CalLBG* p193
CHEYNE William	1376		?GI	?1412	?JKB 1415, CJKB 1424	*CalPMR64–81* p242
TREMAYNE John	1389/90	CS 1387/8		1401		*CalLBF* p273
MAKENADE William	1391/92					*CalLBH* p385
COKAYNE John	?1393			1396	CBEx 1400, JCP 1405	*CalLBH* pp401, 417
SOUTHWORTH Matthew	1397/8					*CalLBH* p444
THORNBURGH Thomas	1403/4					*CalLBF* p214, *CalLBK* p32

PRESTONE John	1405/6			1412	JCP 1415	*CalLBF* p274
BARTONE John senior	1414/5	US by 1405		exempted, 1415		*CalLBI* p143
FRAY John	1420/22	CS 1417+			BEx 1426	*CalLBI* p248 but see p261
SIMOND John	1426		LI			Jor2 fo86
ANNE Alexander	1435/6	US by 1422, CS 1423	GI	elected, 1438		*CalLBK* p194
COKAYNE Thomas	1438		GI			Jor3 fo173v
BOWES John	1440					Jor3 fo46
DANVERS Robert	1442	CS 1441	LI	1443	JCP 1450	Jor3 fo141
BILLYNG Thomas	1450	CS 1443, US by 1446	GI	1453	JKB 1464, CJKB 1469	Jor5 fo46v
URSEWYK Thomas	1454	CS 1453	?GI		CBEx 1471	Jor5 fo196
STARKEY Humphrey	1471		IT	1478	JCP 1483, CBEx 1483	Jor7 fo246
FITZWILLIAM Thomas	1483		IT			Jor9 fo27v
SHEFFELDE Robert	by 1495		IT			*CalLBL* p308
CHALONER John	1508		GI			Rep2 fo44v
BROKE Richard	1510	US 1502	GI	1510	JCP 1520, CBEx 1526	Rep 2 fo93
SHELLEY William	1520	US 1514	IT	1521	JCP 1526	Rep4 fo52v
BAKER John	1526	US 1520	IT		AG 1536	Rep7 fo148
CHOLMONDLEY Roger	1535		LI	1531	CBEx 1545, CJKB 1552	Rep9 fo112v
BROKE Robert	1545	CS 1536	MT	1552	CJKB 1554	Rep11 fo 246

[1] Details of aldermen taken from Beaven, *Aldermen of London*; of serjeants at law, from Baker, *Order of Serjeants at Law*; of inns of court, from *Lincoln's Inn Admissions Register*, I, Foster, *Gray's Inn Admissions Register*, I, Sturgess, *Middle Temple Admissions Register*, I, Thorne, Baker, *Readings & Moots*, II, Baker, *Readers and Readings*.

Appendix 7.2 – *Common serjeants of London, 1319–1550*

NAME	Cmn Serj	Other City Offices	Inn	Serj at Law	Judge &c	Sources[1]
NORTONE Gregory de	1319					*CalLBE* p20
Vacant	*1327*					
IFORD William de	1330					HR CP54 m6v
ACRES Adam de	1351					*CalLBF* p234
MORYCE Thomas	1356			1362		*CalLBG* p79
BRICLESWORTH John de	pre 1363					*CalLBG* p163
WENTEBRIGG John de	1365		?GI			*CalLBG* p199
STRODE Ralph de	1373					*CalLBG* p317
RECHE John	1382					*CalLBH* p23
TREMAYNE John	1387/8	Rec 1390		1401		*CalLBH* pp306, 52
PEEK Robert	1389/90					*CalLBF* p273, LBH fo259
WESTONE John	pre 1402	US by 1394	LI	1425		*CalLBI* p19
FRAY John	1417+	US by 1416, Rec by 1422			BEx 1426	Jor1 fo1v, *CalPMR, 1413–37* p99
ANNE Alexander	1423	US by 1422, Rec by 1436	GI	elected, 1438		Jor2 fo4
METELE John	1435/6		?MT			*CalPMR1412–37* p287,Jor3 fo127v
WILTON John	1437	US by 1431				Jor3 fo188
DANVERS Robert	1441	Rec 1442	LI	1443		Jor3 fo97

MOYLE Richard [Walter?]	1442		?GI	?1443		Jor3 fo142v
BILLYNG Thomas	1443	US by 1446, Rec 1450	GI	1453	JKB 1464, CJKB 1469	Jor4 fo9
NEDEHAM John	1449		GI	1453	JCP 1471	Jor5 fo13v
URSEWYK Thomas	1453	Rec 1454	?GI		CBEx 1471	Jor5 fo113v
INGLETON Robert	1454					Jor5 fo210v
FAIRFAX Guy	1457	US 1459	GI	1463	JKB 1478	Jor6 photo19
RIGBY Thomas	1459	US 1460	?GI			Jor6 photo275
BRYAN Thomas	1460		GI	1463	CJCP 1471	Jor6 photo394
BALDEWYN John	1463		GI			*CalLBL* p36
MOLYNEUX Robert	1469		GI			Jor7 fo194v
HAUGH John [HAWE/S]	1485	US 1485	LI	1486	JCP 1486	Jor9 fo86v
FROWYK Thomas	1485		IT	1495	CJCP 1502	*CalLBL* p227
MAROWE Thomas	1491	US 1496	IT	1503		*CalLBL* p281
GRENE John	?1495		IT			Jor10 fo50v
WHITE Henry	1521	US 1526	IT			Jor12 fo154
WALSINGHAM William	1526	US 1530	GI			Jor12 fo364
ONLEY John	1530	US 1533	IT			LBO fo192
HALL Edward	1533	US 1535	GI			Jor13 fo366v
SOUTHWELL Robert	1535		MT			Jor13 fo444v
BROKE Robert	1536	Rec 1545	MT	1552	CJCP 1554	Jor14 fo13
ATKYNS Thomas	1545	Cmn Plr 1537, US 1547	LI			Jor14 fo146v
MERSSHE John	1547		LI			Rep11 fo344

[1] See also Masters, 'The Common Serjeant'. Details of serjeants at law from Baker, *Order of Serjeants at Law*; of inns of court, from *Lincoln's Inn Admissions Register*, I, Foster, *Gray's Inn Admissions Register*, I, Sturgess, *Middle Temple Admissions Register*, I, Thorne, Baker, *Readings & Moots*, II, Baker, *Readers and Readings*.

Appendix 7.3 – *Undersheriffs of London,* c. *1298–1550*

NAME	Undersheriff	Other City Offices	Inn	Serj at Law	Judge &c	Sources[1]
LONDONSTONE William de	by 1301					*CalEMCR* pp88, 237
CHAUMBRE John de la	by 1309 (?1307)					*CalLBC* p181
?DEPHAM Roger de	?by 1332	Cmn Clk 1335, Rec 1338				*CalLBE* p286
?HARDYNGHAM John de	?by 1335					*CalLBE* p286
MORTON John de	by 1374 (?1370)					*Gt Chron* p43
CRESSEWYK William de	?by 1370					*LPossAss* p46
?LEVYNGTON John	?by 1379					MC1/1 m75
SYSEL William	pre 1391					C1/7 m18
EDMOND John	pre 1392					HR CP117 m8v
WESTONE John	by 1394	CS ?1402				HR CP120 m4
COLREDE Thomas	by 1394					HR CP120 m4
ASTON William	by 1400 (?1398)	Clk 1397				HR CP125 m3v, Jor1 fo1v
SELMAN John	by 1402					HR CP128 m9
BARTONE John	by 1405	Rec 1414/5		exempted, 1415		HR CP131 m3
?CORNWALEYS John	by 1406					*CalLBI* p149
FRAY John	by 1416 (?1414/5)	CS 1417+, Rec 1422			BEx 1426	Jor1 fo1v
ENDERBY William	1417+, pre 1419					*CalLBI* p209
ANNE Alexander	by 1422	CS 1423, Rec ?1435	GI	elected, 1438		HR CP145 m6v

FORTESCUE John	by 1424		LI	1438	CJKB 1442	HR CP149 m5
PERY [ ]	by 1427/8					HR CP152 m3
HALTOFT Gilbert	by 1428		GI		?BEx 1447	*LPossAss* p105
FORSTER John	by 1430		LI			HR CP155 m3
WILTON John	by 1431	CS 1437				HR CP158 m4
MARKHAM John	by 1434		GI		JKB 1444, CJKB 1461	*LPossAss* p113
BURGOYNE Thomas	1433			exempted, 1443		HR CP157 m6
HEYWORTH Robert	pre 1439		LI			Jor3 fo25
BILLYNG Thomas	1449	CS 1443, Rec 1450	GI	1453	JKB 1464, CJKB 1469	*LPossAss* p122
BYRKES Roger	1450		?GI			Jor5 fo47v
FAIRFAX Guy	1459	CS 1457	GI	1463	JKB 1478	Jor6 photo392
RIGBY Thomas	1460	CS 1459	?GI			Jor6 fo394
WATNO John	1469		GI			*CalCR, 1468–76* no482
HAUGH John [HAWE(S)]	1485	CS 1485	LI	1486	JCP 1486	*CalLBL* p227
HEIGHAM Richard	1486		LI			Jor9 fo114
SALL Thomas	1487		?MT		?Queen's AG 1488	Jor9 fo146v
MAROWE Thomas	1496	CS 1491	IT	1503		Jor10 fo77v
DUDLEY Edmund	1496		GI	exempted, 1503		Jor10 fo81v
BROKE Richard	1502	Rec 1510	GI	1510	JCP 1520, CBEx 1526	Jor10 fo246v
LEGH Ralph	1502		IT			Jor10 fo273
NEVYLE Thomas	1509		GI			Jor11 fo90v

Appendix 7.3 (*Cont.*)

NAME	Undersheriff	Other City Offices	Inn	Serj at Law	Judge &c	Sources[1]
MORE Thomas	1510		LI		Chanc 1529	Jor11 fo118v
SHELLEY William	1514	Rec 1520	IT	1521	JCP 1526	LBM fo221v
PAKYNGTON John	1518	BH Counsel 1516/7	IT	exempted, 1531		LBN fo86
BAKER John	1520	Rec 1526	IT		AG 1536	LBN fo136v
WHITE Henry	1526	CS 1521	IT			Jor12 fo364, LBP fo8v
WALSINGHAM William	1530	CS 1526	GI			LBO fo192
ONLEY John	1535	CS 1530	IT			Jor13 fos366v, 444v
HALL Edward	1535	CS 1533	GI			Jor13 fo444v, LBP fo131
CRAYFORD Guy	1537		LI			LBP fo131, Rep11 fo344
ATKYNS Thomas	1547	CS 1545	LI			LBP fo198

[1] Details of serjeants at law from Baker, *Order of Serjeants at Law*; of inns of court, from *Lincoln's Inn Admissions Register*, I, Foster, *Gray's Inn Admissions Register*, I, Sturgess, *Middle Temple Admissions Register*, I, Thorne, Baker, *Readings & Moots*, II, Baker, *Readers and Readings*.

Appendix 8.1 – *Common pleaders of London, 1518–1550*

NAME	Cmn Plr	City Offices	Inn	Sjt at Law	Other Offices	Sources[1]
CHOLMONDLEY Roger	1518		LI	1531	CJKB 1552	Rep3 fo207
MARTYN William	1518	Cmn Att 1498	GI			Rep3 fo213
PETYT John	1526		GI		BEx 1532	Rep7 fos87v, 187
RYSSHTON Thomas	1527	Protho 1513	LI	1540		Rep7 fo 223
WARD Richard	1532		IT			Rep8 fo 259v
CURSON Robert	1532		LI		BEx 1547	Rep8 fo259v, Rep11 fo326
MORRANT Thomas	1533		GI			Rep9 fo10v
ATKYNS Thomas	1537	CS 1545	LI			Rep9 fo242v
CHOLMONDLEY William	1537		LI			Rep9 fo248
HONE William	1542		MT			Rep10 fo269v
FULLER John	1546		IT			Rep11 fo215v
GOODING Richard	?1546		MT			Rep11 fo221
BURNELL Richard	1547		LI			Rep11 fo326
TAWE John	1548		IT			Rep11 fo474v

[1] Details of serjeants at law from Baker, *Order of Serjeants at Law*; of inns of court, from *Lincoln's Inn Admissions Register*, I, Foster, *Gray's Inn Admissions Register*, I, Sturgess, *Middle Temple Admissions Register*, I, Thorne, Baker, *Readings & Moots*, II.

Appendix 8.2 – *Attorneys in the city's courts, 'home' court unknown, 1300–1550*
(Attorneys who only appeared jointly with others are excluded)

NAME	Attorney	City Offices	Sources[1]
GLADWYNE Richard	1272–1311		HR CP1, HR PL34
ROTHINGE Geoffrey de	1272–1316		HR CP1, HR PL37
PEVEREL Ralph	1272–1300		HR CP1, HR PL23
ENEFEUD Terry de	1282–1300		HR PL11, HR PL23
WARE John de	1288–1309		HR PL16, HR PL31
EXCESTRE Henry de	1291–1308		HR CP24, HR CP34
WOLLEWARD Reginald	1292–1332		HR PL18, HR CP56
WALTHAM John de	1294–1318	clk 1309	HR PL19, HR PL39, *CalLBC* p172
CORNHULL John de	1294–1323		HR CP24, HR CP47
HACCHE Matthew de	1295–1304		HR CP23, HR CP29
NEWERKE John de	1298–1310		HR CP24, HR CP35
REILLE William de	1300–1322		HR PL23, HR CP46
BARRE John de la	1302–1312	ward serg 1303/4	HR CP28, HR CP36, HR PL26 m9v
PASSENHAM Henry de	1303–1311		HR PL26, *LAssNuis*
RISLE John de	1305		HR PL27
COOK John [LE KEU]	1309–1323	clk 1307	HR PL32, HR PL44, HR CP37 m3
DEVENYS William	1311–1313		HR CP36, HR CP38
ORPEDEMAN Adam	1312–1319		HR CP37, HR PL41
WESTWODE William de	1312–1332		HR CP32, HR PL51

HESELINGFELD Adam de	1316–1323	sheriff's serg 1307	HR CP41, HR PL44, *CalLBC* p179
GLADWYNE Walter	1315–1342		HR PL36, HR CP66
BURY Thomas de	1315–1339		HR PL37, HR CP63
MOMBY William de	1316–1347		HR PL35, HR CP71
SPALDYNG Joce de	1317–1319		HR PL39, HR PL41
DENYS John	1317–1323		HR CP42, HR CP47
GARBOLDESHAM Adam de	1315–1337		HR PL36, HR CP60
HORWODE John de I	1318–1340	bailiff, Queenhithe 1327	HR CP42, HR CP64, HR CP51 m6
THAME Robert de	1320–1325		HR CP45, HR PL48
GOMEBY Robert de	1320–1330		HR PL42, HR PL51
KELSHULL Simon de	1323–1347		HR CP48, HR CP71
RANDOLF Thomas	1323–1325		HR CP48, HR CP49
STUBBARD John	1324–1336		HR CP49, HR CP60
BLITHE John de	1324–1329		HR PL46, HR PL51
SNODENHAM John de	1325–1334		HR CP49, HR CP58
REDE John de	1328–1338		HR CP52, HR CP62
ALEGATE John de	1329–1345		HR CP53, HR CP69
CROFTON Richard de	1330–1331	clk 1301	HR CP54, HR PL53, *CalLBB* p102
RASNEE William de	1331–1334		HR CP55, *LAssNuis*
CRANLE Nicholas de	1331		HR CP55
LUTTERWORTH Nigel de	1332–1339	clk 1332	HR CP56, HR PL61, HR CP56 m8
WARE Thomas de	1334–1349		HR CP58, HR CP73
GULDEFORD John de	1335–1344	clk 1343	HR PL56, *LPossAss*, HR PL64 m20

Appendix 8.2 (*Cont.*)

NAME	Attorney	City Offices	Sources[1]
BURY Christian de	1335–1345		HR CP60, HR CP69
MANENEDEN John de	1336–1342		HR CP60, HR CP66
HUBERD Thomas	1337		HR PL59
TIFFELD Richard de	1337–1344		HR CP61, HR CP68
SALESBURY John de	1338–1346		HR PL59, HR CP70
HORWODE Alan de	1338–1361	sheriffs' summoner 1361	HR CP62, HR PL83, HR CP85 m6v
HORWODE Richard de	1340–1341	sheriffs' summoner 1357	HR CP63, HR CP65, HR CP81 m8
DAUNCER John	1340–1361	sheriffs' summoner 1361[2]	HR CP64, HR PL83, HR CP85 m6v
SUTTONE Henry de	1341–1362	dep coroner 1349–59	HR PL62, HR PL84, *LPossAss* pp20–68
GREYNGHAM William de	1342–1344	chamber serg 1345	HR CP66, HR CP68, *CalLBF* p124
HASELWODE John de	1342–1348		HR CP66, HR CP72
HEYWORTH Adam de	1342–1343		HR CP66, HR PL65
THRIPPELOWE John de	1343–1349		HR CP66, HR PL71
HORWODE Fulk de	1343		HR CP67
ROUS John	1344–1349		HR PL66, HR PL71
GYLLYNGHAM Richard de	1345–1346		HR PL67, HR CP69
MIDDELTON John de	1345–1353		HR CP69, HR CP77
PRESTONE Robert de	1345–1349		HR CP69, HR CP73
HORWODE William de	1346	clk 1360	HR PL68, HRW&D89/4
GYLLYNGHAM Alan de	1346–1355		*LPossAss*

OLNEYE Richard de	1346–1368	sheriff's serg 1353	HR PL68, HR PL90, HR CP77 m6
WEST John	1347		HR CP71
HOCKELE William de	1350–1375	sheriff's clk/serg 1335, dep coroner 1367–76	HR CP73, HR CP99, HR CP59 m14, HR CP91 m16v
ASSHEWELL John de	1350–1375		HR CP74, HR PL97
GYLLYNGHAM William de	1351–1369		HR PL73, HR PL90
MORTON John de	1351–1361	sheriff's clk 1358	HR PL75, HR CP85, *LAssNuis* p121
RUSTYNGTON Thomas de	1352–1355		HR PL74, HR CP79
HORWODE Hugh de	1352–1367		HR CP74, HR CP91
WATLYNGTON Robert de	1356–1376	sheriffs' summoner 1373–4	HR CP80, HR CP100, *LAssNuis* pp149,155
SERIAUNT John	1358–1372		HR PL80, HR PL94
CRESSEWYK Robert de	1362–1368	mayor's ct pledge to prosecute c. 1370[3]	HR PL84, *LAssNuis* p137, MC1/2 no52
GRANEBY Henry de	1365		HR PL87
MELDEBOURNE Gilbert de	1366–1391	mayor's ct pledge to prosecute c. 1370	HR PL88, HR CP115, MC1/2 no44
FORSTER Richard	1367–1408	sheriffs' summoner c. 1388	HR PL89, HR PL133, HR CP113 mm4–4v
COO Ralph	1368–1379	mayor's ct pledge to prosecute c. 1370	*CalPMR64–81*, HR PL101, MC1/1 no179
WENT William	1370–1379		HR PL92, HR PL101
PALMER William	1369–1400		HR CP93, *LPossAss*
TOTHE John	c. 1370	mayor's ct pledge to prosecute c. 1370	MC1/1 nos110, 140, 171
CHAMBERLEYN John	c. 1370	chamber serg 1369	MC1/2 no71, *CalLBG* p249
BROUN John	c. 1370	sheriff's serg c. 1370	MC1/1, MC1/1 no136

Appendix 8.2 (*Cont.*)

NAME	Attorney	City Offices	Sources[1]
WATLYNGTON John	c. 1370	sgt 1365, common serg 1370	MC1/1, *CalLBG* pp202, 265
MERSSH John	1370–1384	mayor's ct pledge to prosecute c. 1370[4]	MC1/1, HR CP109, MC1/1 nos36,38
MIDDELTON John de	1375	clk 1375	HR PL97
SYMCOKE Nicholas	1376–1407	dep coroner 1378–1400	HR CP100, HR CP131, *LPossAss* pp52–130
CHAPEL John	1377–1379		HR PL100, HR PL101
SHELFORD Henry de	1378–1389	dep coroner 1377	HR CP103, HR PL112, *LPossAss* p46
LEMMON/LUMBARD John	1380		MC1/2 no71
PEROT Henry	1380	cmn clk 1375	HR PL103, *CalLBH* p8
MYLES Thomas	c. 1380		MC1/1, MC1/2
MARCHAUNT John	1380–1393	chamber clk 1381, cmn clk 1399	MC1/1, MC1/2, *CalLBH* p163, *CalLBI* p19
JUEL John	1381–1383		*CalPMR64–81*, *CalPMR1381–1412*
MELRETH Thomas	1382–1399		HR PL104, HR PL121
CLOS John	1382–1422	dep coroner 1392	HR CP106, HR CP146, *CalCR92–96*, p35
EDMOND John	1383	US pre 1392	HR CP107
HORWODE John de II	1388–1390		HR CP113, HR PL112
SYDYNGBORNE John	1389–1406		MC1/2, *LPossAss*
OSBARN Richard	1390–1403	chamber clk 1400	HR PL112, HR CP128, HRW&D129/9
RYKHALL Philip	1390–1394	clk 1393	MC1/1, HR CP119, PROB11/1/9

HOGHAM John [OUGHAM]	1391–1407		MC1/2, HR CP131
BYROM John	1392		HR PL115
NEUTON Robert	1392–1404	clk 1397	MC1/2, HR PL128, HRW&D126/20
SYDYNGBORNE William	1393		*CalPMR81–1412*
IRTON Henry	1395–1400		HR PL119, HR PL124
DODDE Nicholas	1397–1399		HR PL122, HR PL123
STABLE Thomas	1398–1416		HR CP122, HR CP139
DALTON John	1400–1402		HR CP125, HR PL126
HETH John	1400		HR CP125
COKKYS John	c. 1400		HR CP125, CP40/559 m5
ASTON William	1400–1406	clk 1397, US by 1400	HR CP125, HR CP130, HRW&D126/1
WESTONE John	1401	US by 1394, CS pre 1402	HR PL126
KENT John	1402–1404		HR PL126, HR PL128
COLYN William	c. 1403		HR CP129
KNYVYNTON William	1404		HR CP128
VAUX William	1407		HR CP131
KYNGESMYLL William	1407	scrivener pre 1404	*LPossAss*
REDYNG Thomas	1412		HR CP136
FOWELERE William	1417		HR CP140
RYKHALL Robert	1420		HR PL144
PYNCH William	1421		HR CP147
SHIPTON Thomas	1439–1447		HR PL161, *LPossAss*
CLON William	1446	scrivener 1432	*LPossAss*
WELHAM Henry	1448/9		HB1
BULMAN William	1482		HB1

[1] Details of scriveners from Steer, *Scriveners' Paper*.

[2] Acted as a summoner, together with John Lucas, a sheriffs' ct clk (US?).

[3] Acted as a pledge to prosecute, together with Chamber Serg John Chamberleyn (q.v.).

[4] There was a CP att of the same name, active in 1390: HR CP115 mm. 1–1v.

Appendix 8.3 – *Mayor's court attorneys c. 1400–1550*

NAME	Mayor's Ct Att	City/Other Offices	Scrivener	Inn	Sources[1]
CARPENTER John	1403–1415	cmn clk 1417			MC1/2, *LAssNuis*, *CalLBI* p19
KINGESTON William	1402–1408		pre 1404		MC1/2, HR PL133, *Scriveners' Paper* p21
HETH William	1406–1407				MC1/2
COOK Simon	1406–1407				MC1/2
STAFFORD John	1416–1434	clk 1426		?LI	HR CP139, HR PL157, *CalPMR1413–37* p196
HAMOND William	1417–1420			?LI	*CalPMR1413–37*
CROWTON John	1425–1427	clk 1440		?LI	*LAssNuis*, HR CP151, CP40/723 m4v
LANGFORD Robert	1428–1437	clk 1436, chamber clk 1460		LI	HR CP152, HR CP161, *CalPMR1413–37* p292, Jor5 fo47
CHEDWORTH William	1432–1437	chamber clk 1437			HR PL56, HR CP161, Jor3 fo191
BLOUNT Robert	1436–1475[2]	clk 1441, discharged 1476?		?GI	HR PL159, *CalPMR58–82* p94, Baker, private comm.
H[ILSAY?] R[obert?]	c. 1439–1443				MC1/3

LAMBOURNE John	1440–1449	mayor's ct clk 1455, sheriff's clk 1458, secondary 1466	?GI	MC1/3, Jor5 fo210, *CalPMR37–47* p 117, Sheriff's Reg fo78, EH I no653
KYRTON Thomas	1443–1462	mayor's ct clk 1461	LI	HR PL167, HB1, Jor6 fo24
SPYCER Roger al. TONGE	c. 1444	cmn clk 1446	LI	HR PL163, Jor4 fo149
ALEYN John	1454–1457	clk 1454, mayor's ct clk 1461		MC1/3, MC1/3A, Jor5 fo254, *CalPMR58–82* p1
ASTON Robert	c. 1455–1457	mayor's ct clk 1456		MC1/3, MC1/3A, Jor6 ph79
CARTLEAGE Robert	1456–1482	mayor's ct clk 1458, dep coroner 1484	LI	MC1/3A, HB1, *LI Adm Reg* p14, KB9/366 m31
GRENE John	1466–1485	mayor's ct clk 1478		HB1, HR PL169, KB27/867 m82v
HERT John	1467–1476	chamber clk 1478		HB1, *CalLBL* p160
FOX William	1476–1498	clk in GH, 1480/1	CI	HB1, HR PL170, BH Rental 1460–84 p991
HALE John	1485–1514	mayor's ct clk 1512		PL169, HB2, Rep2 fo144
PROUDFOTE John	1488–1502	mayor's ct clk 1488?		HR PL169, HR PL172, Re1 fo139
CLAYBROKE Giles	1492–1513	sheriff's secondary 1510		HR PL170, HR PL173, Rep2 fo101v
JOYNOUR [Thomas?]	1508–1510	mayor's ct clk 1508?		HB2, Rep2 fo141

Appendix 8.3 (*Cont.*)

NAME	Mayor's Ct Att	City/Other Offices	Scrivener	Inn	Sources[1]
SAXTON Peter	1511–1514	mayor's ct clk 1507			HR PL173, HR PL174, Rep2 fo 22v
DEDILL Thomas	1513	mayor's ct clk 1512			HR PL174, Rep2 fo141
BARKBY William	1514–1518	mayor's ct clk 1513	1510	?GI	HB2, *Scriveners' Paper* p25, Rep2 fo167, CCL Reg9 fo 122v
RUTLAND Nicholas	1516–1526	mayor's ct clk 1515, comptroller 1526	1497		HB2, *Scriveners' Paper* p24, Rep3 fo15, Rep3 fo71
HAYES Thomas	1516–1532	mayor's ct clk 1515, comptroller 1533			HB2, Rep3 fo101
MARSHALL William	1518–1519	*Rec's clk to 1517*, mayor's ct clk 1517		LI	HB2, Rep3 fo141v, *LI Adm Reg* p28
GOLDYNG William	1519	mayor's ct clk pre-1519	1516		HB2, Rep4 fo 18v
BAKER Richard	1519–1523	mayor's ct clk 1517		LI	HB2, Rep4 fo 18v
HEYDON William	1521–1529	mayor's ct clk 1521		LI	HB2, Rep5 fo203
SNOWDEN Thomas	1524–1530	mayor's ct clk 1523	1520		HB2, Rep4 fo161, *Scriveners' Paper* p25
WYLLEY James	1526–1528	*Cmn Plr's servant to 1526*, mayor's ct clk 1526			HB2, HB3, Rep6 fo78
PATY Thomas	1529	US's clk to 1529, mayor's ct clk 1529			HB2, HB3, Rep8 fo17
THROWER Thomas	1529–1536	Cmn Clk's clk to 1529, mayor's ct clk 1529		GI	HB2, Rep8 fo39, *GI Adm Reg* p10

ISCHAM Robert	1530–1533	cmn att 1506, clk of ct 1515, mayor's ct clk 1530		HB2, Rep3 fo3v, Rep8 fo78v, Rep2 fo29
GYBBES John	1531–	mayor's ct clk 1530	LyI	HB2, HB3, Rep8 fo133, Baker, private comm.
PYCKERING William	1533–1541	mayor's ct clk 1533	ClI	HB2, HB3, Rep8 fo284v, Baker, private comm.
DYGNAM Thomas	1536	mayor's ct clk 1533, *att in CPs 1555*		HB2, Rep9 fo15, Baker, private comm.
HEYWARD William	1536–1542	mayor's ct clk pre 1537, 2nd clk by 1537	IT	HB2, HB3, Rep9 fo251, Baker, private comm.
BAXTER Robert	1536–1538	mayor's ct clk 1536		HB2, HB3, Rep9 fo161v
DUNMORE William	1540–1544	mayor's ct clk 1538, comptroller 1544		HB3, Rep9 fo250v, Rep11 fo109v
CHRISTOPHER Robert	1542–	mayor's ct clk 1542, sheriff's secondary 1551	GI	HB3, Rep10 fo233, Rep12/2 fo303, Baker, private comm
COYS Roger	1542–	*Cmn Plr's clk to 1542*, mayor's ct clk 1542	LI	HB3, Rep10 fos253v, 254v
BENDOVER John	1544–1547	*?Rec's clk to 1544*, mayor's ct clk 1544		HB3, Rep10 fo254, Rep11 fo109v
BERE William	1547–	*ex-Rec's servant to 1547*, mayor's ct clk 1547		HB3, Rep11 fos 69, 329v

[1] Details of inns of court are from *Lincoln's Inn Admissions Register*, I, Foster, *Gray's Inn Admissions Register*, I, Sturgess, *Middle Temple Admissions Register*, I, Thorne, Baker, *Readings & Moots*, II.

[2] Blount, who was serving as the Goldsmiths' common clerk by 1473, was discharged from the office of enrolling deeds and testaments in 1476 but continued to appear as an attorney in the Husting thereafter: CLRO, HR CP168, m. 44 (1476, appointed attorney 'at the instance of Robert Molyneux and Richard Manet'), HR CP169, m. 1 (1488).

Appendix 8.4 – *Common attorneys, c. 1400–1550*

Name	Cmn Att[1]	City/Other Offices	Scriv'r	Inn	Sources[2]
LOUTH Robert	1376–1420				*LPossAss*, Jor1 fo1v
KIRKEBY John	1388–1424	sheriffs' ct att 1391/2			HR CP113, Jor1 fo69
BERTEVILLE David	*1389*	sgt 1368, keeper of Newgate 1382			*CalLBH* p344, *CalPMR64–81* p104, *CalLBH* p185
HETHYNGHAM John	1400–1433	BH clk/att 1405/6			HR CP125, *LPossAss*, BH WP I fo 79, Jor2 fo28v
STOKYNTON William	1403–1424				HR PL128, Jor2 fo28v
RUSHTON William	1410–1431				*LPossAss*, Jor1 fo1v
STOKE Ralph	*1413*				*CalLBK* p61
MORDON John	1413–1449				HR PL138, *LPossAss*, Jor1 fo1v
HEGGE Richard	*1416*				Jor1 fo1v
HERNYNG Robert	*1416*				Jor1 fo1v
STRENSALL William [TRANSELL]	1416–1424				HR CP140, *LPossAss* p101, Jor2 fo28v
THRELKELD Robert	*1420*	*?att in CPs 1420–40*			Jor1 fo69, CP40/639 m6v, /723 mm2,3
LOUTHER William	*1420–1421*			?LI	HR CP146, Jor1 fo69
KELLOW [William?]	*1424*			?LI	Jor2 fo28v
WAKEFELD [William?]	*1424*	?[city] att in CPs 1410/11			Jor2 fo28v, CP40/599 m3v
HERNYNG Thomas	1435–1442	BH Att Gen 1435/6[3]			*LPossAss* pp114,116, BH WP IV, fo211

BLYTON William	1439–1447		LI	HR PL161, *LPossAss* pp116–124, Baker, private comm.
MORE Thomas[4]	1446–1464	clk 1420, BH att in GH 1460	?LI/GI	*LPossAss* pp121–8, *CalPMR13–37 p85*, BHRental 60–84 fos44,137, *EH* I no653
REEDE John	1447–1449	*?Ex att 1450s*		*LPossAss* pp126–9, Baker, private comm
JENY John [GENNEY]	1447–1466	BH att at GH 1464/5	LI	*LPossAss* p124, *CalPMR58–82* p41, BHRental 60–84 p234
CROKKER John	*1450*		?GI	Recog Roll20 m1v, *EH* I no653
LOVELL Richard	*1453*	sheriff's clk 1444	?LI	*CalLBK* p350, Jor4 fo82
BRADMAN James	1454–1470		?GI	Jor5 fo177, *LPossAss* p131
TALBOT Richard	*1454*			Jor5 fo202v
WARTER Hugh	*1454–1474*		?LI	Recog Roll23 m3v, Jor8 fo81
CHAPMAN Robert	*1454*			Recog Roll23 m3v
CHAUMBRE Thomas	*1455*			Jor5 fo262
STRANGWSH [ ] [STRANGWEYS]	*1457*			Jor6 photo158
LAURENS John	*1460*			Jor6 photo397
COTE Richard	*1460*	sheriff's clk (secondary?) 1439	?LI	Jor6 photo422, Jor3 fo25

Appendix 8.4 (*Cont.*)

Name	Cmn Att[1]	City/ *Other* Offices	Scriv'r	Inn	Sources[2]
CORNYSSH Richard	*1461*				Jor6 photo479
GRENE Richard[5]	*1462–1466*				*CalLBL* p19, *CalPMR58–82* p41
ACTON Thomas jun	*1463*				*CalLBL* p30
MOUNTFORD George	*1465–1470*	*of Gonville College Cambs*		?LI	*CalLBL* p61, HB1, CCL Reg6 fo299v
JOYS John [JOCE]	*1467*	*att in CPs 1463*			Jor7 fo155, KB27/809 m20
PENROSE R[ ]	*1468*				Jor7 fo180v
?GYBON John [GIBBON]	c. 1470	?US of Middlesex c. 1460			C1/46/197, KB9/295 m10
ORCHARD Robert	*1472*	sheriff's clk 1458/9?			Jor8 fo12, Sheriff's Reg fo75v
BURRELL [ ]	*1472*				Jor8 fo12
BARTON [Richard?]	*1472*		1484?		Jor8 fo32v
YONGE W[ ]	*1476*	sheriff's clk 1467, ex att 1485?			Jor8 fo123, Jor7 fo162, Baker, private comm.
CHAPELYN T[ ]	*c. 1477–1510*				Jor8 fo146
ELYOT R[ichard?]	*c. 1477*	*Queen's Att Gen? serj 1503?*		MT	Jor8 fo146v, Ives, *Cmn Lawyers* p60, *R&M* I pxv
CHAMBERLEYN J[ ]	*c. 1479*	*chancery clk, att in CP 1476*		?IT	Jor8 fo205, *R&M* II pxxiv
WALPOLE P[ ]	*1479*				Jor8 fo205

BREMPS J[ ]	*1481*			Jor8 fo251v
GUDMAN Thomas	*-1498*		LI	Rep1 fo34v
PYNCKNEY Robert	*-1500*	*plr in Chancery c.1500*	MT	Rep1 fo71, C1/288/90, *R&M* I pxv
LYSTER Richard	*-1507*	*CBEx, serj, CJKB 1545*	MT	Rep2 fo29, *R&M* I, pxv, *OSaL* p169
GOER John	*-1512*			Rep2 fo141
MARTYN William	*1498–1518*	Cmn Plr 1518	GI	Rep1 fo34, HB2, Rep3 fo213
STAVERTON Richard	*c. 1498*		LI	Rep1 fo41
BARNEWELL [ ]	*pre 1502–1539+*			Rep10 fo74
BELLAMY Richard	*1502–1536+*	Writer of Ct Bills to 1502	LI	Rep1 fo139, HB2, Rep1 fo139
ISCHAM Robert	*1506–1515*	clk of Mayor's Ct 1515		Rep2 fo29, HB2
EVERTON William	*c. 1506*			Rep2 fo29
LYNTON Robert	*1510–1539+*		?ClI	Rep2 fo92, Rep10 fo74, *EH* II no1510
BOLTON James	*1512–*			Rep2 fo 146
AYLEM William	*1513–1514*			Rep2 fo165v, Rep3 fo22v
WALWYN Nicholas	*1513–*	*att in CPs by 1520*		Rep2 fo166, Baker, private comm
PALMER Richard	*1514–1518*			Rep3 fos22v, 217v
COTTON Richard	*1518–1526*			Rep3 fo213v, Rep7 fo88
DYNNE Robert	*1518–*		ClI	Rep3, fo217v, Baker, private comm

Appendix 8.4 (*Cont.*)

Name	Cmn Att[1]	City/Other Offices	Scriv'r	Inn	Sources[2]
MELSHAM John	*1521–*		1519	LI	Rep5 fo103, *Scriveners' Paper* p25
ADAMS John	*1526–*			IT	Rep7 fo88
HERTWELL William	*1527–*				Rep5 fo128
ROBYNS Thomas	*1528–1539*	*att in CPs by 1537*		IT	Rep7 fo268, Rep10 fo107v, Baker, private comm
BLAGG Barnaby	*1534–1536*			IT	Rep9 fos 60v, 150, Baker, private comm.
HUCHECOK John	*1534-?1545*			IT	Rep9 fo85, Rep10 fo238v, Baker, private comm
WENT Thomas	*1535–1554+*	*att in CPs by 1546*	1543		Rep9 fo142, Sheriffs' Ct Rolls 1554, Baker, private comm, *Scriveners' Paper* p26
JAKES John	*1537–*	*chanc's servant 1537*			Rep10 fos6, 8
STRODE William	*1538–1540*				Rep10 fos30, 168v
CURSON William	*c.1538-c.1544*			?ClI	Rep10 fo69v, *LCC* p128, Baker, private comm.
HYDE Stephen	*1539*				Rep10 fo78
MADDY Robert	*1539–*				Rep10 fo79
HYLTON John	*1539–*			?GI	Rep10 fo107v
OSBORNE John	*1539–1544*			LI	Rep10 fo132, Rep11 fo57v
BROKE Humphrey[6]	*1540–1542*				Rep10 fo177, CCL Reg11 fo83, *Scriveners' Paper* p29

PALLADYE Richard	1540–1548			Rep10 fo168v, Rep11 fo405
JENYNS Robert	*1541–*			Rep10 fo201
BALL Thomas	*pre 1543–1544*	*Rec's servant*		Rep10 fos205,309, Rep11 fo15v
RYSBOROUGH Richard	*1543–*	*butler of LI, att/filacer in CPs by 1541*	LI	Rep11 fo15v, Baker, private comm.
COLSELL William	*1544–*		IT	Rep11 fo57v, Baker, private comm.
HUNNESDON Jerome	*1545–*			Rep11 fo158v
HERDELEY George	*1545–*			Rep11 fo159
WILSON [ ]	*1545–*			Rep11 fo173v
BYLLINGTON George	*1546+–*			Rep11 fo289
LEYSON George	*1548–*			Rep11 fo405
SMITH William	*1549–*			Rep12/1 fo99

[1] Details in *italics* indicate (a) date of appointment as a common attorney or (b) offices held outside the city.

[2] Details of inns of court are from *Lincoln's Inn Admissions Register*, I, Foster, *Gray's Inn Admissions Register*, I, Sturgess, *Middle Temple Admissions Register*, I, Thorne, Baker, *Readings & Moots*, II.

[3] In the 1436 lay subsidy, Thomas Hernyng answered as guardian to William Wakefeld, city orphan: Thrupp, *Merchants of Medieval London*, p. 386. It is conceivable, given this and his appointment in 1435, that he was Common Attorney Wakefeld's successor (and possibly also his pupil).

[4] There may have been 2 Thos. Mores: (a) the clk, adm. LI in 1435, (b) the cmn att, active 1446–64, probably a member of GI by 1456.

[5] Grene may have been a member of the Scriveners, as a Richard Grene 'writer of court letter [scrivener]' made his will in 1479: CCL Reg 6, fo. 260v.

[6] Broke may possibly have been a member of the Scriveners, as a William Tisdale [apprentice?] of Humphrey Broke subscribed to the company's oath in 1551: Steer, *Scriveners' Paper*, p. 29.

BIBLIOGRAPHY

UNPUBLISHED PRIMARY SOURCES

Corporation Of London Record Office:

Administrative Records and Custumals:

Journals of the Common Council, 1–16
Repertories, 1–12/2
Liber Dunthorne
Letterbooks A–V

Legal Treatises & Commentaries:

'Remarks Submitted to Authority for Reform' [Anonymous], Misc. MSS 4/37
The Practise [sic] of the Sheriffs Court London: 1657 [Anonymous] (London)

Husting:

Rolls of Common Pleas, 1–168
Rolls of Pleas of Land, 1–168
Books, 1–3
Rolls of Wills and Deeds, 45–211
Calendars of Husting Wills and Deeds, vols. II–VI

Mayor's Court:

Files of Original Bills, MC1/A–MC3A
Portsoken Wardmote Presentments, 1466/7–1483
'Mayor's Court Original Bills – List of Schedules' [A. F. Sutton]

Sheriffs' Court:

Court Roll (1320), Misc. Roll CC
Court Rolls [*Querelae Levatae*], Box 1A
Court Rolls, fragments of, 1501–11, Misc. MSS 327/14 (summons and attachments)

Sheriffs' Register of Writs, MS 205C/15 ('Brevia Regis Vice Comitis de London 37 Hen 6')
'Minutes of Plaints in Compters, 1653–66'
[Poultry] Counter Registers, A and B, 1769–70

Bridge House:

Bridge Masters' Annual Account Rolls (transcript/translation), 1381–9 and 1390–1405
Bridge House Weekly Payments, Vols. I: 1421–30, II: 1412–21, III: 1421–30, IV: 1430–45
Bridge House Rental [and Accounts] (transcript/translation), 1460–84, 1509–25, 1525–40 and 1540–54
Bridge House Accounts, 1484–1509

Guildhall Library:

Fletewode W., 'A Briefe Treatise or Discourse of the Vallidity, Strength and Extent of the Charter of BRIDEWELL, and how farr Repugnant both in Matter, Sense and Meaning to the great Charter of England, by Mr. Serjeant Fleetwood', fos. 1–9v of 'Observations on Statutes and Customs' [from Sir Thomas Phillips' Collection], MS 9384
Archdeaconry of London Court, MS9051/, Registers 1–3, Act Books 1–2
Commissary Court of London, MS9171/, Registers 1–15

Company records:

Microfilm 7146/1–36, Cutlers Accounts, 1442–98
MSS 11570, 11570A, Grocers' Ordinances, Remembrances and Accounts, 1345[–]1557
MSS 11571/1, 11571/2, Grocers' Wardens' Account Books, 1454[–]71
MS 16988/1, Ironmongers' Accounts, 1454–83
Microfilms 297, 298, Merchant Taylors' Accounts, Vols. I–III, 1397[–]1484
MSS 30727/1, 30727/2, Skinners' Company, Receipts and Payments, Vols. I, II, 1491[–]1535
MS 15332, Vintners' Financial records, 1507–[13], fos. 1–27

Churchwardens' Records:

MS 5090/1, Churchwardens' Accounts, All Hallows, London Wall, 1455–1535
MSS 1454/1, 1454/2, Churchwardens' Accounts, St Botolph's, Aldersgate, 1466–7, 1468–72
MS 959/1, Churchwardens' Accounts, St Martin Orgar, 1471 [*recte*, 1469]–1615
MS 4071/1, Churchwardens' Accounts, St Michael's, Cornhill, 1455[–]1608

MS 654/1, Churchwardens' Accounts, St Peter's, West Cheap, 1435–1601
MS 593/1, Churchwardens' Accounts, St Stephen's, Wallbrook, 1474–1538

Hampshire Record Office:

Winchester:

City Court Rolls, W/D1/3–/80, selected rolls
Piepowder Court Rolls, W/D2/1, /7, /8
Recorda, W/D1/108–110, /112–113

British Library:

Additional MS 37493, Yearbook of Law Cases 10–21 Edward IV (Robert Chaloner's Book)
MS Hargrave 105, Yearbook 22 Edward IV–21 Henry VIII
MS Harley 2183, 'Natura Brevium Temp. Edw. I'
MS Harley 5155, Fletewode's Book of Cases, 3–14 Henry VI
MS Harley 5156, Fletewode's Commonplace Book

The National Archives (Public Record Office):

Chancery:

Index to Early Chancery Petitions 1515–29, List and Index Soc. Vol. XXXVIII
Early Chancery Proceedings, C1/4–7, /27–71
[Habeas] Corpus Cum Causa Writ Files, C250/1–5, /12-/14
Corpus Cum Causa Writ Files, C244/91–132 plus selected files /1-/173
Attachias Non Sunt Inventi Writ Files, C251/9–41, selected files, and Cepi Corpus Writ Files, C252/5
Sub Pena Writ Files, C253/1–11, and /21–53, selected files
Dedimus Potestatem Writ Files, C254/134
Certiorari Writ Files, C258/35–45, selected files
Ecclesiastical Miscellanea, C270/22

Common Bench/Pleas:

Plea Rolls, CP40/3, /40, /787, /802, /950, and /800–/882 (Michaelmas terms only, where available)

King's Bench:

Indictments, KB9/167, 295–321, 325–66
Plea Rolls [with Common Pleas], KB26/7–135, selected rolls
Plea Rolls, KB27/1–1152, selected rolls
Panella Writ Files, KB146/4/2/1–/12/1/4, selected files

Southampton Record Office:

Town Court Books, SC7/1/1–9
'Late Fifteenth-Century Formulary', SC2/8

PUBLISHED PRIMARY SOURCES

Amos A. ed., *Fortescue, De Laudibus Legum Angliae* (Cambridge, 1825)
Arnold M. S. ed., *Year Books of Richard II: 2 Richard II, 1378–9*, The Ames Foundation Ser., I (1975)
Baker J. H. ed., *The Reports of Sir John Spelman: volume II*, Selden Soc., XCIV (1978)
Baker J. H. ed., *Reports of Cases from the Time of King Henry VIII, vol. I*, Selden Soc., CXX (2003)
Baker J. H. ed., *Reports of Cases from the Time of King Henry VIII, vol. II*, Selden Soc., CXXI (2004)
Baildon W. P. ed., *Select Cases in Chancery AD 1364 to 1471*, Selden Soc., X (1896)
Baildon W. P. ed., *The Records of the Honourable Society of Lincoln's Inn: the Black Books 1422–1845; volume I, 1422–1586* (London, 1897)
Basile M. E., Bestor J. F., Coquillette D. R, Donahue C. jnr., *Lex Mercatoria and Legal Pluralism* (Cambridge, 1998)
Bateson M., 'A London Municipal Collection of the Reign of King John', *EHR*, **xvii** (1902), pp. 480–511
Bateson M. ed., *Borough Customs*, 2 volumes, Selden Soc., XVII, XXI (1904, 1906)
Bickley F. B. ed., *The Little Red Book of Bristol* (2 vols., Bristol, 1900)
Bird W. H. B. ed., *The Black Book of Winchester* (Winchester, 1925)
Brand P. A. ed., *The Earliest English Law Reports, Volume II: Common Bench Reports 1285–1289 and Undated Reports 1279–1289*, Selden Soc., CXII (1996)
Calendar of the Close Rolls Preserved in the Public Record Office, 1296–1302 (London, 1906)
Calendar of the Close Rolls Preserved in the Public Record Office, 1318–23 (London, 1895)
Calendar of the Close Rolls Preserved in the Public Record Office, 1500–09 (London, 1963)
Calendar of the Coroners' Rolls of the City of London AD 1300–1378, ed. R. R. Sharpe (London, 1913)
Calendar of Early Mayor's Court Rolls, 1298–1307, ed. A. H. Thomas (Cambridge, 1924)
Calendar of Fine Rolls Preserved in the Public Record Office: 1272[–]1509, 22 vols. (London, 1911–62)
Calendar of Letter-Books [A–L] Preserved among the Archives of the Corporation of the City of London at the Guildhall, ed. R. R. Sharpe, 11 vols. (London, 1899–1912)

Calendar of Patent Rolls Preserved in the Public Record Office: 1272–81 (London, 1901)

Calendar of Patent Rolls Preserved in the Public Record Office: 1413[–]22, 2 vols. (Norwich, 1910–11)

Calendar of Patent Rolls Preserved in the Public Record Office: 1422[–]61, 6 vols. (London, 1901–11)

Calendar of Plea and Memoranda Rolls, 1323[–]1437, ed. A. H Thomas (Cambridge, 1926–43)

Calendar of Plea and Memoranda Rolls, 1437[–]1482, ed. P. E. Jones (Cambridge, 1954, 1961)

Calendar of London Trailbaston Trials under Commissions of 1305 and 1306, ed. R. B. Pugh (London, 1975)

Calendar of Wills and Deeds Proved and Enrolled in the Court of Husting, London, 1258–1688, ed. R. R. Sharpe, 2 vols. (London, 1889–90)

Cam H. M. ed., *The Eyre of London, 14 Edward II, A D. 1321: Parts I & II*, Selden Soc., LXXX, LXXXVI (1968, 1989)

Chapman A. B. Wallis ed., *The Black Book of Southampton: Volume I, c. 1388–1414*, Southampton Record Soc. (1912)

Chew H. M. ed., *London Possessory Assizes: A Calendar*, London Record Soc., I (1965)

Chew H. M., Kellaway W. eds., *London Assize of Nuisance 1301–1431*, London Record Soc., X (1973)

Chew H. M., Weinbaum M. eds., *The London Eyre of 1244*, London Record Soc., VI (1970)

Chrimes S. B. ed., *Sir John Fortescue: De Laudibus Legum Anglie* (Cambridge, 1949)

Coke's Reports, Parts 3 & 4 (London, 1738)

Coke's Reports, Parts 5 & 6 (London, 1738)

Coke's Reports, Parts 7 & 8 (London, 1738)

Nicol A. ed., *Curia Regis Rolls Preserved in the Public Record Office: Volume XVII, 1242–3* (London, 1991)

Darlington I. ed., *London Consistory Court Wills, 1492–1547*, London Record Soc., III (1967)

Ellis H. ed., *The New Chronicles of England and France* ... by Robert Fabyan ... (London, 1811)

Fitch M., *Index to the Testamentary Records of the Commissary Court of London: Volume I, 1374–1488*, (London, 1969)

Fitch M., *Testamentary Records in the Archdeaconry Court of London: volume I, (1363)–1649*, British Record Soc., LXXXIX (1979)

Foster J. ed., *The Register of Admissions to Gray's Inn 1521–1889 ...*, 2 parts (London 1889)

Gairdner J. ed., *The Paston Letters*, 6 vols. (Westminster, 1900)

Guy J. A. ed., *Christopher St German on Chancery and Statute*, Selden Soc. Supplementary Series (1985)

Hall, G. D. G. ed., *A Treatise on the Laws and Customs of the Realm of England commonly called Glanvill* (London, 1965)

Hanham A. ed., *The Cely Letters, 1472–1488*, Early English Text Soc., CCLXXIII (1975)

Harding V., Wright L. eds., *London Bridge: Selected Accounts and Rentals, 1381–1538*, London Record Soc., XXXI (1995 for 1994)

Hemmant M. ed., *Select Cases in the Exchequer Chamber ... volume i, 1377–1461*, Selden Soc., LI (1933)

Hemmant M. ed., *Select Cases in the Exchequer Chamber ... volume ii, 1461–1509*, Selden Soc., LXIV (1945)

Hunnisett R. F., Post J. P. eds., *Medieval Legal Records Edited in Memory of C.A.F. Meekings* (London, 1978)

Hudson W., Tingey J. H. eds., *The Records of the City of Norwich*, 2 vols. (Norwich, London, 1906)

Jones P. E., Smith R. eds., *A Guide to the Records of the Corporation of London Records Office and the Guildhall Library Muniment Room* (London, 1951)

Lang R. G. ed., *Two Tudor Subsidy Assessment Rolls for the City of London: 1541 and 1582*, London Record Soc., XXIX (1993 for 1992)

Latham R. E., *Revised Medieval Latin Word-List from British and Irish Sources* (London, 1965)

[*Lincoln's Inn Admission Register*] *The Records of the Honourable Society of Lincoln's Inn, volume I: Admissions from A D. 1420 to A D. 1799* (London, 1896)

Le Livre des Assises et Pleas del' Corone, Moves & Dependants Devant les Justices Sibien en lour CIRCUITS come aylours en temps du Roy Edwarde le Tiers ... (London, 1679)

Les Reports de les Cases contenius en les Ans vint primer, et apres in temps del roy Henry le siz: communement appele, The Seconde part of Henry the Sixt ... (London, 1601)

List of Early Chancery Proceedings, 9 Ric. 11-Edw. IV, List & Index Soc., XII (1901)

List of Early Chancery Proceedings, 1467–1485, List & Index Soc., XVI (London, 1903)

List of Early Chancery Proceedings, 1485–1500, List & Index Soc., XX (London, 1906)

List of Early Chancery Proceedings, 1500–1515, List & Index Series, XXIX (London, 1908)

List of Early Chancery Proceedings, 1544–1553, List & Index Series, LIV (London, 1933)

Littleton T., *Tenures*, ed. E. Wambaugh (Washington, 1903)

Livock D. M. ed., *City Chamberlains' Accounts in the Sixteenth and Seventeenth Centuries*, Bristol Record Soc., XXIV (1966 for 1965)

Lodge E. C., Somerville R. eds., *John of Gaunt's Register, 1379–83: volume ii*, Camden Soc., LVII (1937)

Macray W. D., ed., *Chronicon Abbatiae Ramsiensis*, Rolls Series (London, 1886)

Marsh B. ed./trans., *Records of the Worshipful Company of Carpenters, volume II: Wardens Account Book 1438–1516* (Oxford, 1914)

Masters B. R. ed., *Chamber Accounts of the Sixteenth Century*, London Record Soc., XX (1984)

Neilson N. ed., *Year Book 10 Edward IV and 49 Henry VI: 1470*, Selden Soc., XLVII (1930)

Palgrave F. ed., *Rotuli Curiae Regis*, volumes I and II (London, 1835)

Parsloe G., *Wardens' Accounts of the Worshipful Company of the Founders of the City of London, 1497–1681* (London, 1964)

Poos L. R., Bonfield L. eds., *Select Cases in Manorial Courts, 1250–1550: Property and Family Law*, Selden Soc., CXIV (1997)

Post J. P., 'Courts, Councils and Arbitrations in the Ladbrooke Manor Dispute, 1382–1400', in Hunnisett, Post, *Medieval Legal Records* (above), pp. 290–339

Prideaux Sir Walter S. ed., *Memorials of the Goldsmiths Company ... 1335–1815*, 2 vols. (privately printed [London, 1896–7])

Richardson H. G., Sayles G. O. eds., *Select Cases of Procedure without Writ Under Henry III*, Selden Soc., LX (1941)

Riley H. T. ed., *Memorials of London and London Life in the XIIIth, XIVth and XVth Centuries ... A.D. 1276–1419* (London, 1868)

Riley H. T. ed., *Munimenta Gildhallae Londoniensis: Liber Albus, Liber Custumarum, et Liber Horn*, 4 vols. (London, 1859–62)

Rogers E. F. ed., *Correspondence of Sir Thomas More* (Princeton, 1947)

Rotuli Parliamentorum; ut et Petitiones et placita in Parliamento, 6 volumes (Record Commission, 1783)

Stanford M. ed., *The Ordinances of Bristol 1506–1598*, Bristol Record Soc., XLI (1990)

Stapleton T. ed., *De Antiquis Legibus Liber: Cronica Maiorum & Viscomitum Londoniarum ...* , Camden Soc. (London, 1846)

Statutes of the Realm: Vol. I: 20 Henry III–50 Edward III (1236–1376/7) (1810)

Statutes of the Realm: Vol. II: 1 Richard II–19 Henry VII (1377–1503/4) (1816)

Steer F. ed., *Scriveners' Company Common Paper, 1357–1628, with a Continuation to 1678*, London Record Soc., IV (1968)

Stell P. M. ed. and trans., *Sheriffs' Court Books of the City of York for the Fifteenth Century* (York City Archives, 2000)

Stevenson W. H., ed., *Records of the Borough of Nottingham, Vol. 2, 1399–1485* (Nottingham, 1883)

Stow J., *Annales, or, A Generall Chronicle of England*, ed. E. Howes (London, 1631)

[Stow] A. M., H. D. eds., *The Survey of London ... Begunne first by ... Iohn Stowe*. (London, 1633)

Struder P. ed., *The Oak Book of Southampton, c. A.D. 1300: Volume I*, Southampton Record Soc. (1910)

Sturgess H. A. C. ed., *Register of Admissions to the Honourable Society of the Middle Temple: volume I, Fifteenth Century to 1781* (London, 1949)

Suger S. W. ed., *The Life of Sir Thomas More by his Son-in-Law, William Roper Esq.* (London, 1822)

Thorne S. E., Baker J. H. eds., *Readings and Moots at the Inns of Court in the Fifteenth Century*, Selden Soc., 2 vols., LXXI, CV (1954, 1989)

Thornley I. D. ed., commentary by T. F. T. Plunknett, *Year Books of Richard II: 11 Richard II, 1387–1388*, The Ames Foundation (1937)

Toulmin Smith L., ed., *The Maire of Bristowe Is Kalendar, by Robert Ricart, Town Clerk of Bristol, 18 Edward IV*, Camden Soc., 5th Ser. (1872)

Trapp J. P. ed., *The Complete Works of Sir Thomas More*, 15 vols. (Yale, 1963–86)

Veale E. W. W. ed., *The Great Red Book of Bristol: Introduction, Part I*, Bristol Record Soc., II (1931)

Veale E. W. W. ed., *The Great Red Book of Bristol: Text, Part I*, Bristol Record Soc., IV (1933)

Veale E. W. W. ed., *The Great Red Book of Bristol: Text, Part III*, Bristol Record Soc., XVI (1951)

Weinbaum M. ed., *The London Eyre of 1276*, London Record Soc., XII (1976)

Whittaker W. J. ed., *The Mirror of Justices*, intro. F. W. Maitland, Selden Soc., VII (1895)

Williamson J. B. ed., *The Middle Temple Bench Book, ...* (London, 1937)

Woodbine G. E., Thorne S. E. ed./trans., *Bracton, On the Laws and Customs of England* (4 vols., 1968–77)

SECONDARY SOURCES

Alexander J. J., 'The Dates of County Courts', *BIHR*, **iii** (1925–6), pp. 89–95

Baker J. H., 'The English Legal Profession, 1450–1550' in Prest W. R. ed., *Lawyers in Early Modern Europe and America* (London, 1981), pp. 16–41

Baker J. H., *The Order of Serjeants at Law*, Selden Soc., Supplementary Series, V (London, 1984)

Baker J. H., *The Legal Profession and the Common Law* (London, 1986)

Baker J. H., Milsom S. F. C., *Sources of English Legal History: Private Law to 1750* (London, pb, 1986)

Baker J. H., *Readers and Readings in the Inns of Court and Chancery*, Selden Soc., Supplementary Series, XIII (London, 2000)

Baker J. H., 'The Three Languages of English Law' in *idem, The Common Law Tradition: Lawyers, Books and the Law* (London, Rio Grande, 2000), pp. 225–46

Baker J. H., 'Personal Actions in the High Court of Battle Abbey, 1450–1602' in *idem, The Common Law Tradition: Lawyers, Books and the Law* (London, Rio Grande, 2000), pp. 263–85

Baker J. H., *An Introduction to English Legal History* (4th edn., London, 2002)

Baker J. H., *Oxford History of the Laws of England, vol. VI: 1483–1558* (Oxford, 2003)

Ballard A., *British Borough Charters, 1042–1216* (Cambridge, 1915)

Barron C. M., *The Medieval Guildhall of London* (London, 1974)

Barron, C. M., 'London 1300–1540' in Palliser D., ed., *The Cambridge Urban History of Britain Volume I: 600–1500* (Cambridge, 2000), pp. 395–440

Barron C. M., 'Lay Solidarities: the Wards of Medieval London' in P. Stafford, J. L. Nelson, J. Martindale eds., *Law, Laity and Solidarities: Essays in Honour of Susan Reynolds* (Manchester, 2001), pp. 218–33

Barron C. M., *London in the Later Middle Ages: Government and People 1200–1500* (Oxford, 2004)

Beaven A. B., *The Aldermen of the City of London*, 2 vols. (London, 1908, 1913)

Beckerman J. S., 'The Forty-Shilling Jurisdictional Limit in Medieval English Personal Actions' in D. Jenks ed., *Legal History Studies 1972* (Cardiff, 1975), pp. 110–17

Behrens G., 'An Early Tudor Debate on the Relation between Law and Equity', *JLH*, **xix** (1998)

Beier A. L., 'Social Problems in Elizabethan London' in Barry J., ed., *The Tudor and Stuart Town: A Reader in English Urban History, 1530–1688* (Harlow, 1990), pp. 121–38

Bellamy J. G., *Crime and Public Order in England in the Later Middle Ages* (London, Toronto, 1973)

Bennett E. Z., 'Credit in the Urban Economy: London 1338–1460' (unpublished Yale PhD thesis, 1989)

Blatcher M., *The Court of King's Bench 1450–1550: A Study in Self-Help* (London, 1978)

Bohun [William], *Privilegia Londini: or the Laws, customs, and Priviledges of the City of London* ... , (London, 1702)

Bolton J. L., *The Medieval English Economy 1150–1500* (pb, London, 1980)

Bolton J. L., 'The City and the Crown, 1456–61', *London Journal*, vol. xii (1986), pp. 11–24

Bonfield L., 'What did English villagers mean by "customary law"?' in Razi Z., Smith R. eds., *Medieval Society and the Manor Court* (Oxford, 1996), pp. 103–16

Brand P. A., 'Courtroom and Schoolroom: the Education of Lawyers in England Prior to 1400', *HR*, **lx** (1987), pp. 145–65

Brand P. A., *The Origins of the English Legal Profession* (Oxford, 1992)

Brand, P. A., *The Making of the Common Law* (London, 1993)

Brand, P. A. ed., *The Earliest English Law Reports, vol. II*, Selden Society, CXII (1996)

Brand P. A., *Kings, Barons and Justices* (Cambridge, 2003)

Brandon Woodthorpe, 'Observations on County Courts and Local Municipal Courts as Courts for the Recovery of Small Debts' (London, 1868) (copy available at the CLRO)

Brigden S., *London and the Reformation* (Oxford, 1989)

Britnell R. H., 'Colchester Courts and Court Records, 1310–1525', *Essex Archaeology and History*, **xvii** (1984), pp. 133–40

Britnell R. H., *Growth and Decline in Colchester, 1300–1525* (Cambridge, 1986)

Britnell R., 'The Economy of British Towns 1300–1540' in Palliser D., ed., *The Cambridge Urban History of Britain Volume I: 600–1500* (Cambridge, 2000), pp. 313–33

Brooke C. N. L., Keir G., Reynolds S., 'Henry I's Charter for London', *Journal of the Society of Archivists*, **iv** (1973), pp. 558–78

Brooks C. W., 'The Common Lawyers in England, c. 1558–1642' in Prest W. R. ed., *Lawyers in Early Modern Europe and America* (London, 1981)

Brooks C. W. *Pettyfoggers and Vipers of the Commonwealth: The 'Lower Branch' of the Legal Profession in Early Modern England* (Cambridge, 1986)

Caenegem van, R. C., *The Birth of the English Common Law* (Cambridge, 2nd edn, pb, 1989)

Cam H. M., *Law-Finders and Lawmakers* (London, 1962)

Campbell J., 'Power and Authority 600–1300' in Palliser D., ed., *The Cambridge Urban History of Britain Volume I: 600–1500* (Cambridge, 2000), pp. 51–78

Carlton C. H., 'The Administration of London's Court of Orphans', *GM*, **iv** (1971), pp. 22–35

Champion W. A., 'Litigation in the Boroughs: The Shrewsbury *Curia Parva* 1580–1730, *JLH*, **xv** (1994), pp. 201–22

Champion W. A., 'Recourse to Law and the Meaning of the Great Litigation Decline, 1650–1750: Some Clues from Shrewsbury' in Brooks C. W., Lobban M. eds., *Communities and Courts in Britain 1150–1900* (London, Rio Grande, 1997), pp. 179–98

Chew H. M., 'The Office of Escheator in the City of London during the Middle Ages', *EHR*, **lviii** (1943)

Clanchy M. T., *From Memory to Written Record: England 1066–1307* (Oxford, 2nd edn, pb, 1993)

Clode C. M., *The Early History of the Guild of Merchant Taylors of the Fraternity of St John the Baptist, London ...* , 2 vols. (London, 1888)

Cohen H., *A History of the English Bar and Attornatus to 1450* (London, 1929)

Coleman D. C, *The Economy of England 1450–1750* (London, 1977)

Davies M. ed., *The Merchant Taylors' Company of London: Court Minutes 1486–1493* (Stamford, 2000)

Davies M., 'Lobbying Parliament: the London Companies in the Fifteenth Century' in L. Clark ed., *Parchment and People: Parliament in the Middle Ages* (Edinburgh, 2004), pp. 136–48

Derrett J. D. M., 'Thomas More and the Legislation of the Corporation of London', *GM*, **ii** (1963), pp. 175–80

Dobson R. B., ed., *The Peasants' Revolt of 1381* (2nd edn., Basingstoke, London, 1983)

Doe N., *Fundamental Authority in Late Medieval English Law* (Cambridge, 1990)

Dummelow J., *The Wax Chandlers of London: A Short History of the Worshipful Company of the Wax Chandlers, London* (London, 1973)

Dyer A., *Decline and Growth in English Towns, 1400–1640* (Cambridge, 1991)

Dyer A., 'Appendix: Ranking Lists of English Medieval Towns' in Palliser D., ed., *The Cambridge Urban History of Britain Volume I: 600–1500* (Cambridge, 2000), pp. 747–70

Dyer C., *Standards of Living in the Later Middle Ages: Social Change in England, c. 1200–1520* (Cambridge, 1989)

Elrington C. R. ed., *Victoria County History of Gloucestershire, vol. IV: The City of Gloucester* (Oxford, 1991)

Emerson T., *A Concise Treatise on the Courts of Law in the City of London* (London, 1794)

Foss E., *Tabulae Curiales* (London, 1865)

Foulds T., Hughes J., Jones M., 'Nottingham Borough Court Rolls: The Reign of Henry VI (1422–57)', *Transactions of the Thoroton Society of Nottinghamshire*, **xcvii** (1993), pp. 74–87

Furley J. S. ed., *City Government of Winchester from the Records of the XIV and XV Centuries* (Oxford, 1923)

Gray C. M., *Copyhold, Equity and the Common Law* (Cambridge, Mass., 1963)

Guiseppe M. S., *A Guide to the Manuscripts Preserved in the Public Record Office*, 2 vols., (London, 1923)

Guy J. A., *The Public Career of Sir Thomas More* (Brighton, 1980)

Hanly C., 'The Decline of Civil Jury Trial in Nineteenth-Century England', *JHL*, **xxvi** (2005), pp. 253–78

Harding A., *The Law Courts of Medieval England* (London, New York, 1973)

Harrison C., 'Manor Courts and the Governance of Tudor England' in Brooks C. W., Lobban M. eds., *Communities and Courts in Britain 1150–1900* (London, Rio Grande, 1997), pp. 43–59

Hastings M., *The Court of Common Pleas* (Ithaca, New York, 1947)

Hastings M., 'The Ancestry of Sir Thomas More', *GM*, **ii** (1961), pp. 47–62

Hedley S., 'The "Needs of Commercial Litigants"', *JLH*, **xviii** (1997), pp. 85–95

Helmholz R. H., *Marriage Litigation in Medieval England* (Cambridge, 1974)

Helmholz R. H., 'Usury in the Medieval English Church Courts', *Speculum*, **lx** (1986), pp. 364–80

Henderson E. G., 'Relief from Bonds in the English Chancery: Mid-Sixteenth Century', *AJLH*, **xviii** (1974), pp. 298–306

Herbert W., *History of the Twelve Great Livery Companies of London*, 2 vols. (London, 1937)

Hill J. W. F., *Medieval Lincoln* (Cambridge, 1948)

Holdsworth W. S., *A History of the English Law*, 16 vols. (London, 1922–66)

Holland P., 'Cook's Case in History and Myth', *BIHR*, **lxi** (1988), pp. 21–35.

Holt J. C., *Magna Carta* (7th edn, Cambridge, 1994)

Hopkinson H. L., *Ancient Records of the Merchant Taylors* (privately printed, 1915)

Horwitz H., *Chancery Equity Records and Proceedings 1600–1800* (2nd edn, PRO, 1998)

Hughes S. E., 'Guildhall and Chancery English, 1377–1422', *GSLH*, **iv** (1980), pp. 53–62

Hyams P., 'What did Edwardian Villagers Understand by Law?' in Z. Razi, R. Smith eds., *Medieval Society and the Manor Court* (Oxford, 1996), pp. 69–102

Hunnisett R. F., 'The Reliability of Inquisitions as Historical Evidence' in Bullough D. A., Storey R. L. eds., *The Study of Medieval Records: Essays in Honour of Kathleen Major* (Oxford, 1971), pp. 206–35

Imray J. M., 'Les Bones Gentes de la Mercerye . . . ' in Hollaender A. E. J., Kellaway W. eds., *Studies in London History Presented to Philip Edmund Jones* (London, 1969), pp. 156–78

Ives E. W., 'The Common Lawyers in Pre-Reformation England', *TRHS*, 5th series, **xviii** (1968), pp. 145–73

Ives E. W., *The Common Lawyers of Pre-Reformation England: Thomas Kebell: A Case Study* (Cambridge, 1983)

Jenks S., 'Bills of Custody in the Reign of Henry VI', *JHL*, **xxiii** (2002), pp. 197–222

Johnson A. H., *The History of the Worshipful Company of the Drapers of London, volume I*, (Oxford, 1914)

Jones P. E., 'The City Courts of Law', *The Law Journal*, **xciii** (1943), pp. 301–2

Jones P. E., R. Smith, *A Guide to the Records in the Corporation of London Record Office and the Guildhall Library Muniment Room* (London, 1951)

Jones W. J., 'A Note on the Demise of Manorial Jurisdictions: the Impact of Chancery', *AJLH*, **x** (1966), pp. 297–318

Jurkowski M., Smith C. L., Crook D., eds., *Lay Taxes in England and Wales, 1188–1688* (TNA (PRO), 1998)

Kaye J. M., '*Res Addiratae* and Recovery of Stolen Goods', *LQR*, **lxxxvi** (1970), pp. 379–403

Keene D. J., 'A New Study of London before the Great Fire', *Urban History Yearbook* (1984), pp. 11–21, esp. 18–19

Keene D. J., 'Cheapside before the Great Fire' (ESCR booklet, 1985)

Kellaway W., 'The Coroner in Medieval London' in Hollaender A. E. J., Kellaway W. eds., *Studies in London History Presented to Philip Edmund Jones*, (London, 1969), pp. 75–91

Kellaway W., 'John Carpenter's Liber Albus', *GSLH*, **iii** (1978), pp. 67–84

Ker N. R., '*Liber Custumarum*, and other Manuscripts formerly at the Guildhall', *GM*, **iii** (1954), pp. 37–45

Ker N. R., *Medieval Manuscripts in British Libraries, Vol. I* (Oxford, 1969)

Kermode J. I., 'Some Obvious Observations on the Formation of Oligarchies in Late Medieval Towns' in J. A. F. Thomson ed., *Towns and Townspeople in the Fifteenth Century* (Gloucester, 1988), pp. 87–106

Kermode J. I., 'Medieval Indebtedness: the Regions *versus* London' in N. Rogers ed., *England in the Fifteenth Century* (Stamford, 1994), pp. 72–88

Kiralfy A., 'Custom in Medieval English Law', *JLH*, **xix** (1988), pp. 26–49

Lang R. G. ed., *Two Tudor Subsidy Assessment Rolls for the City of London: 1541 and 1582*, LRS, xxix (1993)

Lobel M. D. ed., *The City of London from Prehistoric Times to c. 1520* (Oxford, 1991)

Lyell L. with Watson F. D., *Acts of Court of the Mercers Company, 1453–1527* (Cambridge, 1936)

Maitland F. W., *Historical Essays* ('English Law and the Renaissance'), introduced by H. M. Cam (Cambridge, 1957), pp. 134–51

Maitland F. W., *The Forms of Action at Common Law*, ed. A. H. Chaytor, W. T. Whittaker (Cambridge, 1971)

Martin G. H., *The Husting Rolls of Wills and Deeds, 1252–1485: Guide to the Microfilm Edition* (Cambridge, 1990)

Masters B. R., 'The Common Serjeant', *GM*, **xi** (1967), pp. 379–89

Masters B. R., 'The Secondary', *GM*, **xi** (1968), pp. 425–37

McFarlane K. B., *The Nobility of Later Medieval England* (Oxford, 1973)

Meekings C. A. F. (notes by J. H. Baker), 'A King's Bench Formulary', *JLH*, **vi** (1985), pp. 86–104

Milsom S. F. C., *Historical Foundations of the Common Law* (2nd edn, London, 1981)

Morris W. A., *The Medieval English Sheriff to 1300* (Manchester, 1927)

Munro J. H. A., *Wool, Cloth and Gold: The Struggle for Bullion in Anglo-Burgundian Trade, 1340–1478* (Toronto, 1972)

Nicholas D., *The Later Medieval City, 1300–1500* (Harlow, 1997)

Nightingale P., 'The Origins of the Court of Husting', *EHR*, **cii** (1987)

Nightingale P., 'Capitalists, Crafts and Constitutional Change in Late Fourteenth-Century London', *Past and Present*, **cxxii-cxxv** (1989)

Ormrod W. M., 'The Use of English: Language, Law, and Political Culture in Fourteenth-Century England', *Speculum*, **lxxvii** (2003), pp. 750–84

Palmer R. C., *The County Courts of Medieval England 1150–1350* (Princeton NJ, 1982)

Palmer R. C., *English Law in the Age of the Black Death, 1348–81* (Chapel Hill/London, 1993)

Pearl V., 'Change and Stability in Seventeenth-Century London', in Barry J. ed., *The Tudor and Stuart Town: A Reader in English Urban History, 1530–1688* (Harlow, 1990)

Plucknett T. F. T., *Statutes and Their Interpretation in the First Half of the Fourteenth Century* (Cambridge, 1922)

Plucknett T. F. T., *The English Trial and Comparative Law* (Cambridge, 1952)

Plucknett T. F. T., *Legislation of Edward I* (Oxford, 2nd edn, 1962)

Pollard A. F, 'The Growth of the Court of Requests', *EHR*, **lvi** (1941)

Pollock Sir Frederick, Maitland F. W., *The History of the English Law before the Time of Edward I*, 2 vols. (2nd edn, Cambridge, 1923)

Post J. B., 'Equitable Resorts before 1450' in Ives E. W. and Manchester A. H. eds., *Law, Litigants and the Legal Profession* (Royal Historical Soc., xxxvi, 1983), pp. 68–79

Postan M. M, 'The Economic and Political Relations of England and the Hanse from 1400 to 1475', in Powers E. E. and Postan M. M. eds., *Studies in English Trade in the Fifteenth Century* (London, 1966), pp. 91–154

Prest W. R, *The Rise of the Barristers: A Social History of the English Bar 1590–1640* (Oxford, 1986)

Pronay N., 'The Chancellor, the Chancery, and the Council at the End of the Fifteenth Century', in Hearder H., Loyn H. R. eds., *British Government and Administration: Studies Presented to S. B.* Chrimes (Cardiff, 1974), pp. 87–103

Pugh R. B. ed., *Victoria County History of Yorkshire: The City of York* (Oxford, 1961)

Ramsay N. L., 'The English Legal Profession, c. 1340–c. 1450' (unpublished PhD thesis, Oxford, 1985)

Ramsay N. L., 'What Was the Legal Profession?' in Hicks M. ed., *Profit, Piety and the Professions* (Gloucester, 1990), pp. 62–71

Rawcliffe C., 'Medicine and Medical Practice in Later Medieval London', *GSLH*, **v** (1981), pp. 13–25

Reddaway T. F., *The Early History of the Goldsmiths Company 1327–1509* & Walker L. E. M. ed., *The Book of Ordinances 1478–8* (London, 1975)

Reynolds S., 'Henry I's Charter for London', *Journal of the Society of Archivists*, **iv** (1973), pp. 558–78

Richardson H. G., Sayles G. O. eds., *Select Cases of Procedure without Writ under Henry III*, Selden Soc., LX (1941)

Rigby S. H., 'Urban "Oligarchy" in Late Medieval England' in Thomson J. A. F. ed., *Towns and Townspeople in the Fifteenth Century* (Gloucester, 1988), pp. 62–86

Rigby S. H., Ewan E., 'Government, Power and Authority 1300–1540' in Palliser, D., ed., *The Cambridge Urban History of Britain Volume I: 600–1500* (Cambridge, 2000), pp. 291–312

Rodgers C. P., 'Humanism, History and the Common Law', *JLH*, **vi** (1985), pp. 130–56

Round J. H., *The Commune of London and Other Studies* (Westminster, 1899)

Sainty J. C., *Officers of the Exchequer*, List & Index Soc. Special Ser., XVIII (1983)

Sayles G., 'The Sources of Two Revisions of the Statute of Gloucester, 1278', *EHR*, **lii** (1937), pp. 467–74

Seabourne G., 'Controlling Commercial Morality in Late Medieval London: the Usury Trials of 1421', *JLH*, **xix** (1998), pp. 116–42

Seabourne G., *Royal Regulation of Loans and Sales in Medieval England* (Woodbridge, 2003)

Seipp D. J., 'Crime in the Year Books' in Stebbings C. ed., *Law Reporting in Britain* (London, 1995), pp. 15–34

Shepard A., 'Cambridge University Courts 1560–1640', *JLH*, **xix** (1998), pp. 62–74

Slatter M., 'The Norwich Court of Requests – A Tradition Continued', *JHL*, **v** (1984), pp. 97–107

Smith C., 'Medieval Coroners' Records: Legal Fiction or Historical Fact?' in Dunn D. E. S., ed., *Courts, Counties and the Capital in the Later Middle Ages* (Stroud, New York, 1996), pp. 93–115

Sutherland D. W., 'Mesne Process upon Personal Actions in the Early Common Law', *LQR*, **lxxxii** (1966), pp. 482–96

Sutherland D. W., *The Assize of Novel Disseisin* (Oxford, 1973)

Tai Lui, 'The Founding of the London Provincial Assembly, 1645–47' in R. C. Richardson, ed., *The English Civil War: Local Aspects* (Stroud, 1997)

Tait J., *The Medieval English Borough: Studies on its Origin and Constitutional History* (Manchester, 1936)

Thrupp S., *The Merchant Class of Medieval London* (University of Michigan, 1989)

Tittler R., 'The Sequestration of Juries in Early Modern England', *BIHR*, **lxi** (1988), pp. 301–5

Torr J. H., 'The Sheriffs (City of London) Court is a Substantive Court of Original and Special Jurisdiction . . . ' (1867)

Tucker P., 'Government and Politics: London, 1461–1483' (unpublished London PhD thesis, 1995)

Tucker P., 'Relationships between London's Courts and the Westminster Courts in the Reign of Edward IV' in Dunn D. E. S. ed., *Courts, Counties and the Capital in the Later Middle Ages* (Stroud, 1996), pp. 117–37

Tucker P., 'London's Courts of Law in the Fifteenth Century: The Litigant's Perspective' in Brooks C. W., Lobban M. eds., *Communities and Courts in Britain 1150–1900* (London, Rio Grande, 1997), pp. 25–41

Tucker P., 'The Early History of the Court of Chancery: A Comparative Study', *EHR*, **cxv** (2000), pp. 791–811

Tucker P., 'First Steps towards an English Legal Profession: The Case of the London 'Ordinance of 1280', *EHR*, **cxxi** (2006), pp. 361–84

Tucker P., 'London and "The Making of the Common Law"' in Davies M., Prescott A., eds., *London and the Kingdom: Essays in honour of Professor Caroline M. Barron (The Harlaxton Symposium 2004)* [forthcoming]

Virgoe R., 'Some Ancient Indictments in the King's Bench referring to Kent, 1450–2', *Kent Archaeological Society Record Series, xxviii* (1964), pp. 214–65

Vising J., *Anglo-Norman Language and Literature* (London, 1923)

Weever J., *Ancient Funeral Monuments* (2nd edn, London, 1767)

Williams G. A., *Medieval London: from Commune to Capital* (London, 1963)

Williams E., *Early Holborn and the Legal Quarter of London*... 2 vols. (London, 1927)

Index

For EU product safety concerns, contact us at Calle de José Abascal, 56–1°, 28003 Madrid, Spain or eugpsr@cambridge.org.

www.ingramcontent.com/pod-product-compliance
Lightning Source LLC
LaVergne TN
LVHW011511200926
848484LV00001B/8
9780521866682